RIN-NE

りんね

Story and Art by
Rumiko Takahashi

RIN-NE

Characters

Rokumon
六文
Black Cat by Contract who helps Rinne with his work.

Tsubasa Jumonji
十文字翼
A young exorcist with strong feelings for Sakura. He competes aggressively with Rinne when it comes to love or dealing with ghosts.

Kain
架印
A shinigami who keeps track of human life spans. Kain's mother was conned by Rinne's father, Sabato, and Kain holds a fierce grudge against him.

Rinne Rokudo
六道りんね
His job is to lead restless spirits who wander in this world to the Wheel of Reincarnation. His grandmother is a shinigami, a god of death, and his grandfather was human. Rinne is also a penniless first-year high school student living in the school club building.

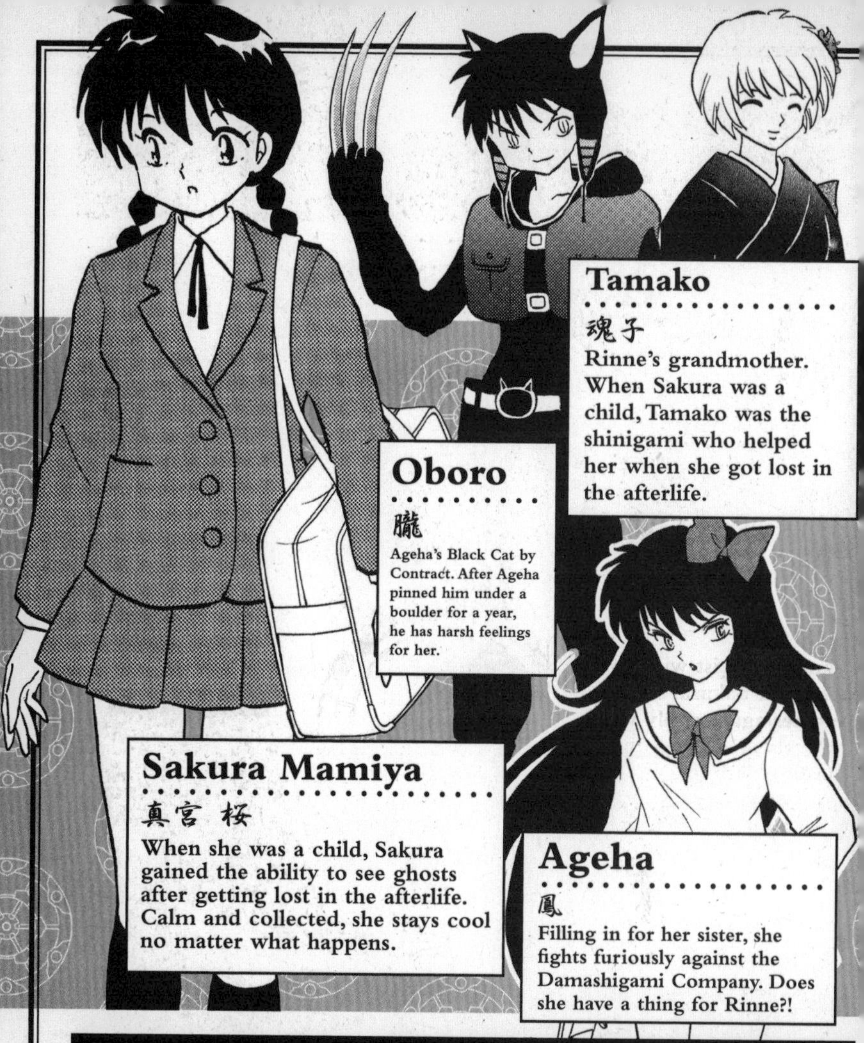

Tamako

魂子

Rinne's grandmother. When Sakura was a child, Tamako was the shinigami who helped her when she got lost in the afterlife.

Oboro

朧

Ageha's Black Cat by Contract. After Ageha pinned him under a boulder for a year, he has harsh feelings for her.

Sakura Mamiya

真宮 桜

When she was a child, Sakura gained the ability to see ghosts after getting lost in the afterlife. Calm and collected, she stays cool no matter what happens.

Ageha

鳳

Filling in for her sister, she fights furiously against the Damashigami Company. Does she have a thing for Rinne?!

The Story So Far

Together, Sakura, the girl who can see ghosts, and Rinne the shinigami (sort of) spend their days helping spirits that can't pass on reach the afterlife, and deal with all kinds of strange phenomena at their school.

Rinne deals with the case of a ghostly skater and helps a spirit from the Taisho era pass on to the afterlife. Then Rinne is caught in the middle of a spat between Ageha and her Black Cat by Contract Oboro, who is mad at her for pinning him under a rock for a year. As a result of this angry quarrel, Ageha gets swallowed by a giant ghost mongoose...

RIN-NE

Contents

CHAPTER 89: A BLACK CAT'S LIFE

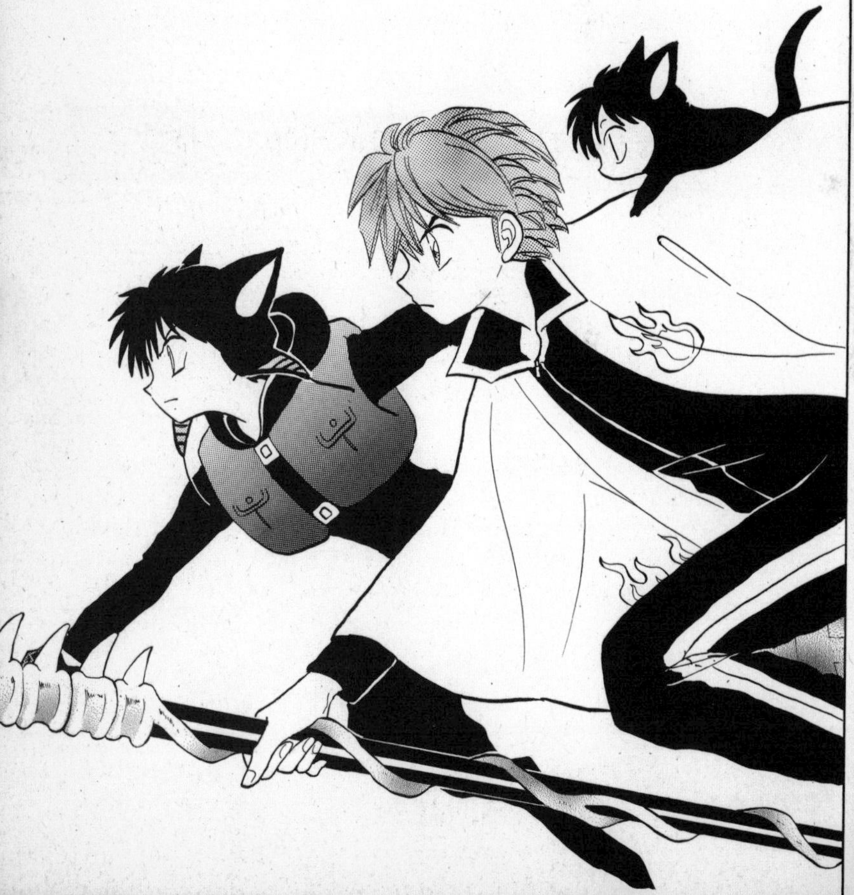

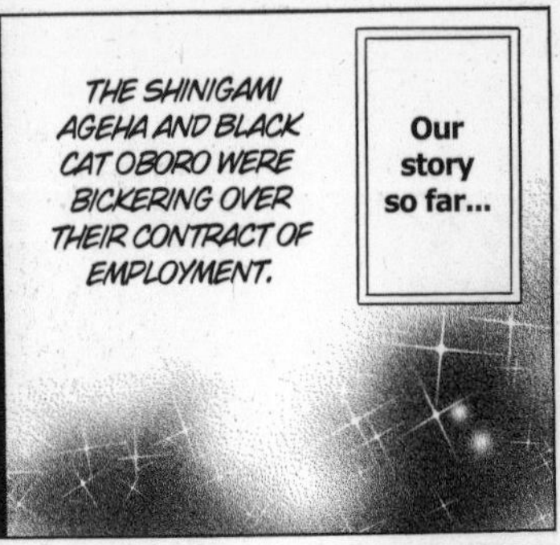
Our story so far...
THE SHINIGAMI AGEHA AND BLACK CAT OBORO WERE BICKERING OVER THEIR CONTRACT OF EMPLOYMENT.
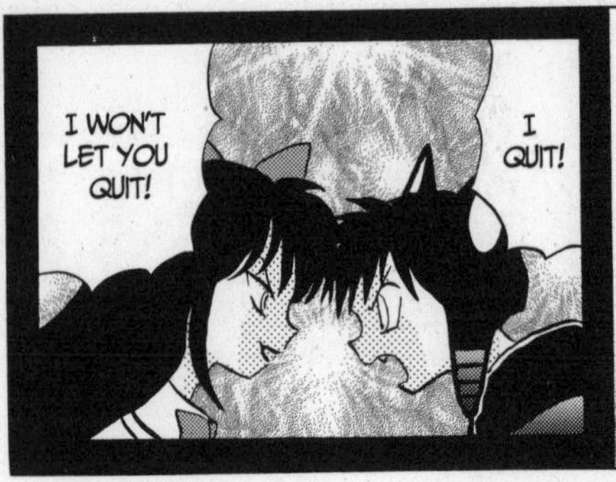
I QUIT!
I WON'T LET YOU QUIT!
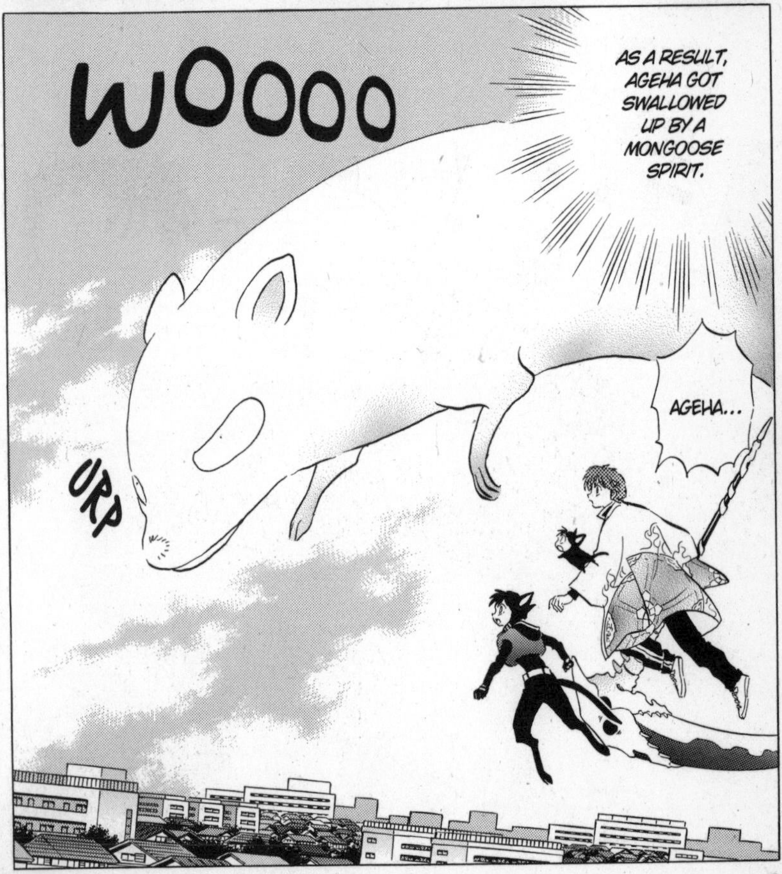
AS A RESULT, AGEHA GOT SWALLOWED UP BY A MONGOOSE SPIRIT.
WOOOO
AGEHA...
URP

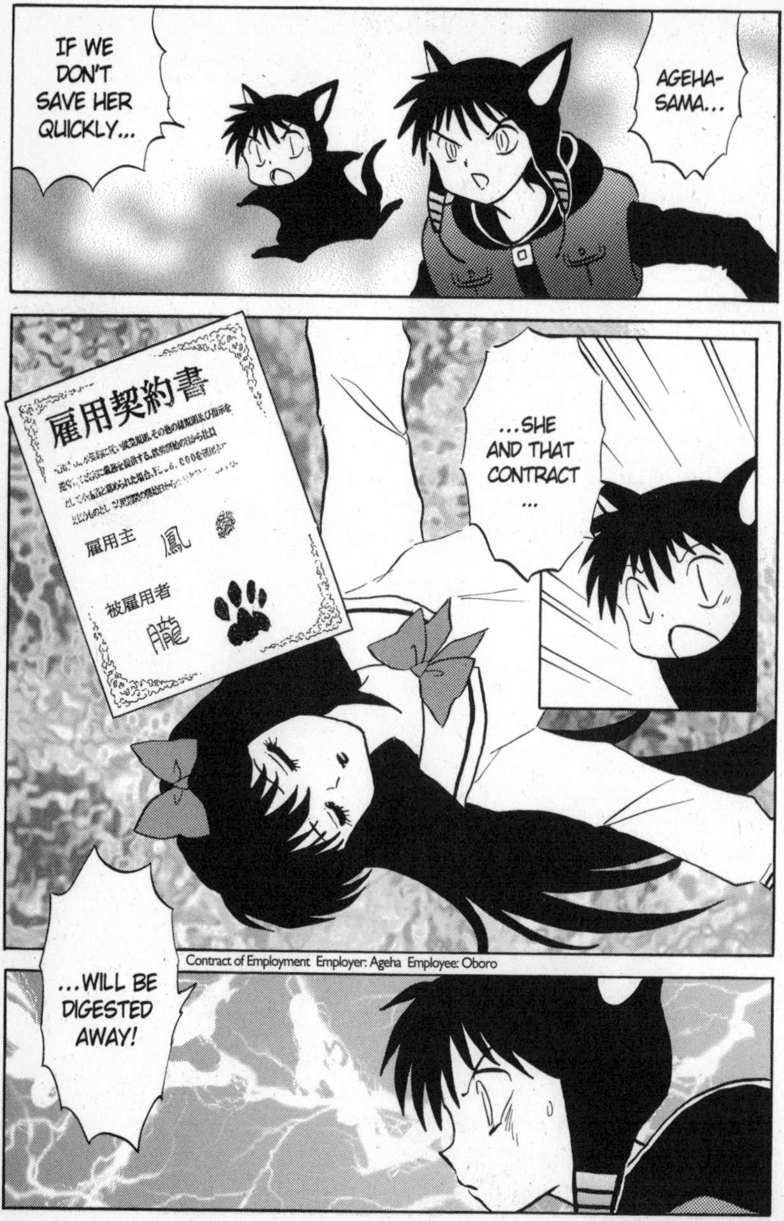
AGEHA-SAMA...
IF WE DON'T SAVE HER QUICKLY...
雇用契約書
雇用主 鳳
被雇用者 朧
...SHE AND THAT CONTRACT ...
Contract of Employment Employer: Ageha Employee: Oboro
...WILL BE DIGESTED AWAY!

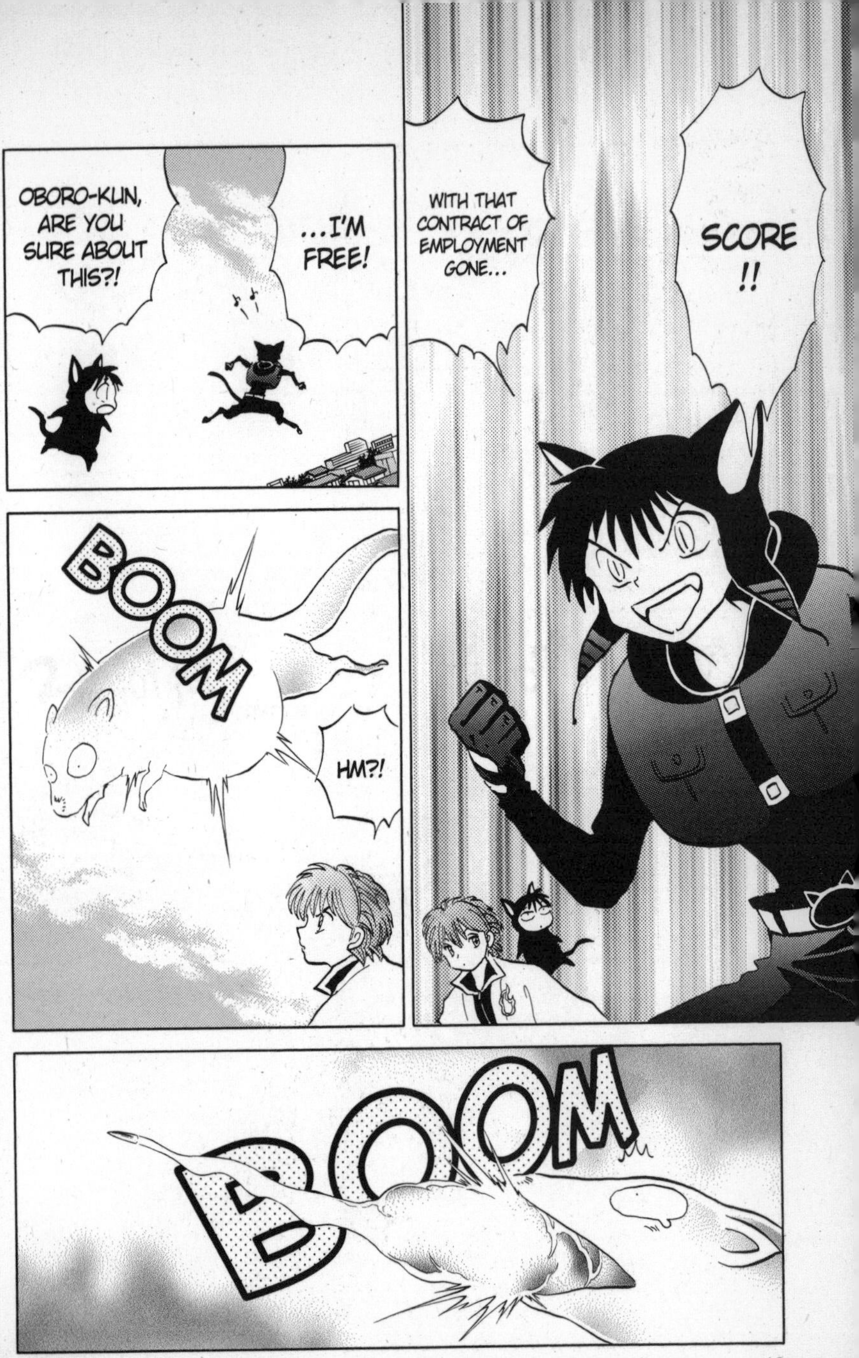
SCORE !!
WITH THAT CONTRACT OF EMPLOYMENT GONE...
...I'M FREE!
OBORO-KUN, ARE YOU SURE ABOUT THIS?!
BOOM
HM?!
BOOM

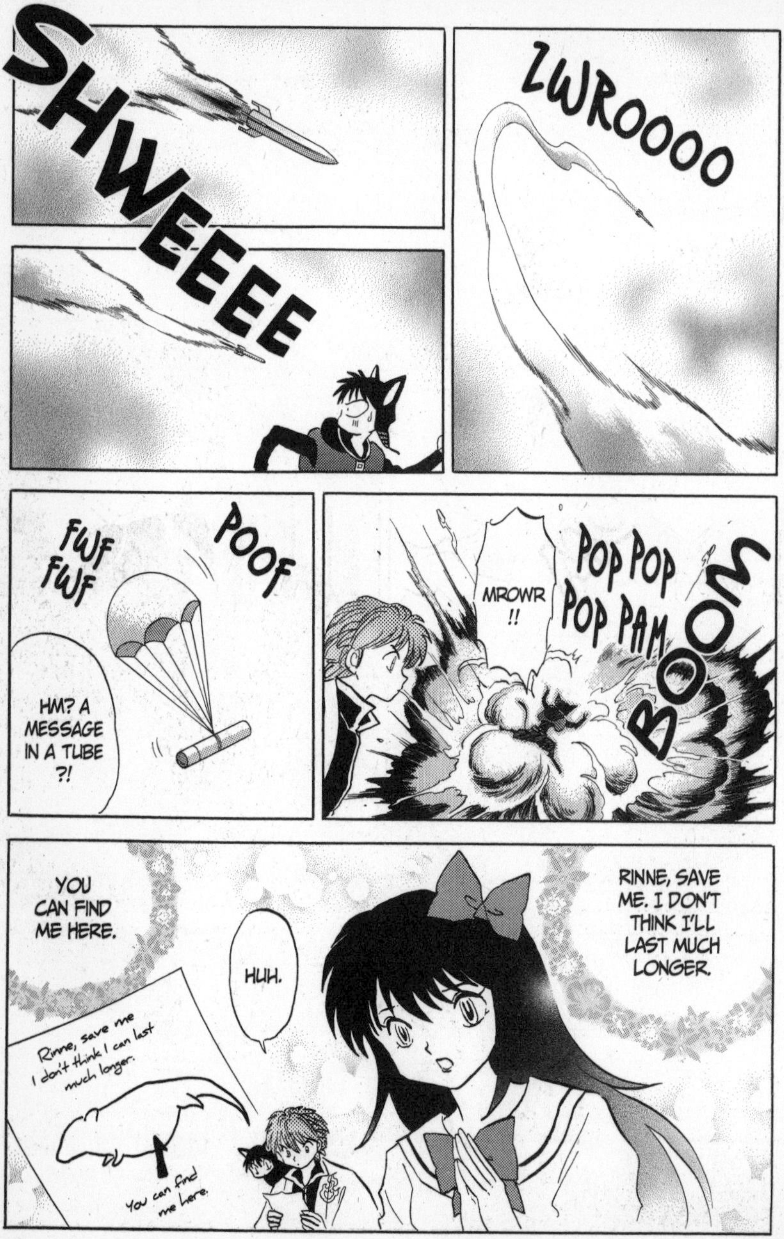
ZWROOOO
SHWEEEE
POP POP POP PAM
BOOM
MROWR !!
POOF
FWF FWF
HM? A MESSAGE IN A TUBE ?!
RINNE, SAVE ME. I DON'T THINK I'LL LAST MUCH LONGER.
HUH.
YOU CAN FIND ME HERE.
Rinne, save me I don't think I can last much longer.
You can find me here.

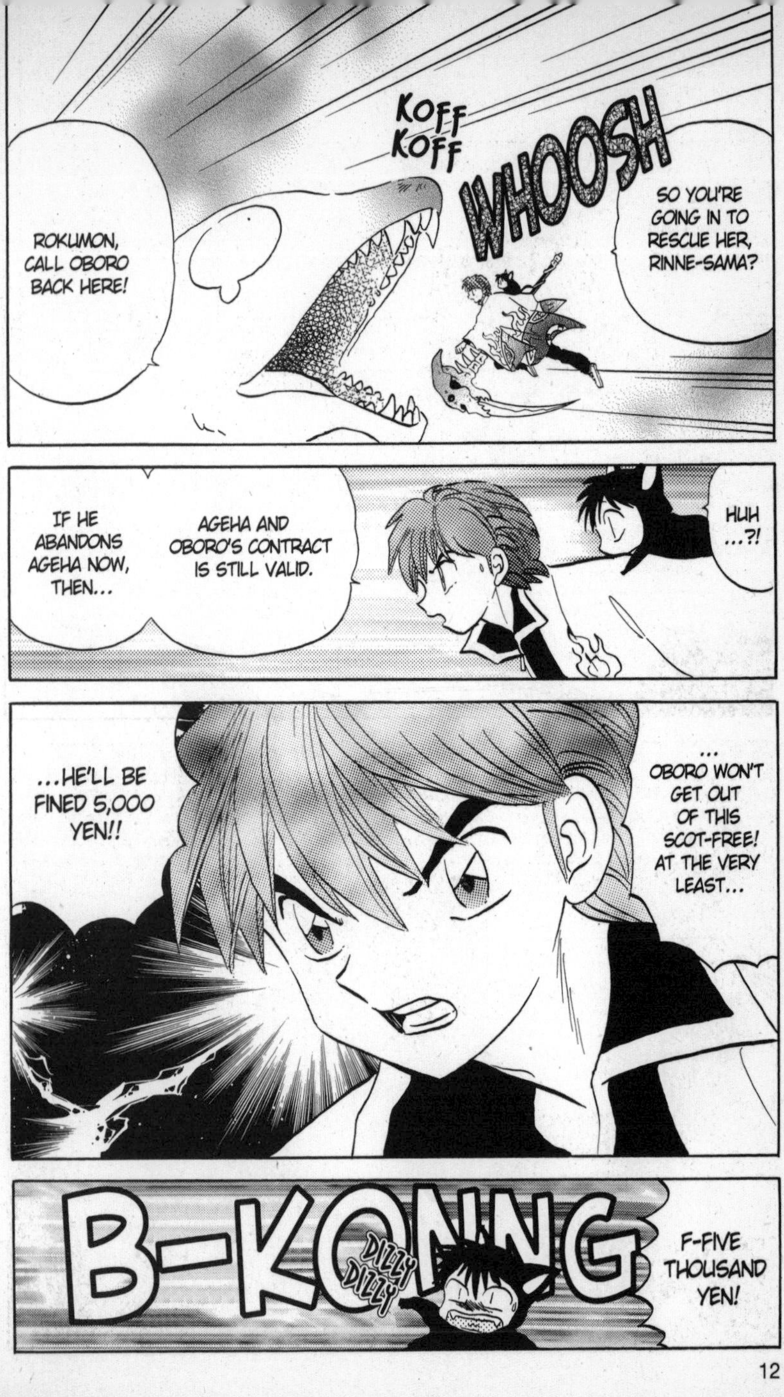
SO YOU'RE GOING IN TO RESCUE HER, RINNE-SAMA?
KOFF KOFF
WHOOSH
ROKUMON, CALL OBORO BACK HERE!
HUH ...?!
AGEHA AND OBORO'S CONTRACT IS STILL VALID.
IF HE ABANDONS AGEHA NOW, THEN...
... OBORO WON'T GET OUT OF THIS SCOT-FREE! AT THE VERY LEAST...
...HE'LL BE FINED 5,000 YEN!!
F-FIVE THOUSAND YEN!
DIZZY DIZZY
B-KONNG

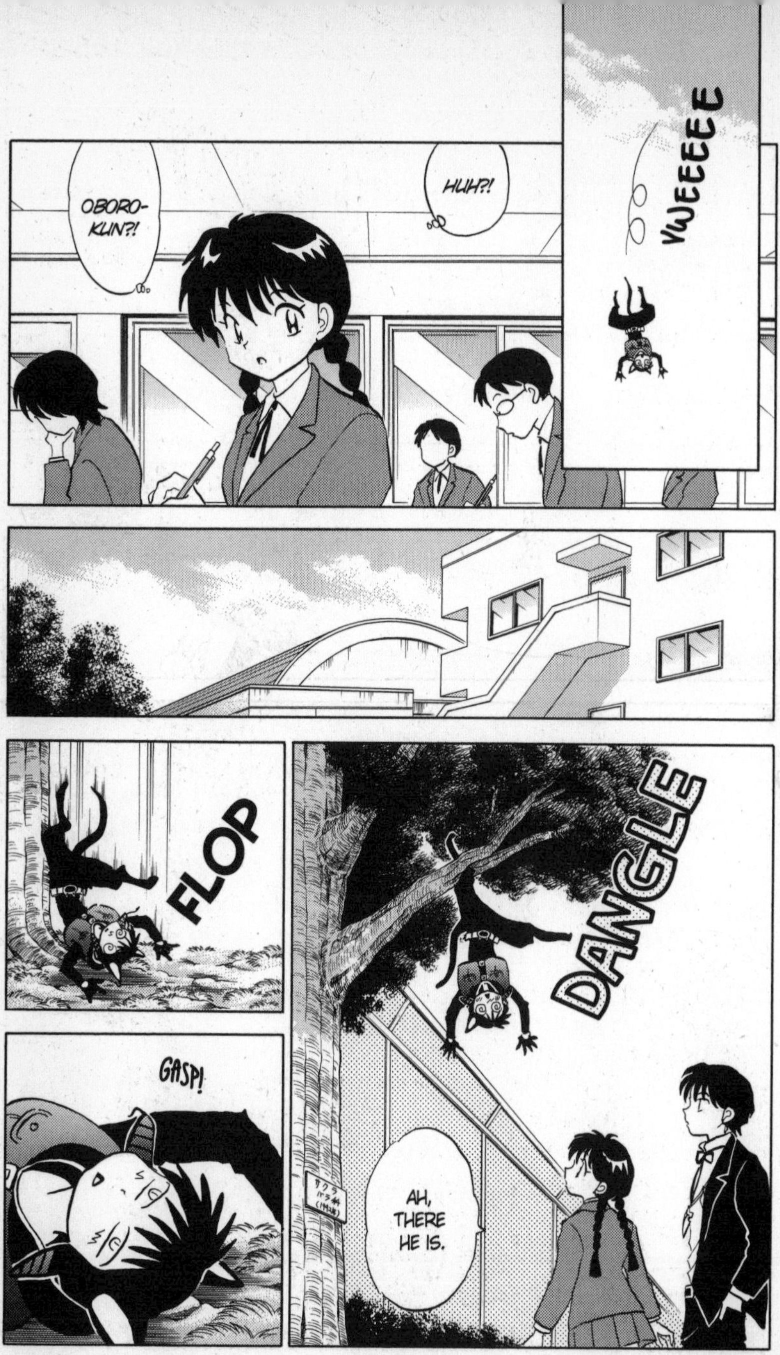
VWEEEEE
HUH?!
OBORO-KUN?!
DANGLE
AH, THERE HE IS.
FLOP
GASP!

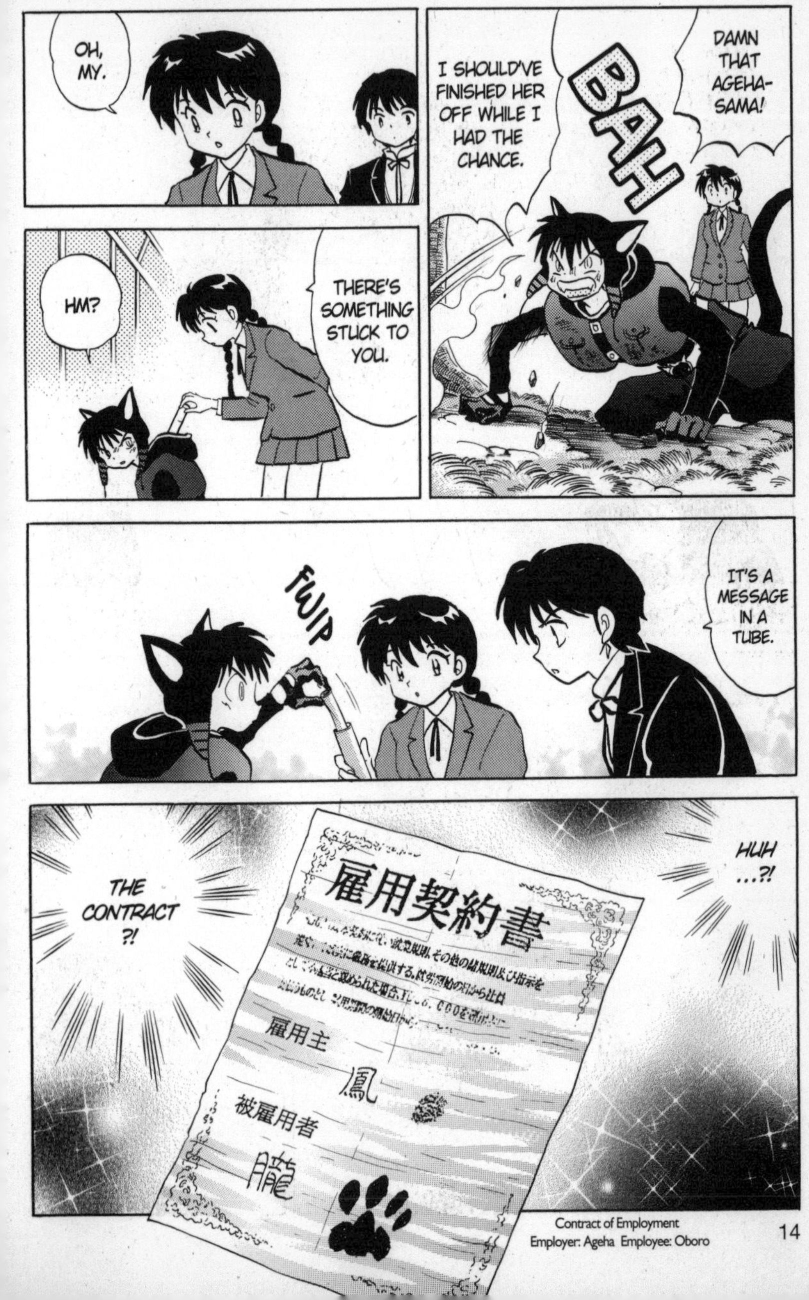
DAMN THAT AGEHA-SAMA!
BAH
I SHOULD'VE FINISHED HER OFF WHILE I HAD THE CHANCE.
OH, MY.
THERE'S SOMETHING STUCK TO YOU.
HM?
IT'S A MESSAGE IN A TUBE.
FWIP
HUH ...?!
THE CONTRACT ?!
雇用契約書
雇用主
鳳
被雇用者
朧

Contract of Employment
Employer: Ageha Employee: Oboro

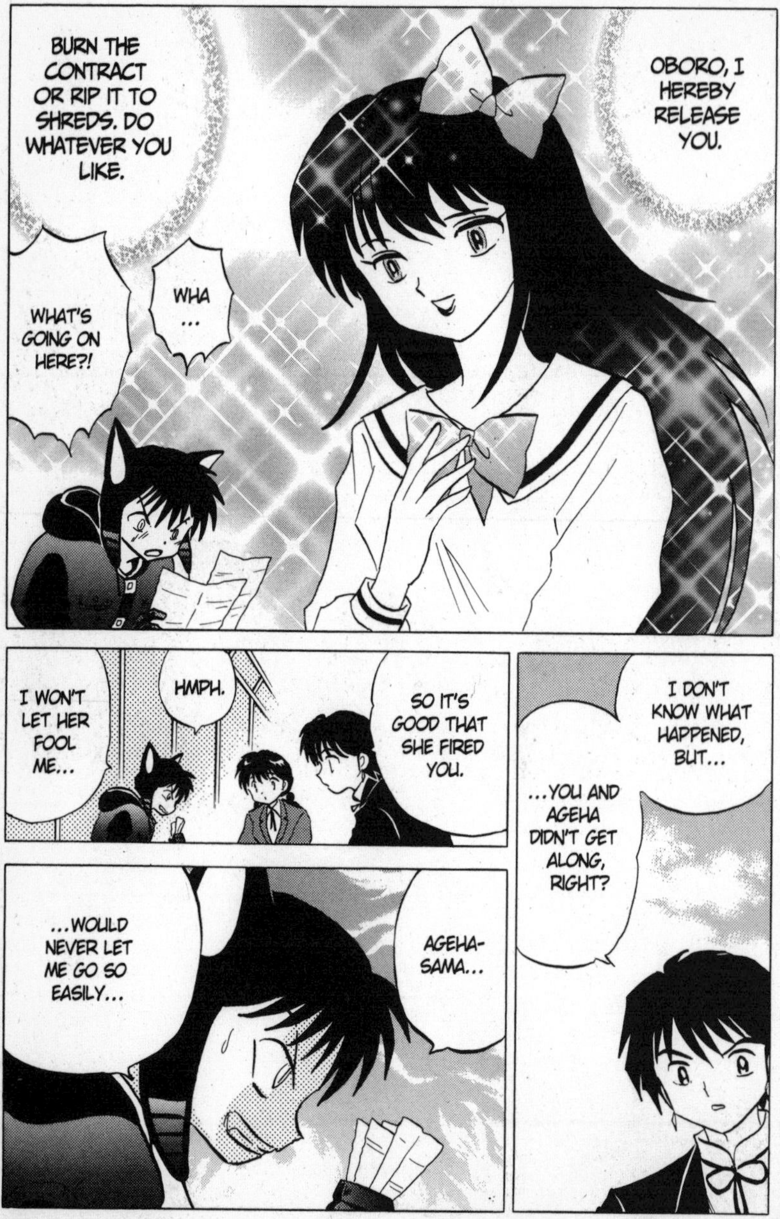
OBORO, I HEREBY RELEASE YOU.
BURN THE CONTRACT OR RIP IT TO SHREDS. DO WHATEVER YOU LIKE.
WHA...
WHAT'S GOING ON HERE?!
I DON'T KNOW WHAT HAPPENED, BUT...
...YOU AND AGEHA DIDN'T GET ALONG, RIGHT?
SO IT'S GOOD THAT SHE FIRED YOU.
HMPH.
I WON'T LET HER FOOL ME...
AGEHA-SAMA...
...WOULD NEVER LET ME GO SO EASILY...

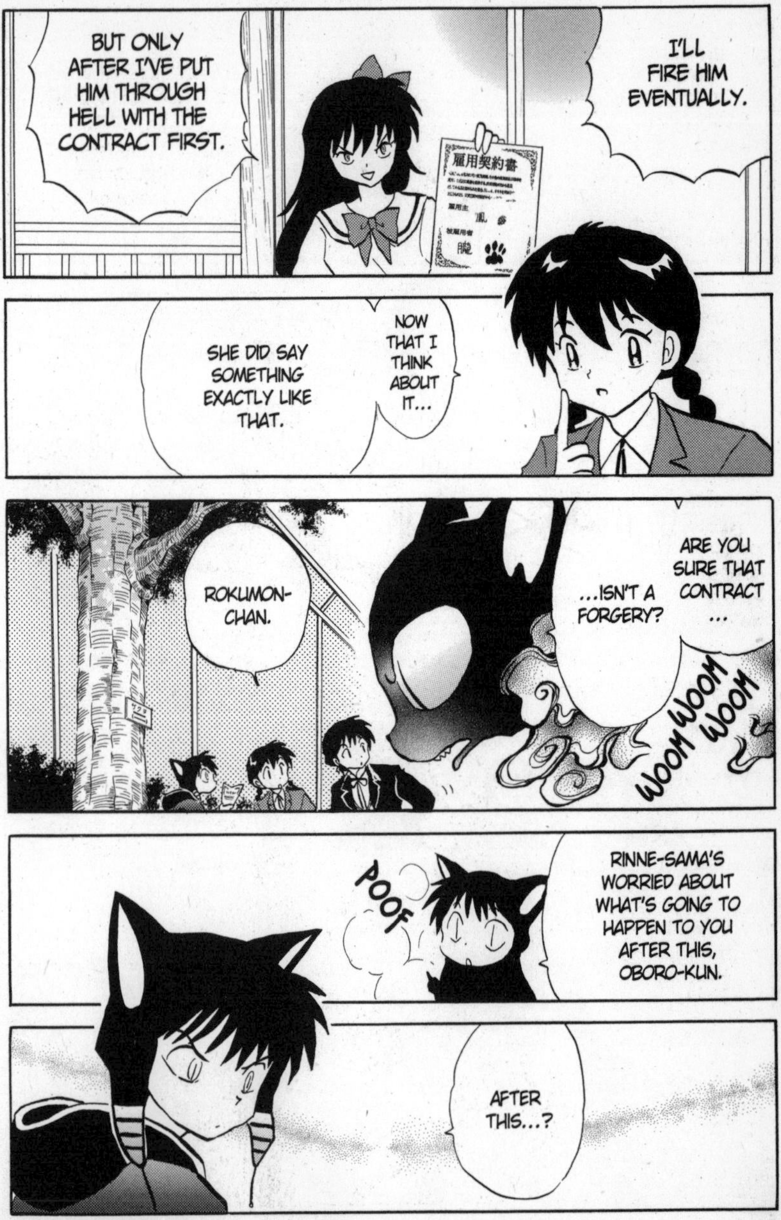
I'LL FIRE HIM EVENTUALLY.
BUT ONLY AFTER I'VE PUT HIM THROUGH HELL WITH THE CONTRACT FIRST.
雇用契約書
NOW THAT I THINK ABOUT IT...
SHE DID SAY SOMETHING EXACTLY LIKE THAT.
ARE YOU SURE THAT CONTRACT ...
...ISN'T A FORGERY?
WOOM WOOM WOOM
ROKUMON-CHAN.
RINNE-SAMA'S WORRIED ABOUT WHAT'S GOING TO HAPPEN TO YOU AFTER THIS, OBORO-KUN.
POOF
AFTER THIS...?

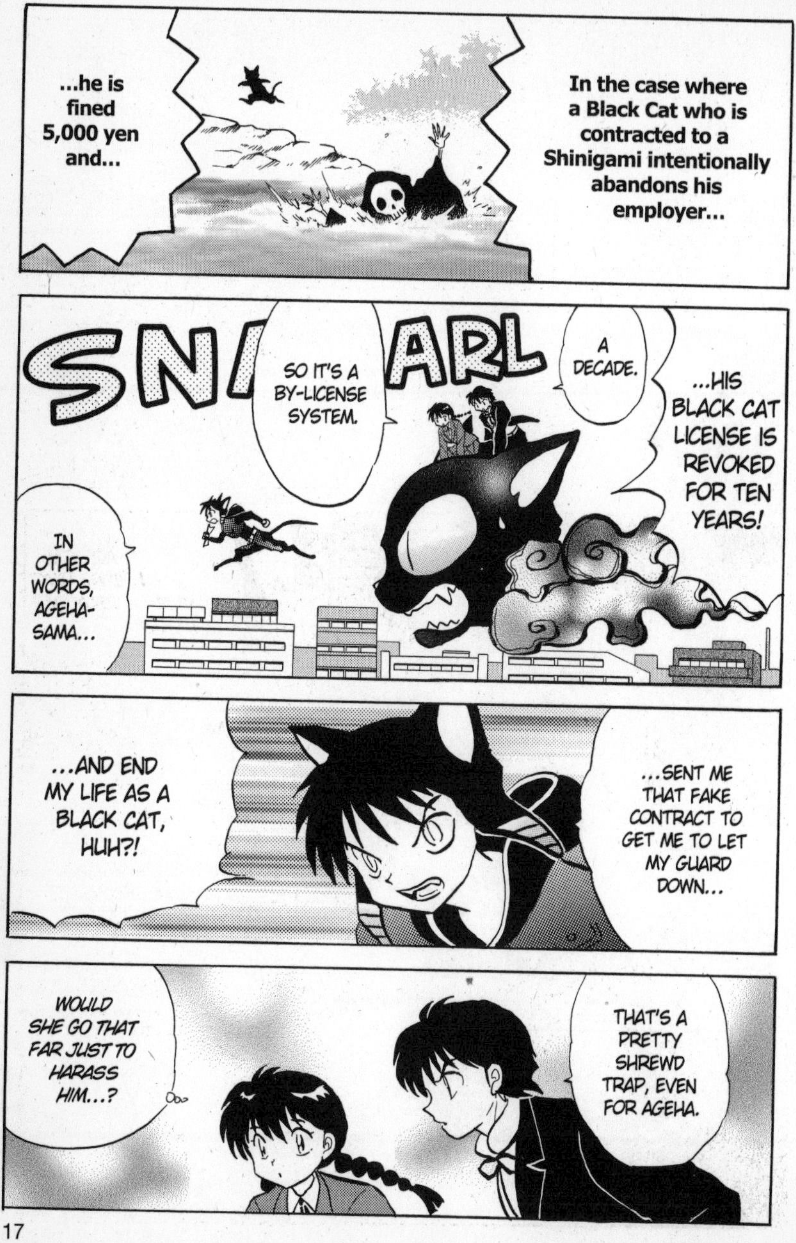
In the case where a Black Cat who is contracted to a Shinigami intentionally abandons his employer...
...he is fined 5,000 yen and...
...HIS BLACK CAT LICENSE IS REVOKED FOR TEN YEARS!
A DECADE.
SN ARL
SO IT'S A BY-LICENSE SYSTEM.
IN OTHER WORDS, AGEHA-SAMA...
...SENT ME THAT FAKE CONTRACT TO GET ME TO LET MY GUARD DOWN...
...AND END MY LIFE AS A BLACK CAT, HUH?!
THAT'S A PRETTY SHREWD TRAP, EVEN FOR AGEHA.
WOULD SHE GO THAT FAR JUST TO HARASS HIM...?

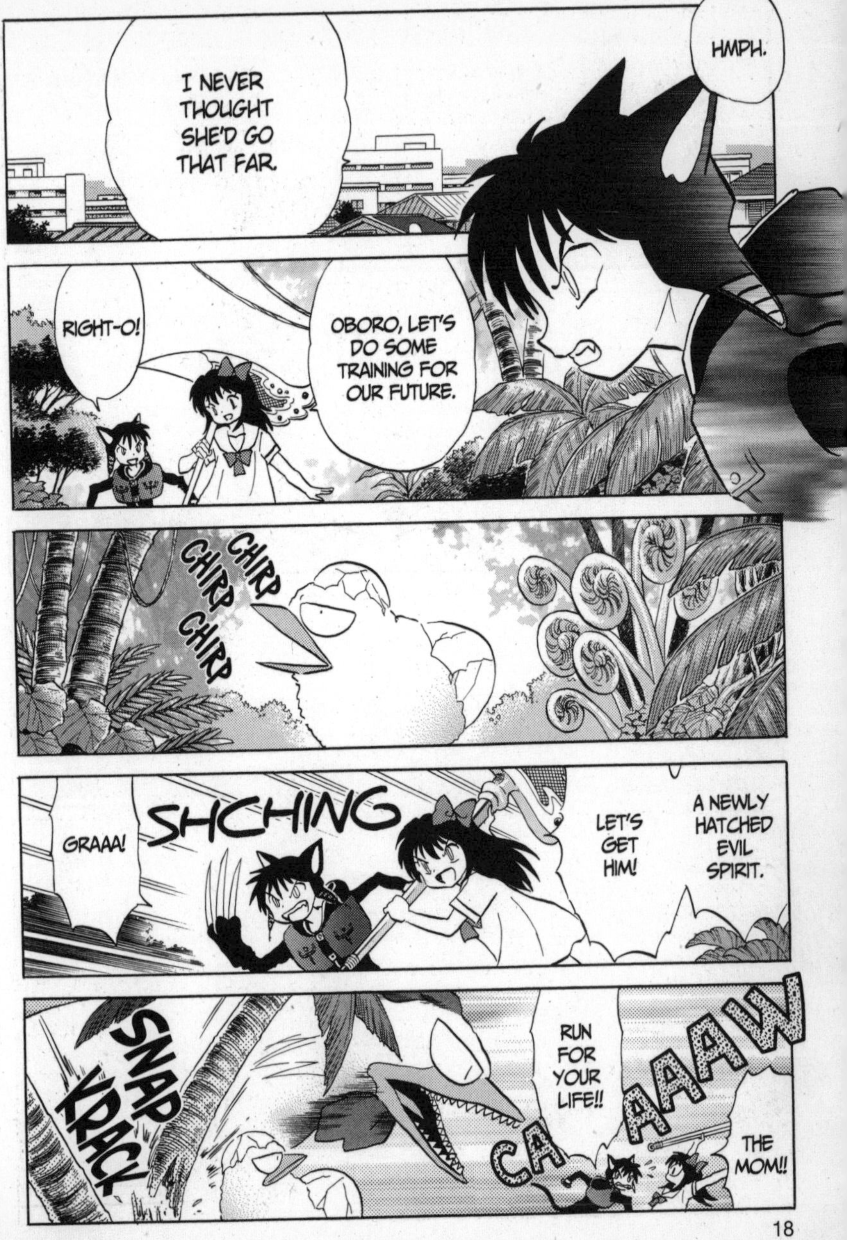
I NEVER THOUGHT SHE'D GO THAT FAR.
HMPH.
OBORO, LET'S DO SOME TRAINING FOR OUR FUTURE.
RIGHT-O!
CHIRP CHIRP CHIRP CHIRP
A NEWLY HATCHED EVIL SPIRIT.
LET'S GET HIM!
SHCHING
GRAAA!
CAAAAAW
THE MOM!!
RUN FOR YOUR LIFE!!
SNAP KRACK

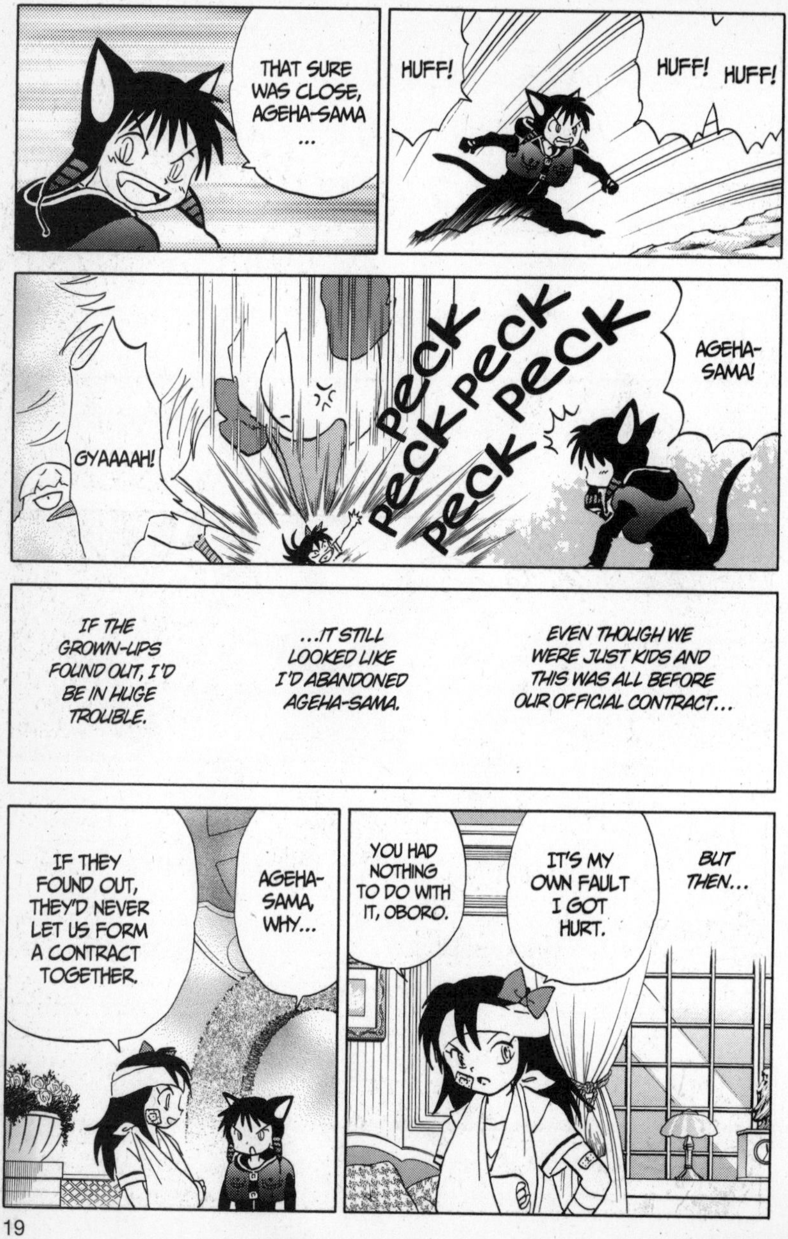
HUFF! HUFF! HUFF!
THAT SURE WAS CLOSE, AGEHA-SAMA ...
AGEHA-SAMA!
PECK PECK PECK PECK PECK PECK
GYAAAAH!
EVEN THOUGH WE WERE JUST KIDS AND THIS WAS ALL BEFORE OUR OFFICIAL CONTRACT...
...IT STILL LOOKED LIKE I'D ABANDONED AGEHA-SAMA.
IF THE GROWN-UPS FOUND OUT, I'D BE IN HUGE TROUBLE.
BUT THEN...
IT'S MY OWN FAULT I GOT HURT.
YOU HAD NOTHING TO DO WITH IT, OBORO.
AGEHA-SAMA, WHY...
IF THEY FOUND OUT, THEY'D NEVER LET US FORM A CONTRACT TOGETHER.

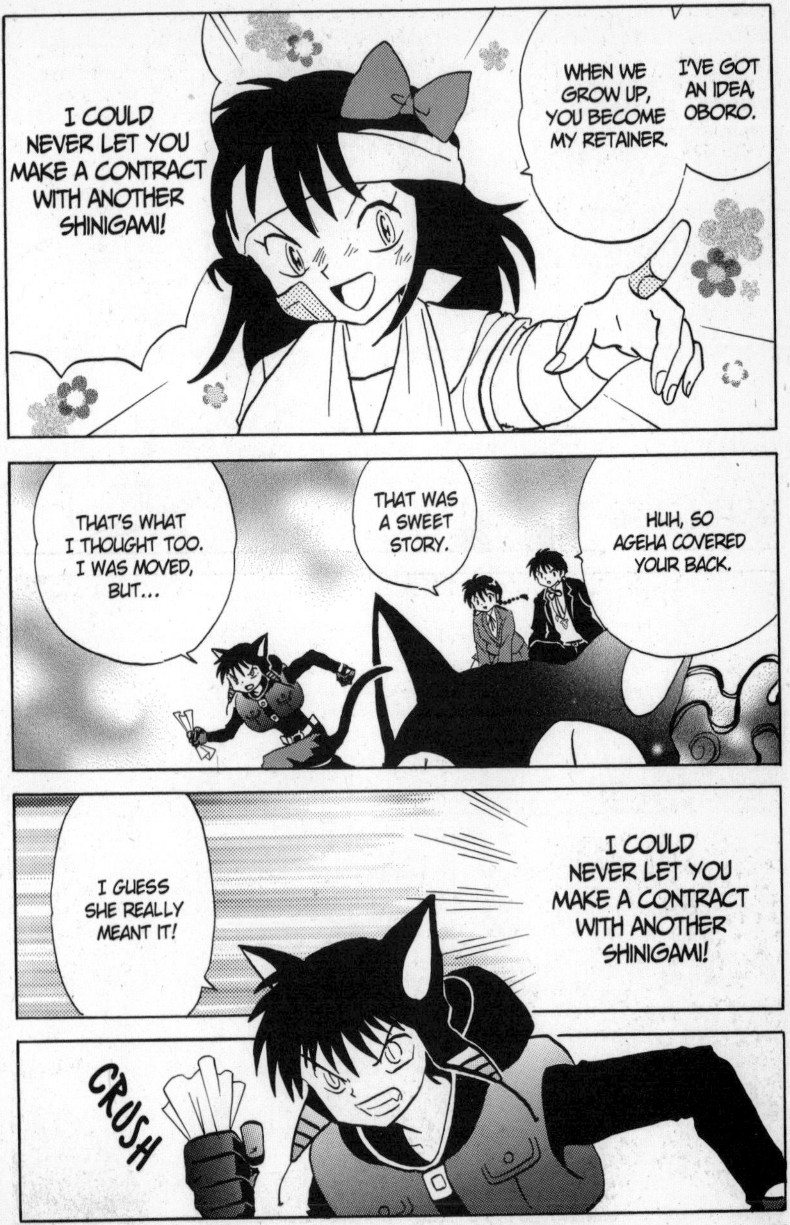
I'VE GOT AN IDEA, OBORO.
WHEN WE GROW UP, YOU BECOME MY RETAINER.
I COULD NEVER LET YOU MAKE A CONTRACT WITH ANOTHER SHINIGAMI!
HUH, SO AGEHA COVERED YOUR BACK.
THAT WAS A SWEET STORY.
THAT'S WHAT I THOUGHT TOO. I WAS MOVED, BUT...
I COULD NEVER LET YOU MAKE A CONTRACT WITH ANOTHER SHINIGAMI!
I GUESS SHE REALLY MEANT IT!
CRUSH

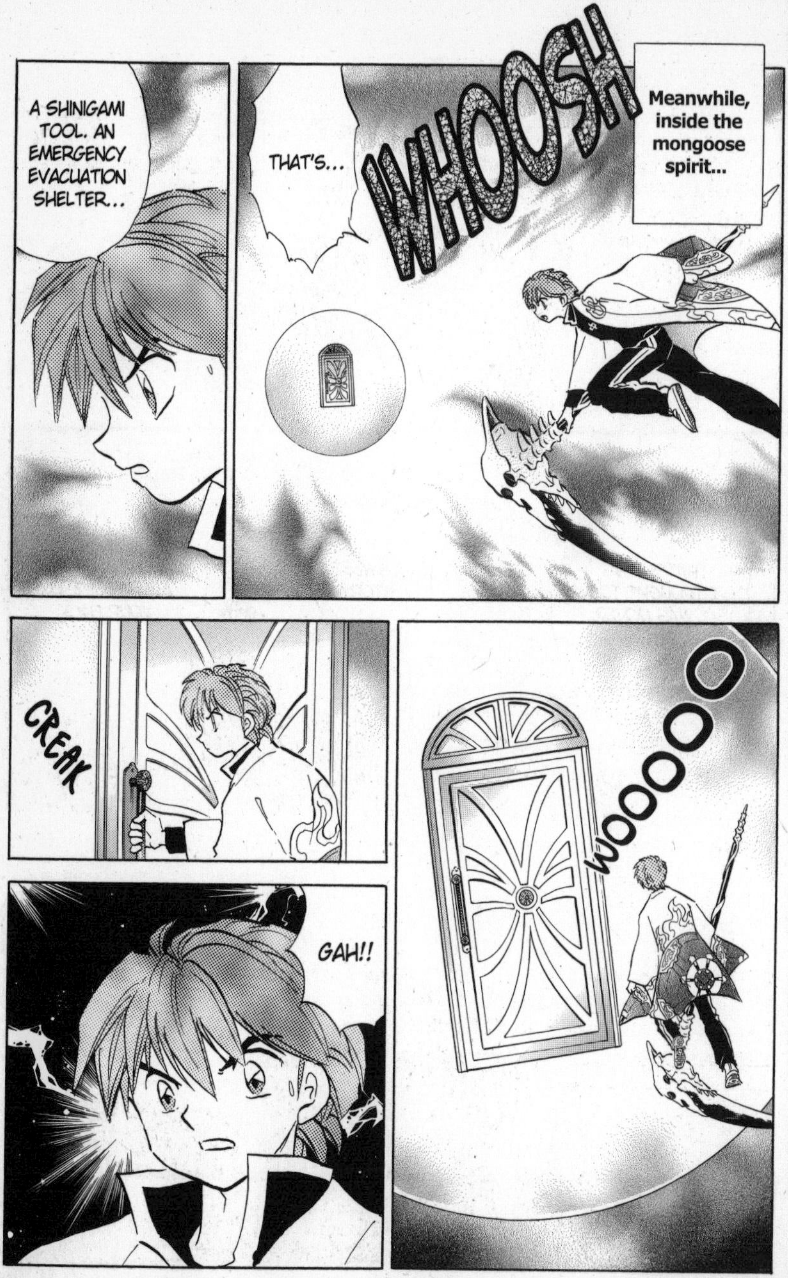

Meanwhile, inside the mongoose spirit...
WHOOSH
THAT'S...
A SHINIGAMI TOOL. AN EMERGENCY EVACUATION SHELTER...
WOOOOO
CREAK
GAH!!

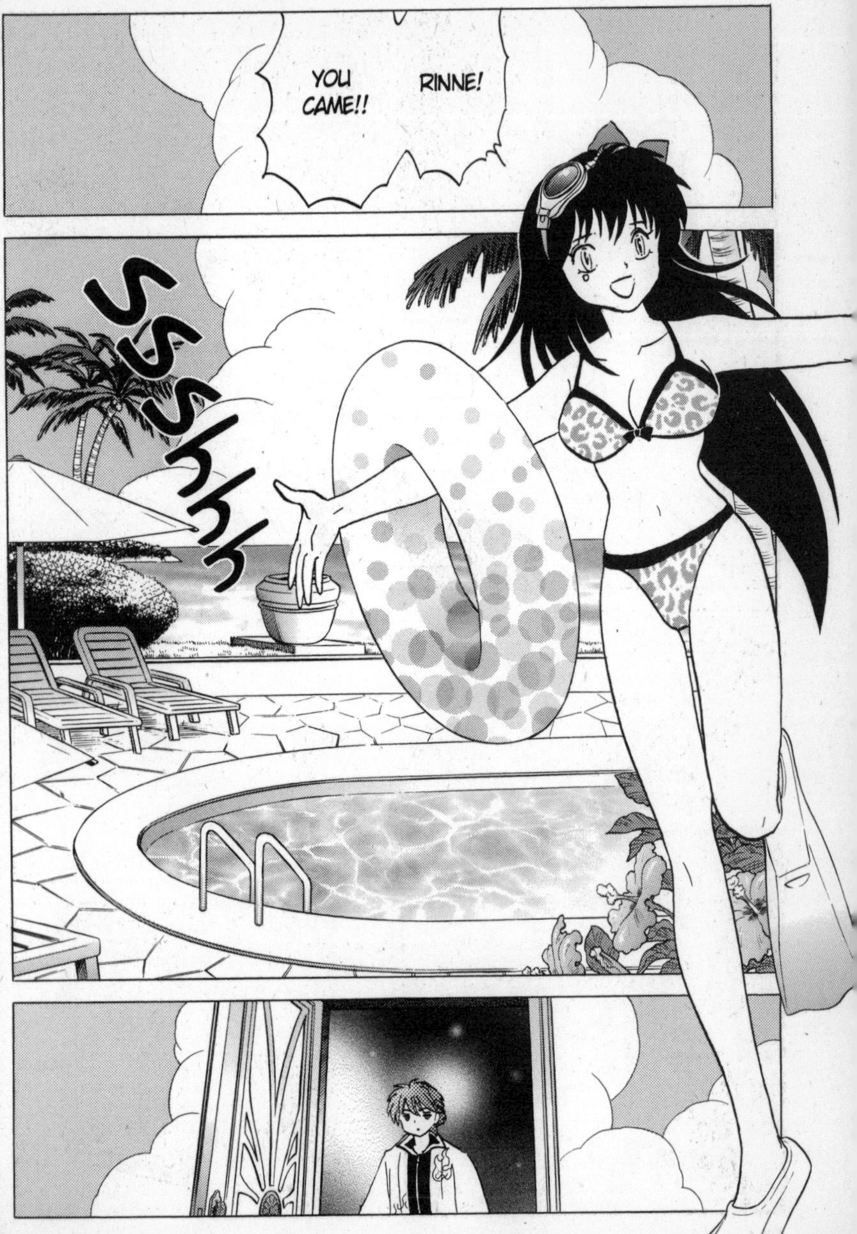
RINNE!
YOU CAME!!
SSShhhh

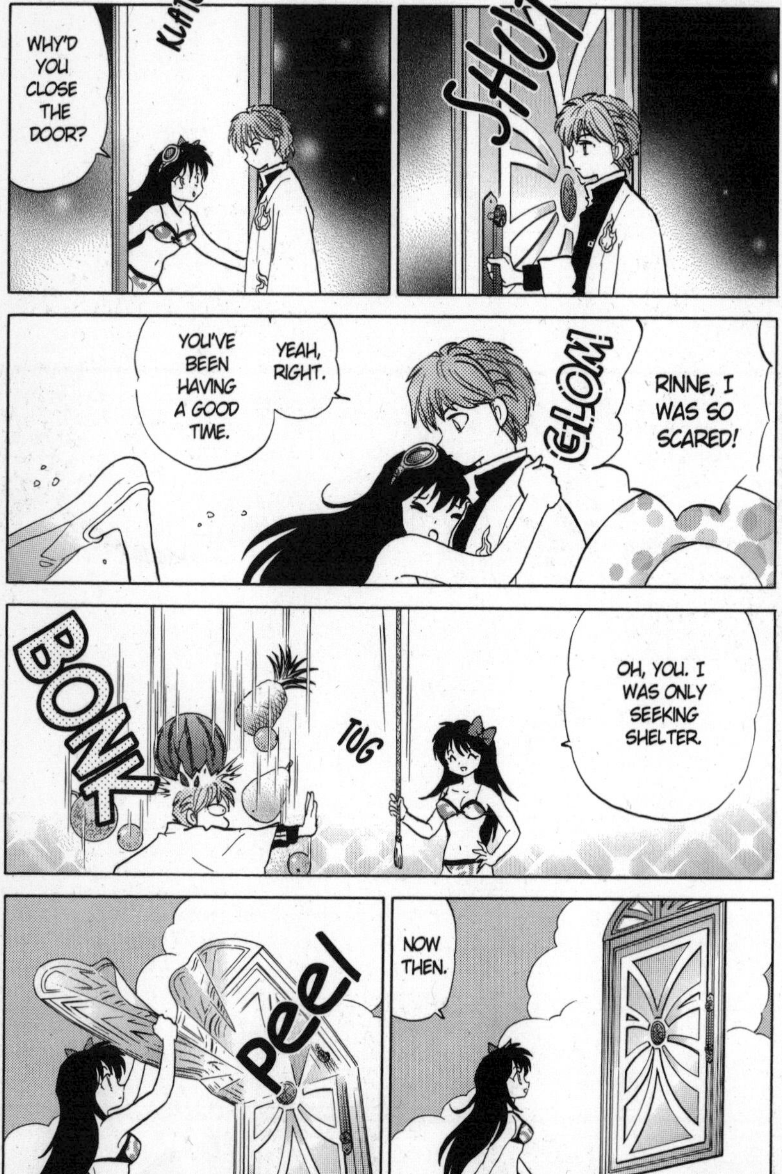
SHUT
KLATCH
WHY'D YOU CLOSE THE DOOR?
RINNE, I WAS SO SCARED!
GLOM!
YEAH, RIGHT.
YOU'VE BEEN HAVING A GOOD TIME.
OH, YOU. I WAS ONLY SEEKING SHELTER.
TUG
BONK
NOW THEN.
Peel

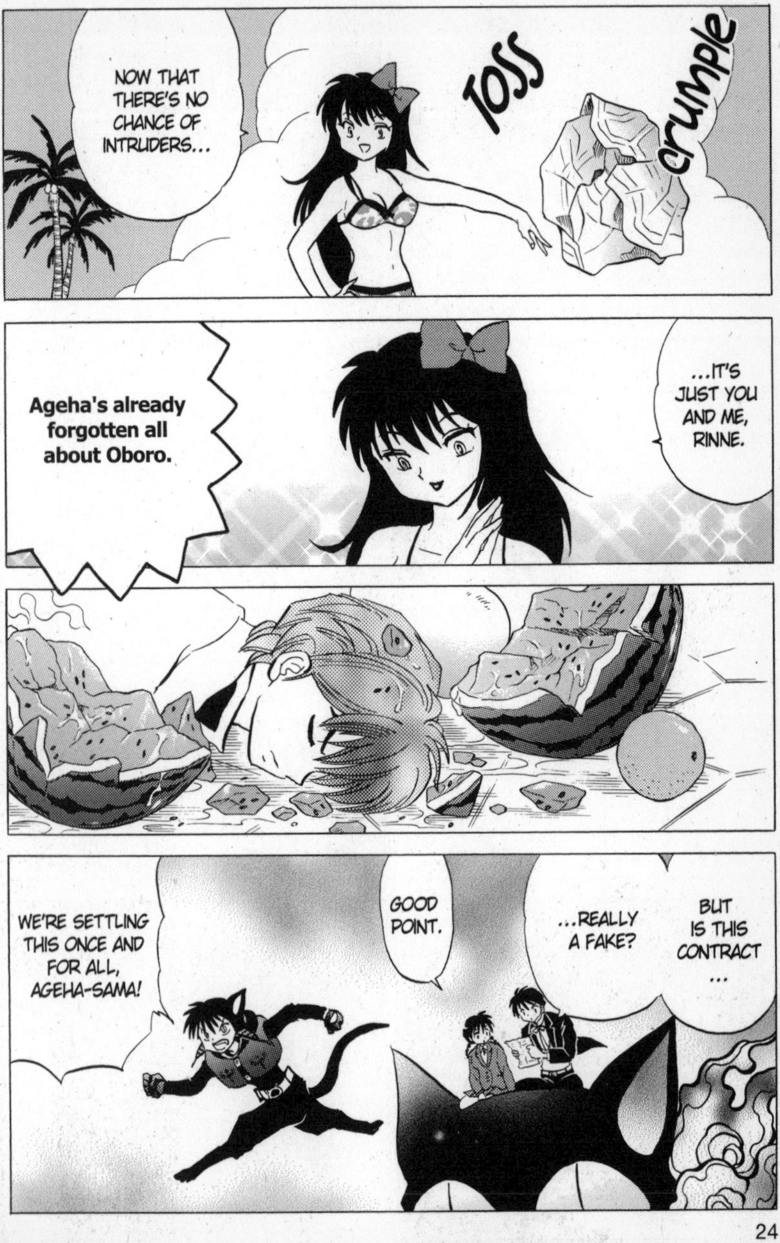
crumple
TOSS
NOW THAT THERE'S NO CHANCE OF INTRUDERS...
...IT'S JUST YOU AND ME, RINNE.
Ageha's already forgotten all about Oboro.
BUT IS THIS CONTRACT ...
...REALLY A FAKE?
GOOD POINT.
WE'RE SETTLING THIS ONCE AND FOR ALL, AGEHA-SAMA!

CHAPTER 90: PARTNERS

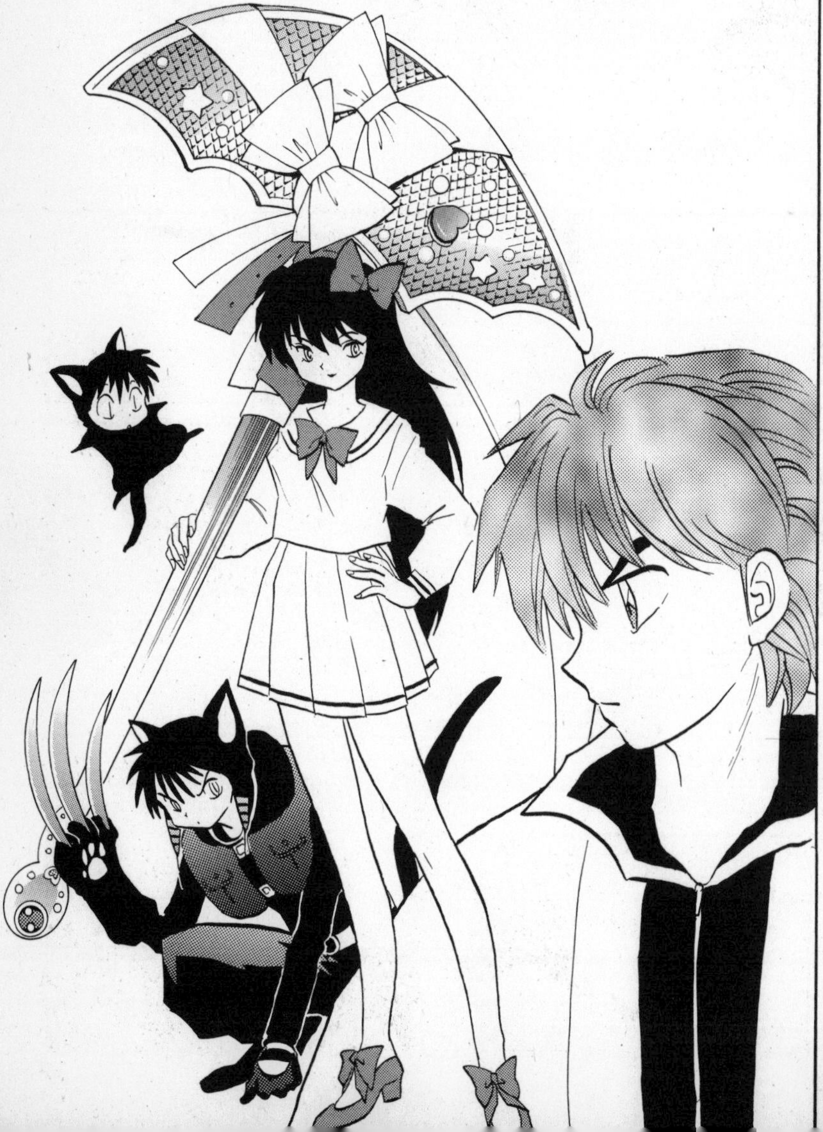

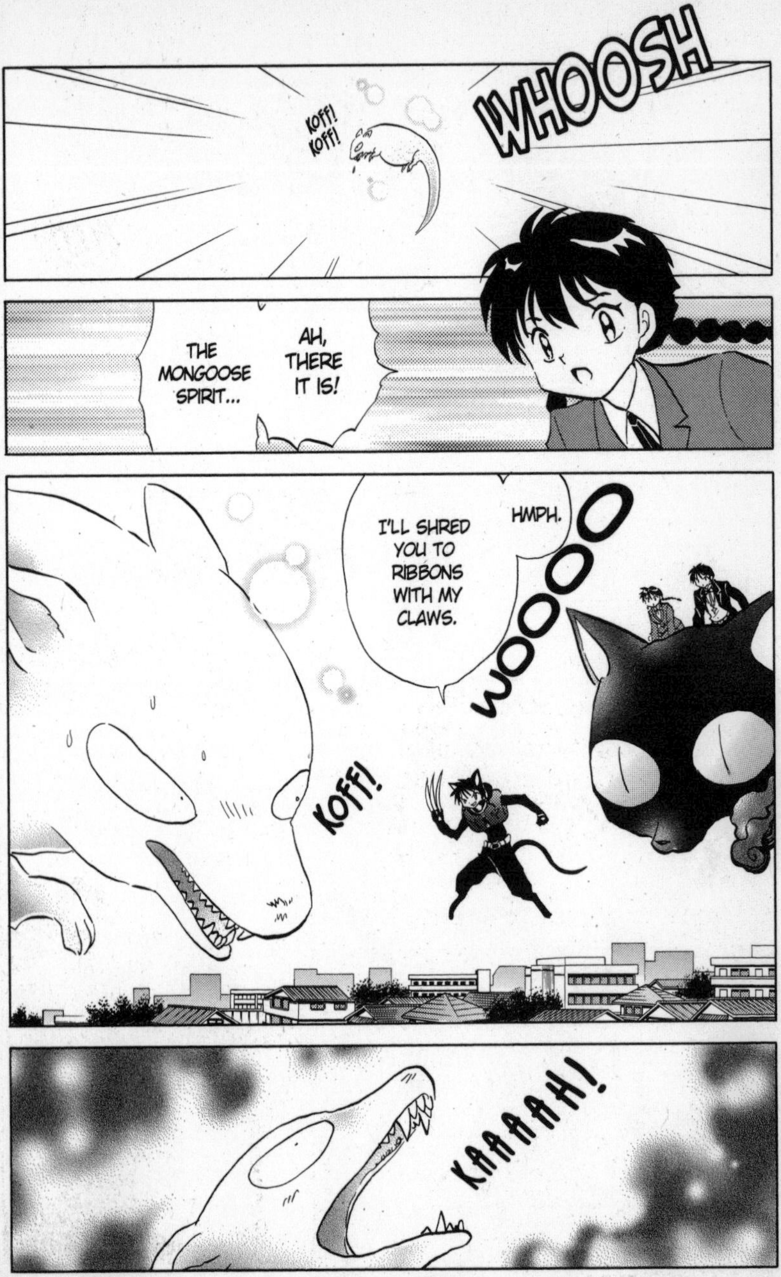
WHOOSH
KOFF! KOFF!
AH, THERE IT IS!
THE MONGOOSE SPIRIT...
HMPH.
I'LL SHRED YOU TO RIBBONS WITH MY CLAWS.
WOOOOO
KOFF!
KAAAAH!

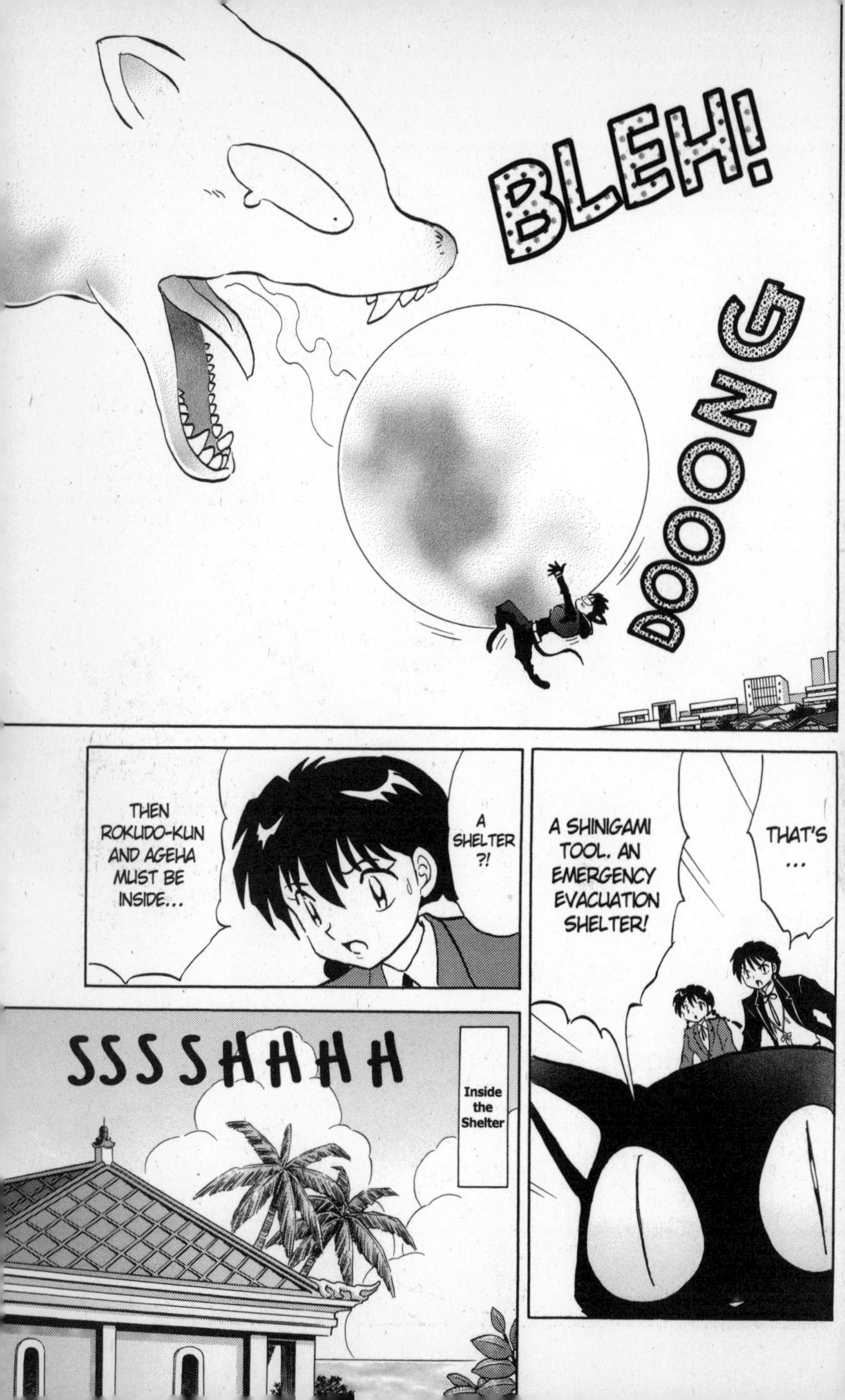
BLEH!
DOOOONG
THAT'S ...
A SHINIGAMI TOOL. AN EMERGENCY EVACUATION SHELTER!
A SHELTER ?!
THEN ROKUDO-KUN AND AGEHA MUST BE INSIDE...
Inside the Shelter
SSSSHHHH

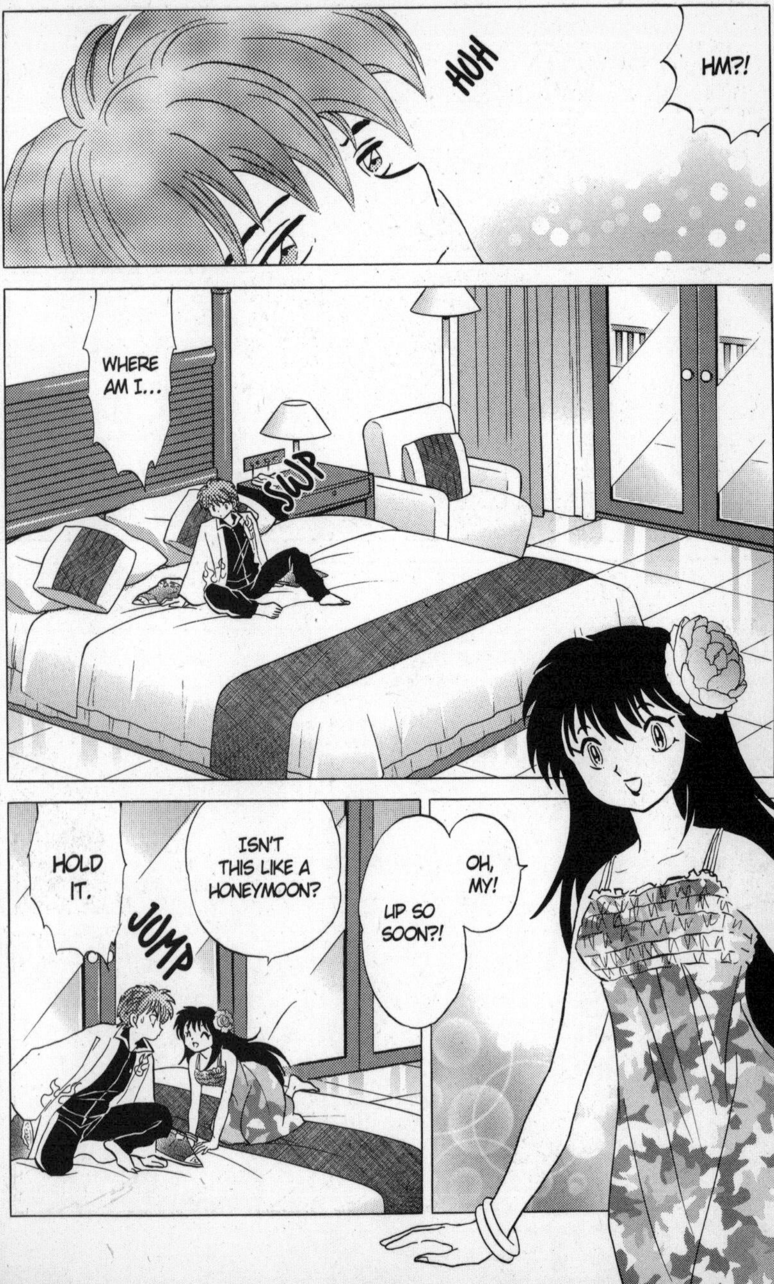
HM?!
HUH
WHERE AM I...
SWP
OH, MY!
UP SO SOON?!
ISN'T THIS LIKE A HONEYMOON?
JUMP
HOLD IT.

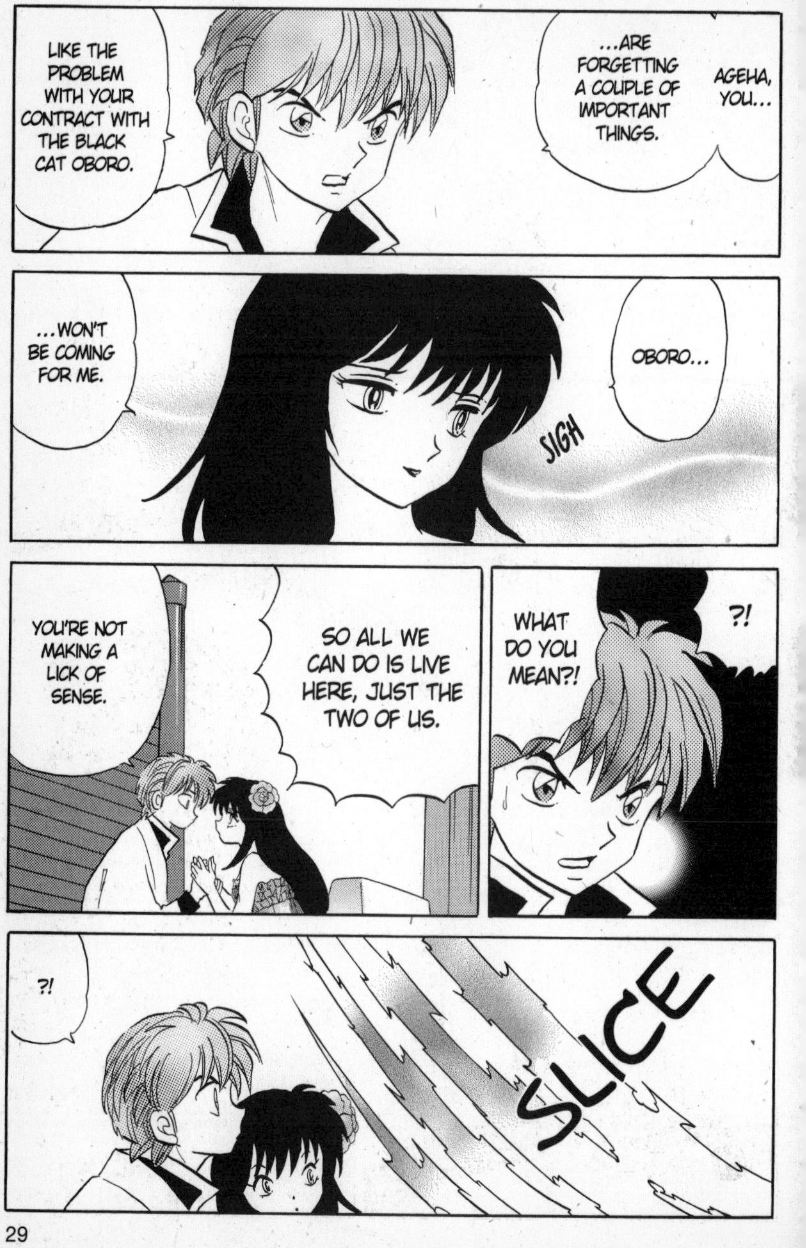

AGEHA, YOU...
...ARE FORGETTING A COUPLE OF IMPORTANT THINGS.
LIKE THE PROBLEM WITH YOUR CONTRACT WITH THE BLACK CAT OBORO.
OBORO...
SIGH
...WON'T BE COMING FOR ME.
?!
WHAT DO YOU MEAN?!
SO ALL WE CAN DO IS LIVE HERE, JUST THE TWO OF US.
YOU'RE NOT MAKING A LICK OF SENSE.
SLICE
?!

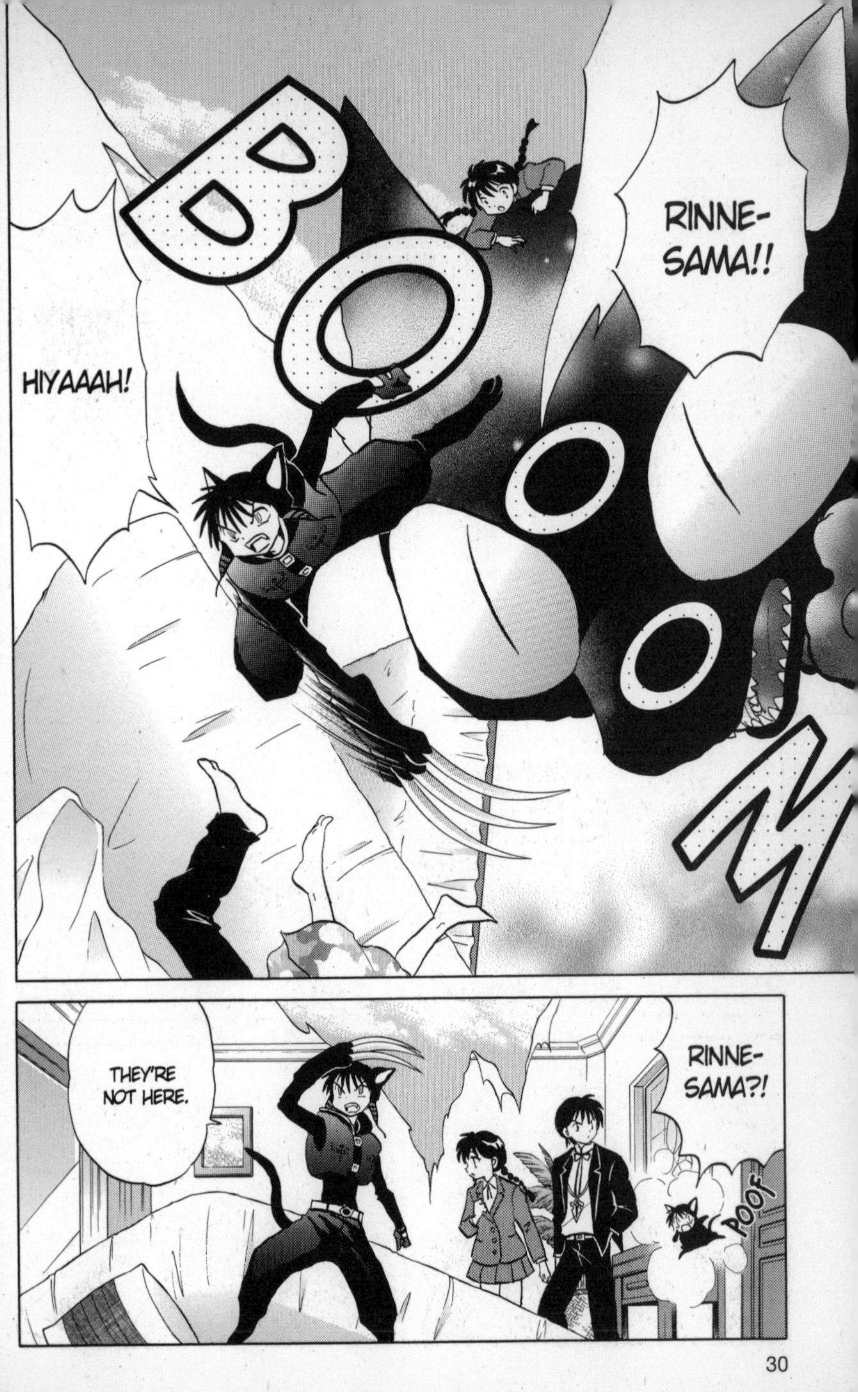
RINNE-SAMA!!
BOOOOM
HIYAAAH!
RINNE-SAMA?!
POOF
THEY'RE NOT HERE.

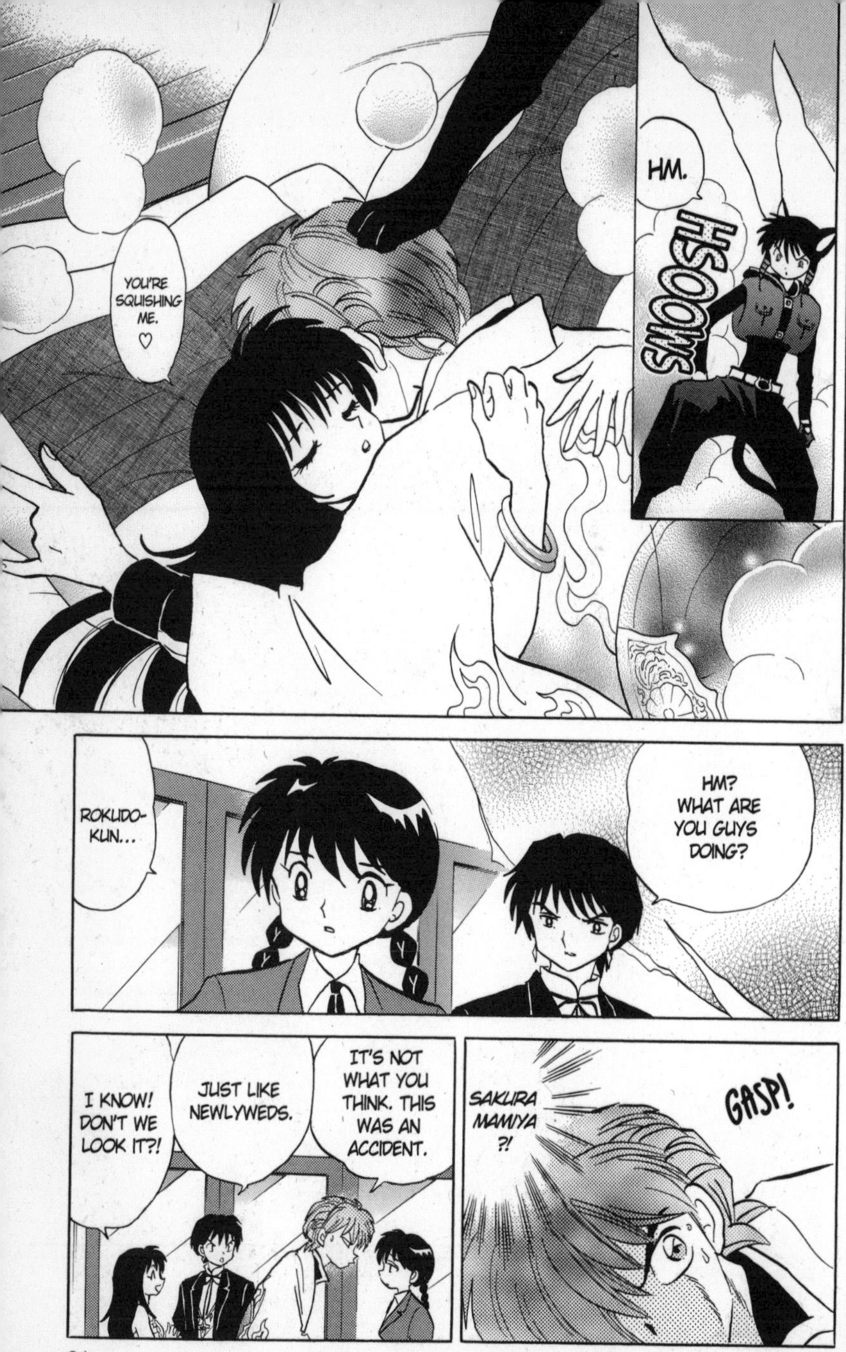
HM.
SWOOSH
YOU'RE SQUISHING ME. ♡
HM? WHAT ARE YOU GUYS DOING?
ROKUDO-KUN...
GASP!
SAKURA MAMIYA?!
IT'S NOT WHAT YOU THINK. THIS WAS AN ACCIDENT.
JUST LIKE NEWLYWEDS.
I KNOW! DON'T WE LOOK IT?!

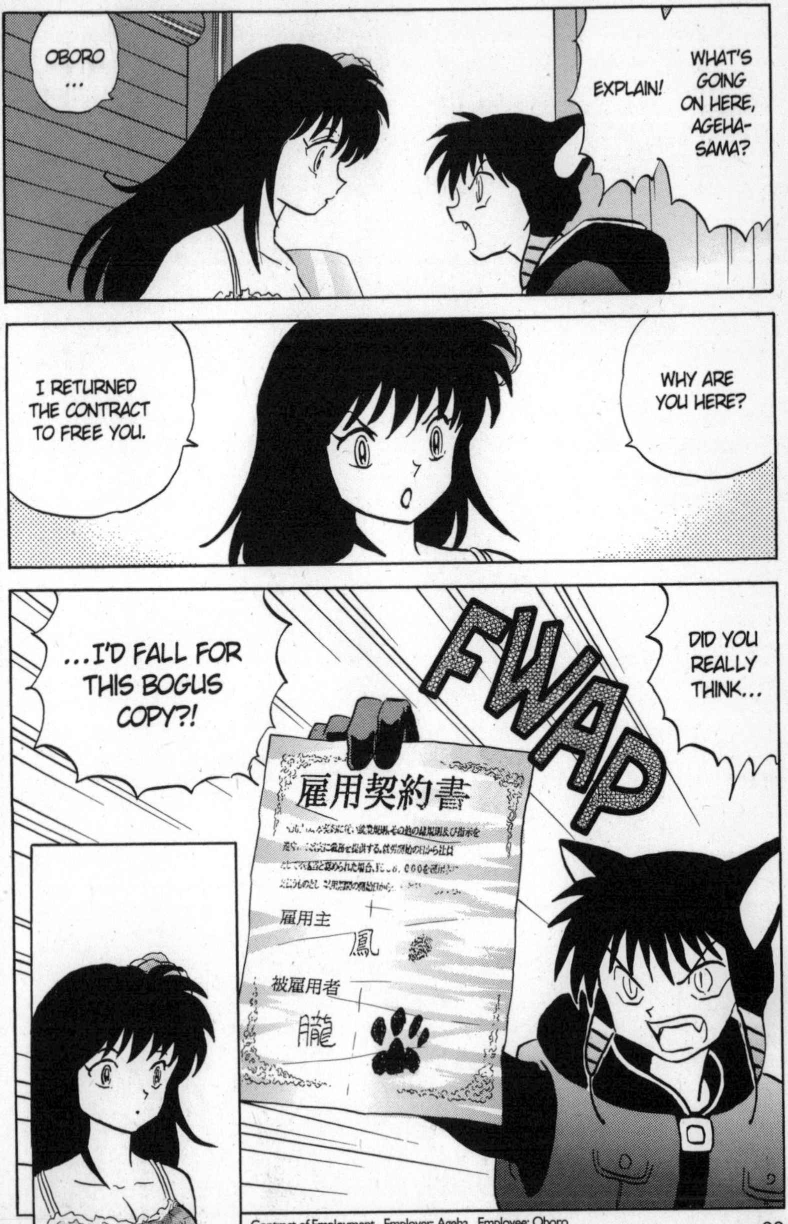
WHAT'S GOING ON HERE, AGEHA-SAMA?
EXPLAIN!
OBORO ...
WHY ARE YOU HERE?
I RETURNED THE CONTRACT TO FREE YOU.
DID YOU REALLY THINK...
FWAP
...I'D FALL FOR THIS BOGUS COPY?!
雇用契約書
雇用主
鳳
被雇用者
朧
Contract of Employment Employer: Ageha Employee: Oboro

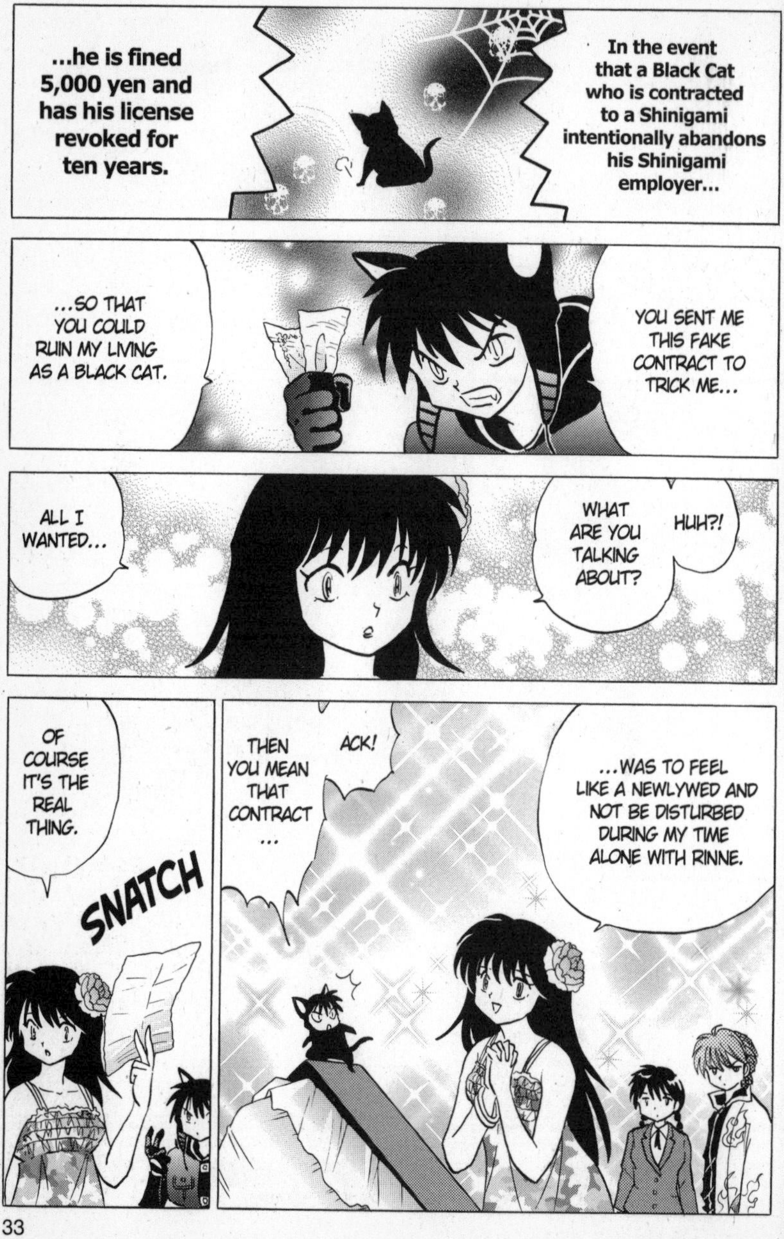
In the event that a Black Cat who is contracted to a Shinigami intentionally abandons his Shinigami employer...
...he is fined 5,000 yen and has his license revoked for ten years.
YOU SENT ME THIS FAKE CONTRACT TO TRICK ME...
...SO THAT YOU COULD RUIN MY LIVING AS A BLACK CAT.
HUH?!
WHAT ARE YOU TALKING ABOUT?
ALL I WANTED...
...WAS TO FEEL LIKE A NEWLYWED AND NOT BE DISTURBED DURING MY TIME ALONE WITH RINNE.
ACK!
THEN YOU MEAN THAT CONTRACT ...
OF COURSE IT'S THE REAL THING.
SNATCH

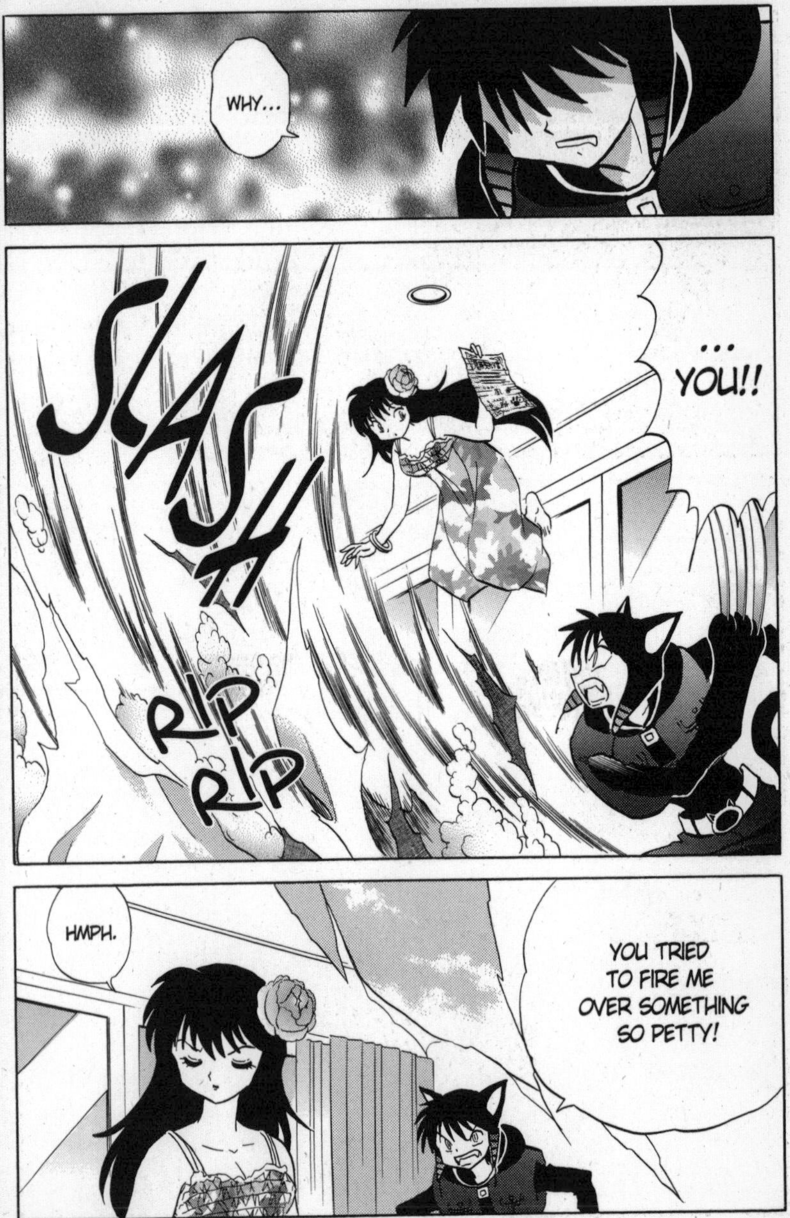
WHY...
... YOU!!
SLASH
RIP RIP
YOU TRIED TO FIRE ME OVER SOMETHING SO PETTY!
HMPH.

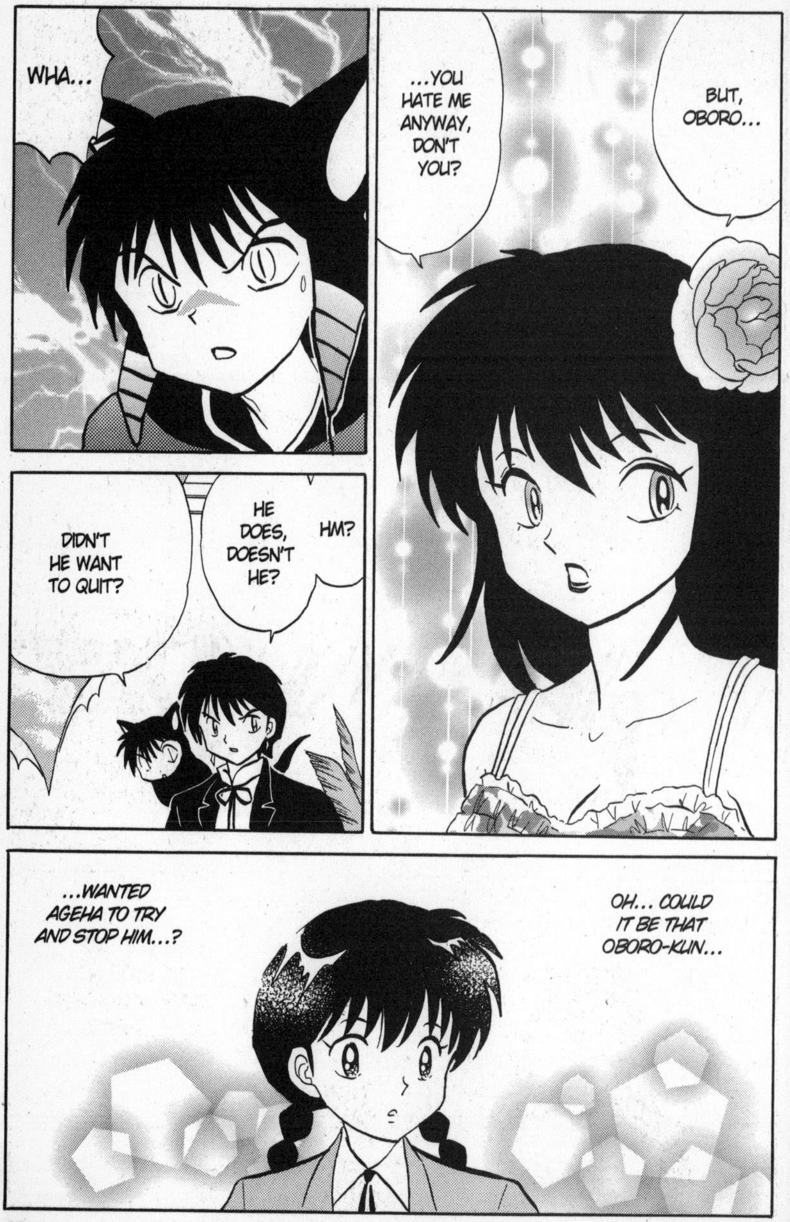
BUT, OBORO...
...YOU HATE ME ANYWAY, DON'T YOU?
WHA...
HM?
HE DOES, DOESN'T HE?
DIDN'T HE WANT TO QUIT?
OH... COULD IT BE THAT OBORO-KUN...
...WANTED AGEHA TO TRY AND STOP HIM...?

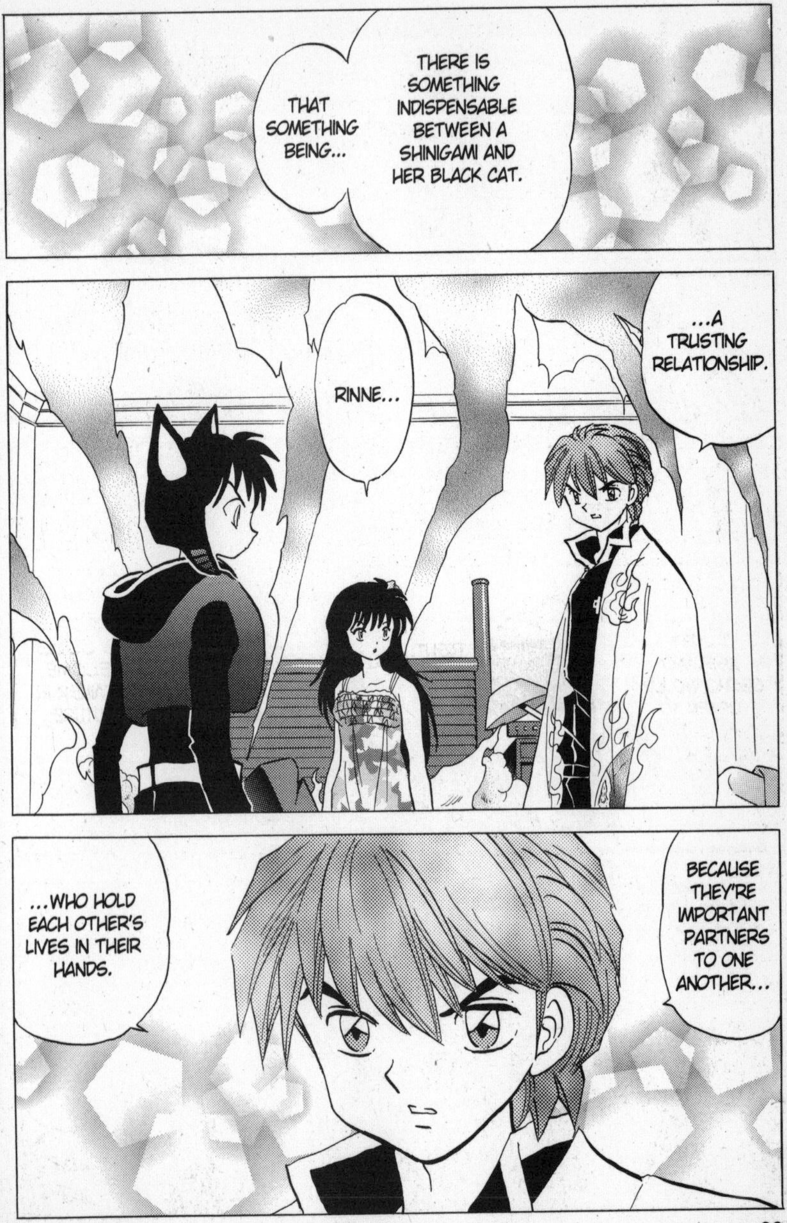
THERE IS SOMETHING INDISPENSABLE BETWEEN A SHINIGAMI AND HER BLACK CAT.
THAT SOMETHING BEING...
...A TRUSTING RELATIONSHIP.
RINNE...
BECAUSE THEY'RE IMPORTANT PARTNERS TO ONE ANOTHER...
...WHO HOLD EACH OTHER'S LIVES IN THEIR HANDS.

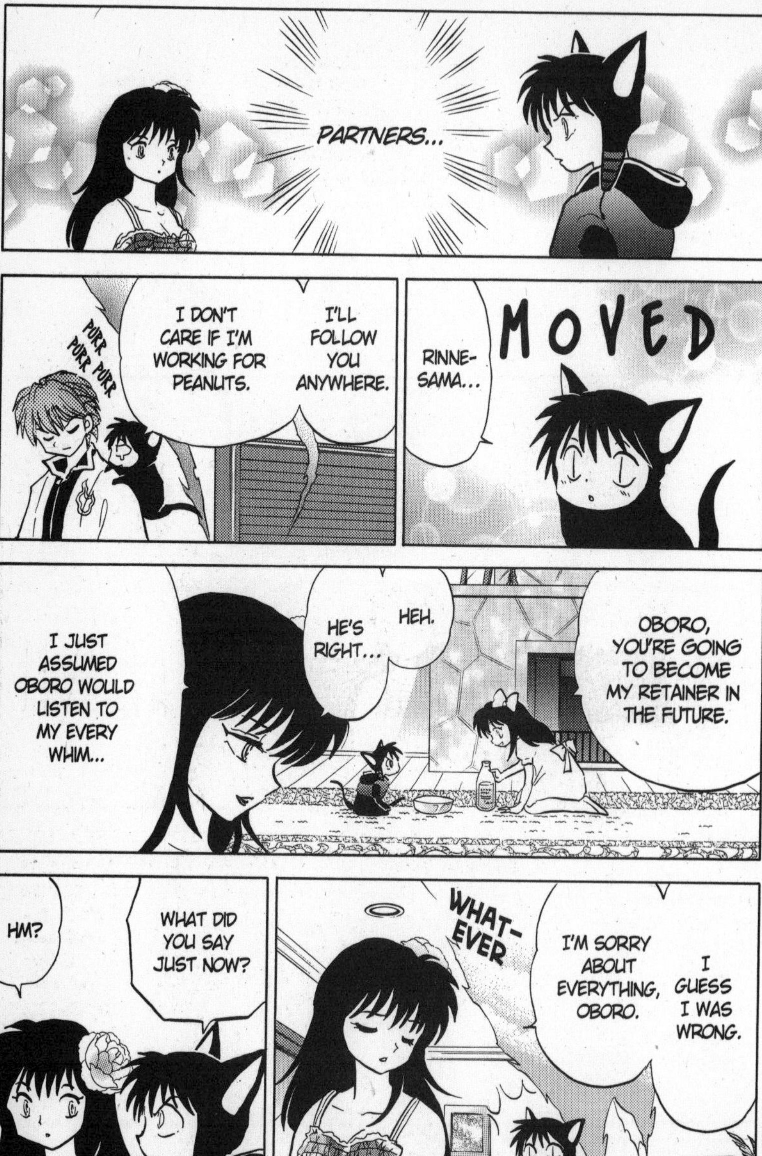
PARTNERS...
MOVED
RINNE-SAMA...
I'LL FOLLOW YOU ANYWHERE.
I DON'T CARE IF I'M WORKING FOR PEANUTS.
PURR PURR PURR
OBORO, YOU'RE GOING TO BECOME MY RETAINER IN THE FUTURE.
HEH.
HE'S RIGHT...
I JUST ASSUMED OBORO WOULD LISTEN TO MY EVERY WHIM...
WHAT-EVER
I GUESS I WAS WRONG.
I'M SORRY ABOUT EVERYTHING, OBORO.
WHAT DID YOU SAY JUST NOW?
HM?

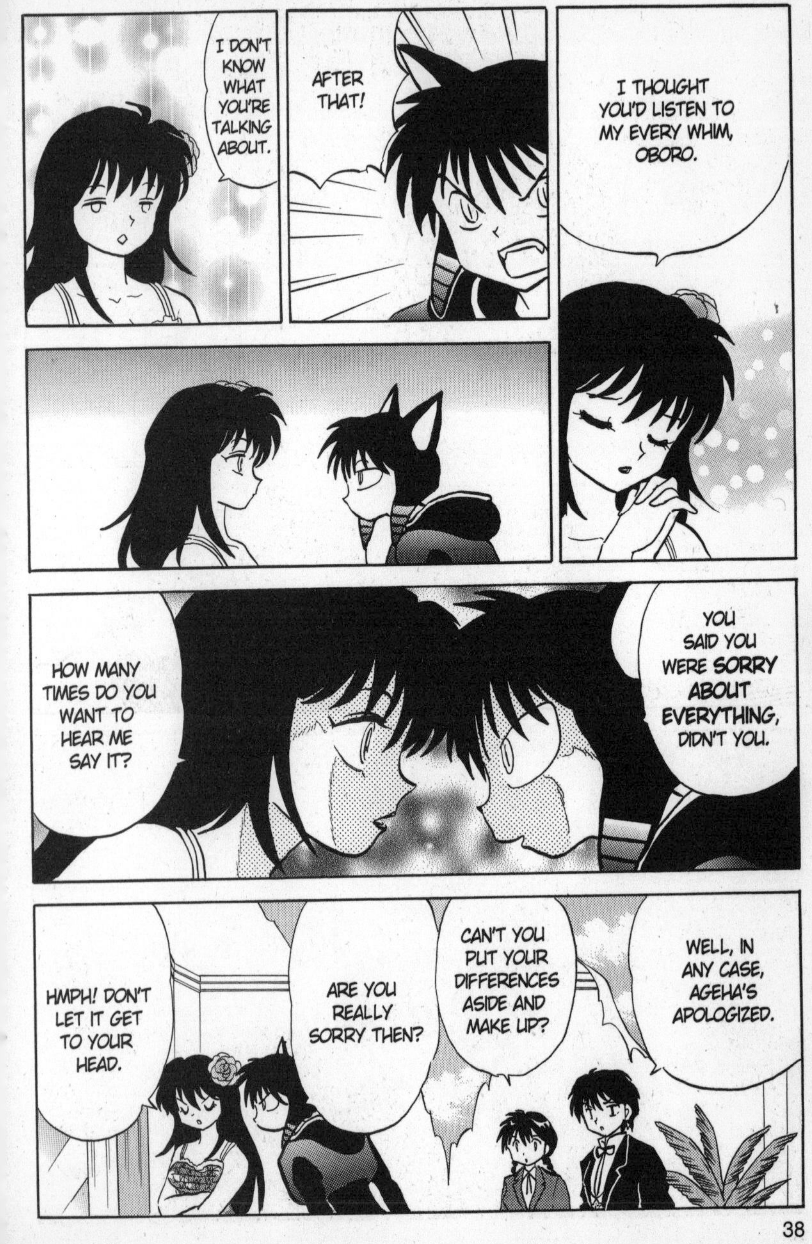
I THOUGHT YOU'D LISTEN TO MY EVERY WHIM, OBORO.
AFTER THAT!
I DON'T KNOW WHAT YOU'RE TALKING ABOUT.
YOU SAID YOU WERE **SORRY ABOUT EVERYTHING**, DIDN'T YOU.
HOW MANY TIMES DO YOU WANT TO HEAR ME SAY IT?
WELL, IN ANY CASE, AGEHA'S APOLOGIZED.
CAN'T YOU PUT YOUR DIFFERENCES ASIDE AND MAKE UP?
ARE YOU REALLY SORRY THEN?
HMPH! DON'T LET IT GET TO YOUR HEAD.

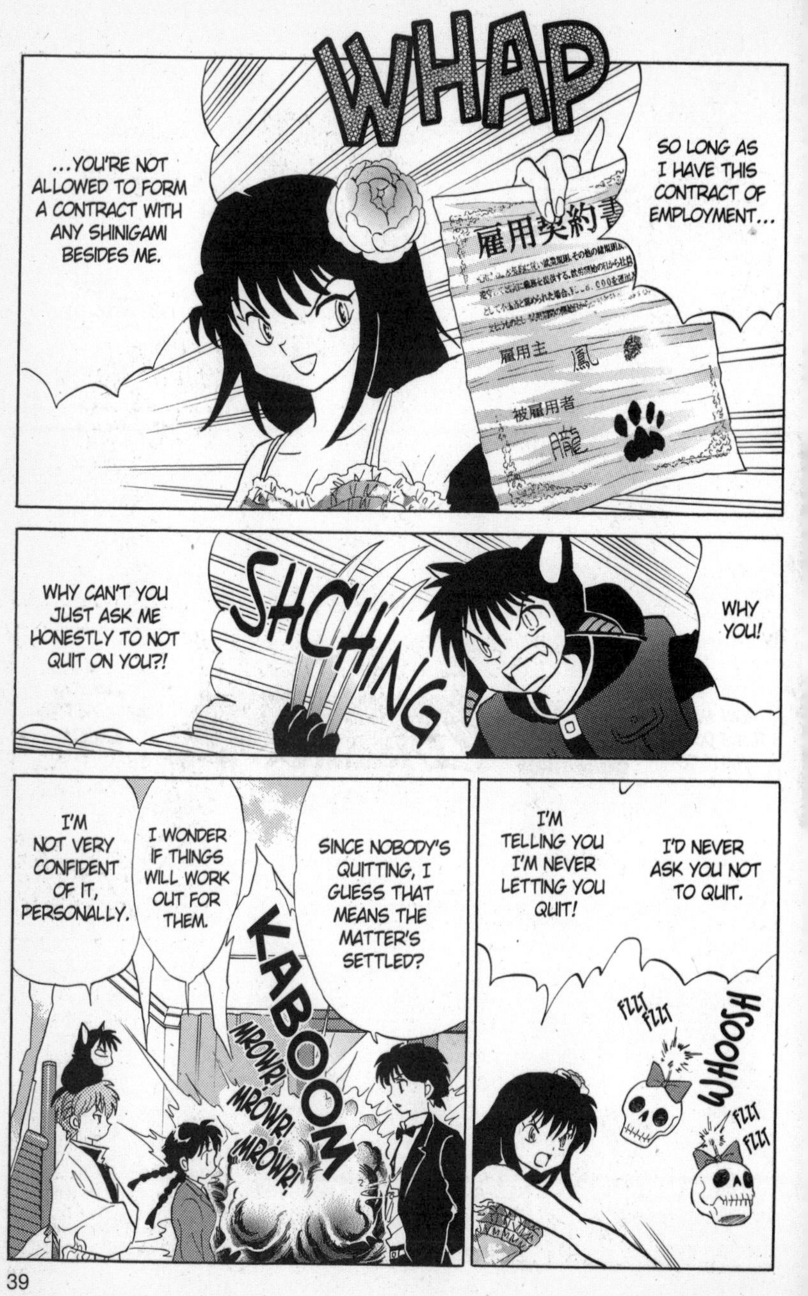
WHAP
SO LONG AS I HAVE THIS CONTRACT OF EMPLOYMENT...
...YOU'RE NOT ALLOWED TO FORM A CONTRACT WITH ANY SHINIGAMI BESIDES ME.
雇用契約書
雇用主 鳳
被雇用者 朧
WHY YOU!
SHCHING
WHY CAN'T YOU JUST ASK ME HONESTLY TO NOT QUIT ON YOU?!
I'D NEVER ASK YOU NOT TO QUIT.
I'M TELLING YOU I'M NEVER LETTING YOU QUIT!
WHOOSH
FZZT FZZT
FZZT FZZT
SINCE NOBODY'S QUITTING, I GUESS THAT MEANS THE MATTER'S SETTLED?
I WONDER IF THINGS WILL WORK OUT FOR THEM.
I'M NOT VERY CONFIDENT OF IT, PERSONALLY.
KABOOM
MROWR! MROWR! MROWR!

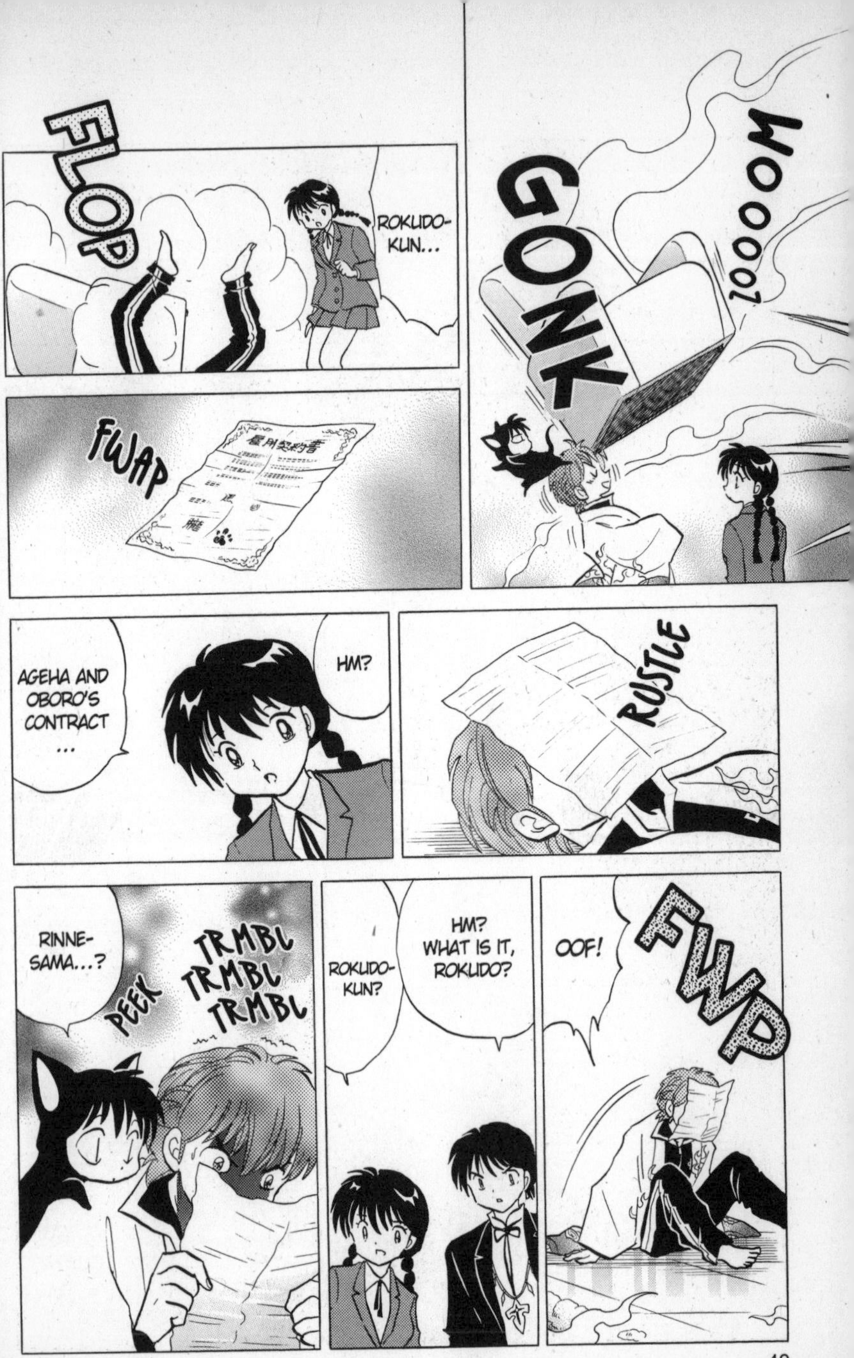

GONK
ZOOOOOM
FLOP
ROKUDO-KUN...
FWAP
RUSTLE
HM?
AGEHA AND OBORO'S CONTRACT ...
FWP
OOF!
HM? WHAT IS IT, ROKUDO?
ROKUDO-KUN?
RINNE-SAMA...?
TRMBL TRMBL TRMBL
PEEK

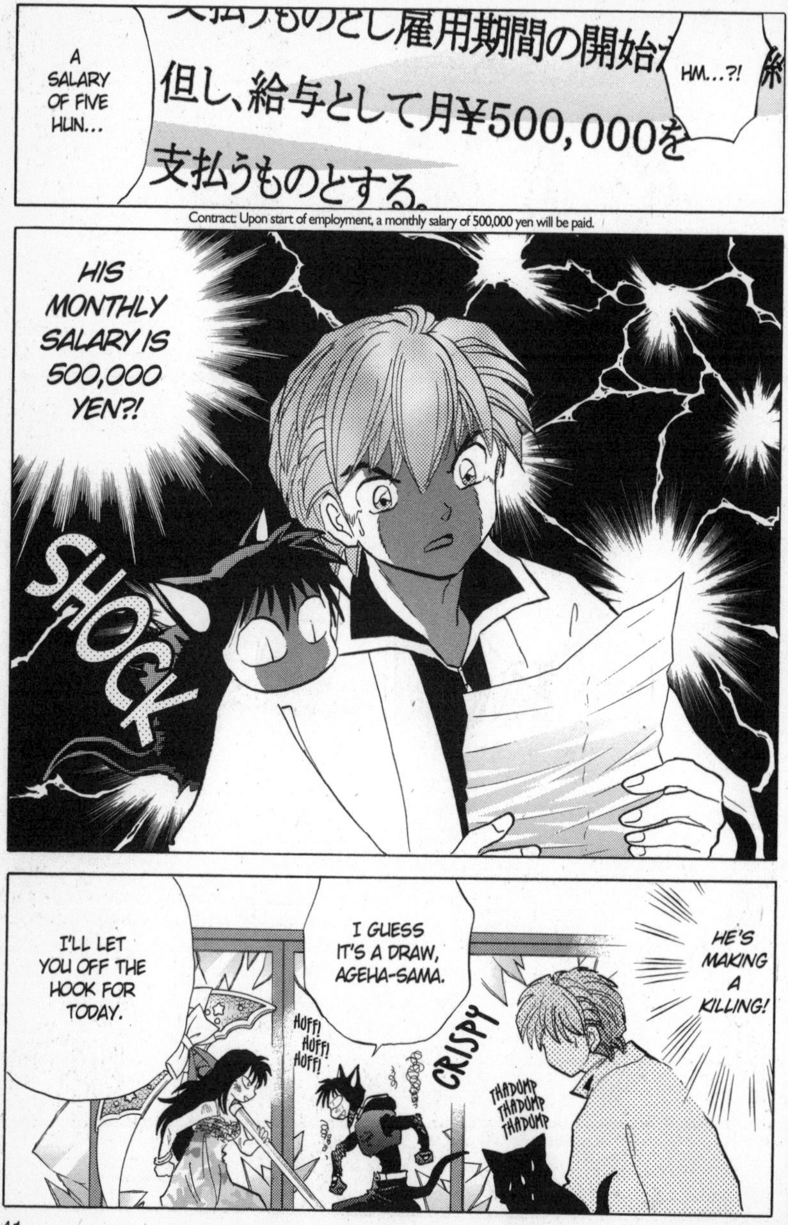
HM...?!
但し、給与として月¥500,000を
支払うものとする。
A SALARY OF FIVE HUN...
Contract: Upon start of employment, a monthly salary of 500,000 yen will be paid.
HIS MONTHLY SALARY IS 500,000 YEN?!
SHOCK
HE'S MAKING A KILLING!
THADUMP THADUMP THADUMP
CRISPY
I GUESS IT'S A DRAW, AGEHA-SAMA.
HUFF! HUFF! HUFF!
I'LL LET YOU OFF THE HOOK FOR TODAY.

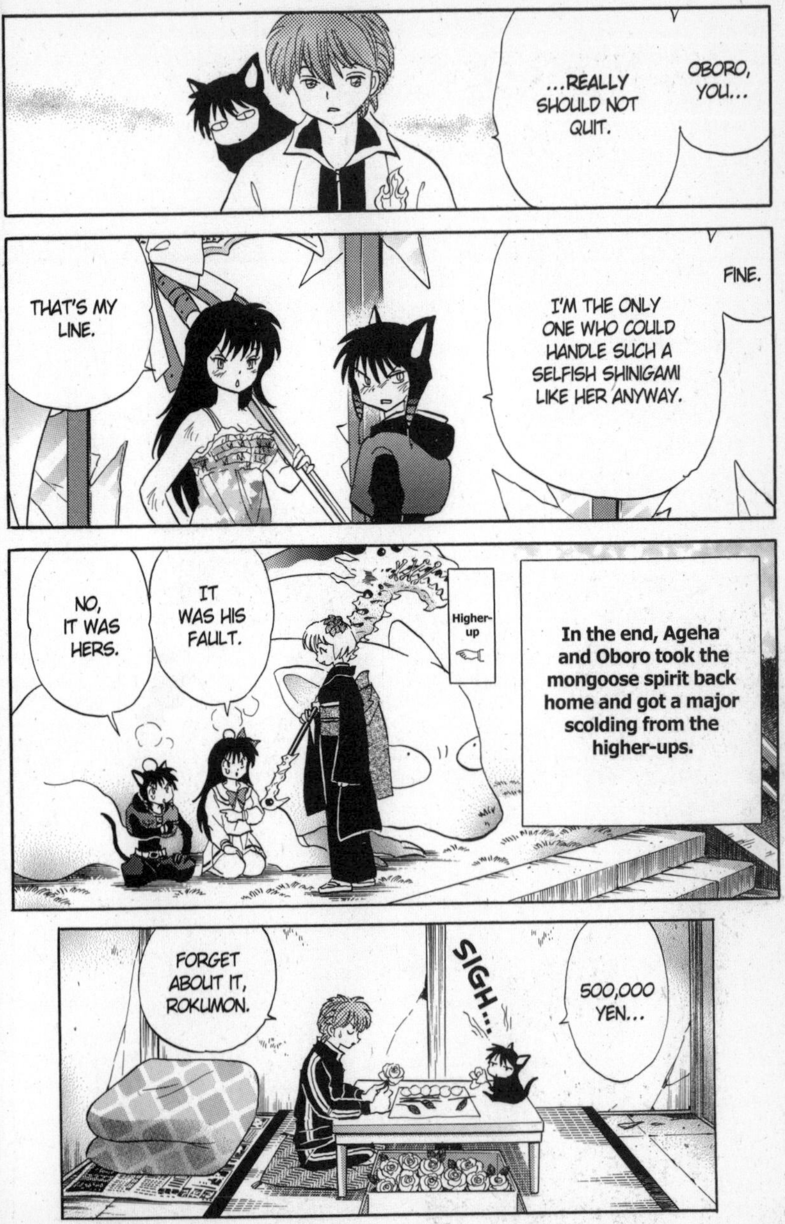
OBORO, YOU...
...REALLY SHOULD NOT QUIT.
FINE.
I'M THE ONLY ONE WHO COULD HANDLE SUCH A SELFISH SHINIGAMI LIKE HER ANYWAY.
THAT'S MY LINE.
In the end, Ageha and Oboro took the mongoose spirit back home and got a major scolding from the higher-ups.
Higher-up
IT WAS HIS FAULT.
NO, IT WAS HERS.
500,000 YEN...
SIGH...
FORGET ABOUT IT, ROKUMON.

CHAPTER 91: THE MISSING BUS STOP

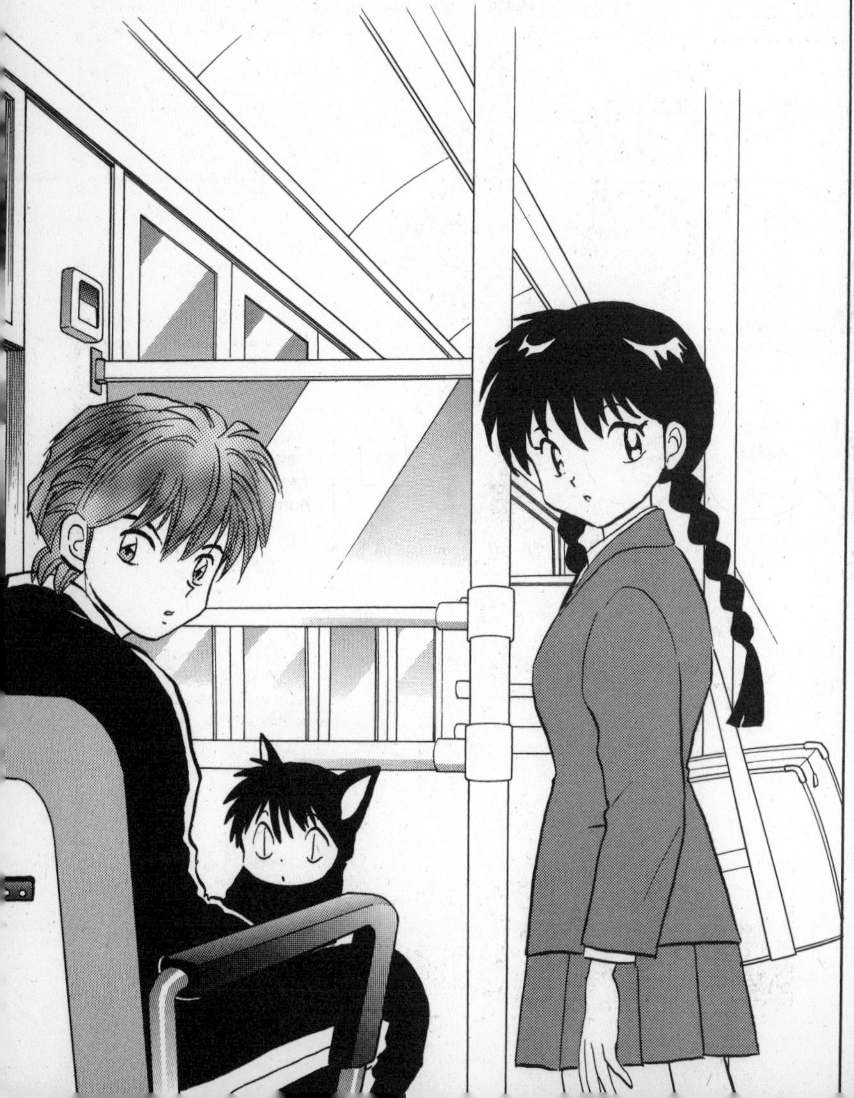

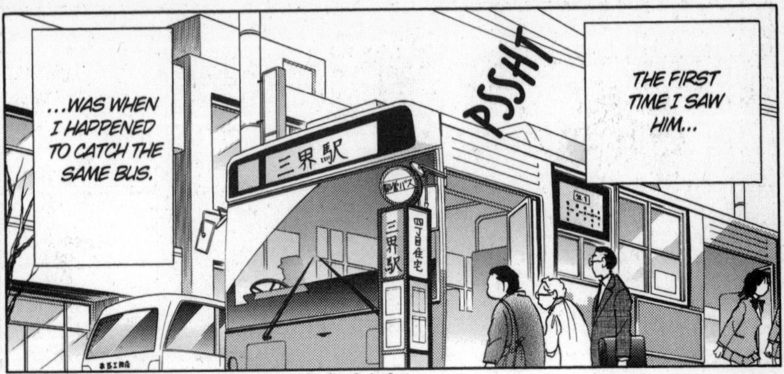
THE FIRST TIME I SAW HIM...
PSHT
三界駅
...WAS WHEN I HAPPENED TO CATCH THE SAME BUS.
Bus Sign: Sankai Station

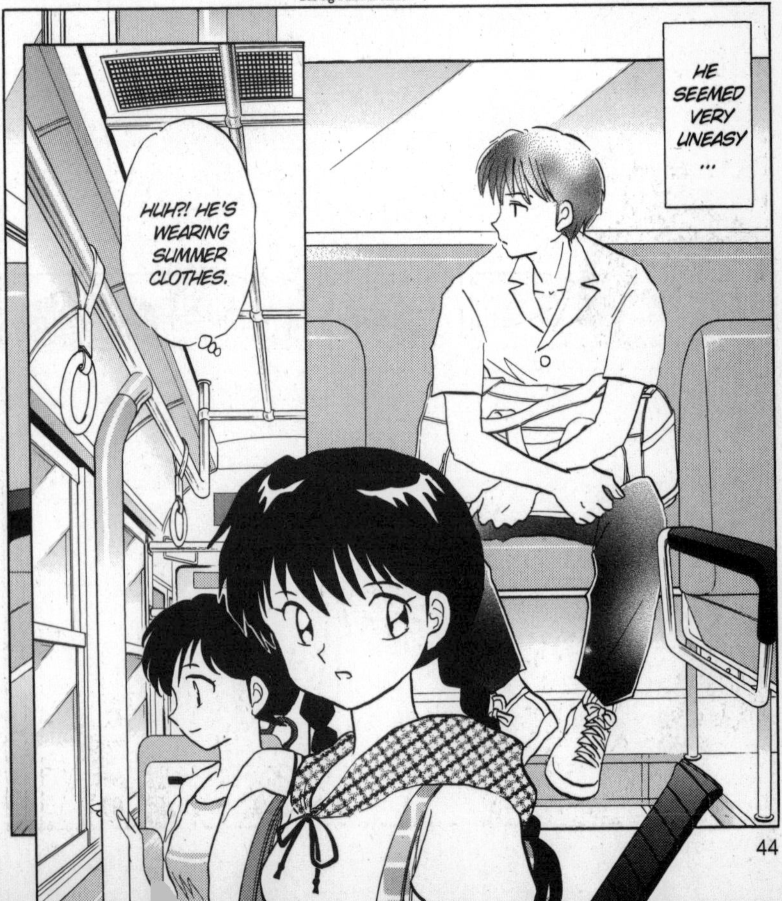
HE SEEMED VERY UNEASY ...
HUH?! HE'S WEARING SUMMER CLOTHES.

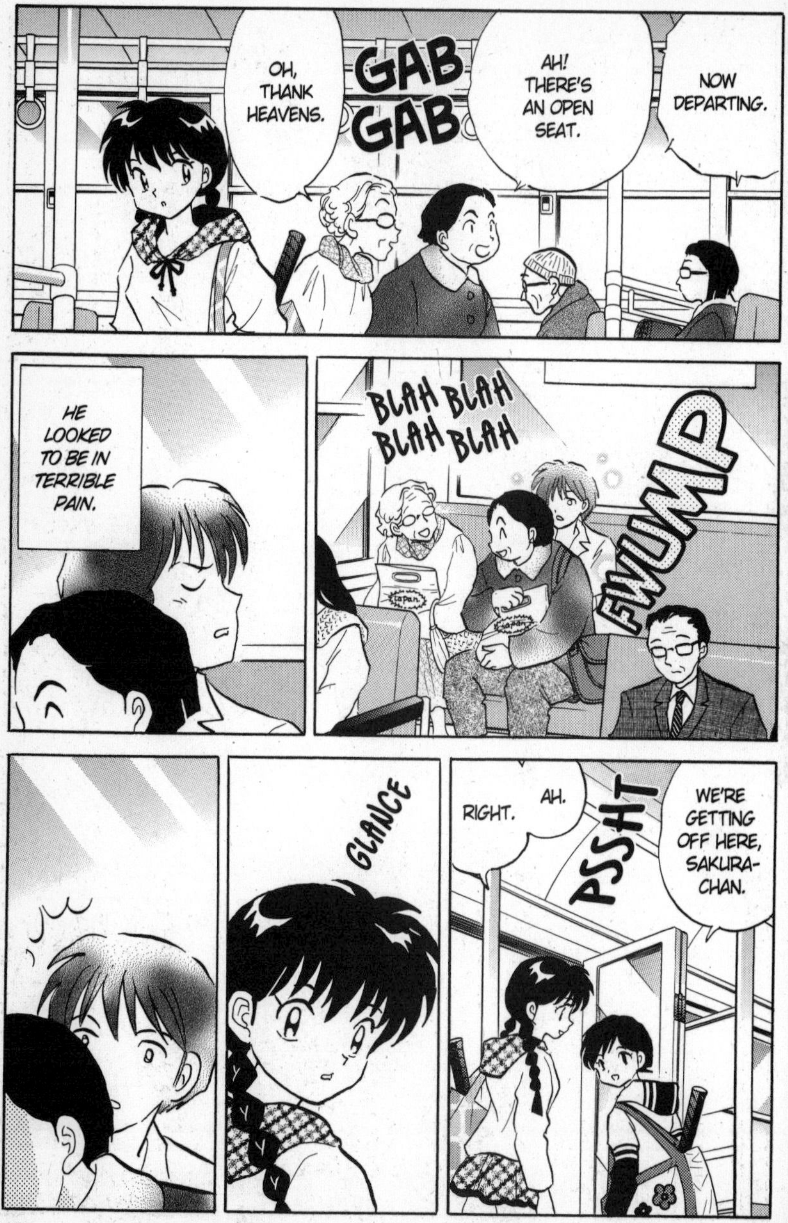
NOW DEPARTING.
AH! THERE'S AN OPEN SEAT.
GAB GAB
OH, THANK HEAVENS.
FWUMP
BLAH BLAH BLAH BLAH
HE LOOKED TO BE IN TERRIBLE PAIN.
WE'RE GETTING OFF HERE, SAKURA-CHAN.
PSSHT
AH.
RIGHT.
GLANCE

Signs: Sankai Station Tennis Courts

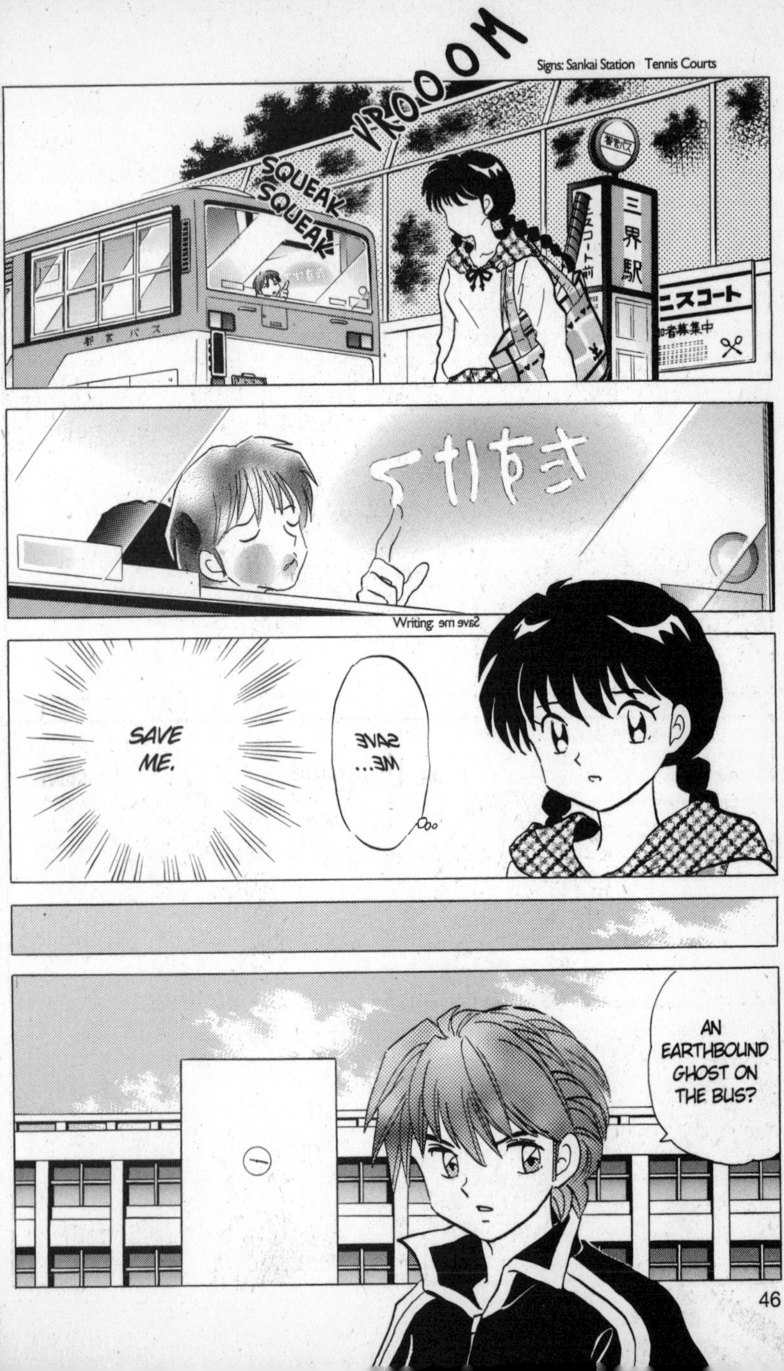
VROOOM
SQUEAK SQUEAK
三界駅
SAVE ME...
SAVE ME.
AN EARTHBOUND GHOST ON THE BUS?

Writing: Save me

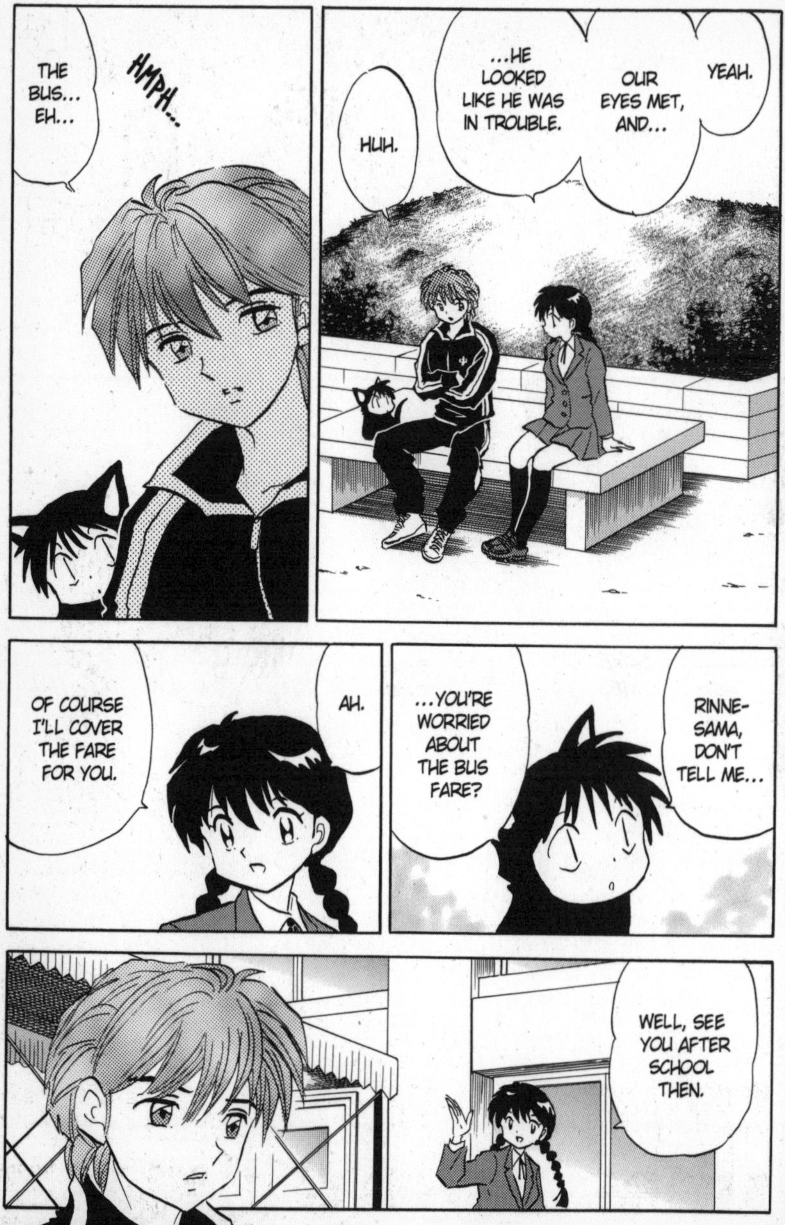
YEAH.
OUR EYES MET, AND...
...HE LOOKED LIKE HE WAS IN TROUBLE.
HUH.
HMPH...
THE BUS... EH...
RINNE-SAMA, DON'T TELL ME...
...YOU'RE WORRIED ABOUT THE BUS FARE?
AH.
OF COURSE I'LL COVER THE FARE FOR YOU.
WELL, SEE YOU AFTER SCHOOL THEN.

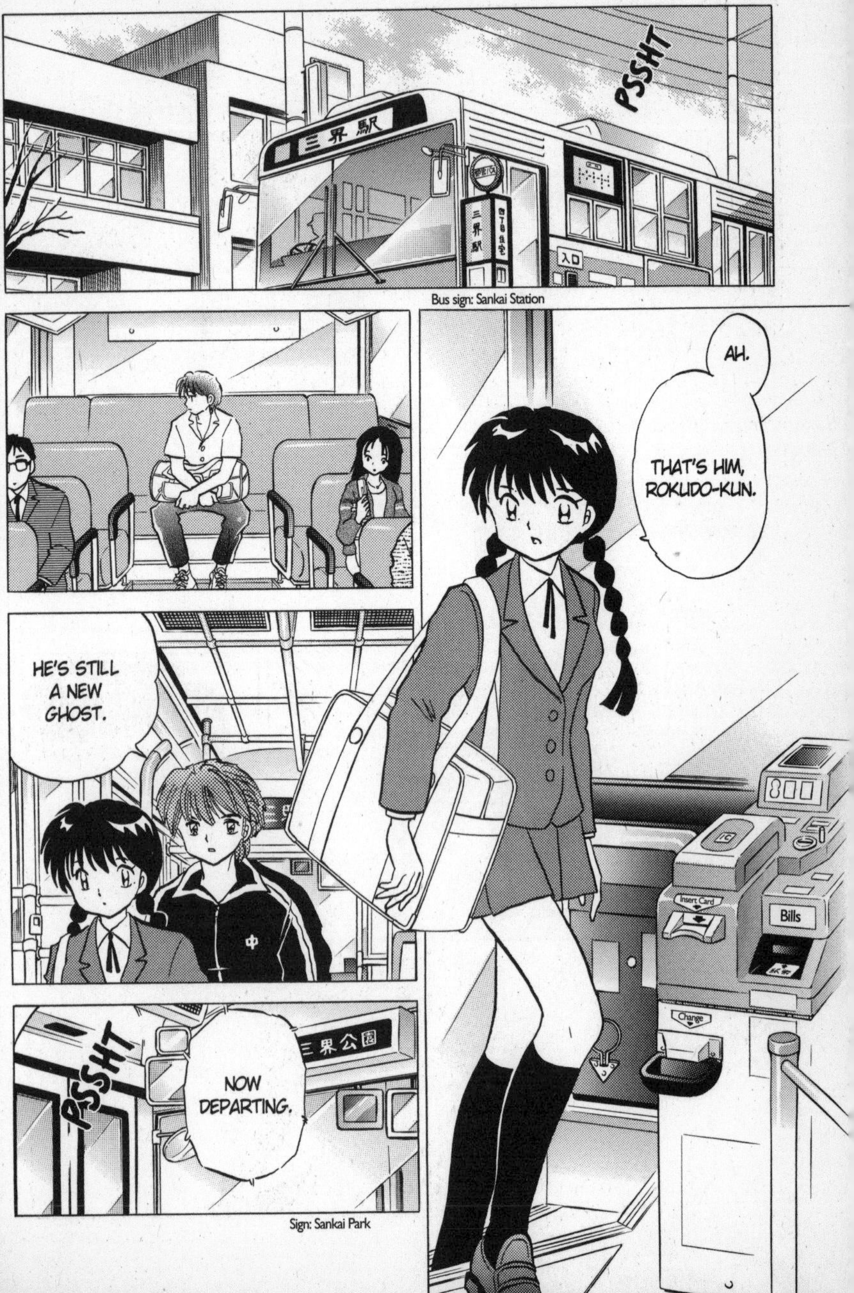
PSSHT
三界駅
AH.
THAT'S HIM, ROKUDO-KUN.
800
Insert Card
Bills
Change
HE'S STILL A NEW GHOST.
PSSHT
NOW DEPARTING.
Bus sign: Sankai Station

Sign: Sankai Park

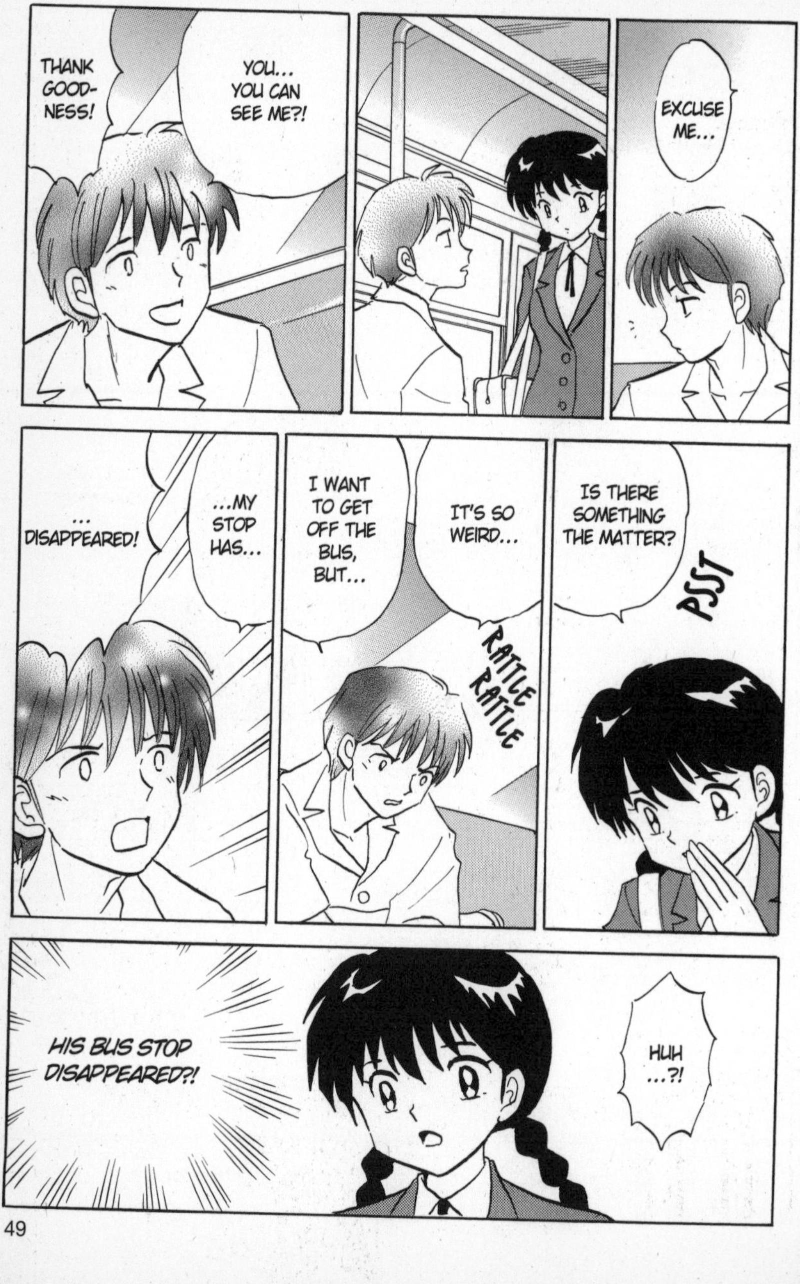
EXCUSE ME...
YOU... YOU CAN SEE ME?!
THANK GOODNESS!
IS THERE SOMETHING THE MATTER?
PSST
IT'S SO WEIRD...
RATTLE RATTLE
I WANT TO GET OFF THE BUS, BUT...
...MY STOP HAS...
...DISAPPEARED!
HUH ...?!
HIS BUS STOP DISAPPEARED?!

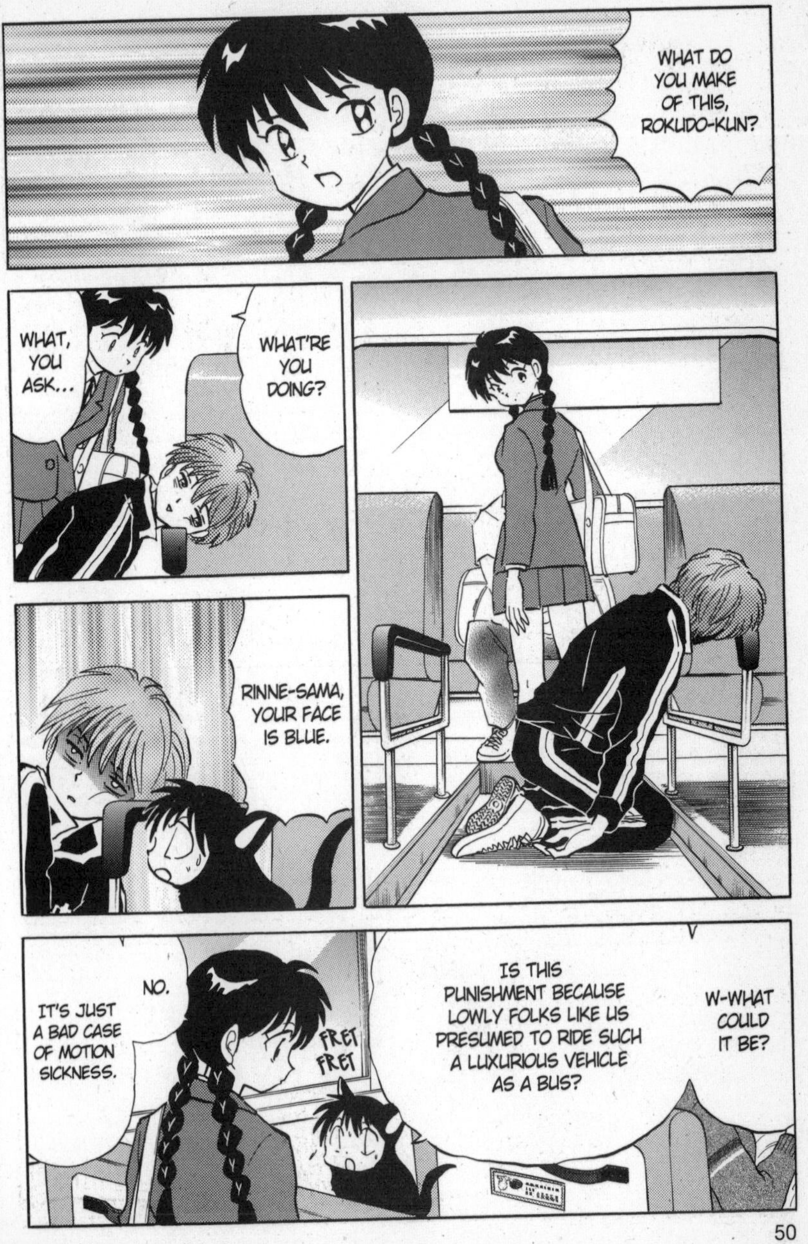
WHAT DO YOU MAKE OF THIS, ROKUDO-KUN?
WHAT'RE YOU DOING?
WHAT, YOU ASK...
RINNE-SAMA, YOUR FACE IS BLUE.
W-WHAT COULD IT BE?
IS THIS PUNISHMENT BECAUSE LOWLY FOLKS LIKE US PRESUMED TO RIDE SUCH A LUXURIOUS VEHICLE AS A BUS?
FRET FRET
NO.
IT'S JUST A BAD CASE OF MOTION SICKNESS.

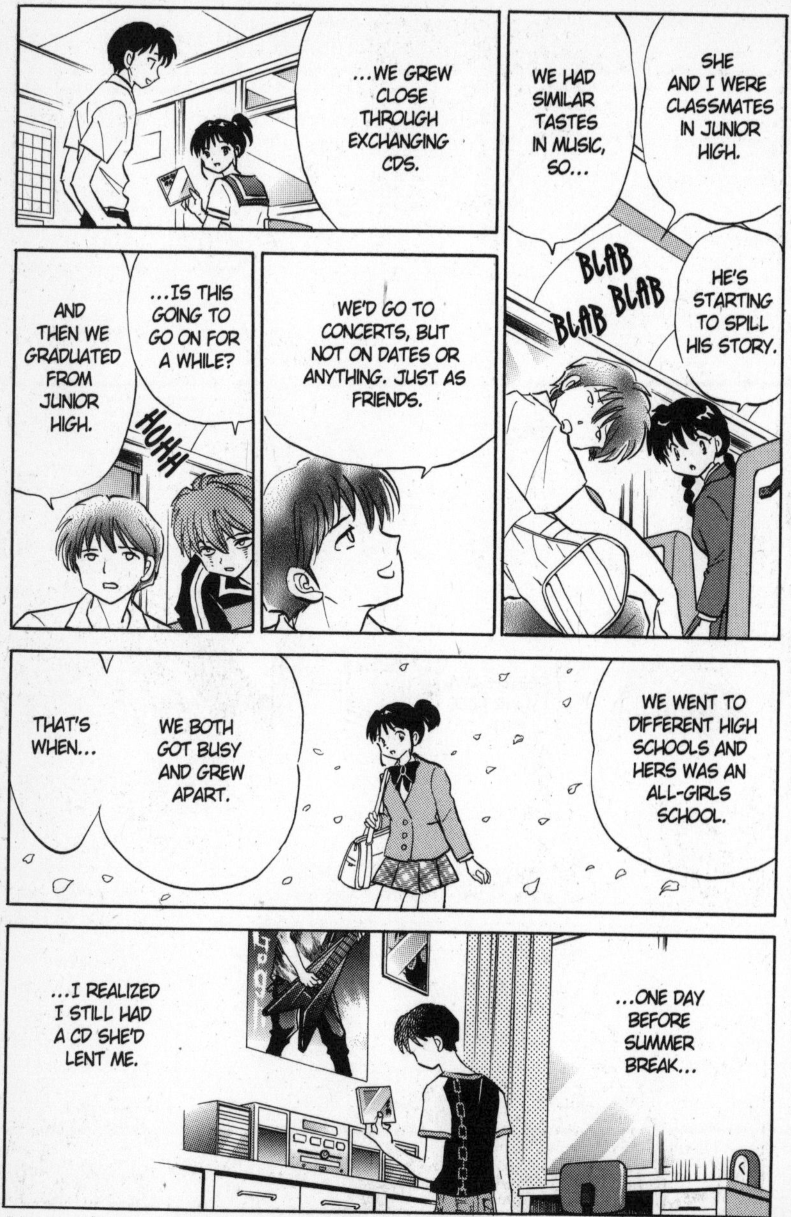
SHE AND I WERE CLASSMATES IN JUNIOR HIGH.
WE HAD SIMILAR TASTES IN MUSIC, SO...
BLAB BLAB BLAB
HE'S STARTING TO SPILL HIS STORY.
...WE GREW CLOSE THROUGH EXCHANGING CDS.
WE'D GO TO CONCERTS, BUT NOT ON DATES OR ANYTHING. JUST AS FRIENDS.
...IS THIS GOING TO GO ON FOR A WHILE?
AND THEN WE GRADUATED FROM JUNIOR HIGH.
HUHH
WE WENT TO DIFFERENT HIGH SCHOOLS AND HERS WAS AN ALL-GIRLS SCHOOL.
WE BOTH GOT BUSY AND GREW APART.
THAT'S WHEN...
...ONE DAY BEFORE SUMMER BREAK...
...I REALIZED I STILL HAD A CD SHE'D LENT ME.

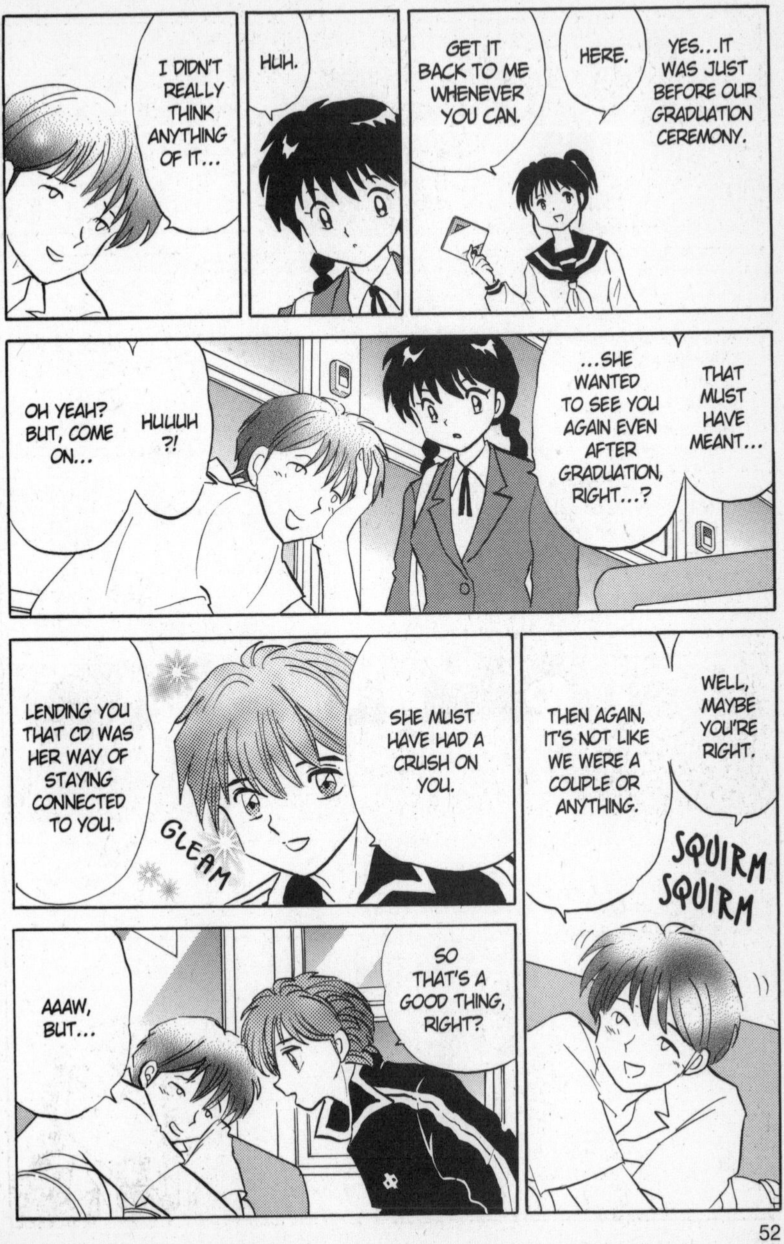
YES...IT WAS JUST BEFORE OUR GRADUATION CEREMONY.
HERE.
GET IT BACK TO ME WHENEVER YOU CAN.
HUH.
I DIDN'T REALLY THINK ANYTHING OF IT...
THAT MUST HAVE MEANT...
...SHE WANTED TO SEE YOU AGAIN EVEN AFTER GRADUATION, RIGHT...?
HUUUH?!
OH YEAH? BUT, COME ON...
WELL, MAYBE YOU'RE RIGHT.
THEN AGAIN, IT'S NOT LIKE WE WERE A COUPLE OR ANYTHING.
SQUIRM SQUIRM
SHE MUST HAVE HAD A CRUSH ON YOU.
LENDING YOU THAT CD WAS HER WAY OF STAYING CONNECTED TO YOU.
GLEAM
SO THAT'S A GOOD THING, RIGHT?
AAAW, BUT...

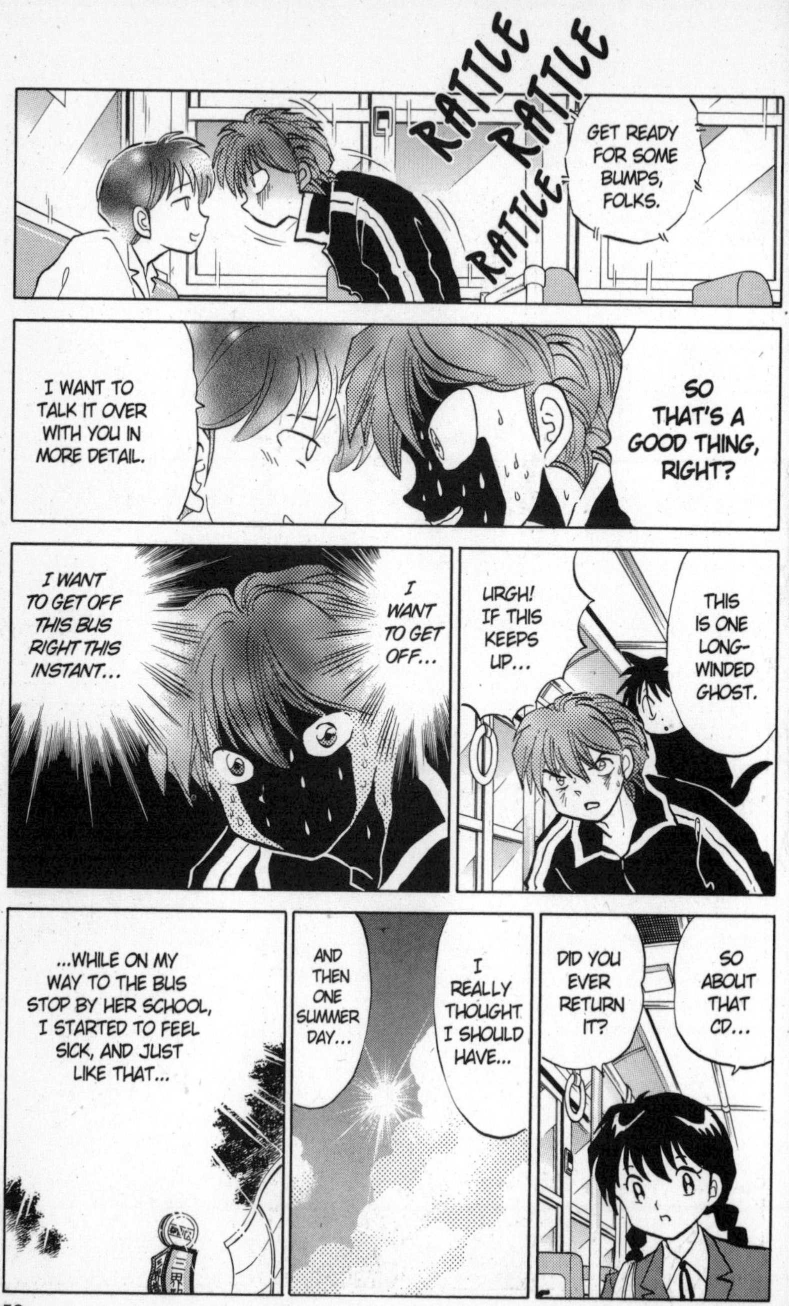

RATTLE RATTLE RATTLE
GET READY FOR SOME BUMPS, FOLKS.
SO THAT'S A GOOD THING, RIGHT?
I WANT TO TALK IT OVER WITH YOU IN MORE DETAIL.
THIS IS ONE LONG-WINDED GHOST.
URGH! IF THIS KEEPS UP...
I WANT TO GET OFF...
I WANT TO GET OFF THIS BUS RIGHT THIS INSTANT...
SO ABOUT THAT CD...
DID YOU EVER RETURN IT?
I REALLY THOUGHT I SHOULD HAVE...
AND THEN ONE SUMMER DAY...
...WHILE ON MY WAY TO THE BUS STOP BY HER SCHOOL, I STARTED TO FEEL SICK, AND JUST LIKE THAT...

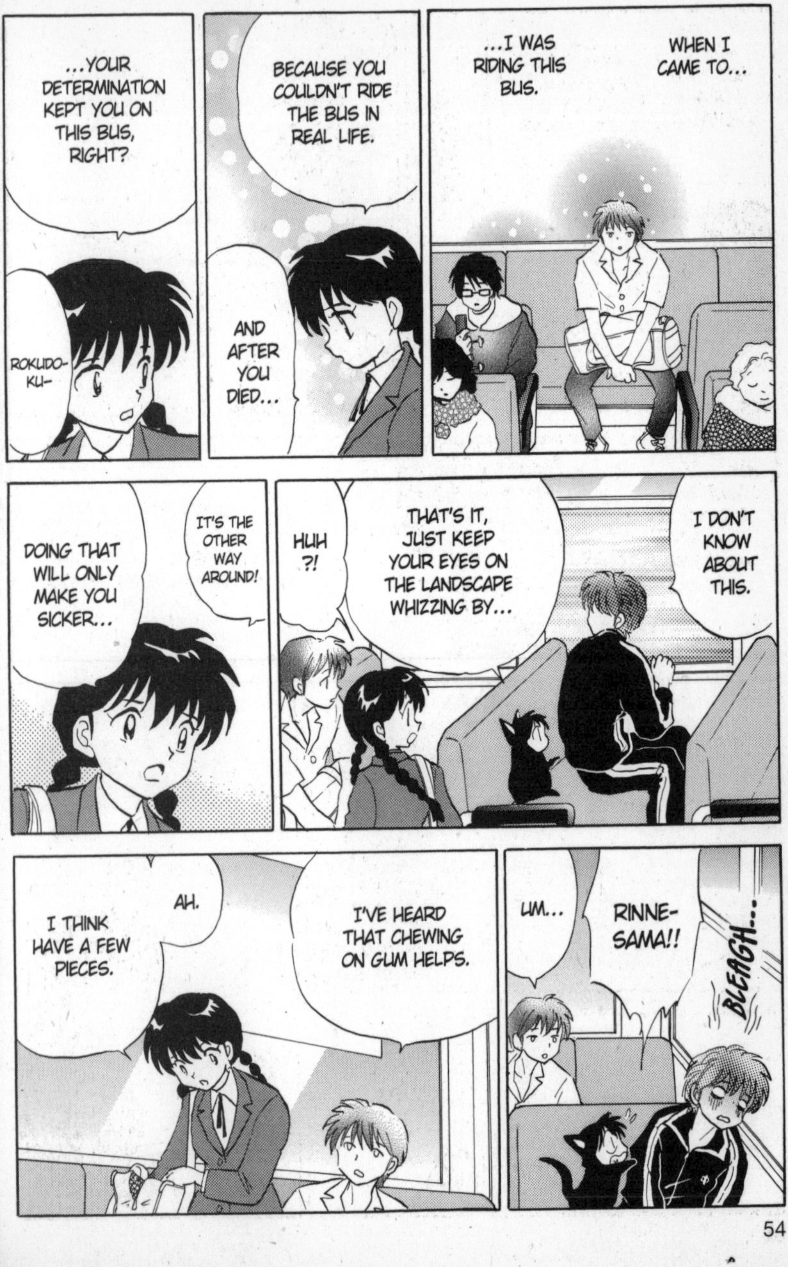
WHEN I CAME TO...
...I WAS RIDING THIS BUS.
BECAUSE YOU COULDN'T RIDE THE BUS IN REAL LIFE.
AND AFTER YOU DIED...
...YOUR DETERMINATION KEPT YOU ON THIS BUS, RIGHT?
ROKUDO-KU-
I DON'T KNOW ABOUT THIS.
THAT'S IT, JUST KEEP YOUR EYES ON THE LANDSCAPE WHIZZING BY...
HUH ?!
IT'S THE OTHER WAY AROUND!
DOING THAT WILL ONLY MAKE YOU SICKER...
RINNE-SAMA!!
UM...
BLEAGH...
I'VE HEARD THAT CHEWING ON GUM HELPS.
AH.
I THINK HAVE A FEW PIECES.

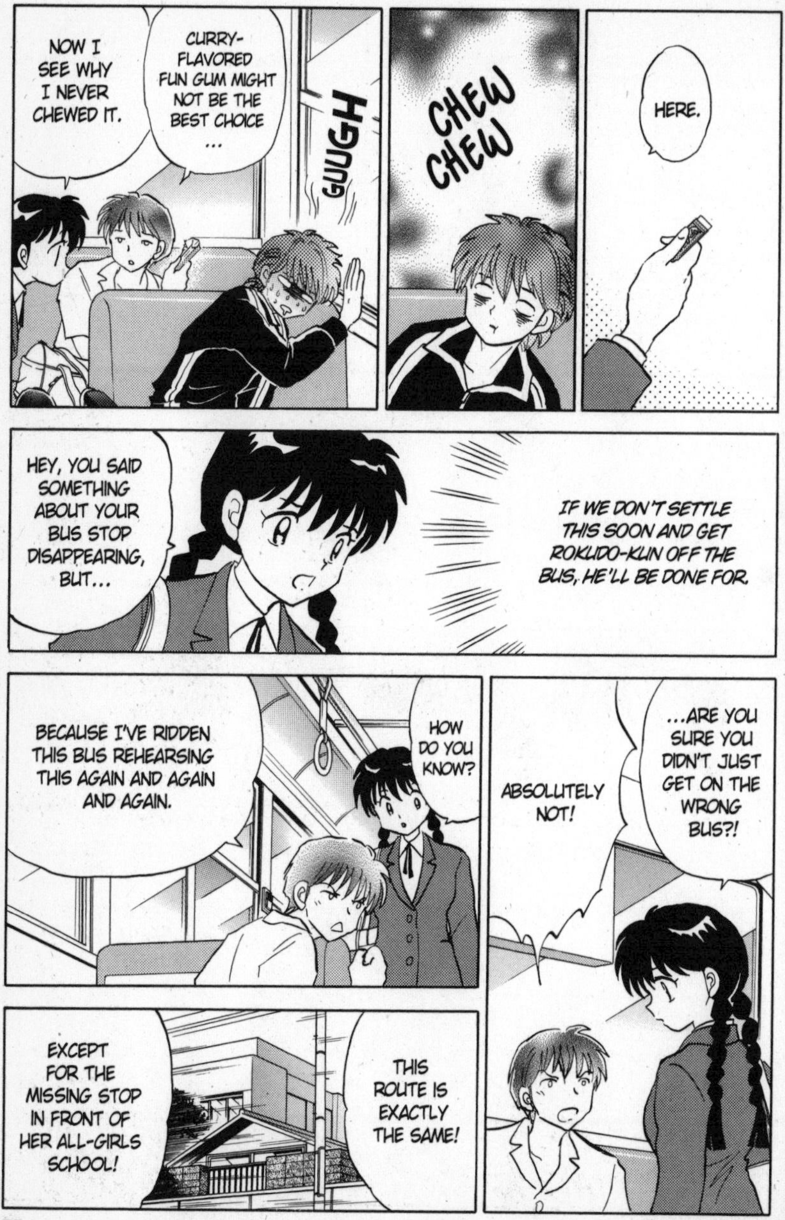
HERE.
CHEW CHEW
CURRY-FLAVORED FUN GUM MIGHT NOT BE THE BEST CHOICE ...
GUUUGH
NOW I SEE WHY I NEVER CHEWED IT.
IF WE DON'T SETTLE THIS SOON AND GET ROKUDO-KUN OFF THE BUS, HE'LL BE DONE FOR.
HEY, YOU SAID SOMETHING ABOUT YOUR BUS STOP DISAPPEARING, BUT...
...ARE YOU SURE YOU DIDN'T JUST GET ON THE WRONG BUS?!
ABSOLUTELY NOT!
HOW DO YOU KNOW?
BECAUSE I'VE RIDDEN THIS BUS REHEARSING THIS AGAIN AND AGAIN AND AGAIN.
THIS ROUTE IS EXACTLY THE SAME!
EXCEPT FOR THE MISSING STOP IN FRONT OF HER ALL-GIRLS SCHOOL!

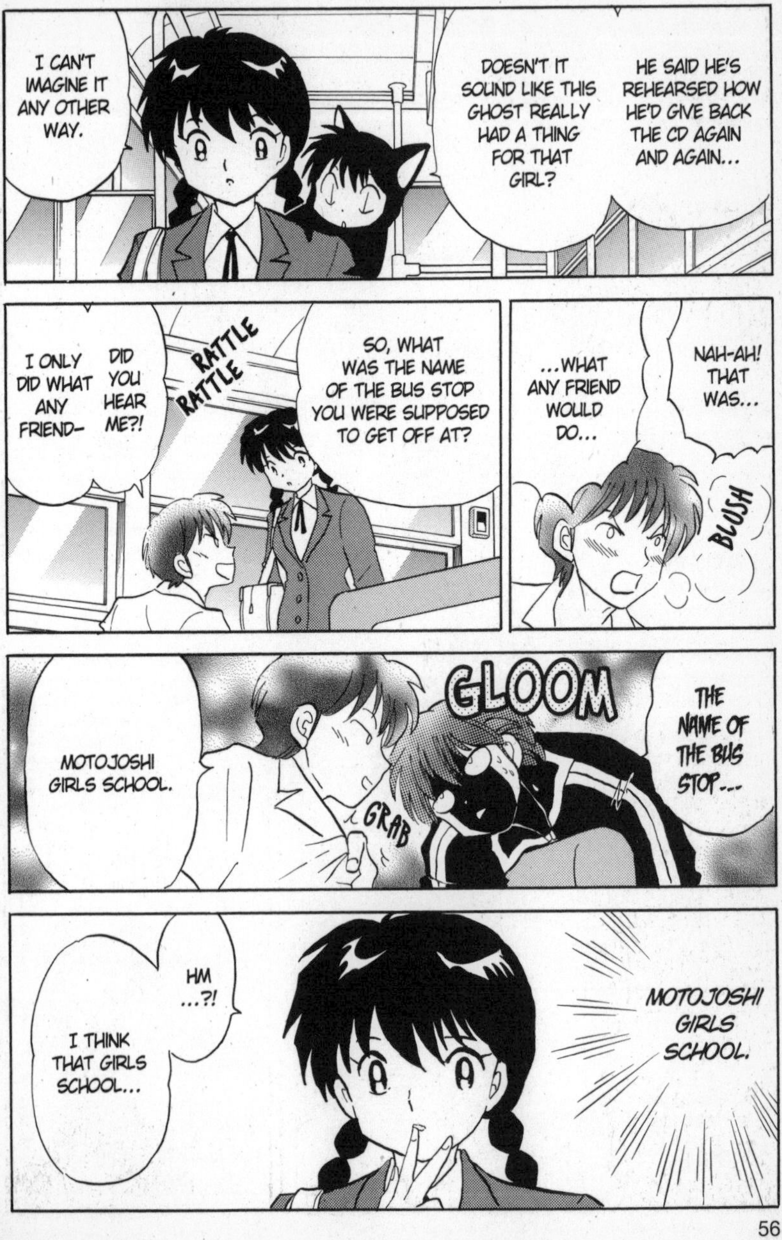
HE SAID HE'S REHEARSED HOW HE'D GIVE BACK THE CD AGAIN AND AGAIN...
DOESN'T IT SOUND LIKE THIS GHOST REALLY HAD A THING FOR THAT GIRL?
I CAN'T IMAGINE IT ANY OTHER WAY.
NAH-AH! THAT WAS...
...WHAT ANY FRIEND WOULD DO...
BLUSH
SO, WHAT WAS THE NAME OF THE BUS STOP YOU WERE SUPPOSED TO GET OFF AT?
RATTLE RATTLE
DID YOU HEAR ME?!
I ONLY DID WHAT ANY FRIEND-
THE NAME OF THE BUS STOP...
GLOOM
GRAB
MOTOJOSHI GIRLS SCHOOL.
MOTOJOSHI GIRLS SCHOOL.
HM...?!
I THINK THAT GIRLS SCHOOL...

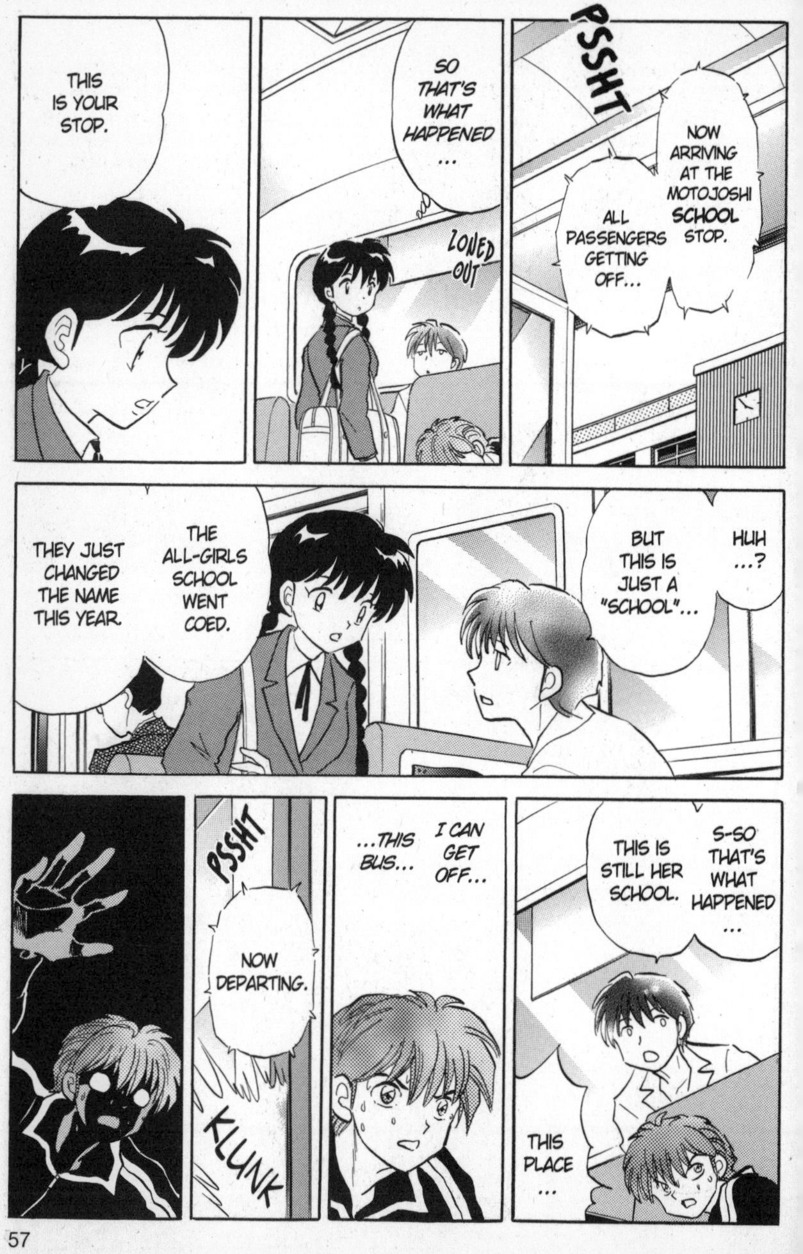
PSSHT
NOW ARRIVING AT THE MOTOJOSHI SCHOOL STOP.
ALL PASSENGERS GETTING OFF...
SO THAT'S WHAT HAPPENED...
ZONED OUT
THIS IS YOUR STOP.
HUH...?
BUT THIS IS JUST A "SCHOOL"...
THE ALL-GIRLS SCHOOL WENT COED.
THEY JUST CHANGED THE NAME THIS YEAR.
S-SO THAT'S WHAT HAPPENED...
THIS IS STILL HER SCHOOL.
THIS PLACE...
I CAN GET OFF...
...THIS BUS...
PSSHT
NOW DEPARTING.
KLUNK

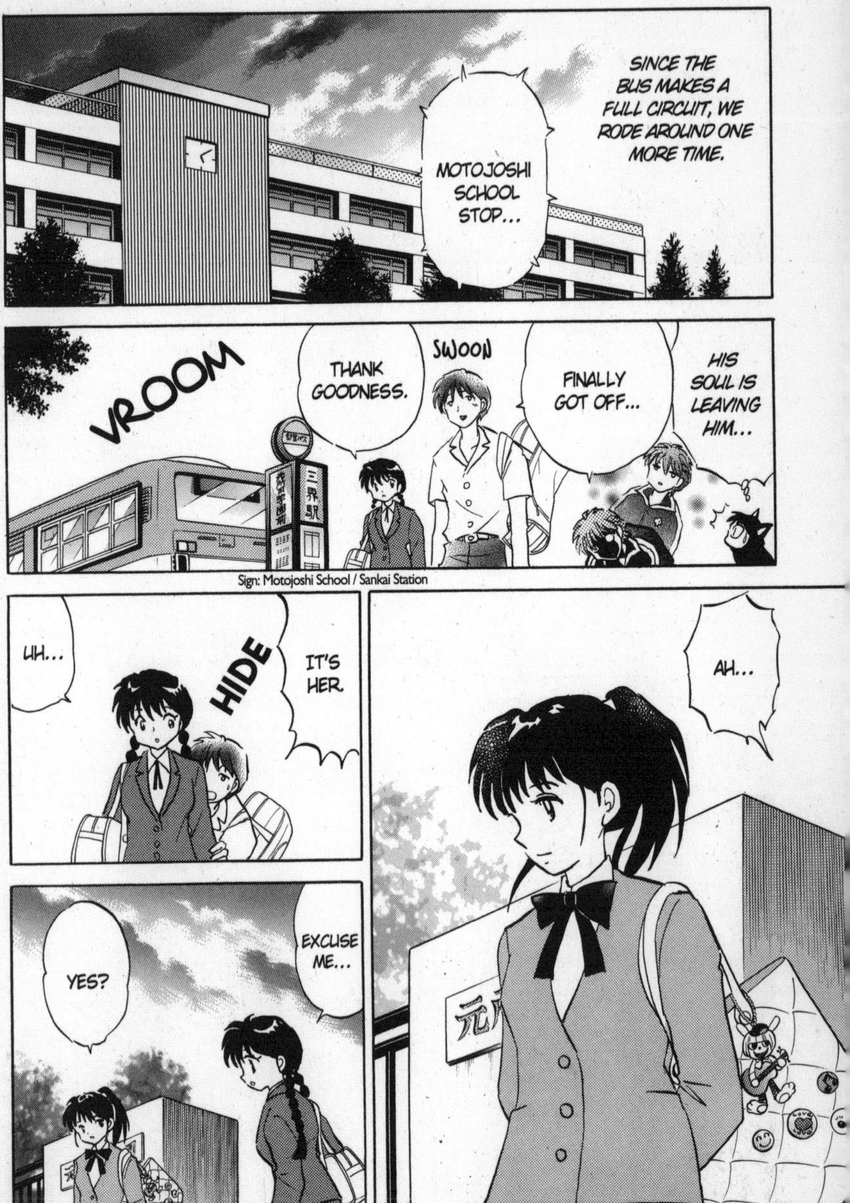

SINCE THE BUS MAKES A FULL CIRCUIT, WE RODE AROUND ONE MORE TIME.
MOTOJOSHI SCHOOL STOP...
HIS SOUL IS LEAVING HIM...
FINALLY GOT OFF...
SWOON
THANK GOODNESS.
VROOM
AH...
IT'S HER.
HIDE
UH...
EXCUSE ME...
YES?

Sign: Motojoshi School / Sankai Station

Sign: MOTOJO

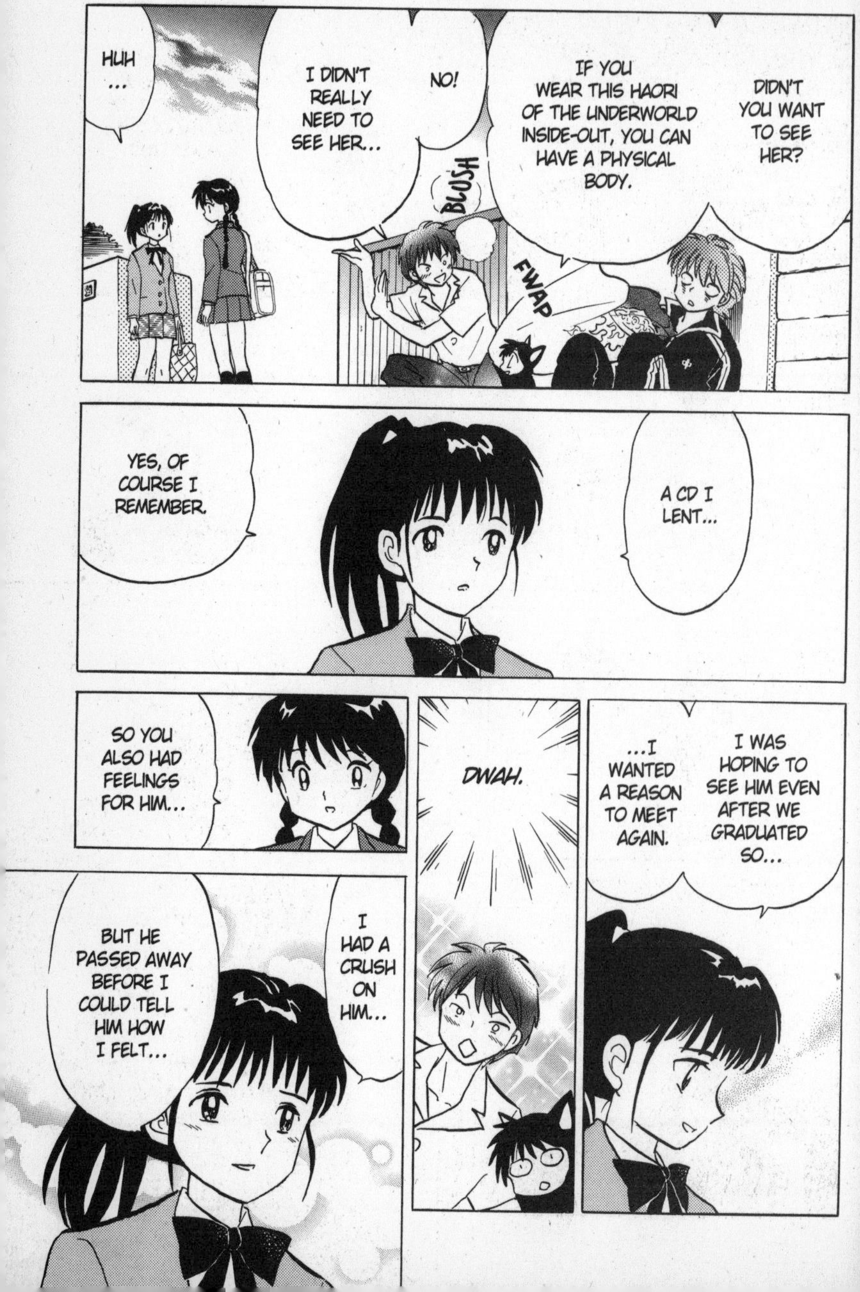
DIDN'T YOU WANT TO SEE HER?
IF YOU WEAR THIS HAORI OF THE UNDERWORLD INSIDE-OUT, YOU CAN HAVE A PHYSICAL BODY.
FWAP
NO!
BLUSH
I DIDN'T REALLY NEED TO SEE HER...
HUH ...
A CD I LENT...
YES, OF COURSE I REMEMBER.
I WAS HOPING TO SEE HIM EVEN AFTER WE GRADUATED SO...
...I WANTED A REASON TO MEET AGAIN.
DWAH.
SO YOU ALSO HAD FEELINGS FOR HIM...
I HAD A CRUSH ON HIM...
BUT HE PASSED AWAY BEFORE I COULD TELL HIM HOW I FELT...

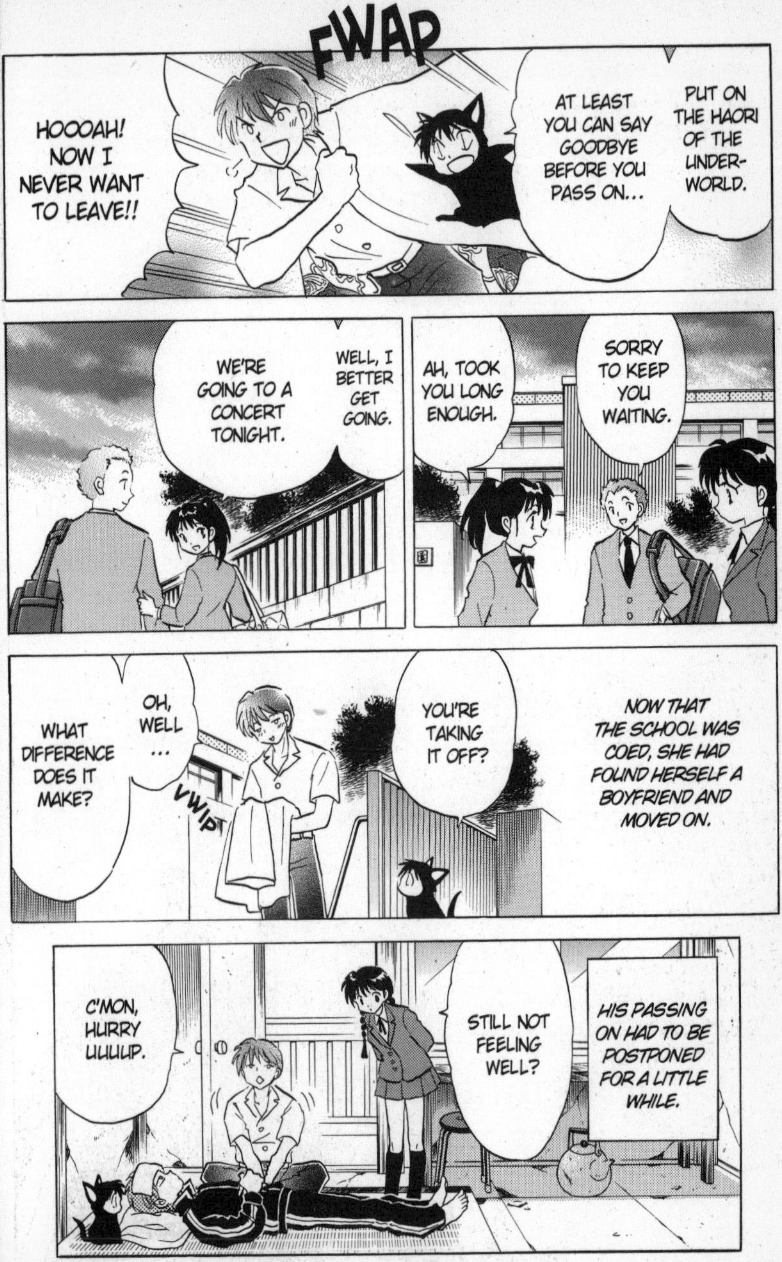
FWAP
PUT ON THE HAORI OF THE UNDER-WORLD.
AT LEAST YOU CAN SAY GOODBYE BEFORE YOU PASS ON...
HOOOAH! NOW I NEVER WANT TO LEAVE!!
SORRY TO KEEP YOU WAITING.
AH, TOOK YOU LONG ENOUGH.
WELL, I BETTER GET GOING.
WE'RE GOING TO A CONCERT TONIGHT.
NOW THAT THE SCHOOL WAS COED, SHE HAD FOUND HERSELF A BOYFRIEND AND MOVED ON.
YOU'RE TAKING IT OFF?
VWIP
OH, WELL ...
WHAT DIFFERENCE DOES IT MAKE?
HIS PASSING ON HAD TO BE POSTPONED FOR A LITTLE WHILE.
STILL NOT FEELING WELL?
C'MON, HURRY UUUUP.

CHAPTER 92: THE DIGITAL CAMERA GHOST

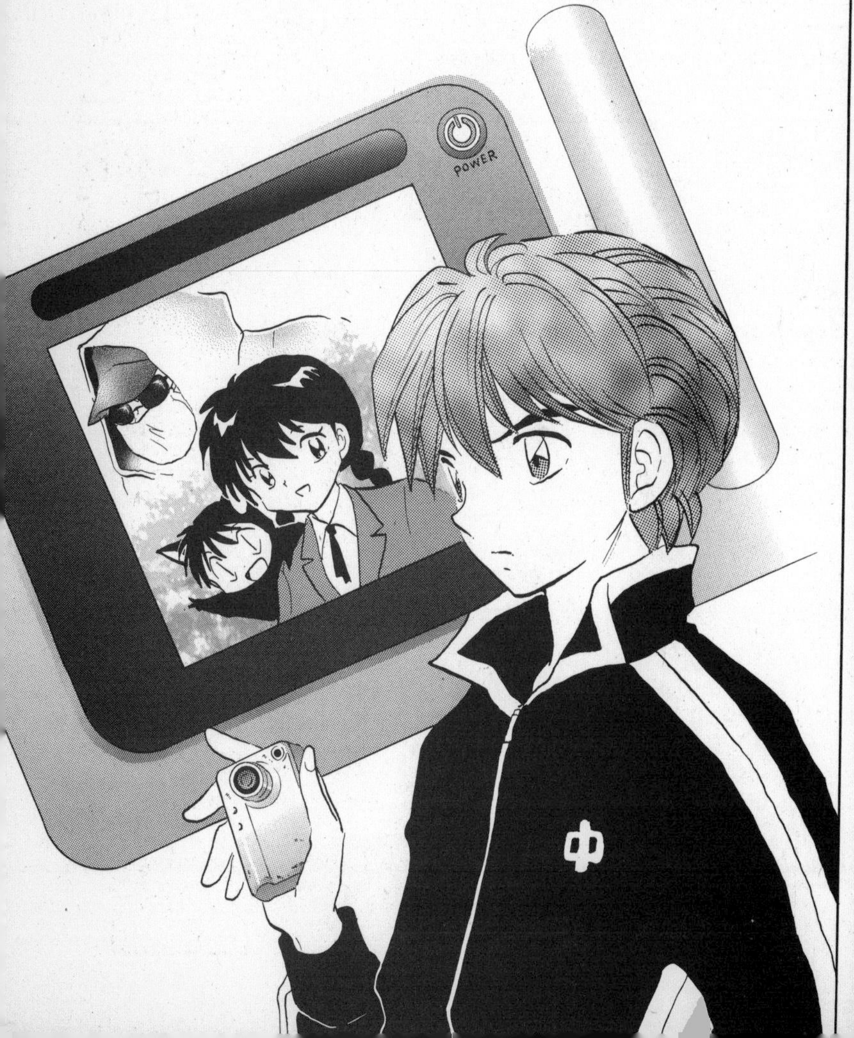
POWER

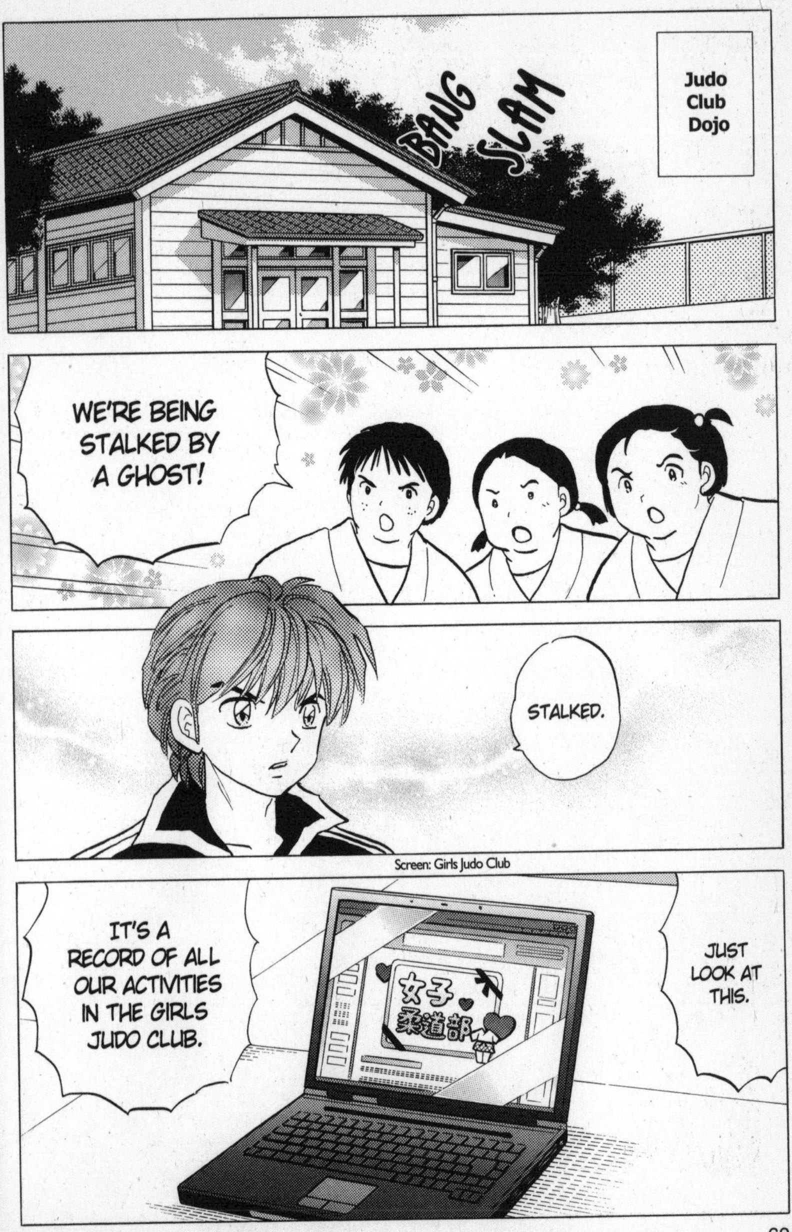
Judo Club Dojo
SLAM
BANG
WE'RE BEING STALKED BY A GHOST!
STALKED.
Screen: Girls Judo Club
JUST LOOK AT THIS.
女子柔道部
IT'S A RECORD OF ALL OUR ACTIVITIES IN THE GIRLS JUDO CLUB.

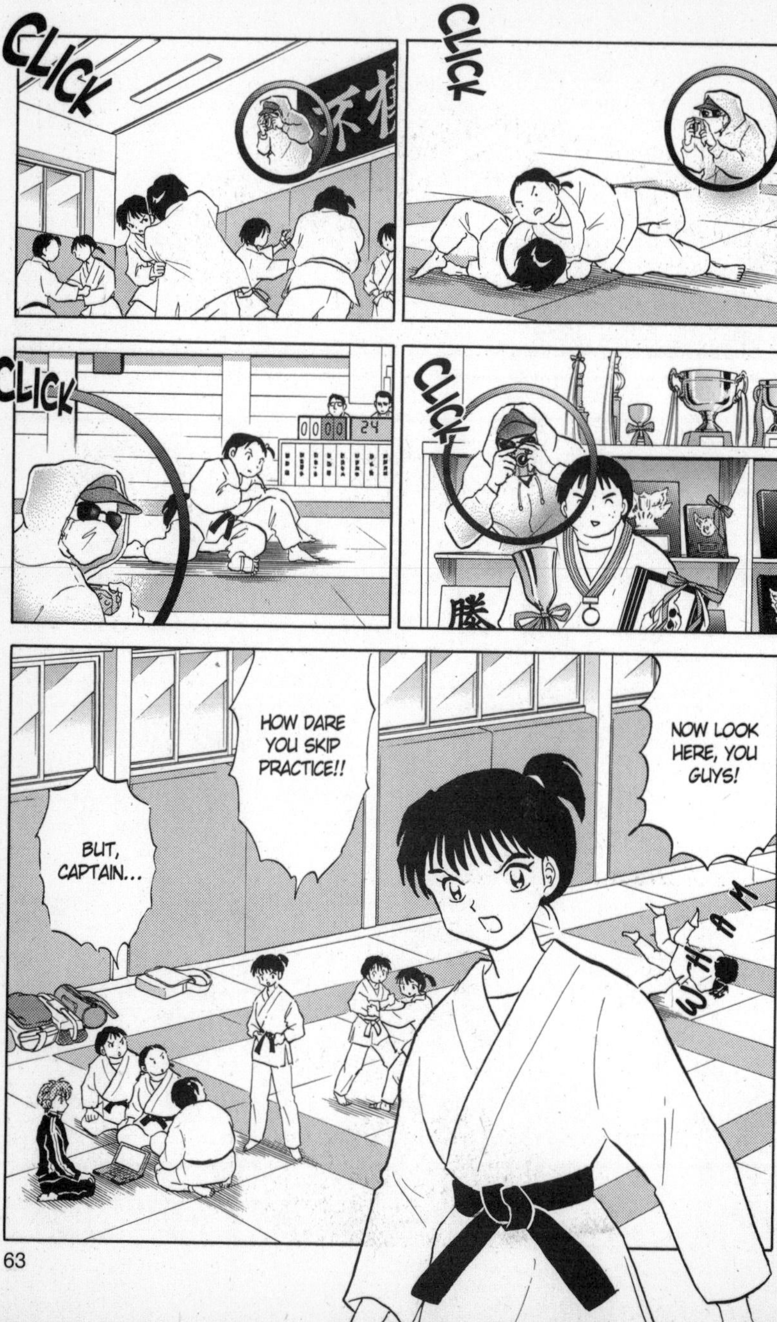
CLICK
CLICK
CLICK
CLICK
勝
NOW LOOK HERE, YOU GUYS!
WHAM
HOW DARE YOU SKIP PRACTICE!!
BUT, CAPTAIN...

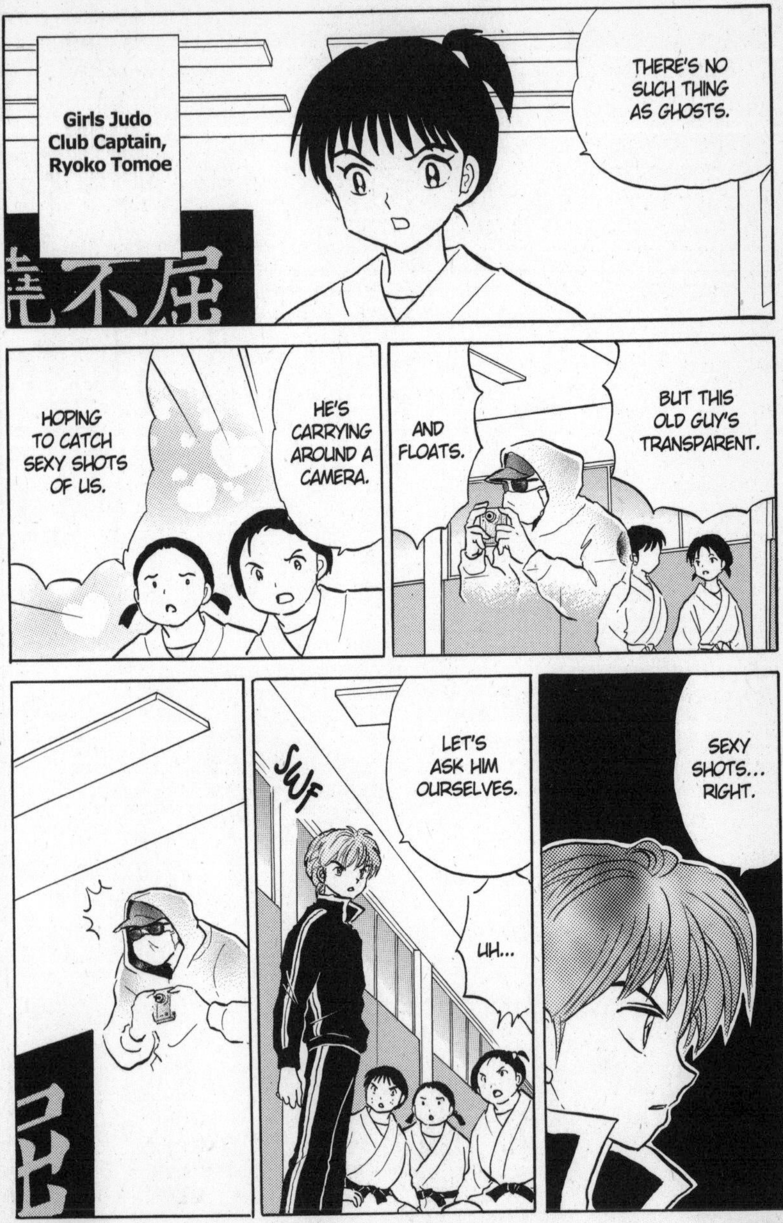
THERE'S NO SUCH THING AS GHOSTS.
Girls Judo Club Captain, Ryoko Tomoe
不屈
BUT THIS OLD GUY'S TRANSPARENT.
AND FLOATS.
HE'S CARRYING AROUND A CAMERA.
HOPING TO CATCH SEXY SHOTS OF US.
SEXY SHOTS... RIGHT.
LET'S ASK HIM OURSELVES.
SWF
UH...

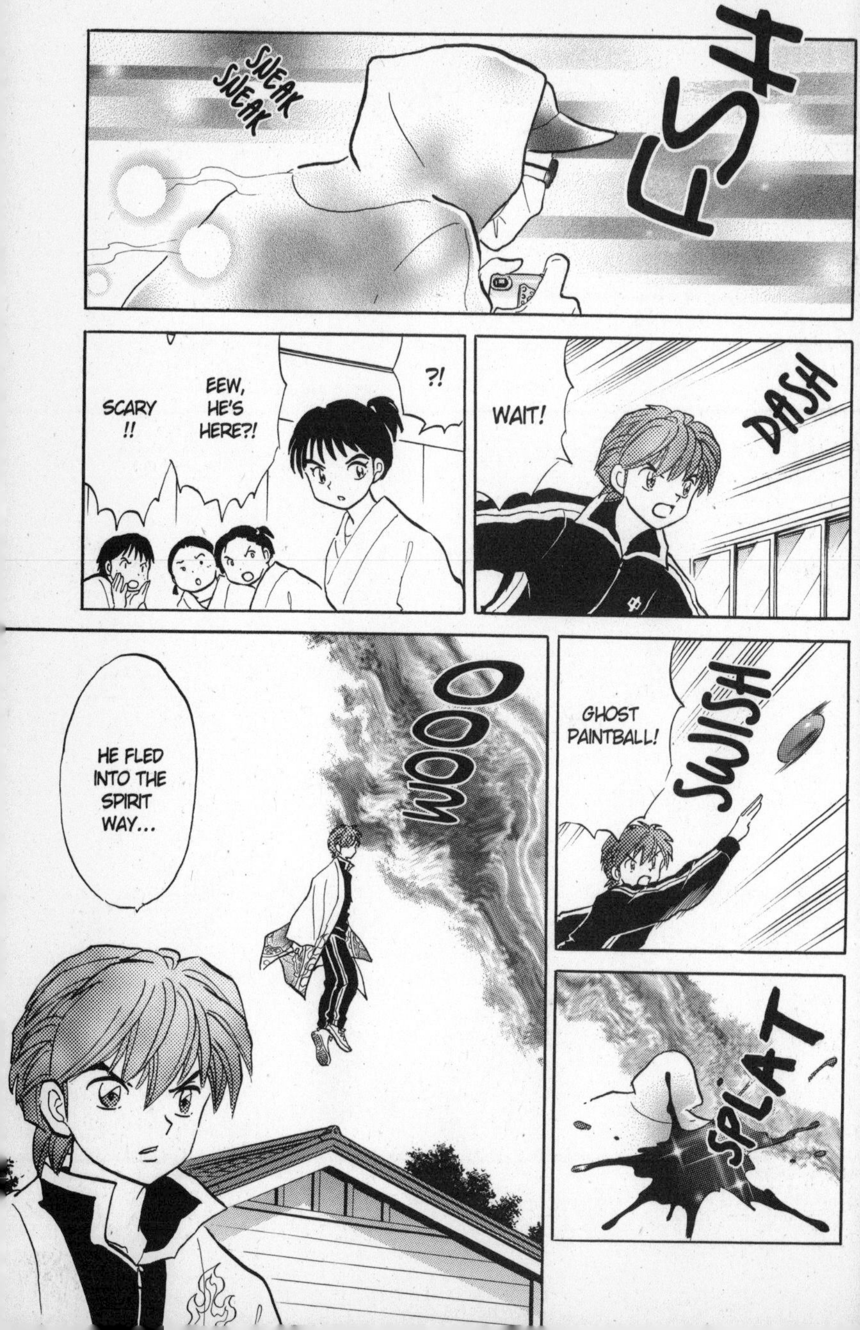
SNEAK SNEAK
WAIT!
DASH
?!
EEW, HE'S HERE?!
SCARY !!
GHOST PAINTBALL!
SWISH
SPLAT
WOOOM
HE FLED INTO THE SPIRIT WAY...

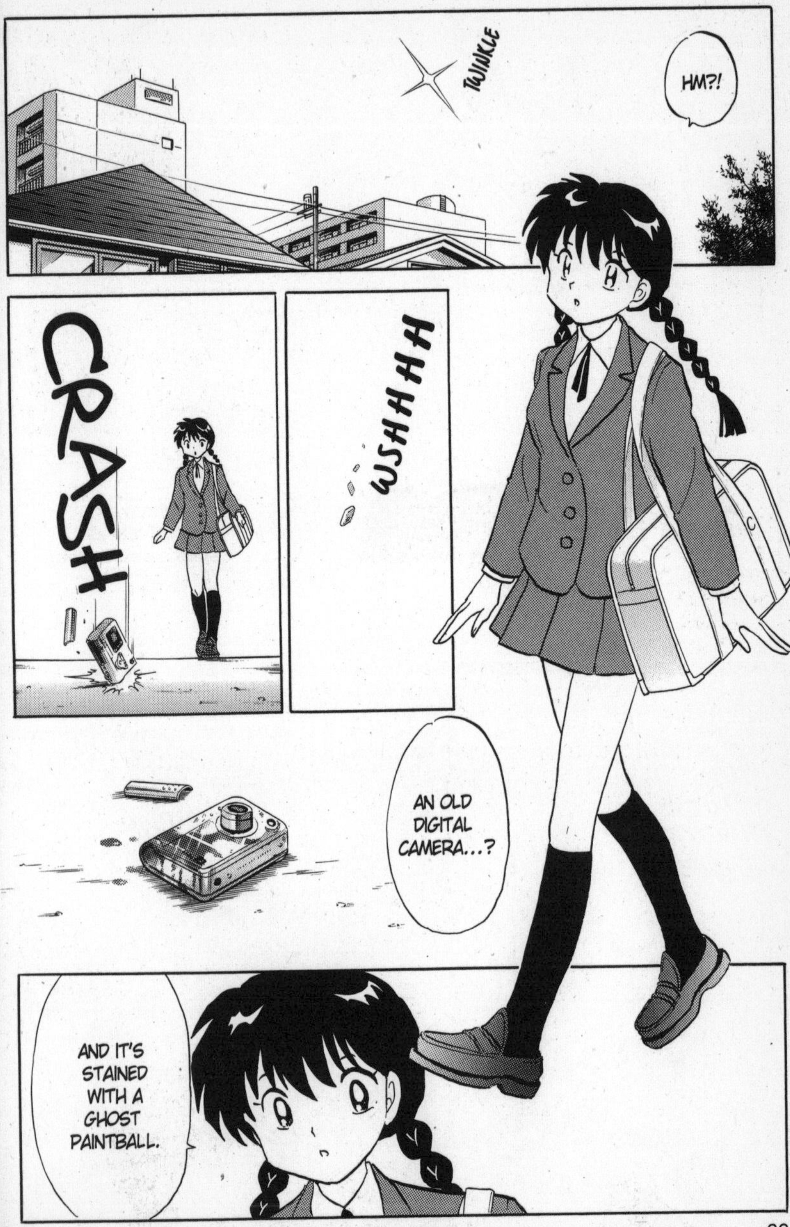
HM?!
TWINKLE
WSHHHHH
CRASH
AN OLD DIGITAL CAMERA...?
AND IT'S STAINED WITH A GHOST PAINTBALL.

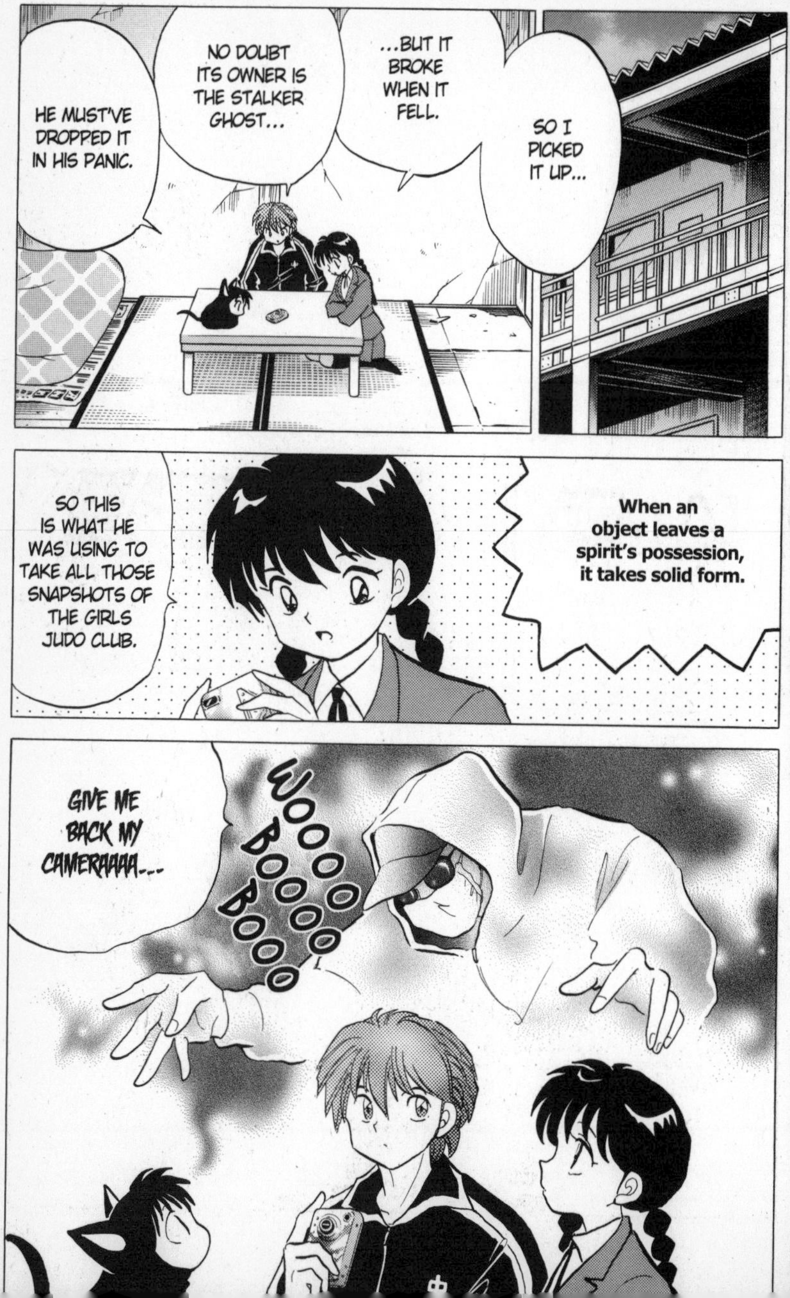
SO I PICKED IT UP...
...BUT IT BROKE WHEN IT FELL.
NO DOUBT ITS OWNER IS THE STALKER GHOST...
HE MUST'VE DROPPED IT IN HIS PANIC.
When an object leaves a spirit's possession, it takes solid form.
SO THIS IS WHAT HE WAS USING TO TAKE ALL THOSE SNAPSHOTS OF THE GIRLS JUDO CLUB.
WOOOOO BOOOOO BOOOO
GIVE ME BACK MY CAMERAAAA...

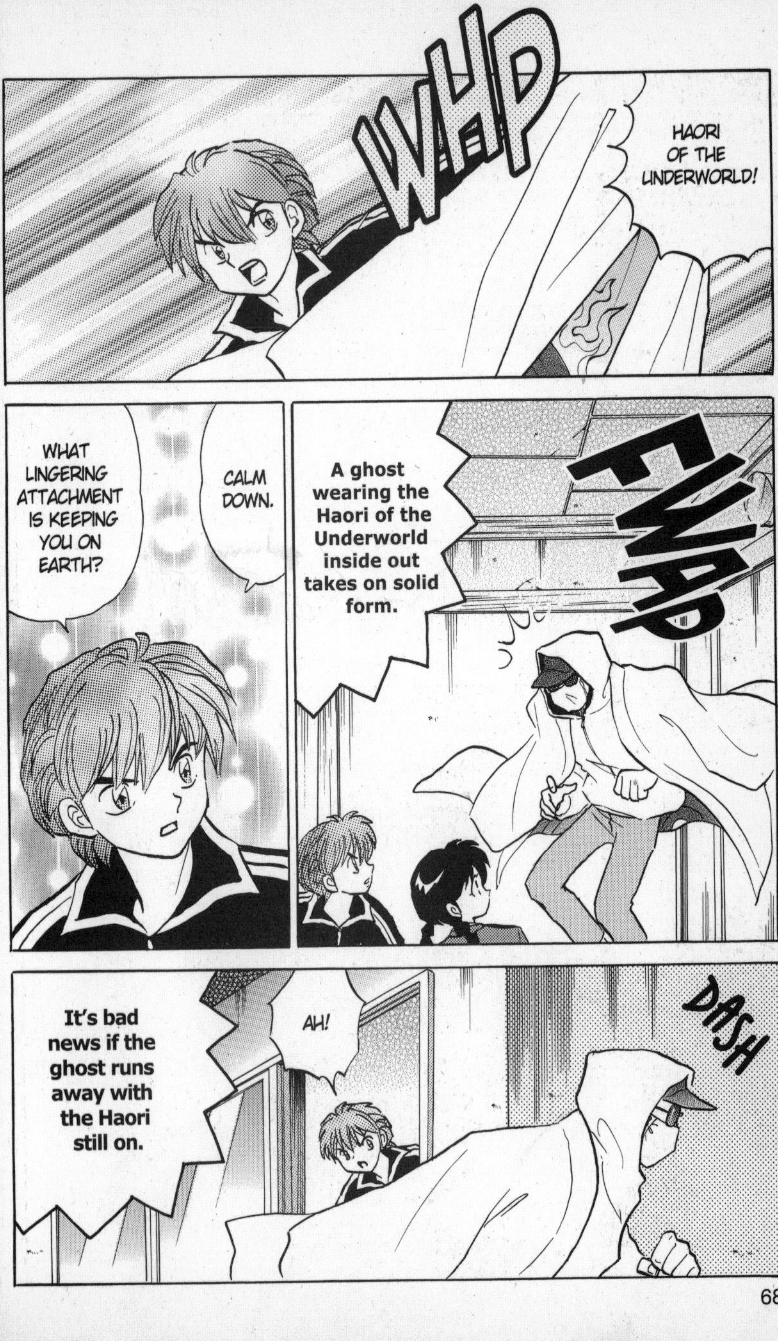
WHP
HAORI OF THE UNDERWORLD!
FWAP
A ghost wearing the Haori of the Underworld inside out takes on solid form.
CALM DOWN.
WHAT LINGERING ATTACHMENT IS KEEPING YOU ON EARTH?
DASH
AH!
It's bad news if the ghost runs away with the Haori still on.

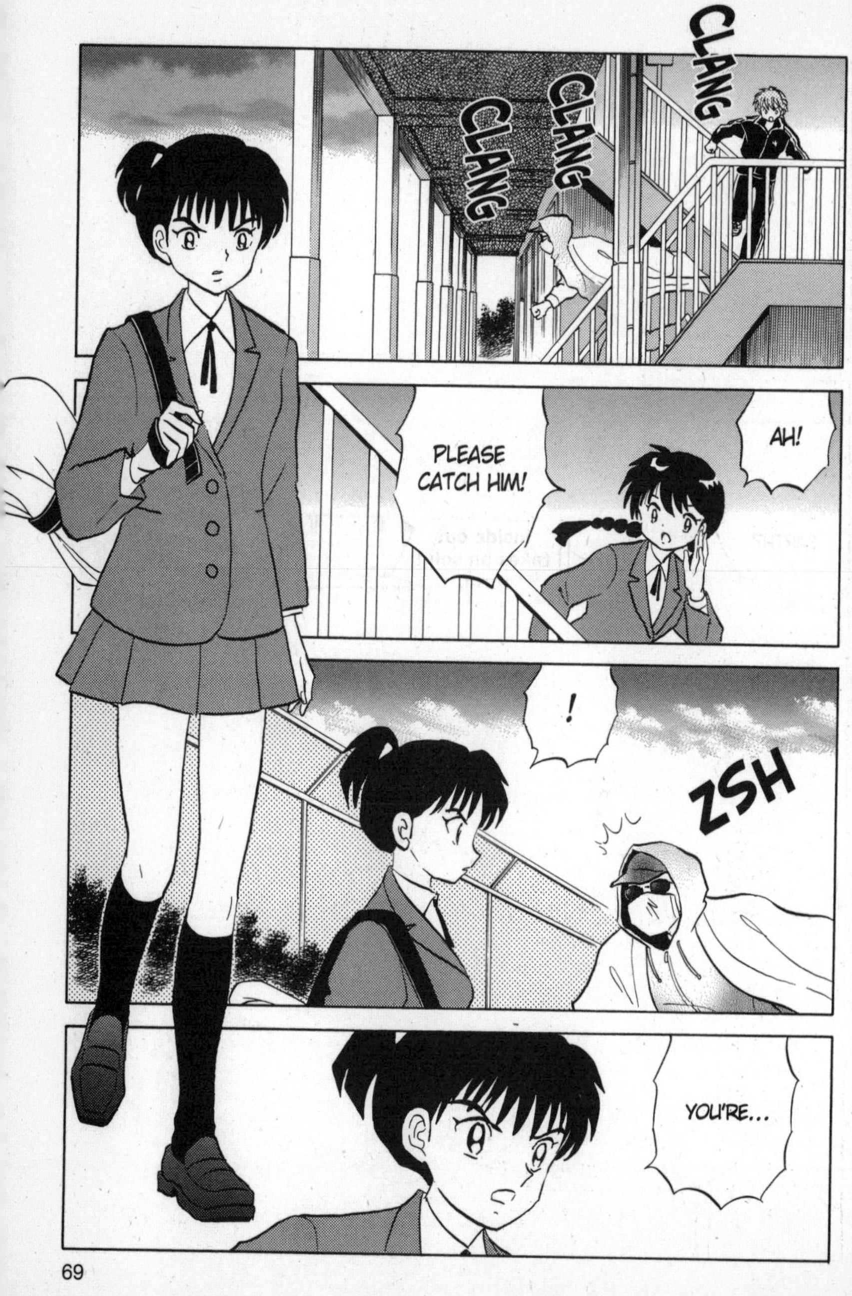
CLANG
CLANG
CLANG
AH!
PLEASE CATCH HIM!
ZSH
!
YOU'RE...

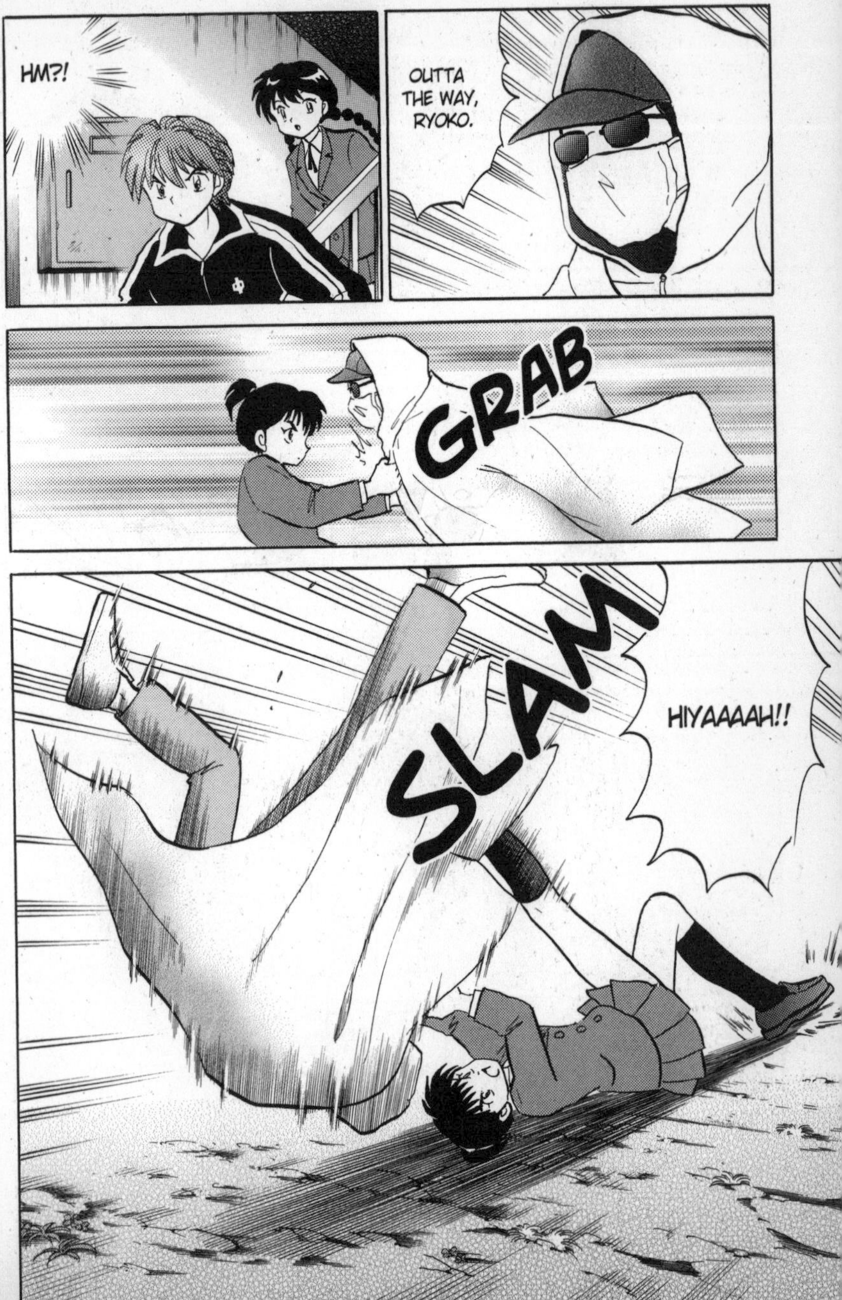
OUTTA THE WAY, RYOKO.
HM?!
GRAB
HIYAAAAH!!
SLAM

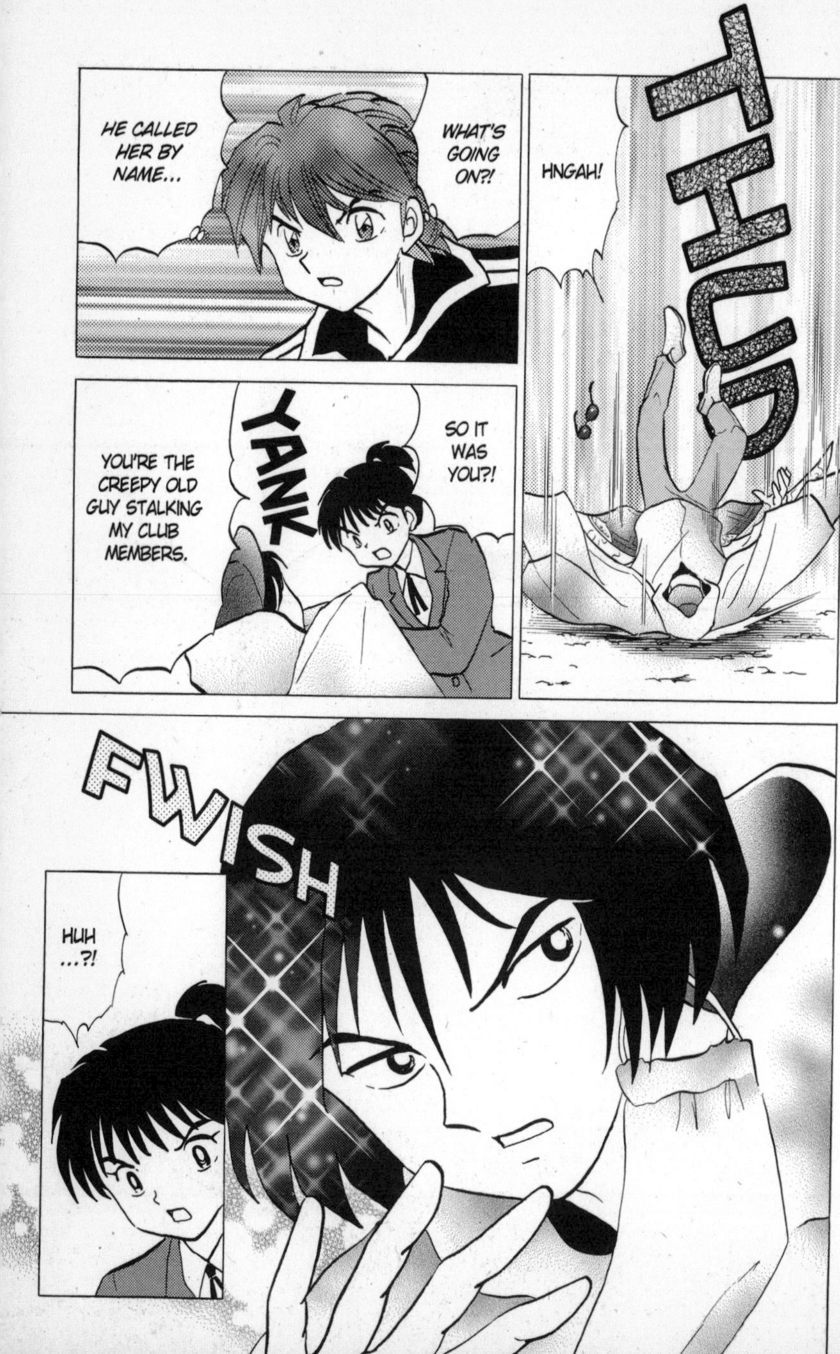
THUD
HNGAH!
WHAT'S GOING ON?!
HE CALLED HER BY NAME...
SO IT WAS YOU?!
YANK
YOU'RE THE CREEPY OLD GUY STALKING MY CLUB MEMBERS.
FWISH
HUH ...?!

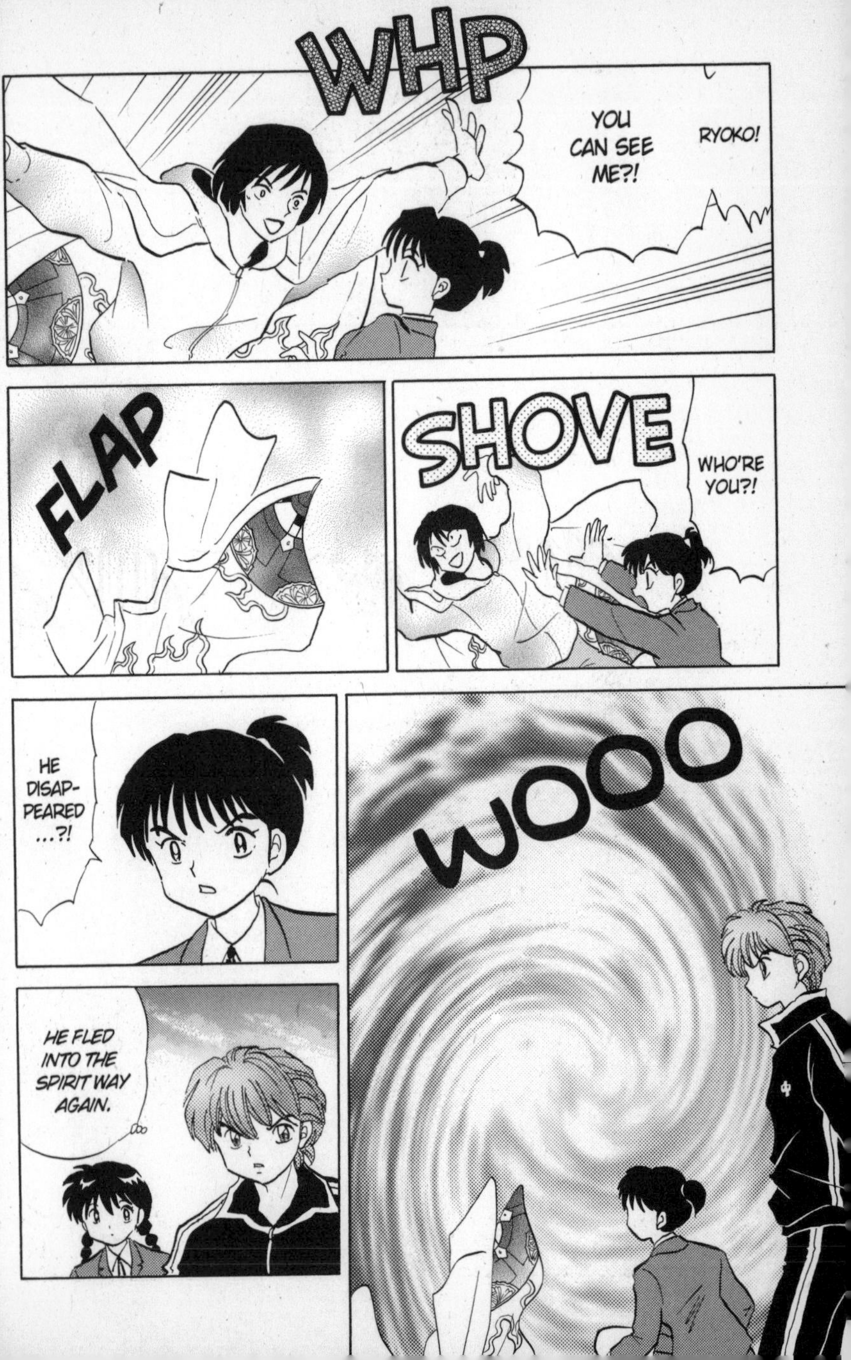
WHP
RYOKO!
YOU CAN SEE ME?!
SHOVE
WHO'RE YOU?!
FLAP
WOOO
HE DISAP-PEARED ...?!
HE FLED INTO THE SPIRIT WAY AGAIN.

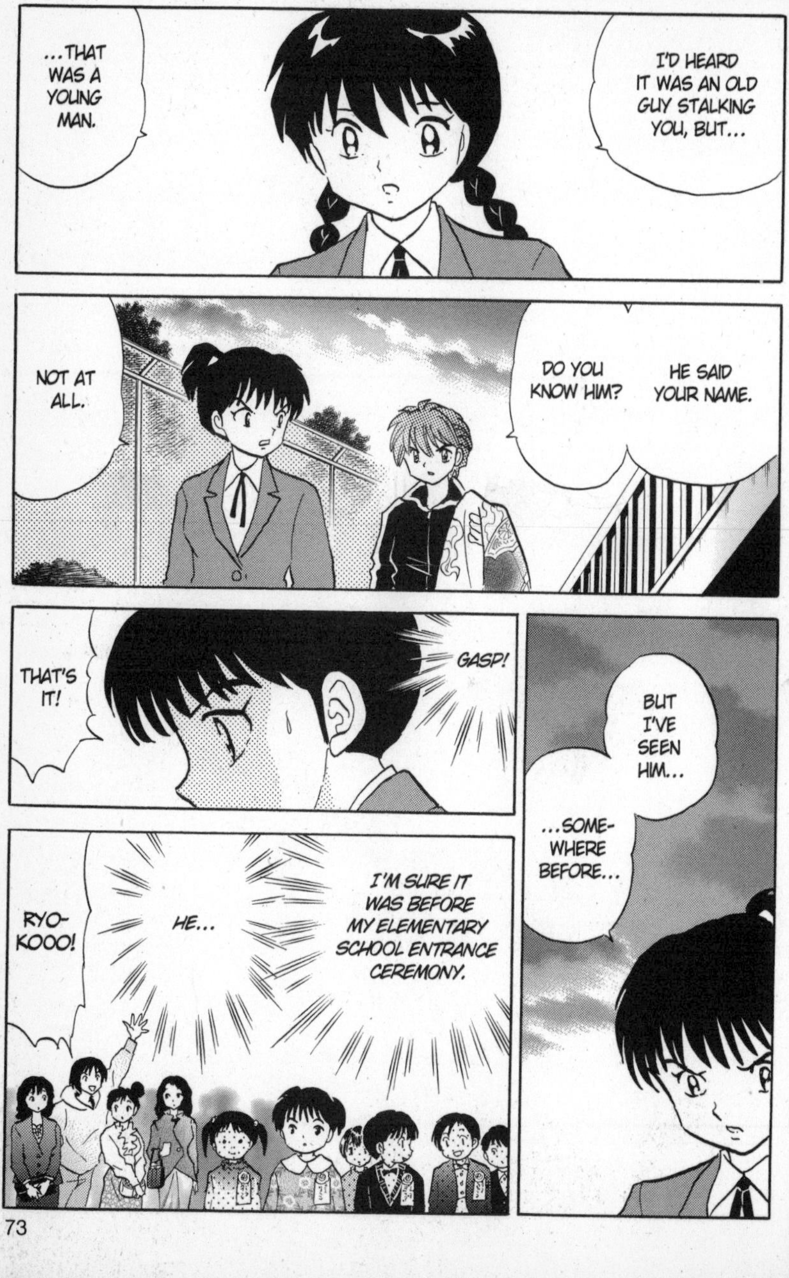
I'D HEARD IT WAS AN OLD GUY STALKING YOU, BUT...
...THAT WAS A YOUNG MAN.
HE SAID YOUR NAME.
DO YOU KNOW HIM?
NOT AT ALL.
BUT I'VE SEEN HIM...
...SOME-WHERE BEFORE...
GASP!
THAT'S IT!
I'M SURE IT WAS BEFORE MY ELEMENTARY SCHOOL ENTRANCE CEREMONY.
HE...
RYO-KOOO!

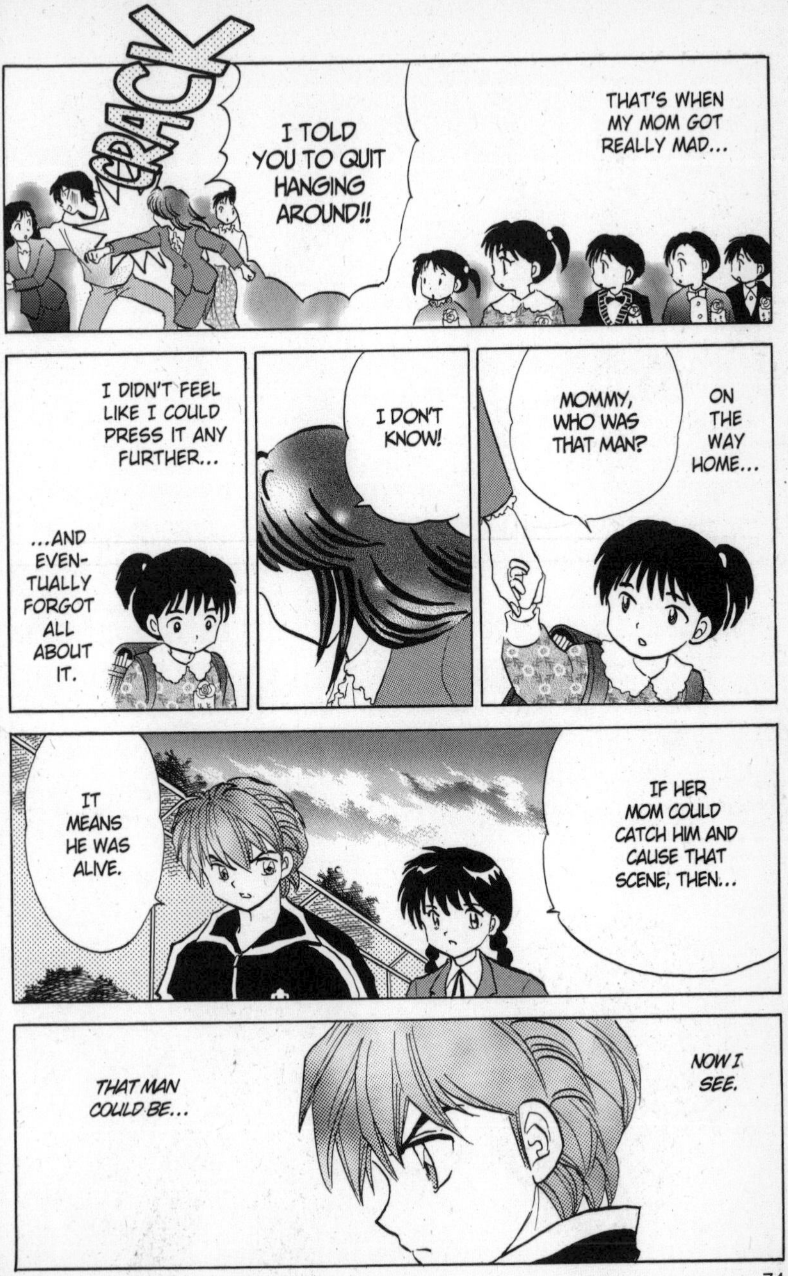
THAT'S WHEN MY MOM GOT REALLY MAD...
I TOLD YOU TO QUIT HANGING AROUND!!
CRACK
ON THE WAY HOME...
MOMMY, WHO WAS THAT MAN?
I DON'T KNOW!
I DIDN'T FEEL LIKE I COULD PRESS IT ANY FURTHER...
...AND EVEN-TUALLY FORGOT ALL ABOUT IT.
IF HER MOM COULD CATCH HIM AND CAUSE THAT SCENE, THEN...
IT MEANS HE WAS ALIVE.
NOW I SEE.
THAT MAN COULD BE...

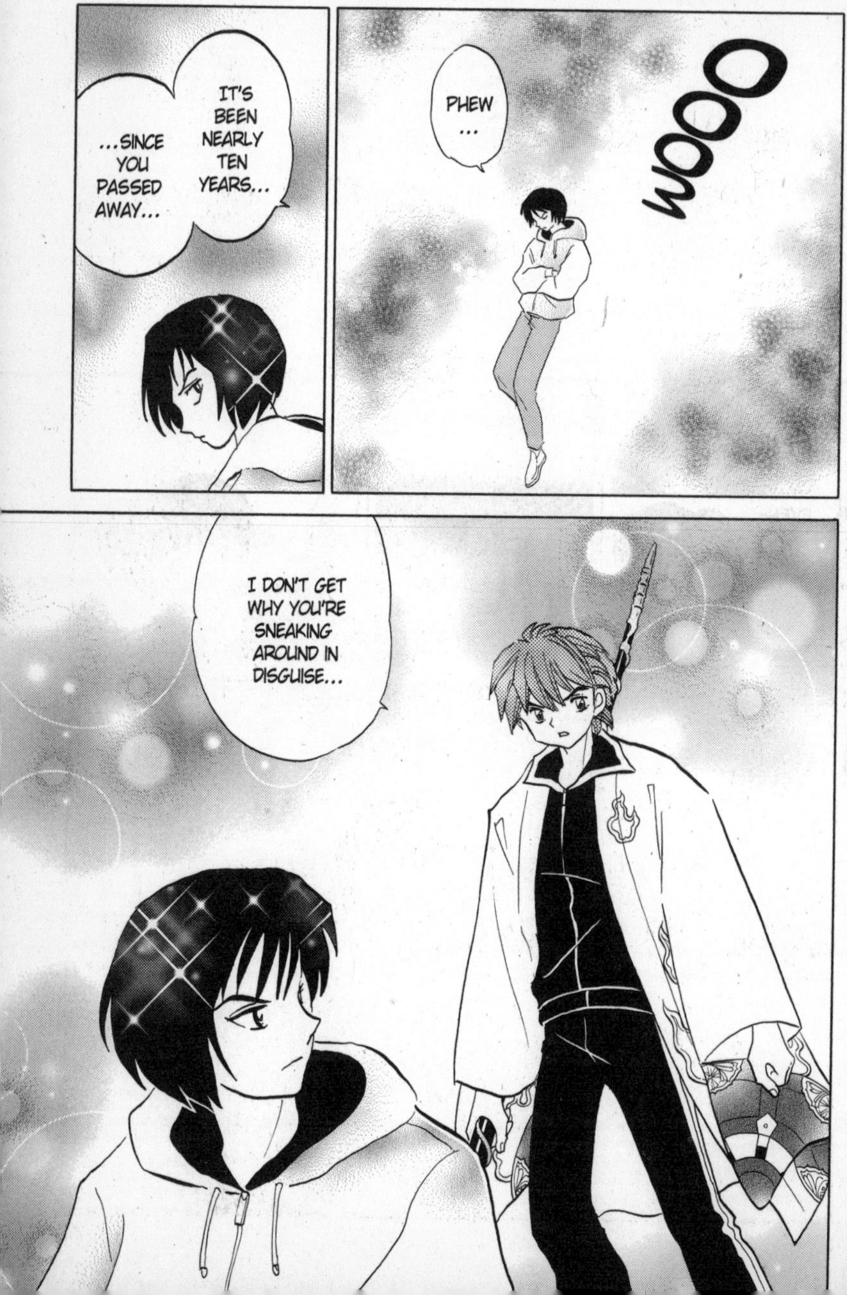
WOOOM
PHEW ...
IT'S BEEN NEARLY TEN YEARS...
...SINCE YOU PASSED AWAY...
I DON'T GET WHY YOU'RE SNEAKING AROUND IN DISGUISE...

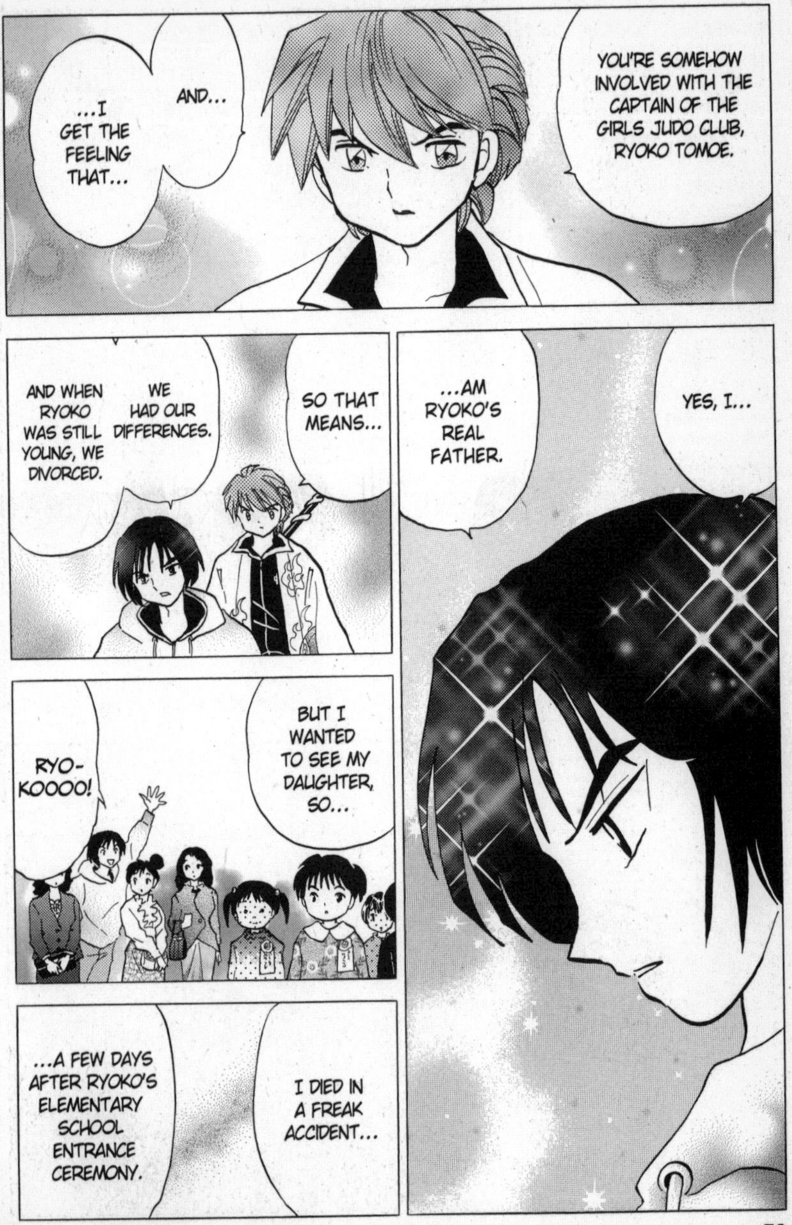
YOU'RE SOMEHOW INVOLVED WITH THE CAPTAIN OF THE GIRLS JUDO CLUB, RYOKO TOMOE.
AND...
...I GET THE FEELING THAT...
YES, I...
...AM RYOKO'S REAL FATHER.
SO THAT MEANS...
WE HAD OUR DIFFERENCES.
AND WHEN RYOKO WAS STILL YOUNG, WE DIVORCED.
BUT I WANTED TO SEE MY DAUGHTER, SO...
RYO-KOOOO!
I DIED IN A FREAK ACCIDENT...
...A FEW DAYS AFTER RYOKO'S ELEMENTARY SCHOOL ENTRANCE CEREMONY.

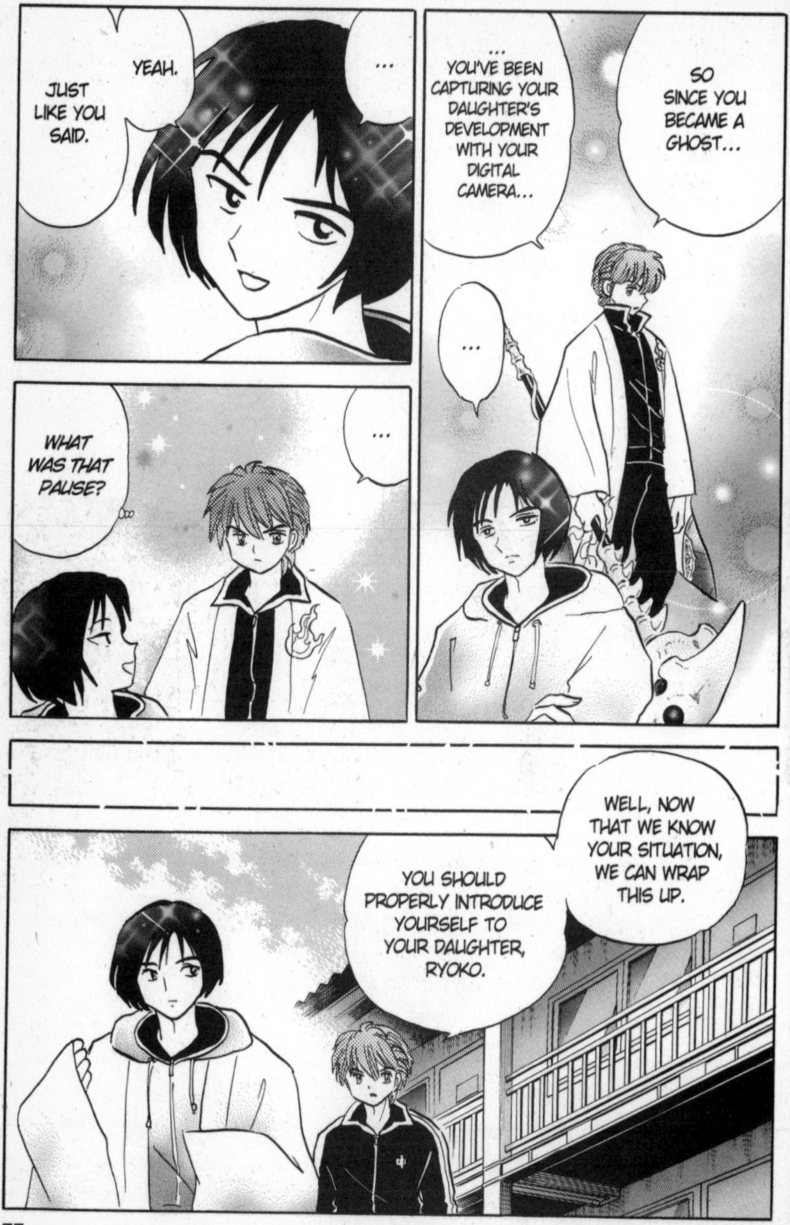
SO SINCE YOU BECAME A GHOST...
... YOU'VE BEEN CAPTURING YOUR DAUGHTER'S DEVELOPMENT WITH YOUR DIGITAL CAMERA...
...
...
YEAH.
JUST LIKE YOU SAID.
...
WHAT WAS THAT PAUSE?
WELL, NOW THAT WE KNOW YOUR SITUATION, WE CAN WRAP THIS UP.
YOU SHOULD PROPERLY INTRODUCE YOURSELF TO YOUR DAUGHTER, RYOKO.

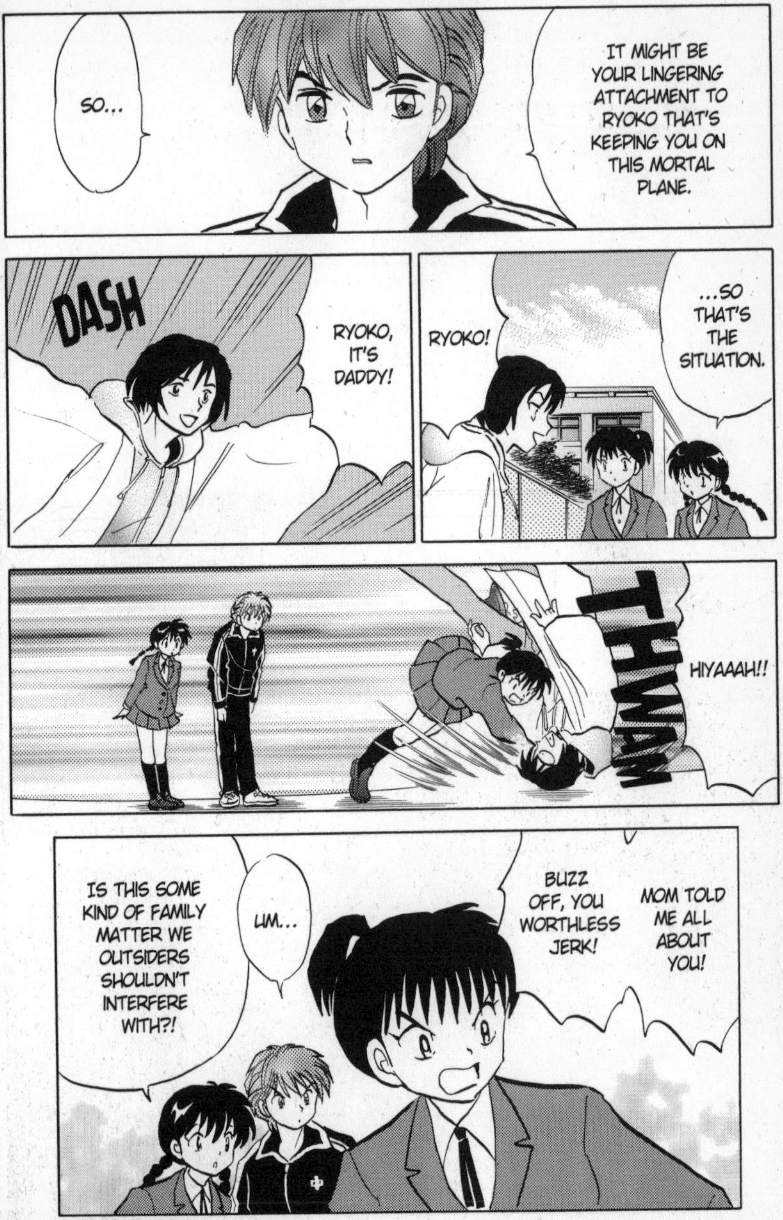
IT MIGHT BE YOUR LINGERING ATTACHMENT TO RYOKO THAT'S KEEPING YOU ON THIS MORTAL PLANE.
SO...
...SO THAT'S THE SITUATION.
RYOKO!
RYOKO, IT'S DADDY!
DASH
HIYAAAH!!
THWAM
MOM TOLD ME ALL ABOUT YOU!
BUZZ OFF, YOU WORTHLESS JERK!
UM...
IS THIS SOME KIND OF FAMILY MATTER WE OUTSIDERS SHOULDN'T INTERFERE WITH?!

CHAPTER 93: MESSAGE

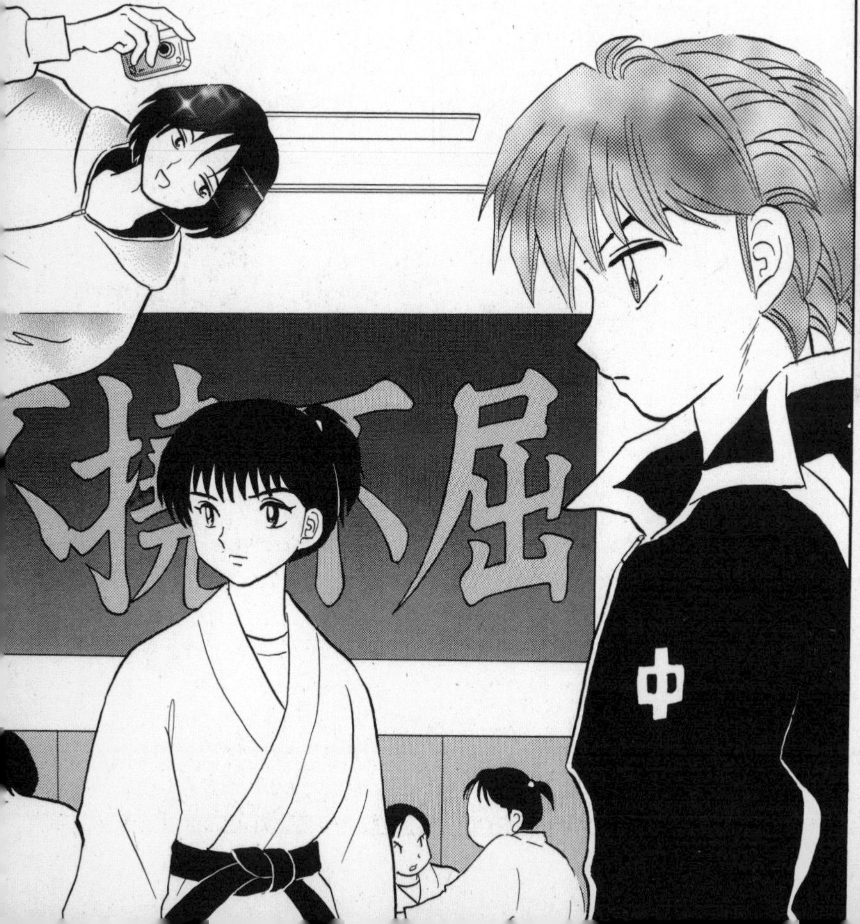

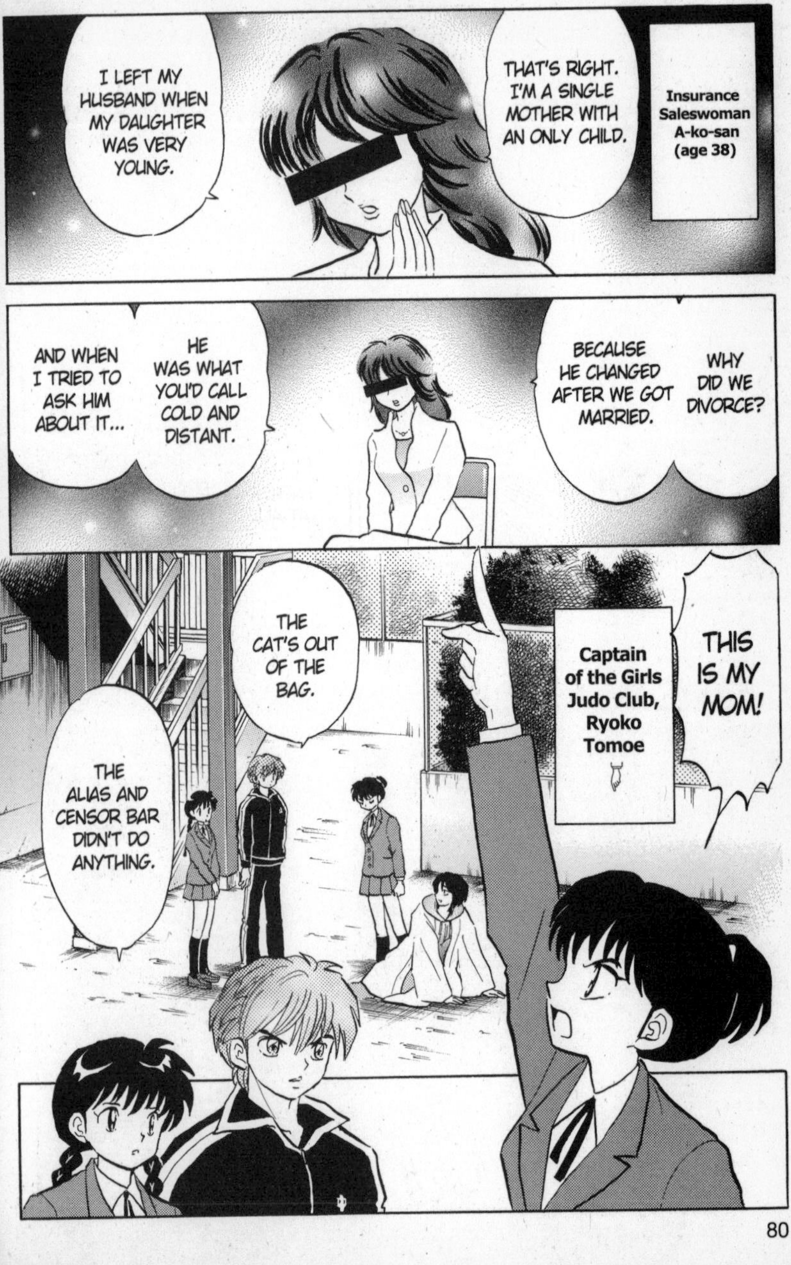
Insurance Saleswoman A-ko-san (age 38)
THAT'S RIGHT. I'M A SINGLE MOTHER WITH AN ONLY CHILD.
I LEFT MY HUSBAND WHEN MY DAUGHTER WAS VERY YOUNG.
WHY DID WE DIVORCE?
BECAUSE HE CHANGED AFTER WE GOT MARRIED.
HE WAS WHAT YOU'D CALL COLD AND DISTANT.
AND WHEN I TRIED TO ASK HIM ABOUT IT...
THIS IS MY MOM!
Captain of the Girls Judo Club, Ryoko Tomoe
THE CAT'S OUT OF THE BAG.
THE ALIAS AND CENSOR BAR DIDN'T DO ANYTHING.

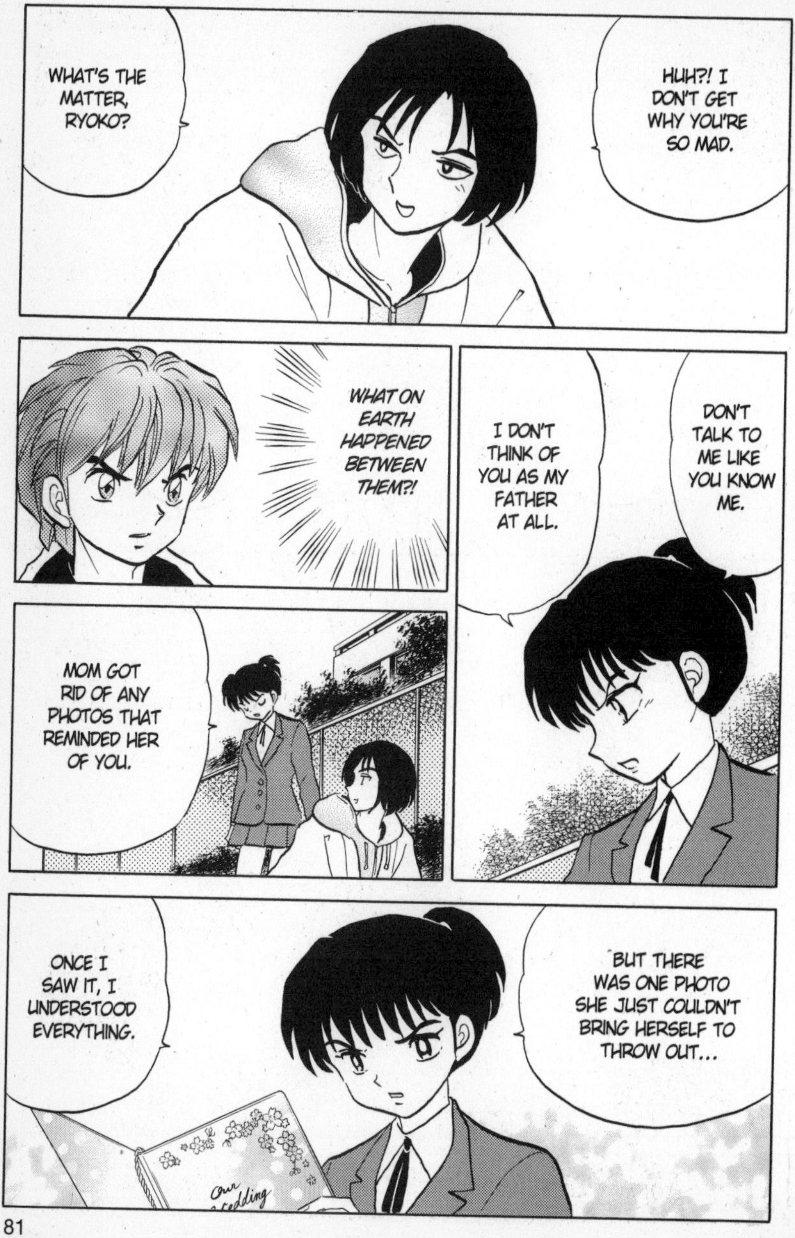
HUH?! I DON'T GET WHY YOU'RE SO MAD.
WHAT'S THE MATTER, RYOKO?
DON'T TALK TO ME LIKE YOU KNOW ME.
I DON'T THINK OF YOU AS MY FATHER AT ALL.
WHAT ON EARTH HAPPENED BETWEEN THEM?!
MOM GOT RID OF ANY PHOTOS THAT REMINDED HER OF YOU.
BUT THERE WAS ONE PHOTO SHE JUST COULDN'T BRING HERSELF TO THROW OUT...
ONCE I SAW IT, I UNDERSTOOD EVERYTHING.

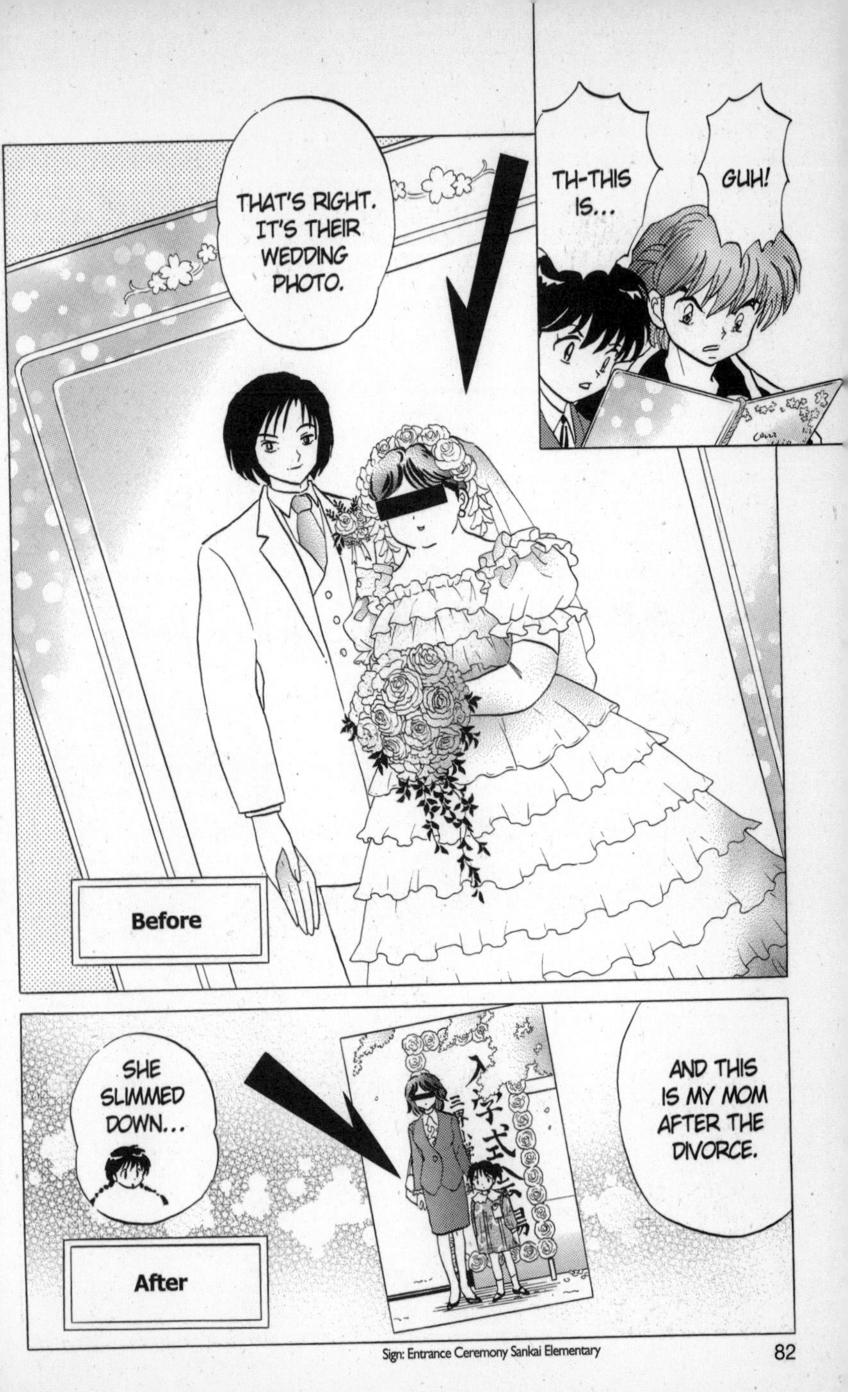
GUH!
TH-THIS IS...
THAT'S RIGHT. IT'S THEIR WEDDING PHOTO.
Before
AND THIS IS MY MOM AFTER THE DIVORCE.
入学式会場
SHE SLIMMED DOWN...
After

Sign: Entrance Ceremony Sankai Elementary

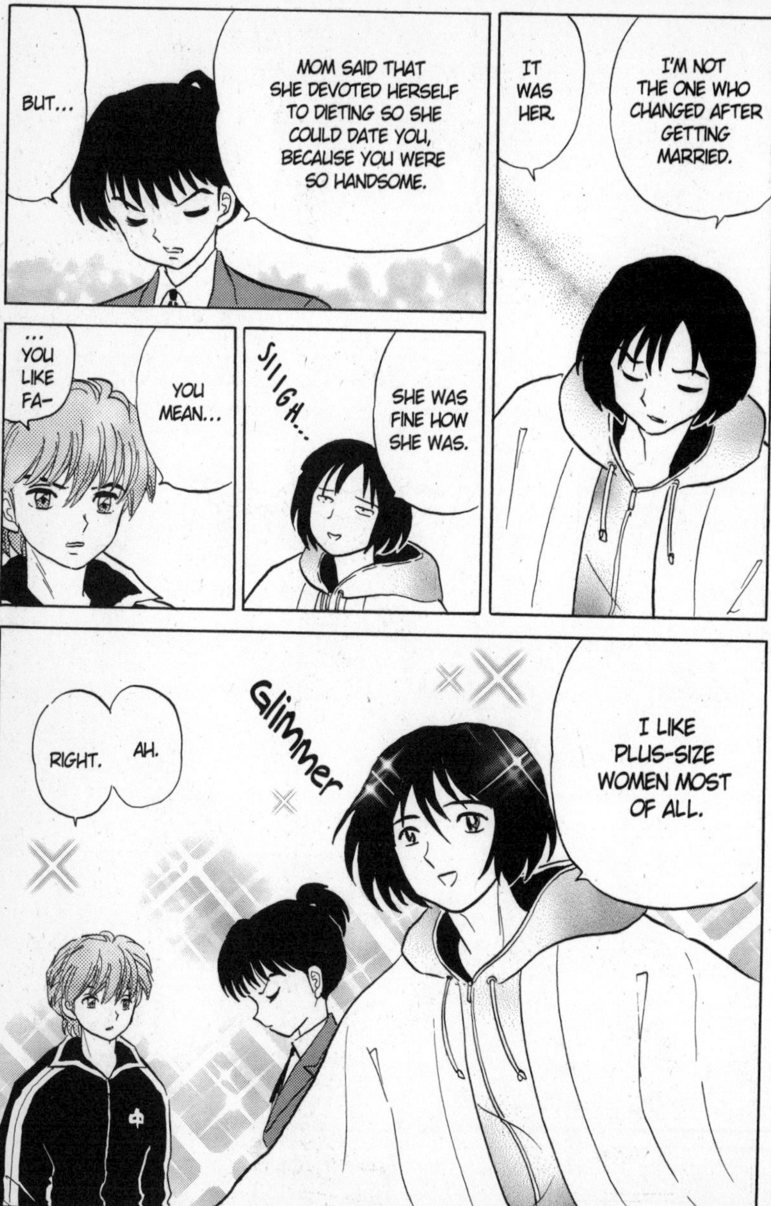
I'M NOT THE ONE WHO CHANGED AFTER GETTING MARRIED.
IT WAS HER.
MOM SAID THAT SHE DEVOTED HERSELF TO DIETING SO SHE COULD DATE YOU, BECAUSE YOU WERE SO HANDSOME.
BUT...
SHE WAS FINE HOW SHE WAS.
SIIIGH...
YOU MEAN...
... YOU LIKE FA-
I LIKE PLUS-SIZE WOMEN MOST OF ALL.
Glimmer
AH.
RIGHT.

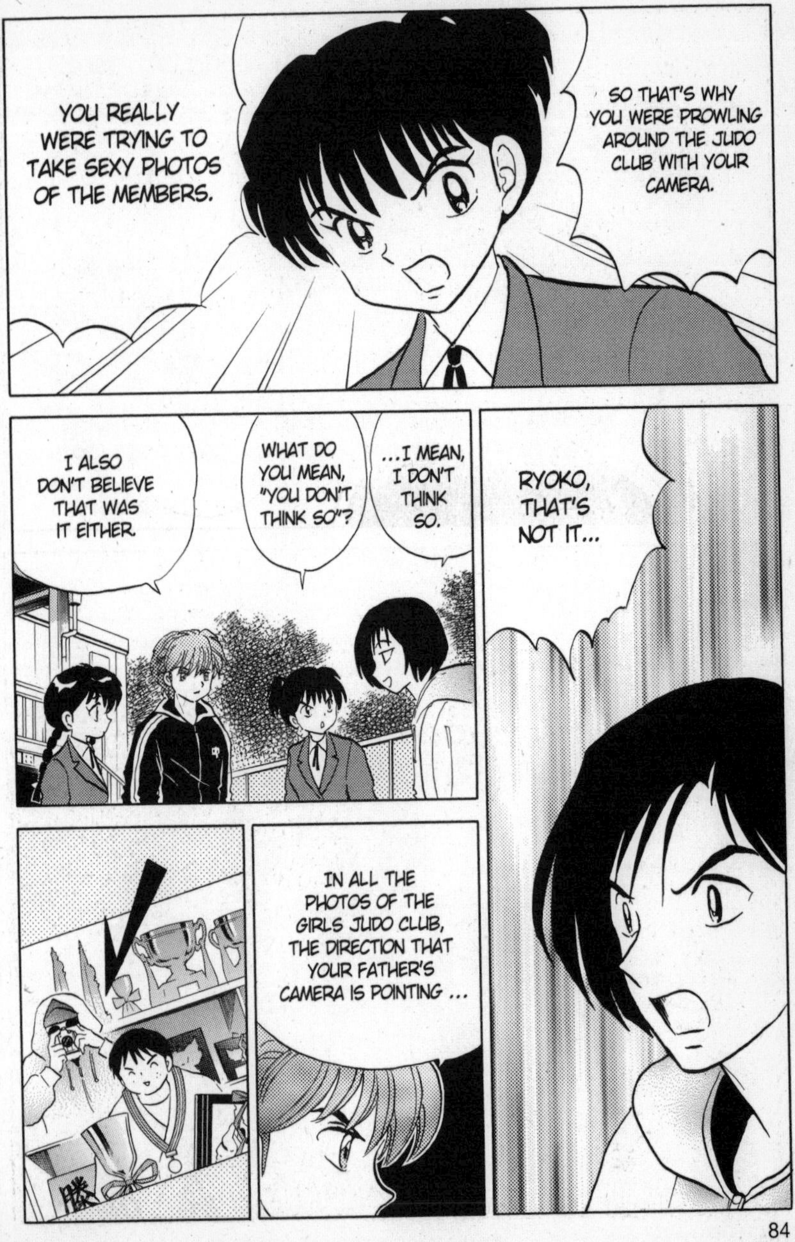
SO THAT'S WHY YOU WERE PROWLING AROUND THE JUDO CLUB WITH YOUR CAMERA.
YOU REALLY WERE TRYING TO TAKE SEXY PHOTOS OF THE MEMBERS.
RYOKO, THAT'S NOT IT...
...I MEAN, I DON'T THINK SO.
WHAT DO YOU MEAN, "YOU DON'T THINK SO"?
I ALSO DON'T BELIEVE THAT WAS IT EITHER.
IN ALL THE PHOTOS OF THE GIRLS JUDO CLUB, THE DIRECTION THAT YOUR FATHER'S CAMERA IS POINTING ...

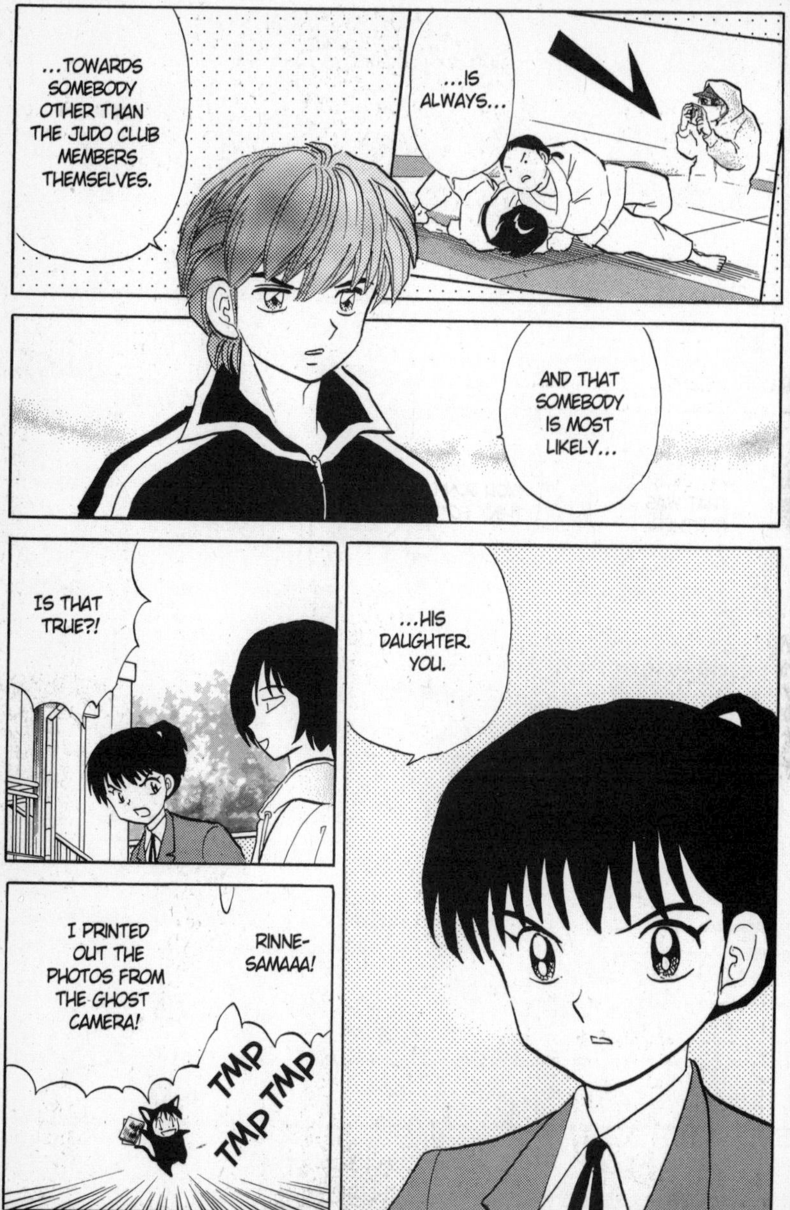
...IS ALWAYS...
...TOWARDS SOMEBODY OTHER THAN THE JUDO CLUB MEMBERS THEMSELVES.
AND THAT SOMEBODY IS MOST LIKELY...
...HIS DAUGHTER. YOU.
IS THAT TRUE?!
RINNE-SAMAAA!
I PRINTED OUT THE PHOTOS FROM THE GHOST CAMERA!
TMP TMP TMP

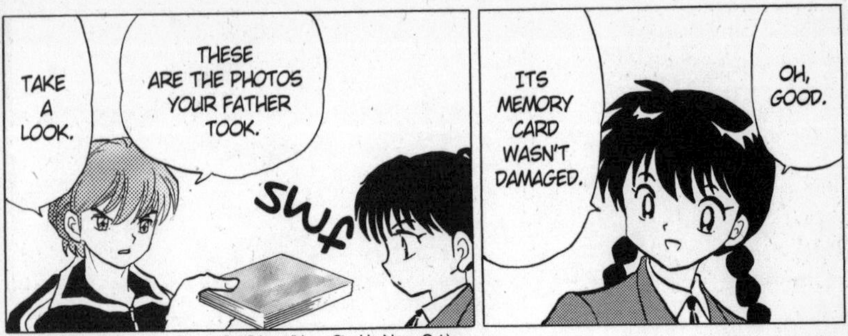
OH, GOOD.
ITS MEMORY CARD WASN'T DAMAGED.
THESE ARE THE PHOTOS YOUR FATHER TOOK.
TAKE A LOOK.
swf

Banner: *Futo Fukutsu* (Never Give Up, Never Quit)

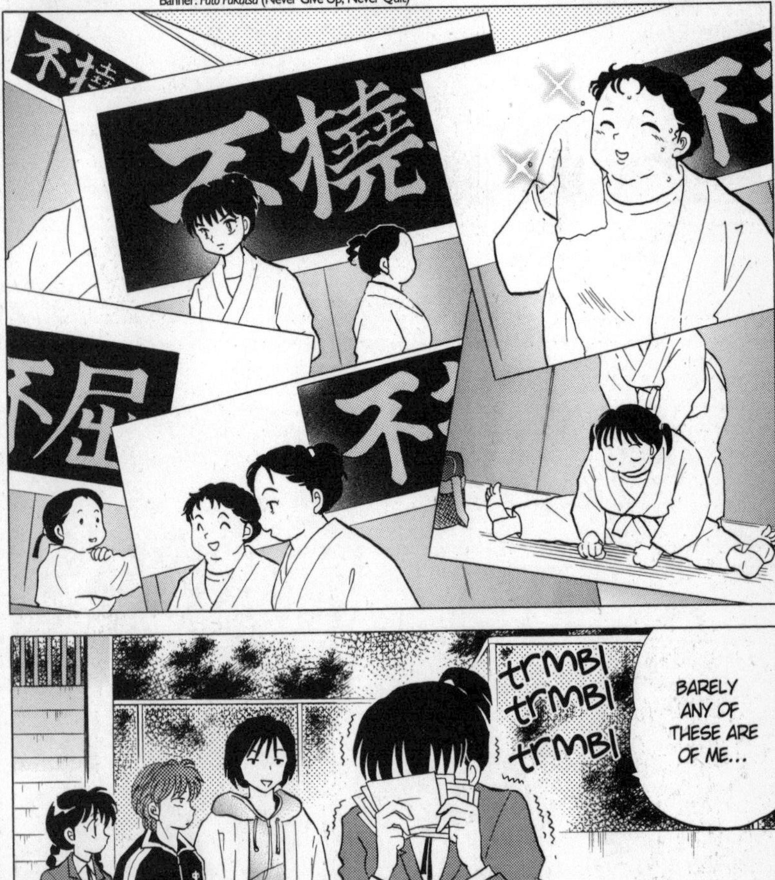
不撓
不屈
BARELY ANY OF THESE ARE OF ME...
trmbl
trmbl
trmbl

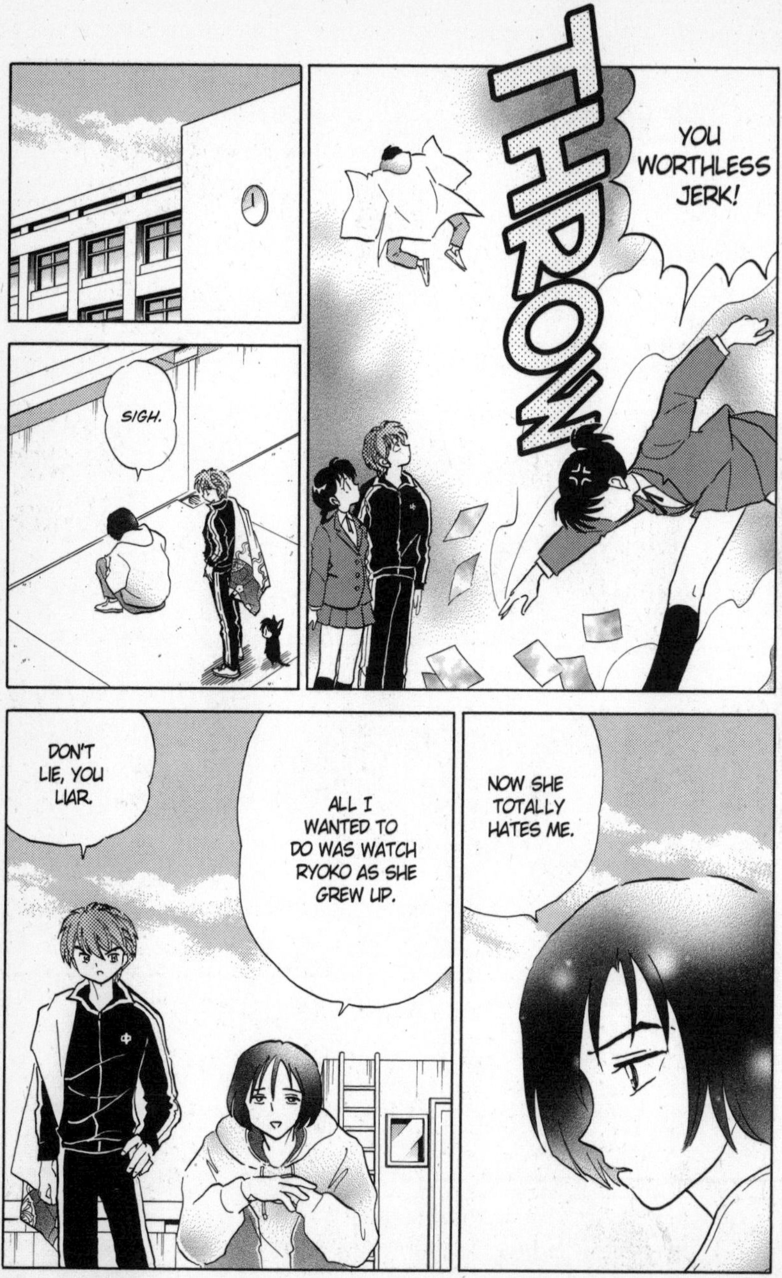

YOU WORTHLESS JERK!
THROW
SIGH.
NOW SHE TOTALLY HATES ME.
ALL I WANTED TO DO WAS WATCH RYOKO AS SHE GREW UP.
DON'T LIE, YOU LIAR.

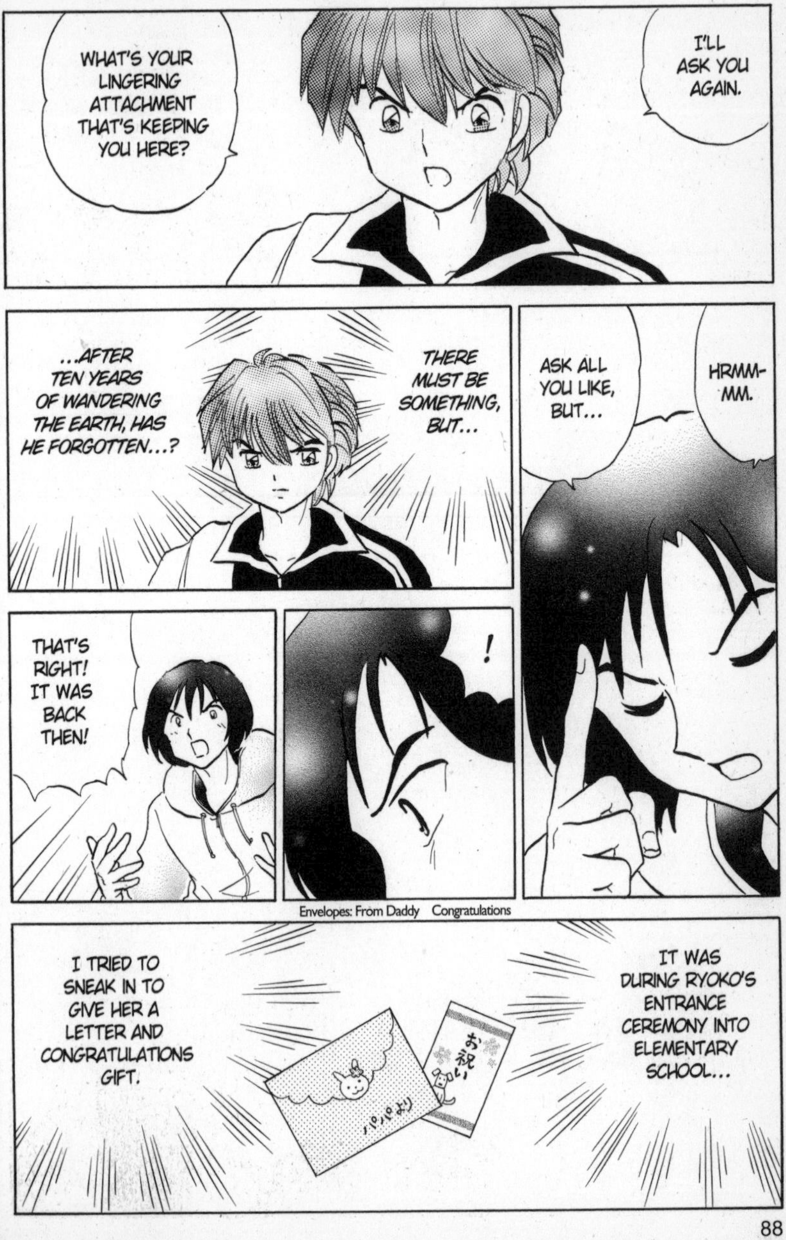
I'LL ASK YOU AGAIN.
WHAT'S YOUR LINGERING ATTACHMENT THAT'S KEEPING YOU HERE?
HRMM-MM.
ASK ALL YOU LIKE, BUT...
THERE MUST BE SOMETHING, BUT...
...AFTER TEN YEARS OF WANDERING THE EARTH, HAS HE FORGOTTEN...?
!
THAT'S RIGHT! IT WAS BACK THEN!
Envelopes: From Daddy Congratulations
IT WAS DURING RYOKO'S ENTRANCE CEREMONY INTO ELEMENTARY SCHOOL...
I TRIED TO SNEAK IN TO GIVE HER A LETTER AND CONGRATULATIONS GIFT.
お祝い
パパより

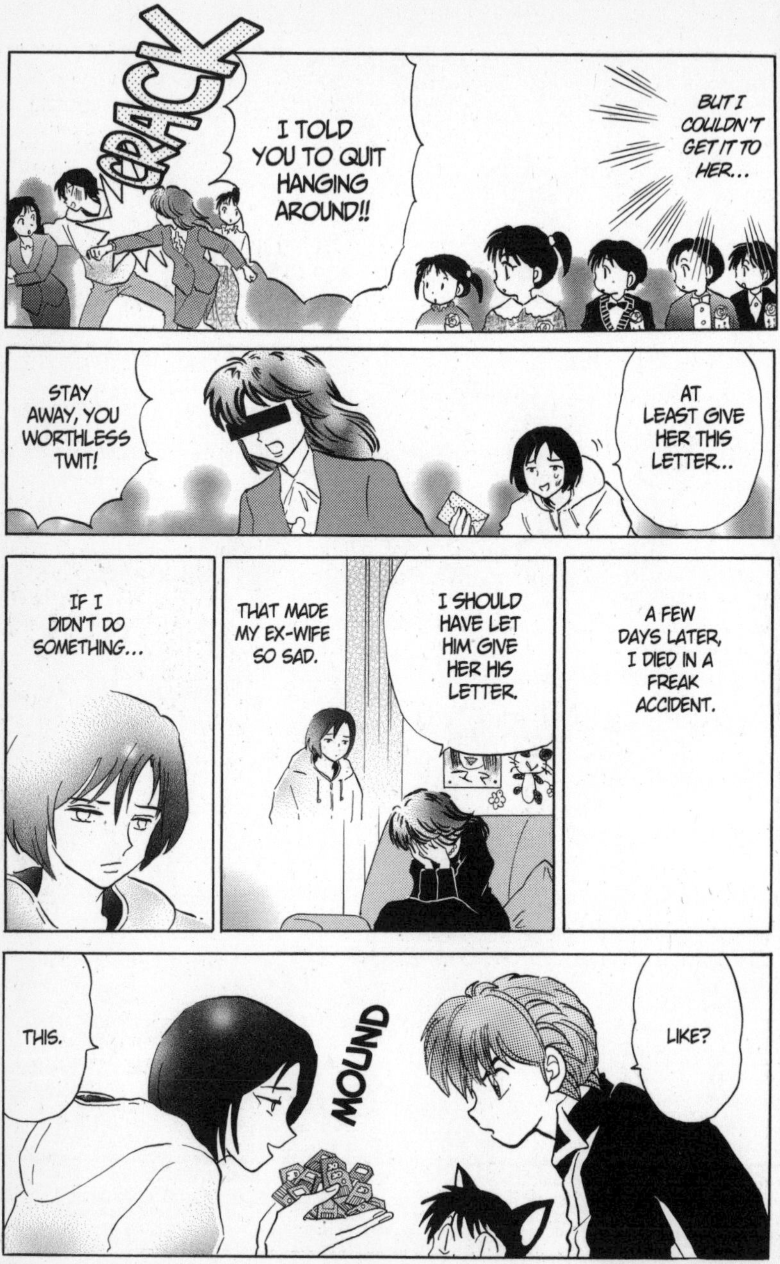
BUT I COULDN'T GET IT TO HER...
CRACK
I TOLD YOU TO QUIT HANGING AROUND!!
AT LEAST GIVE HER THIS LETTER..
STAY AWAY, YOU WORTHLESS TWIT!
A FEW DAYS LATER, I DIED IN A FREAK ACCIDENT.
I SHOULD HAVE LET HIM GIVE HER HIS LETTER.
THAT MADE MY EX-WIFE SO SAD.
IF I DIDN'T DO SOMETHING...
LIKE?
MOUND
THIS.

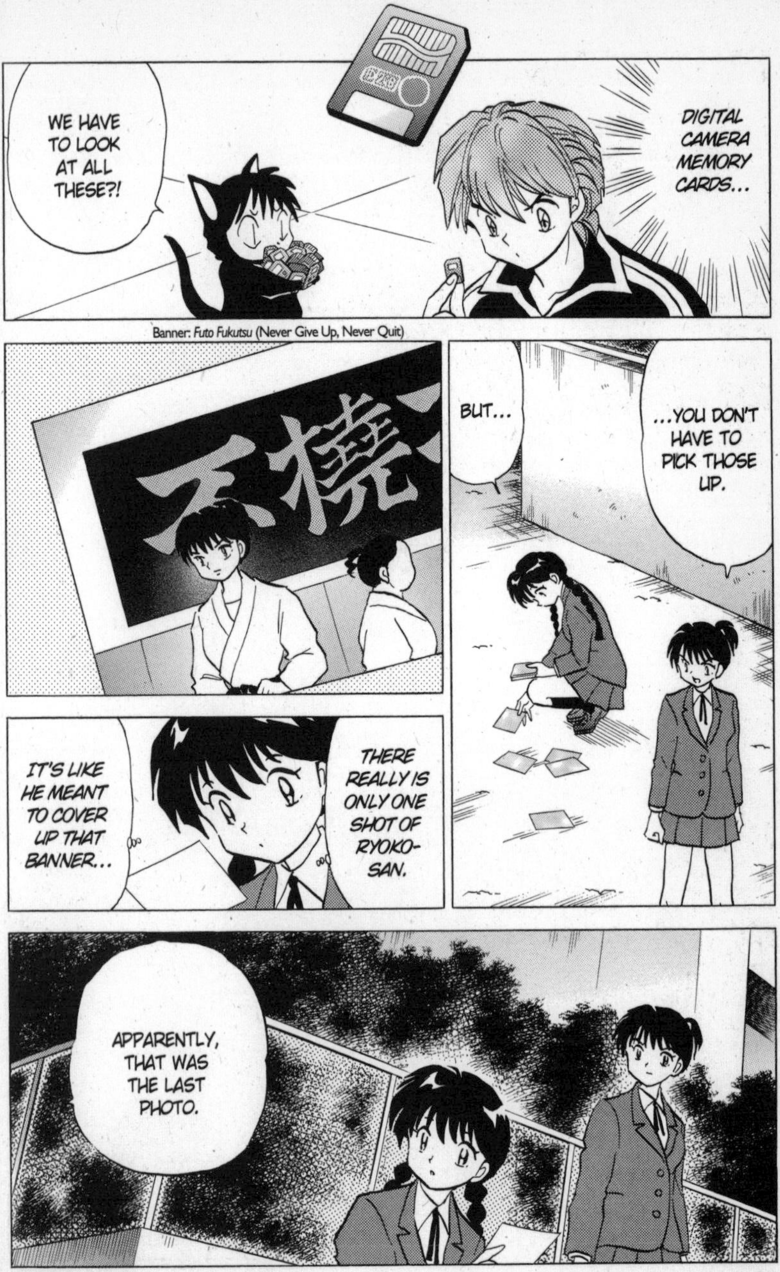
DIGITAL CAMERA MEMORY CARDS...
WE HAVE TO LOOK AT ALL THESE?!
...YOU DON'T HAVE TO PICK THOSE UP.
BUT...
Banner: *Futo Fukutsu* (Never Give Up, Never Quit)
THERE REALLY IS ONLY ONE SHOT OF RYOKO-SAN.
IT'S LIKE HE MEANT TO COVER UP THAT BANNER...
APPARENTLY, THAT WAS THE LAST PHOTO.

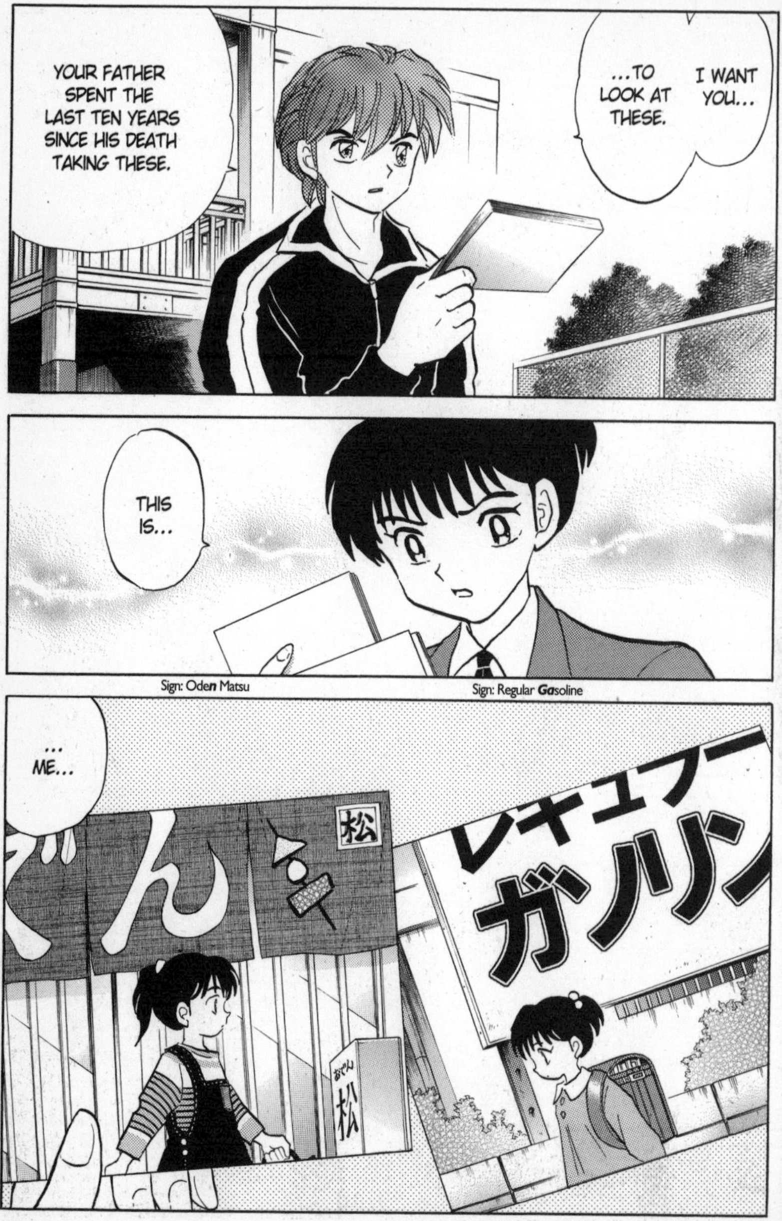
I WANT YOU...
...TO LOOK AT THESE.
YOUR FATHER SPENT THE LAST TEN YEARS SINCE HIS DEATH TAKING THESE.
THIS IS...
Sign: Regular Gasoline
Sign: Oden Matsu
... ME...

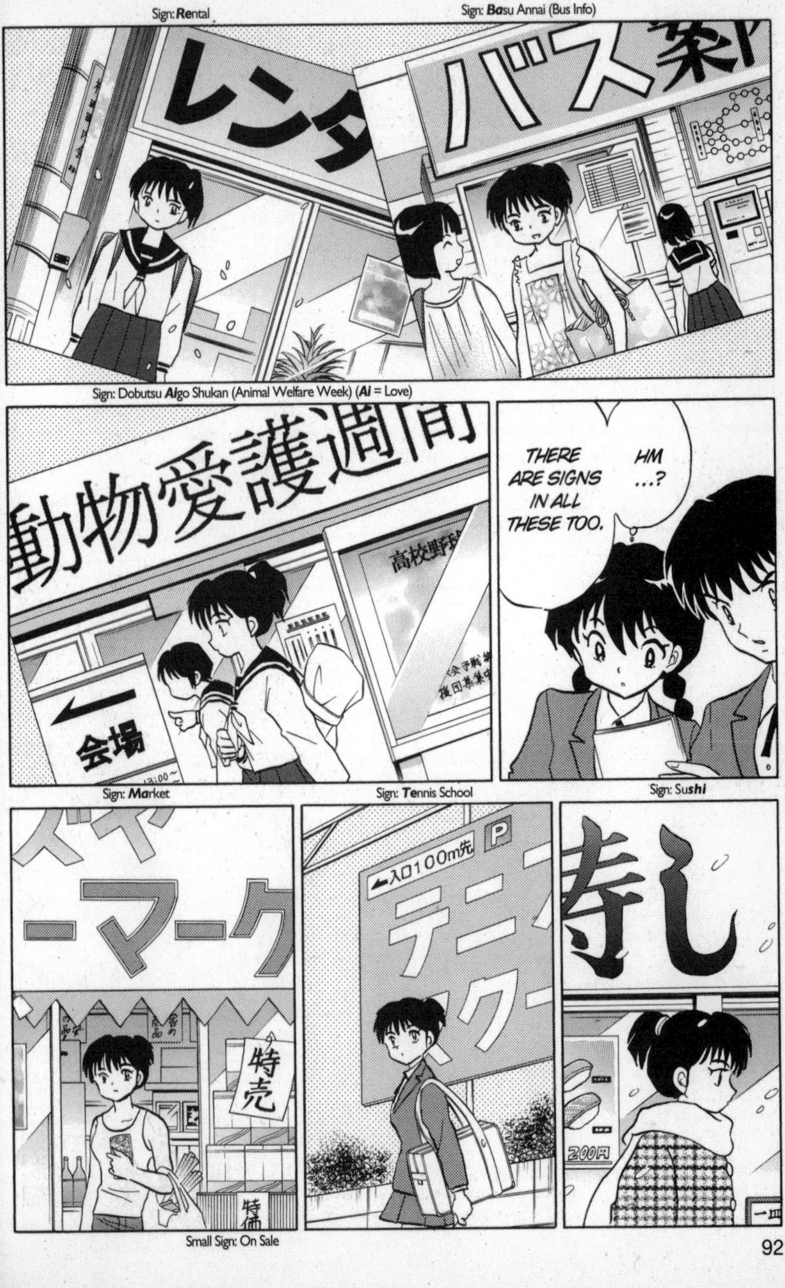
Sign: Basu Annai (Bus Info)
Sign: Rental
HM ...?
THERE ARE SIGNS IN ALL THESE TOO.
Sign: Dobutsu Aigo Shukan (Animal Welfare Week) (Ai = Love)
動物愛護週間
会場
Sign: Sushi
寿し
200円
Sign: Tennis School
←入口100m先
Sign: Market
特売
Small Sign: On Sale

NOTE: The way the first kanji character is covered up makes it look like the katakana character [ス] *su*.

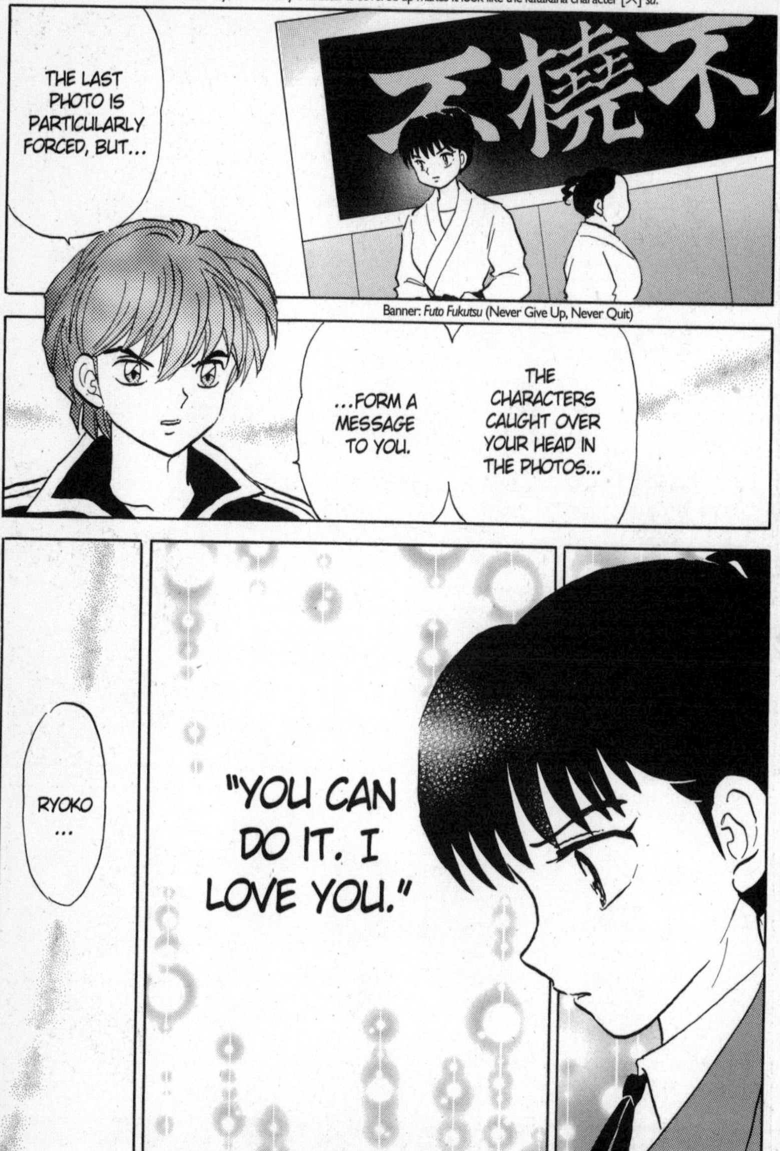

不撓不
THE LAST PHOTO IS PARTICULARLY FORCED, BUT...
Banner: *Futo Fukutsu* (Never Give Up, Never Quit)
THE CHARACTERS CAUGHT OVER YOUR HEAD IN THE PHOTOS...
...FORM A MESSAGE TO YOU.
"YOU CAN DO IT. I LOVE YOU."
NOTE: In all the photos, Ryoko is located directly beneath one particular character that together spell out (in Japanese) "*ga-n-ba-re ai-shi-te-ma-su*," or "You can do it, I love you."
RYOKO ...

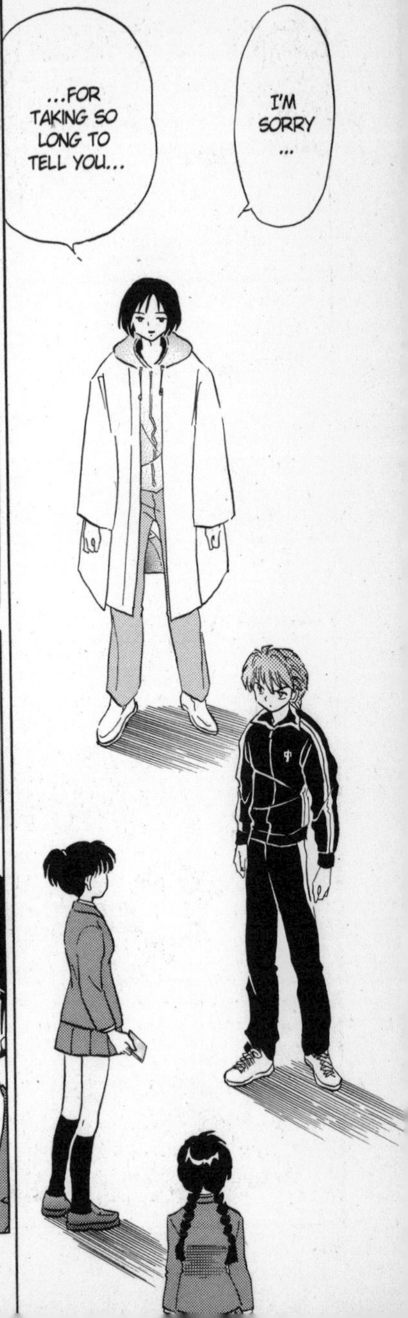
I'M SORRY ...
...FOR TAKING SO LONG TO TELL YOU...

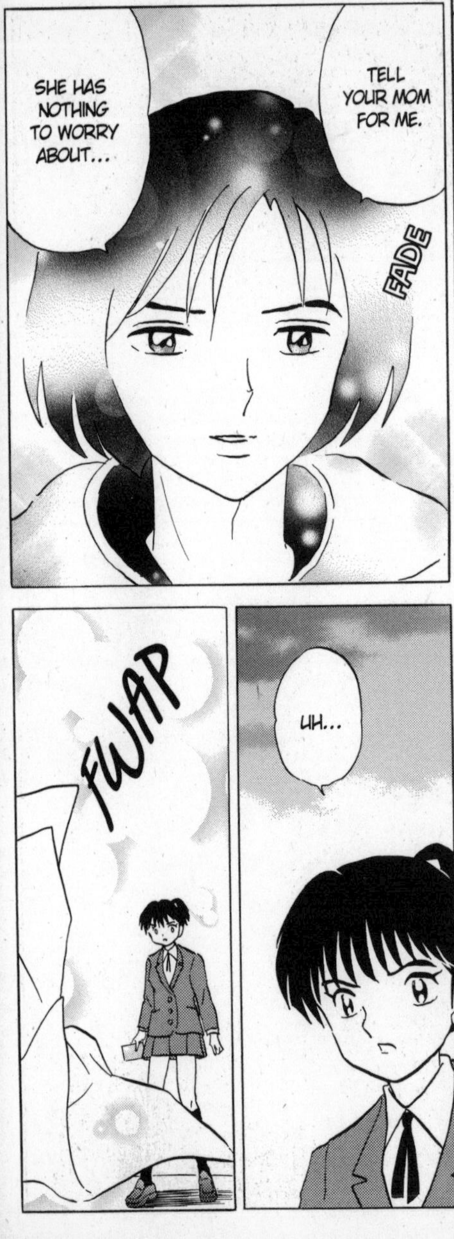
TELL YOUR MOM FOR ME.
SHE HAS NOTHING TO WORRY ABOUT...
FADE
UH...
FWAP

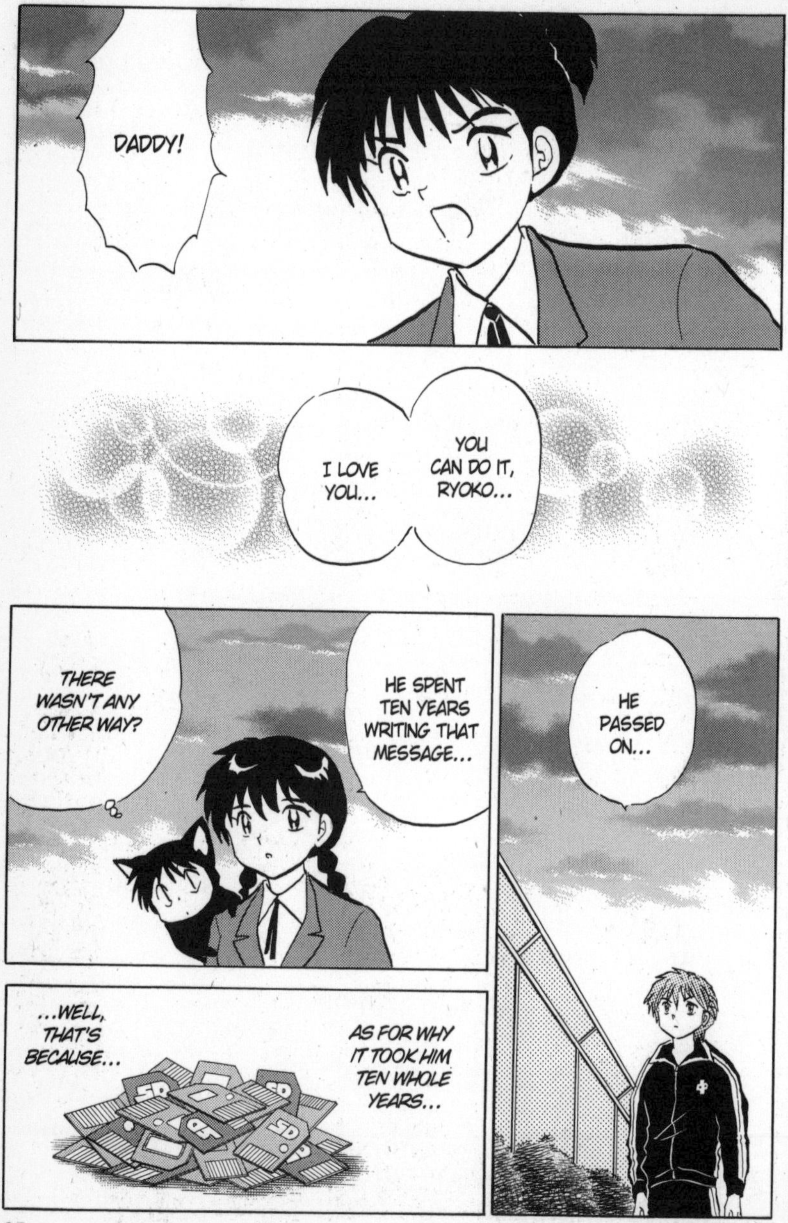
DADDY!
YOU CAN DO IT, RYOKO...
I LOVE YOU...
HE PASSED ON...
HE SPENT TEN YEARS WRITING THAT MESSAGE...
THERE WASN'T ANY OTHER WAY?
AS FOR WHY IT TOOK HIM TEN WHOLE YEARS...
...WELL, THAT'S BECAUSE...

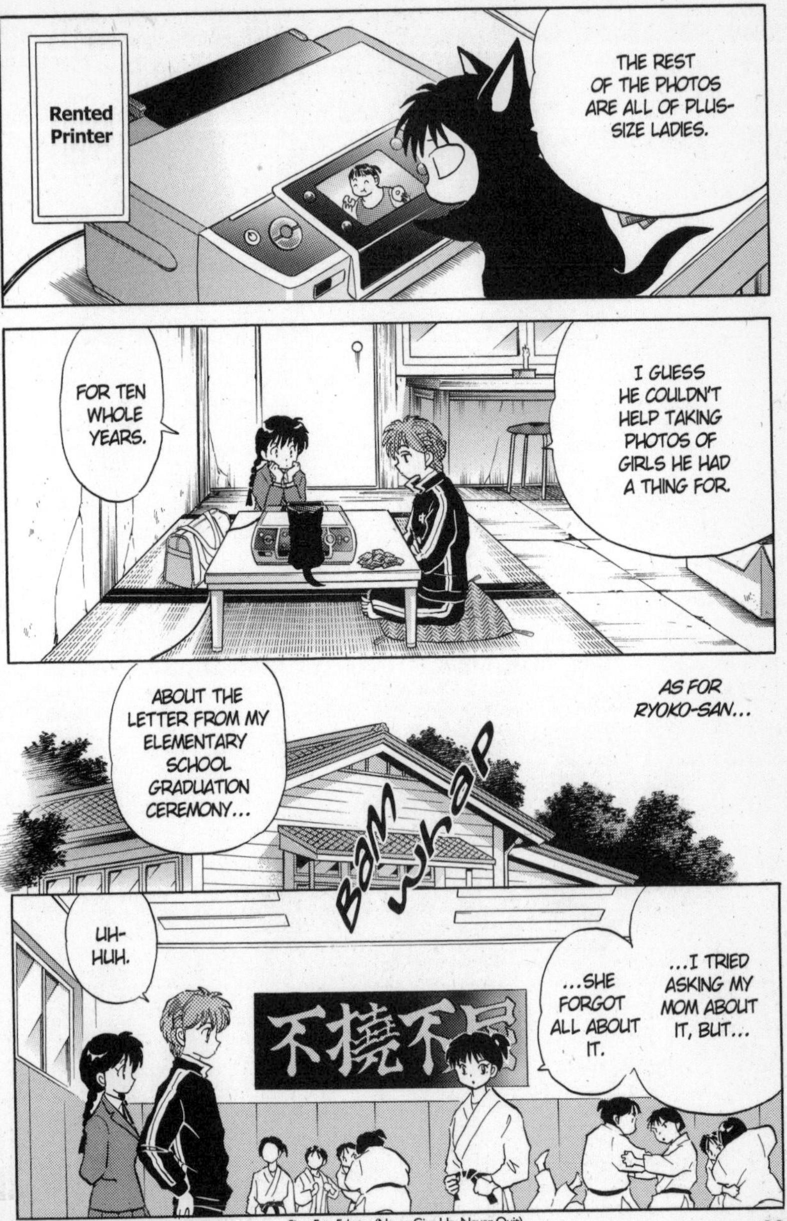
THE REST OF THE PHOTOS ARE ALL OF PLUS-SIZE LADIES.
Rented Printer
I GUESS HE COULDN'T HELP TAKING PHOTOS OF GIRLS HE HAD A THING FOR.
FOR TEN WHOLE YEARS.
AS FOR RYOKO-SAN...
ABOUT THE LETTER FROM MY ELEMENTARY SCHOOL GRADUATION CEREMONY...
Bam
wrap
...I TRIED ASKING MY MOM ABOUT IT, BUT...
...SHE FORGOT ALL ABOUT IT.
不撓不
UH-HUH.

Sign: *Futo Fukutsu* (Never Give Up, Never Quit)

CHAPTER 94: THE MISSING DUES

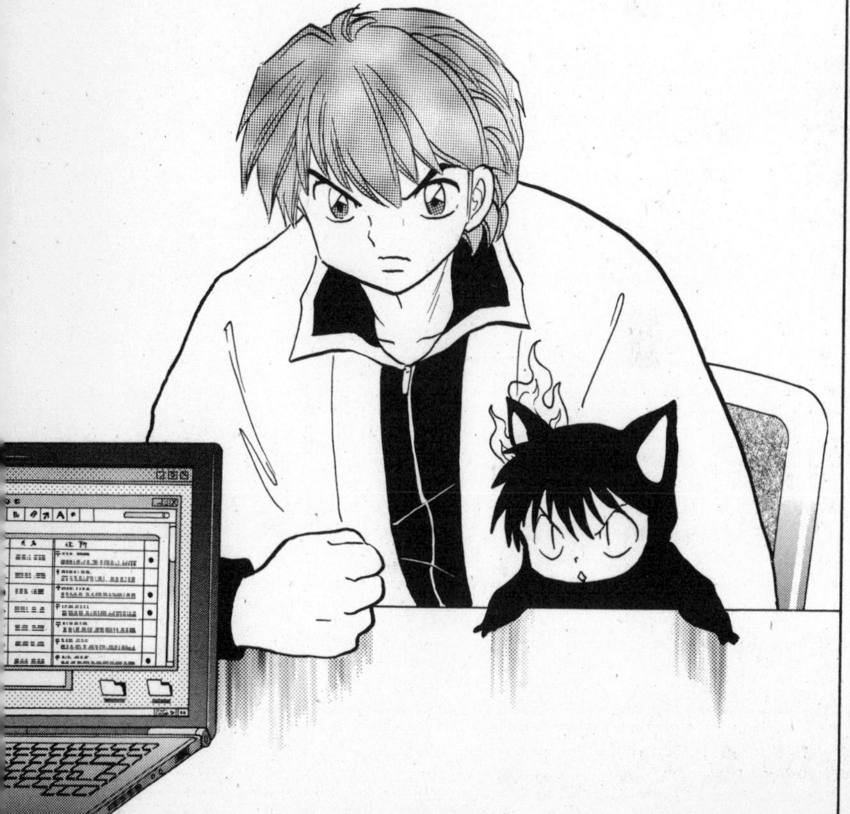

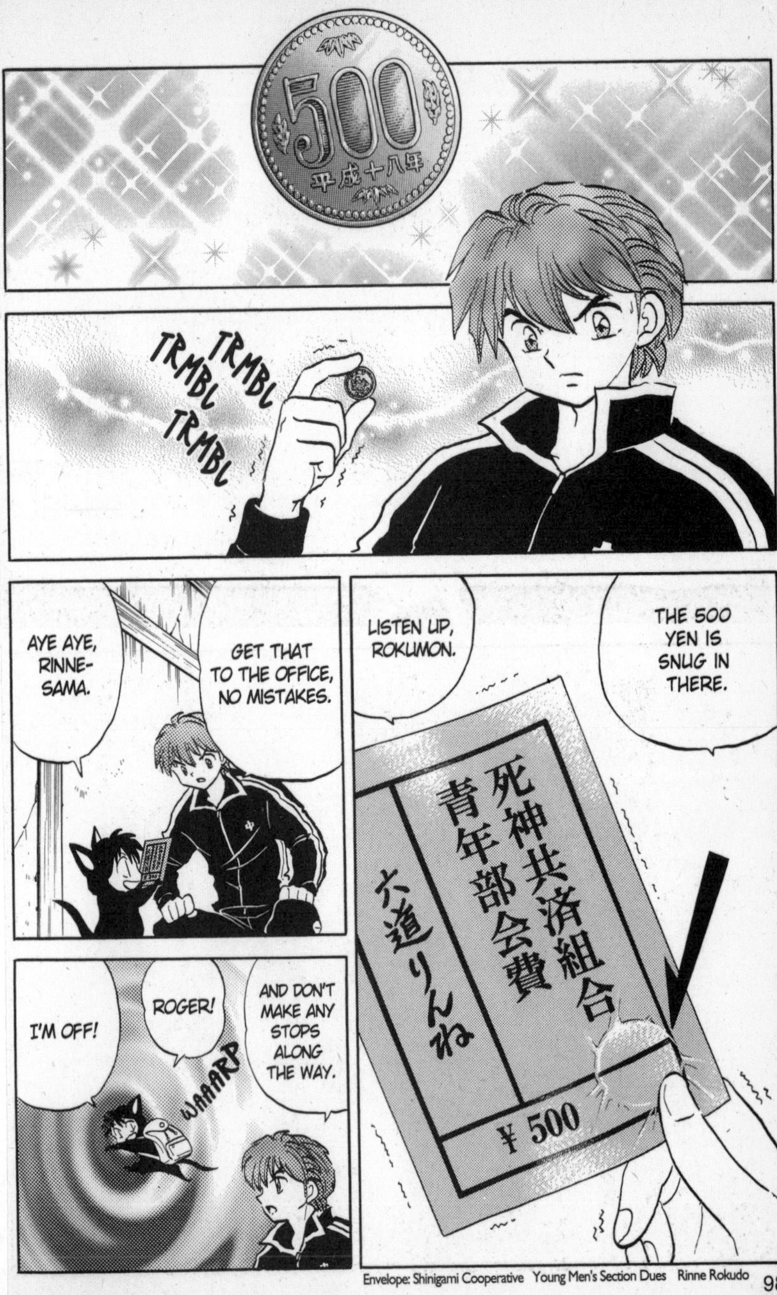
500
平成十八年
TRMBL
TRMBL
TRMBL
THE 500 YEN IS SNUG IN THERE.
LISTEN UP, ROKUMON.
死神共済組合
青年部会費
六道りんね
¥ 500
GET THAT TO THE OFFICE, NO MISTAKES.
AYE AYE, RINNE-SAMA.
AND DON'T MAKE ANY STOPS ALONG THE WAY.
ROGER!
WAAARP
I'M OFF!

Envelope: Shinigami Cooperative Young Men's Section Dues Rinne Rokudo

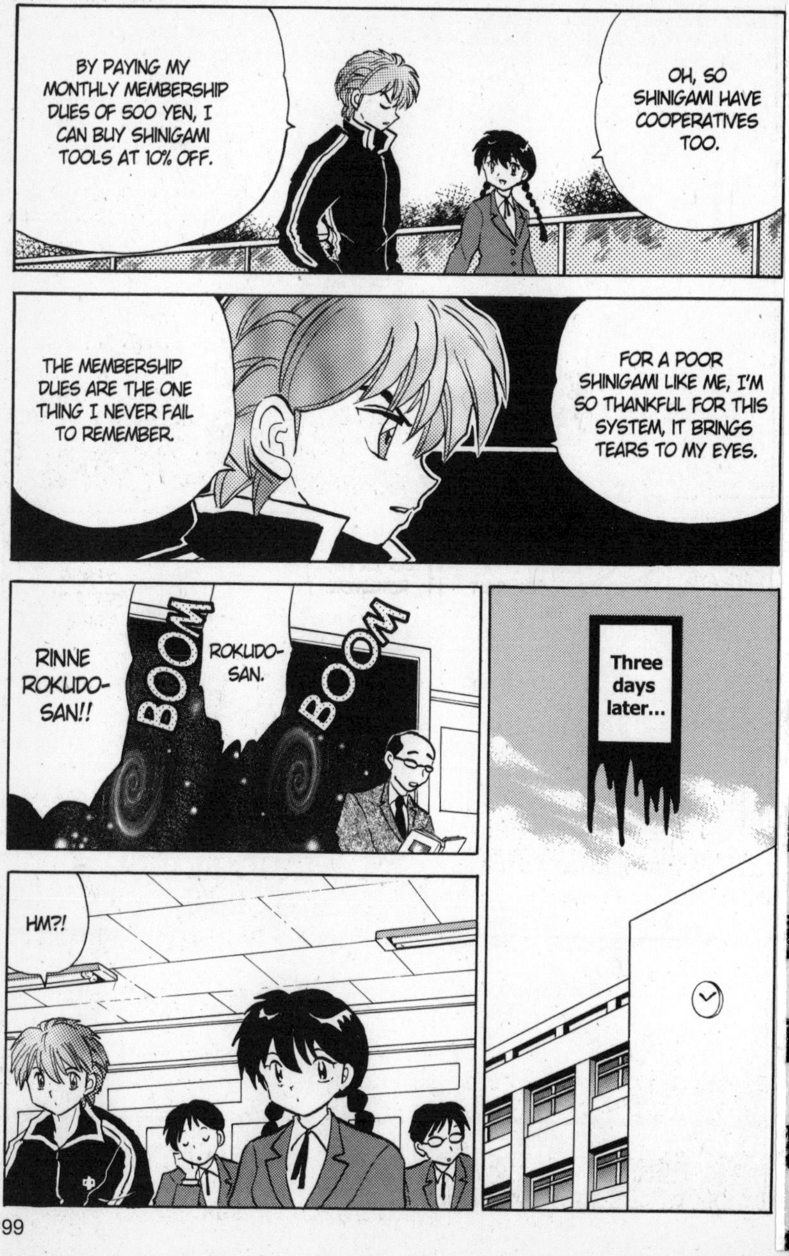
OH, SO SHINIGAMI HAVE COOPERATIVES TOO.
BY PAYING MY MONTHLY MEMBERSHIP DUES OF 500 YEN, I CAN BUY SHINIGAMI TOOLS AT 10% OFF.
FOR A POOR SHINIGAMI LIKE ME, I'M SO THANKFUL FOR THIS SYSTEM, IT BRINGS TEARS TO MY EYES.
THE MEMBERSHIP DUES ARE THE ONE THING I NEVER FAIL TO REMEMBER.
Three days later...
BOOM
ROKUDO-SAN.
BOOM
RINNE ROKUDO-SAN!!
HM?!

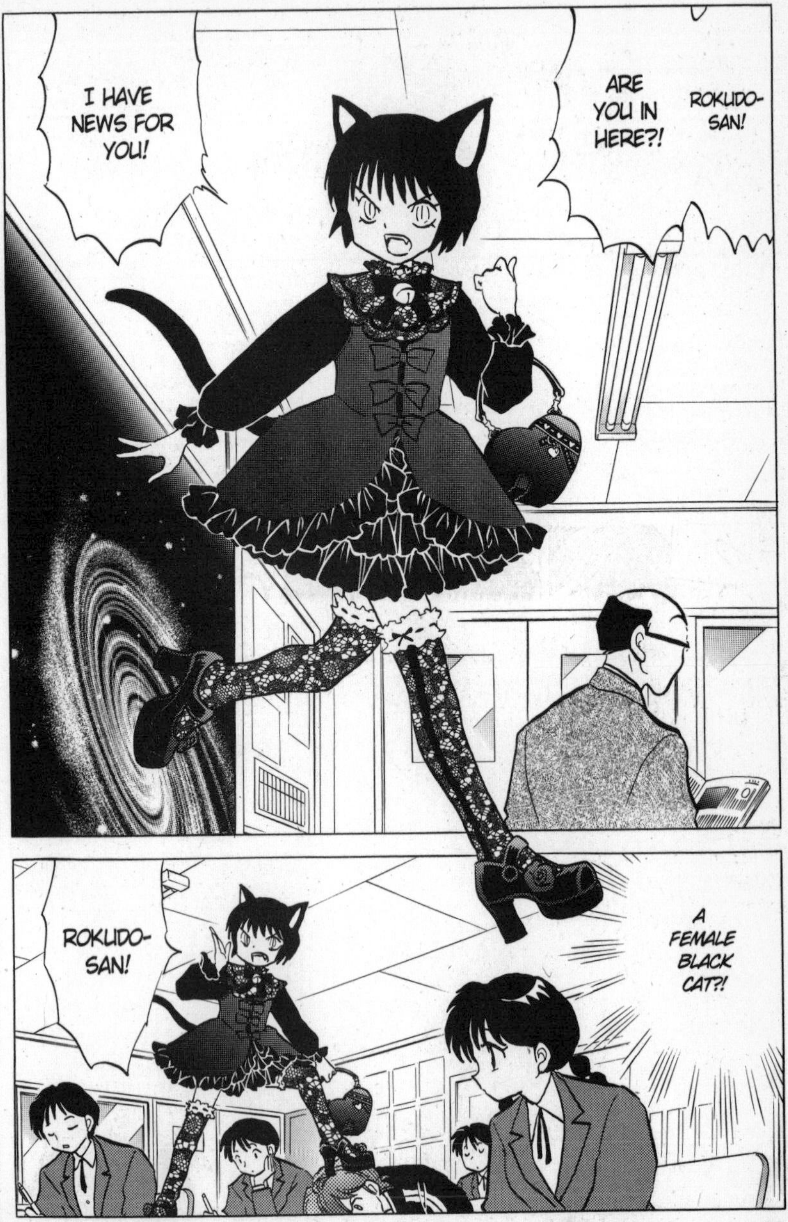
ROKUDO-SAN!
ARE YOU IN HERE?!
I HAVE NEWS FOR YOU!
A FEMALE BLACK CAT?!
ROKUDO-SAN!

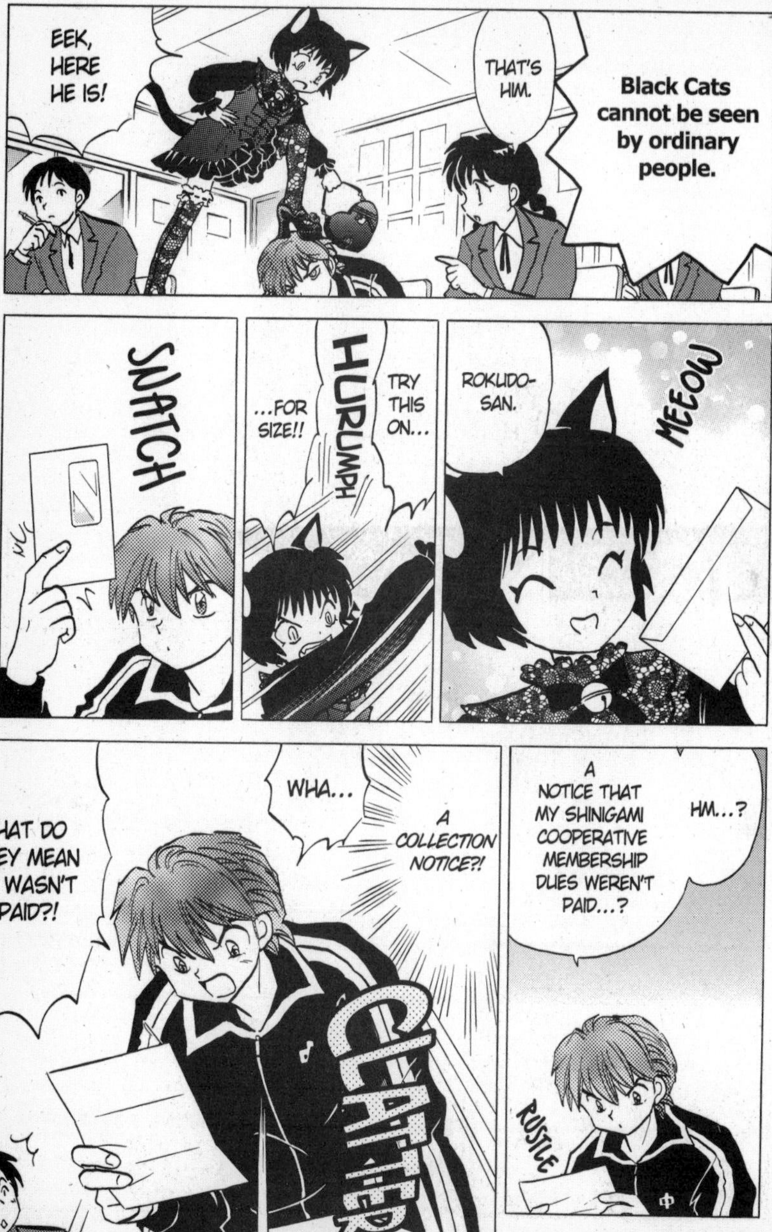
Black Cats cannot be seen by ordinary people.
THAT'S HIM.
EEK, HERE HE IS!
MEEOW
ROKUDO-SAN.
TRY THIS ON...
HURUMPH
...FOR SIZE!!
SNATCH
HM...?
A NOTICE THAT MY SHINIGAMI COOPERATIVE MEMBERSHIP DUES WEREN'T PAID...?
RUSTLE
WHA...
A COLLECTION NOTICE?!
WHAT DO THEY MEAN IT WASN'T PAID?!
CLATTER

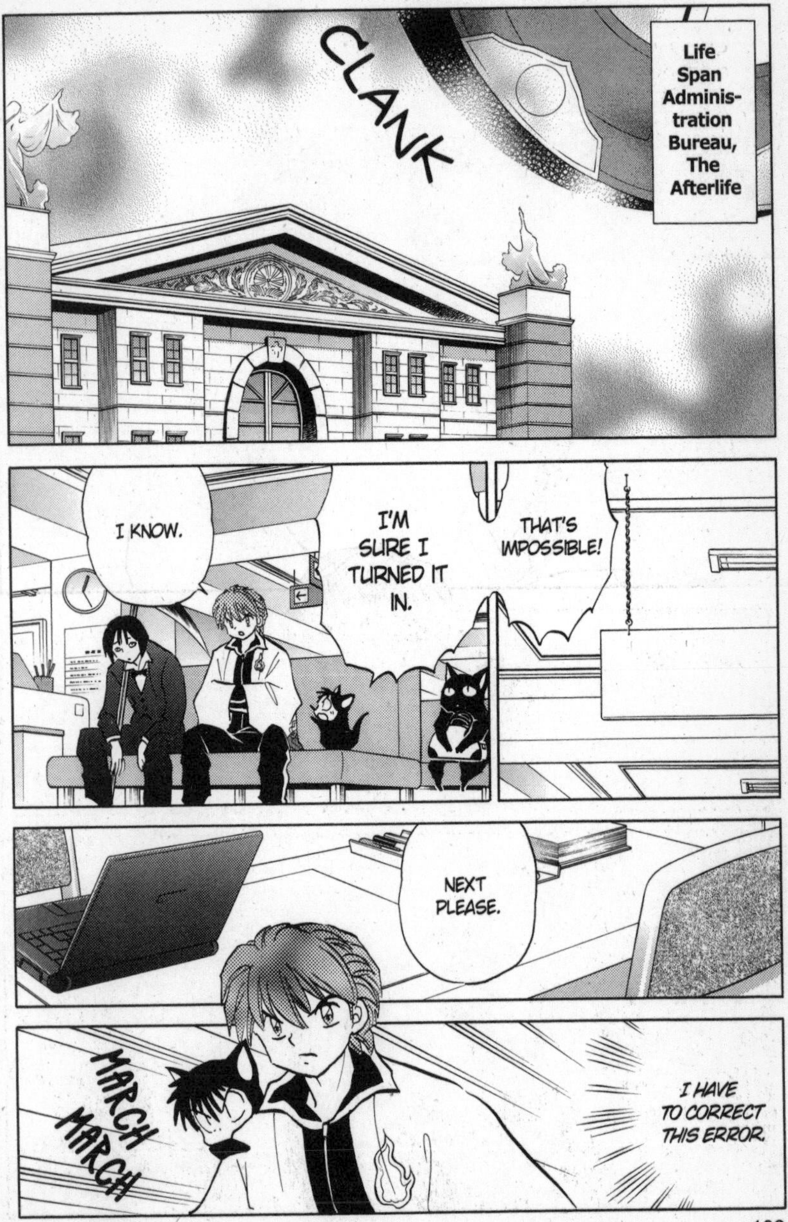
Life Span Adminis-tration Bureau, The Afterlife
CLANK
THAT'S IMPOSSIBLE!
I'M SURE I TURNED IT IN.
I KNOW.
NEXT PLEASE.
I HAVE TO CORRECT THIS ERROR.
MARCH MARCH

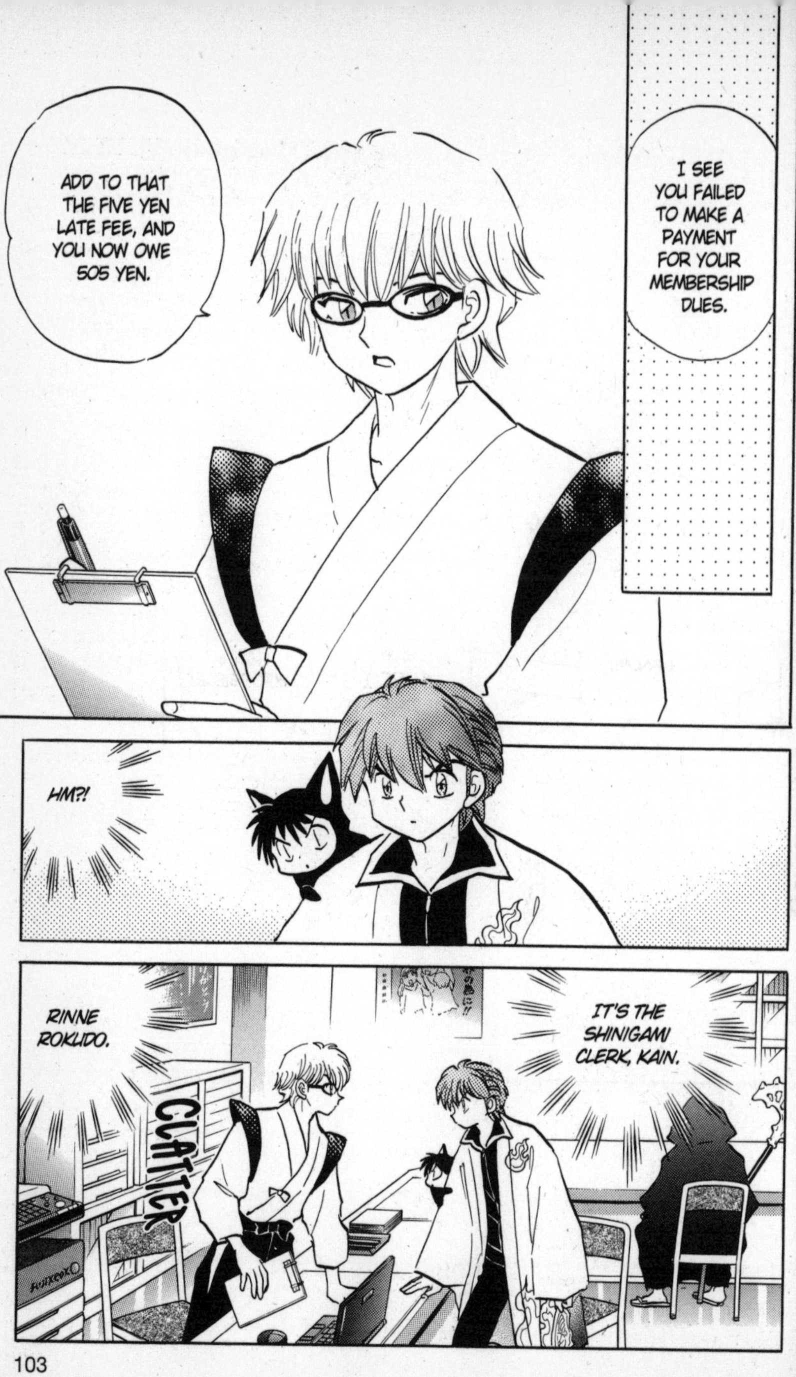
I SEE YOU FAILED TO MAKE A PAYMENT FOR YOUR MEMBERSHIP DUES.
ADD TO THAT THE FIVE YEN LATE FEE, AND YOU NOW OWE 505 YEN.
HM?!
IT'S THE SHINIGAMI CLERK, KAIN.
RINNE ROKUDO.
CLATTER

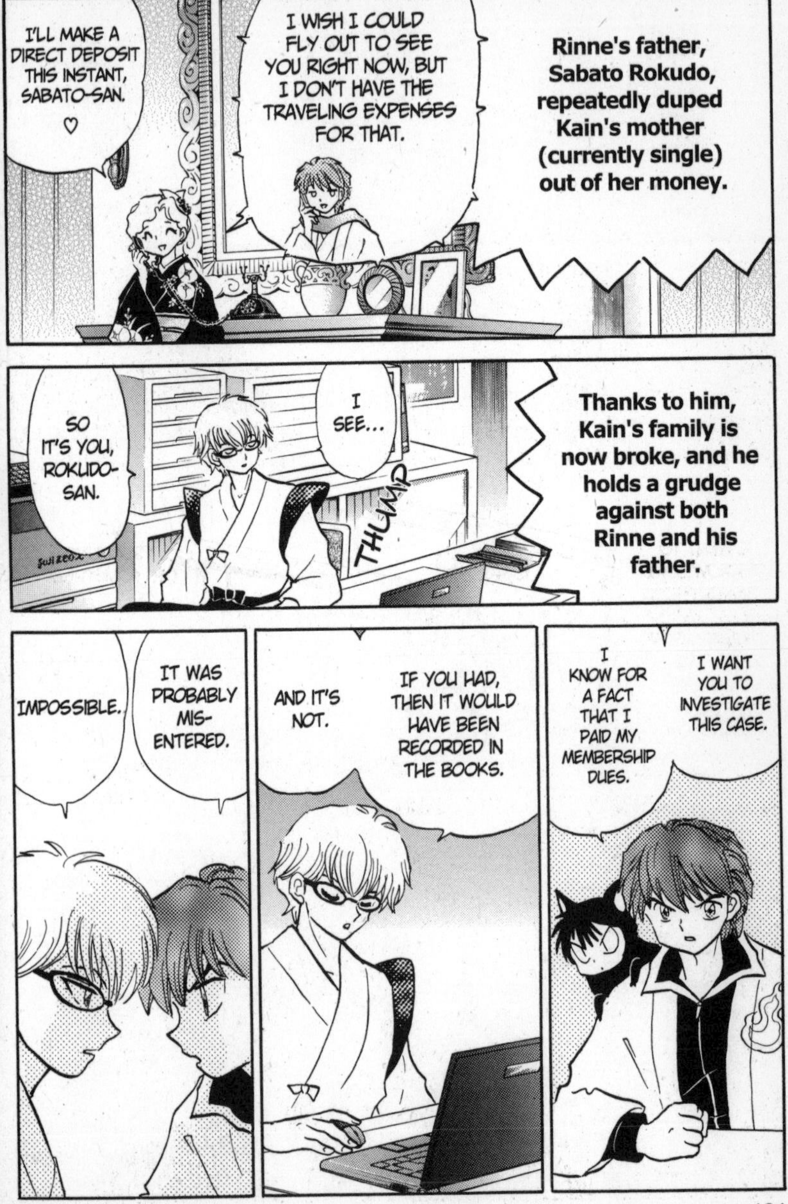
Rinne's father, Sabato Rokudo, repeatedly duped Kain's mother (currently single) out of her money.
I WISH I COULD FLY OUT TO SEE YOU RIGHT NOW, BUT I DON'T HAVE THE TRAVELING EXPENSES FOR THAT.
I'LL MAKE A DIRECT DEPOSIT THIS INSTANT, SABATO-SAN. ♡
Thanks to him, Kain's family is now broke, and he holds a grudge against both Rinne and his father.
I SEE...
THUMP
SO IT'S YOU, ROKUDO-SAN.
I WANT YOU TO INVESTIGATE THIS CASE.
I KNOW FOR A FACT THAT I PAID MY MEMBERSHIP DUES.
IF YOU HAD, THEN IT WOULD HAVE BEEN RECORDED IN THE BOOKS.
AND IT'S NOT.
IT WAS PROBABLY MIS-ENTERED.
IMPOSSIBLE.

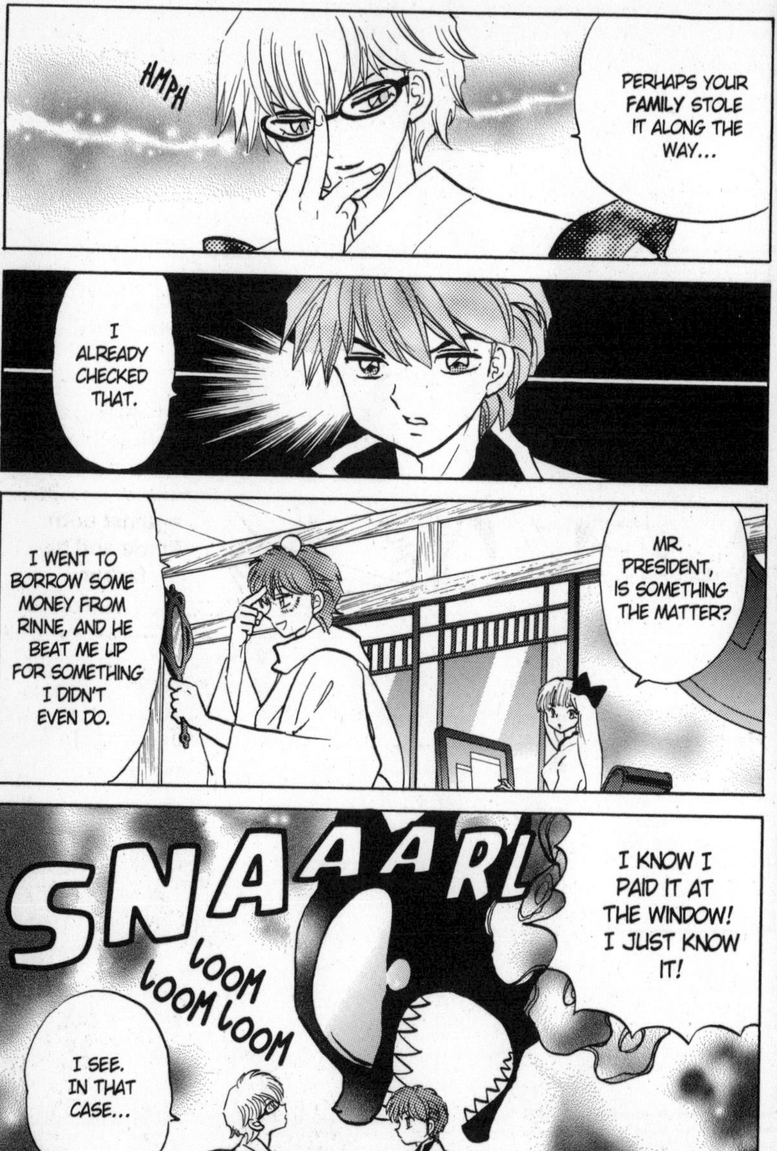
PERHAPS YOUR FAMILY STOLE IT ALONG THE WAY...
HMPH
I ALREADY CHECKED THAT.
MR. PRESIDENT, IS SOMETHING THE MATTER?
I WENT TO BORROW SOME MONEY FROM RINNE, AND HE BEAT ME UP FOR SOMETHING I DIDN'T EVEN DO.
I KNOW I PAID IT AT THE WINDOW! I JUST KNOW IT!
SNAAARL
LOOM LOOM LOOM
I SEE. IN THAT CASE...

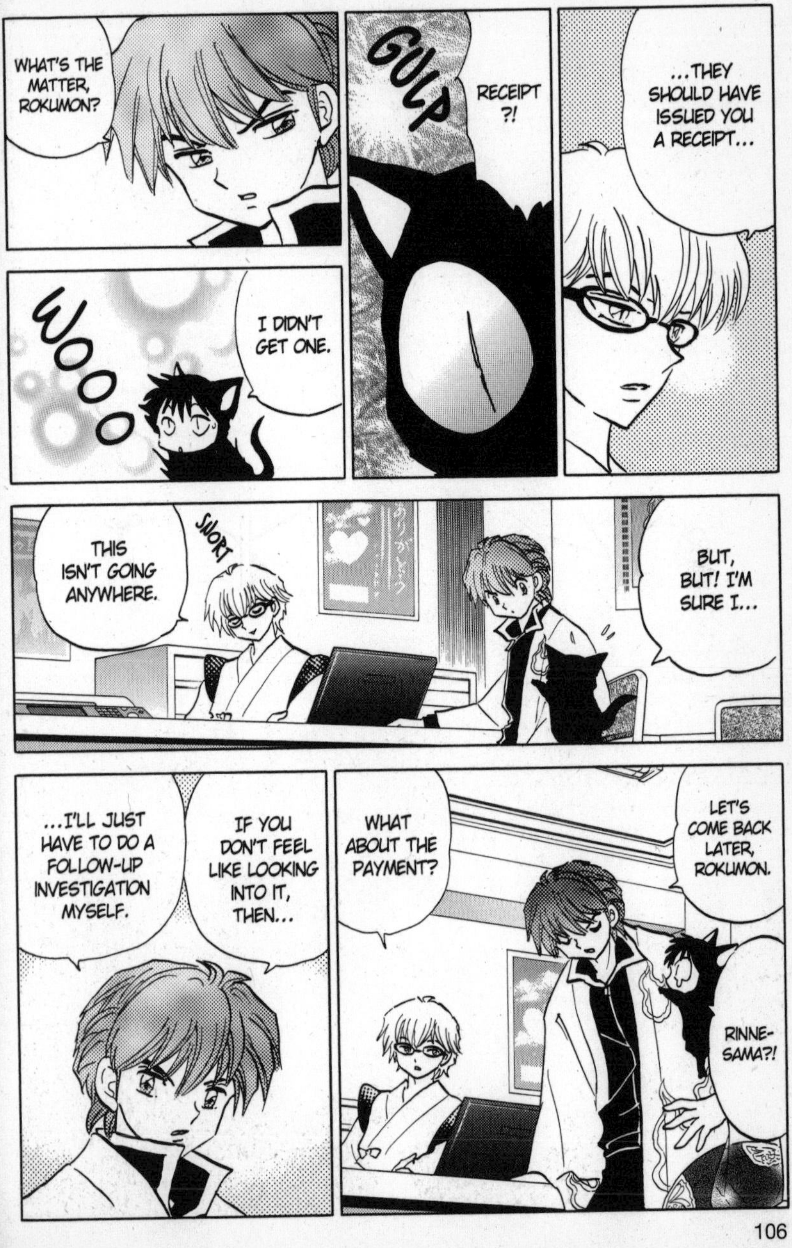
...THEY SHOULD HAVE ISSUED YOU A RECEIPT...
GULP
RECEIPT ?!
WHAT'S THE MATTER, ROKUMON?
WOOOO
I DIDN'T GET ONE.
BUT, BUT! I'M SURE I...
SNORT
THIS ISN'T GOING ANYWHERE.
LET'S COME BACK LATER, ROKUMON.
WHAT ABOUT THE PAYMENT?
RINNE-SAMA?!
IF YOU DON'T FEEL LIKE LOOKING INTO IT, THEN...
...I'LL JUST HAVE TO DO A FOLLOW-UP INVESTIGATION MYSELF.

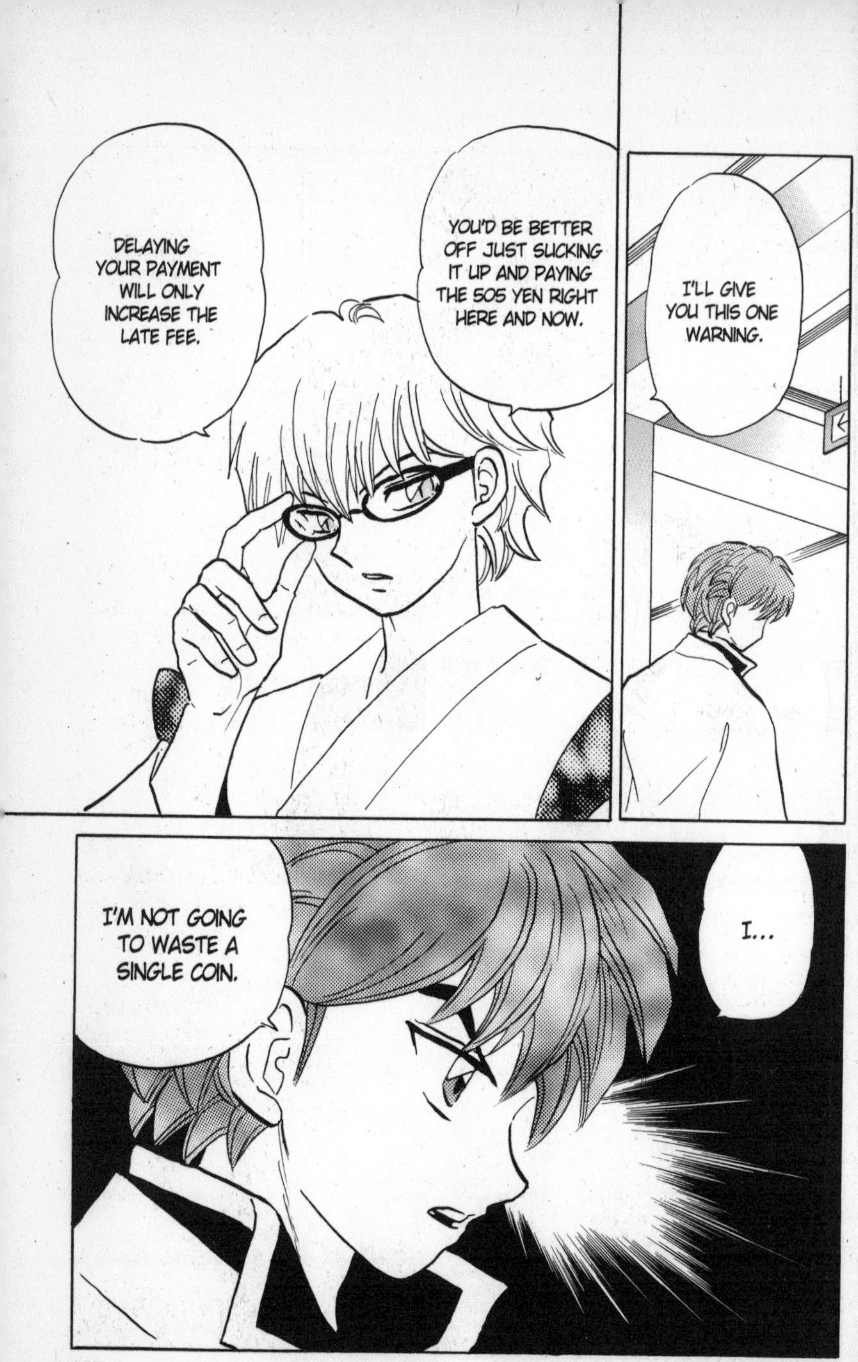
I'LL GIVE YOU THIS ONE WARNING.
YOU'D BE BETTER OFF JUST SUCKING IT UP AND PAYING THE 505 YEN RIGHT HERE AND NOW.
DELAYING YOUR PAYMENT WILL ONLY INCREASE THE LATE FEE.
I...
I'M NOT GOING TO WASTE A SINGLE COIN.

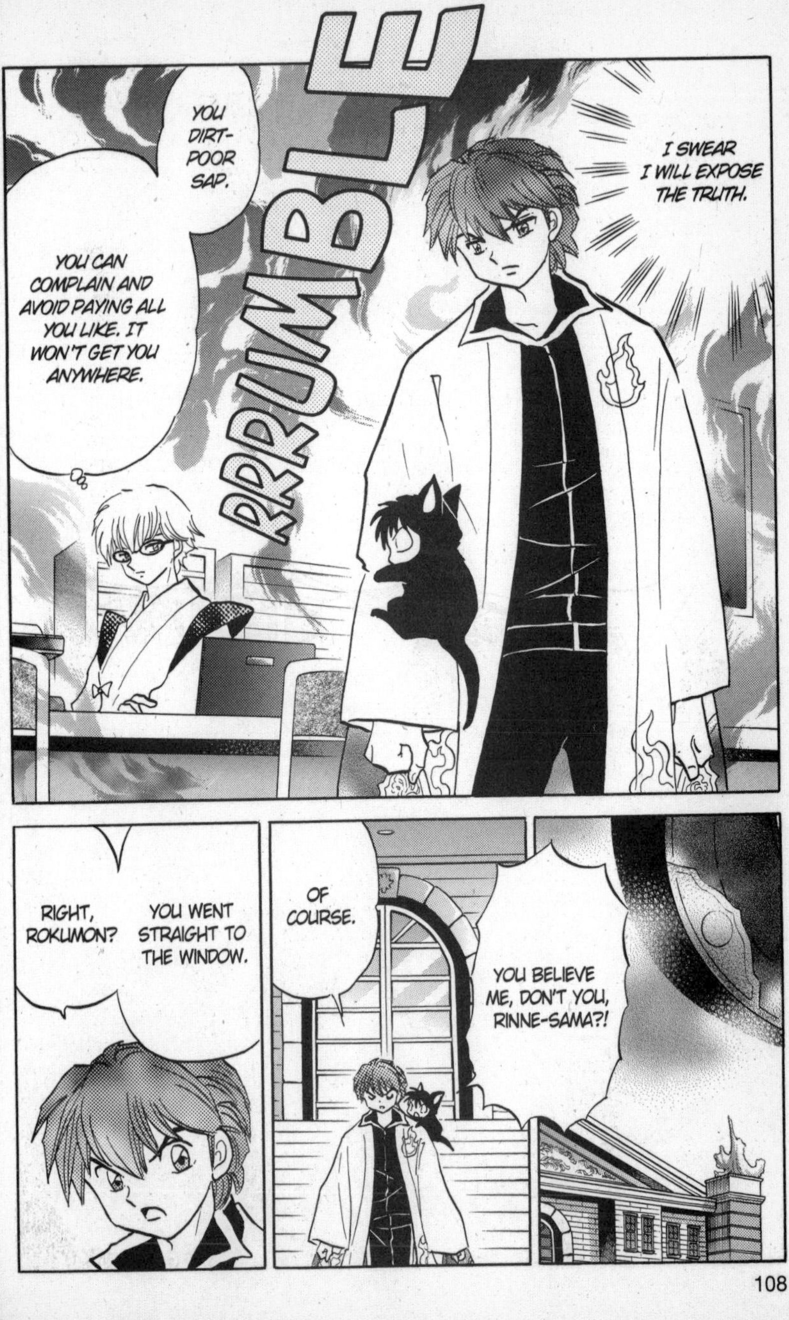
I SWEAR I WILL EXPOSE THE TRUTH.
RRRUMBLE
YOU DIRT-POOR SAP.
YOU CAN COMPLAIN AND AVOID PAYING ALL YOU LIKE. IT WON'T GET YOU ANYWHERE.
YOU BELIEVE ME, DON'T YOU, RINNE-SAMA?!
OF COURSE.
YOU WENT STRAIGHT TO THE WINDOW.
RIGHT, ROKUMON?

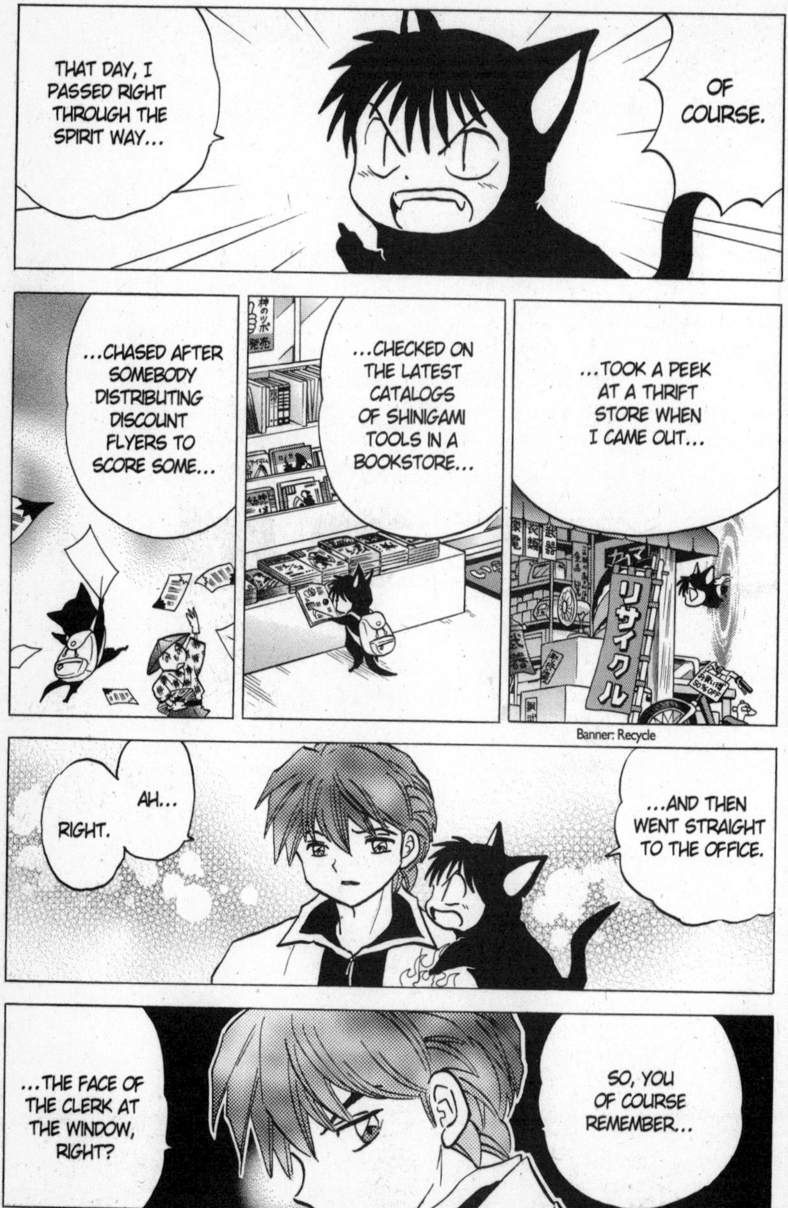
OF COURSE.
THAT DAY, I PASSED RIGHT THROUGH THE SPIRIT WAY...
...TOOK A PEEK AT A THRIFT STORE WHEN I CAME OUT...
...CHECKED ON THE LATEST CATALOGS OF SHINIGAMI TOOLS IN A BOOKSTORE...
...CHASED AFTER SOMEBODY DISTRIBUTING DISCOUNT FLYERS TO SCORE SOME...
...AND THEN WENT STRAIGHT TO THE OFFICE.
AH... RIGHT.
SO, YOU OF COURSE REMEMBER...
...THE FACE OF THE CLERK AT THE WINDOW, RIGHT?
Banner: Recycle

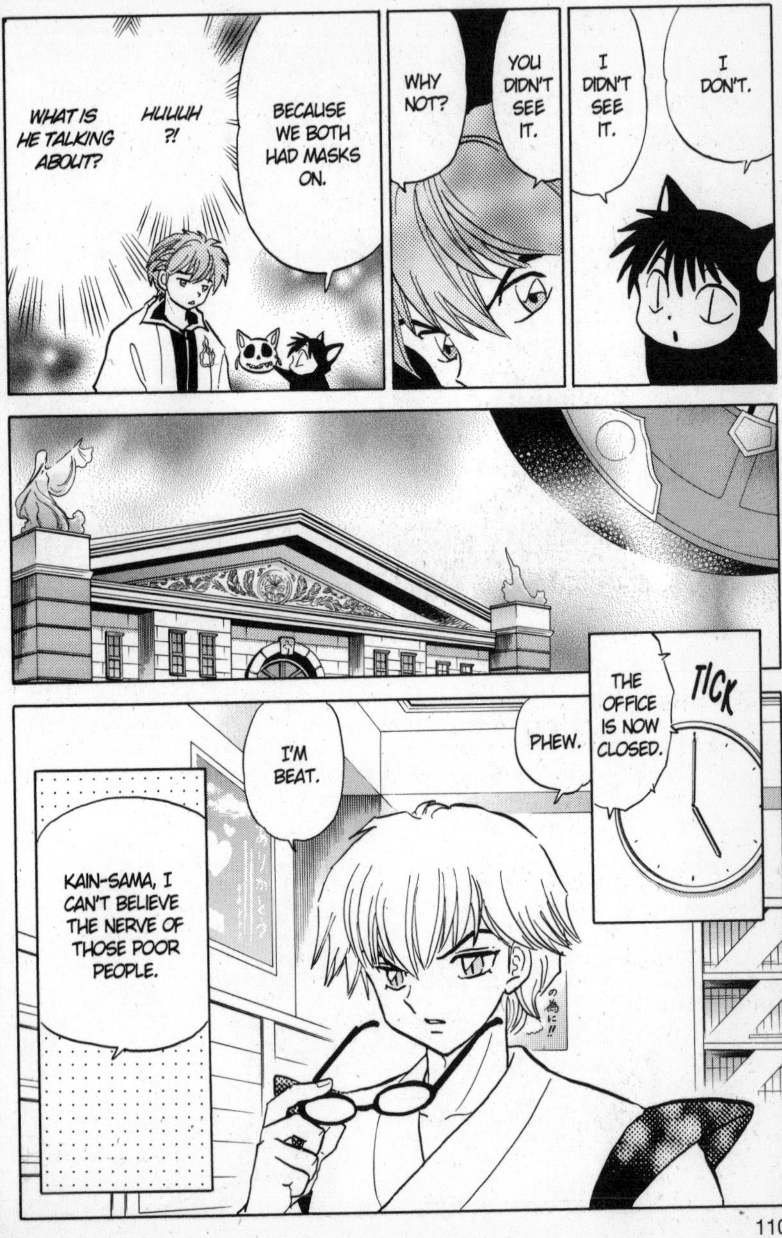
I DON'T.
I DIDN'T SEE IT.
YOU DIDN'T SEE IT.
WHY NOT?
BECAUSE WE BOTH HAD MASKS ON.
HUUUH?!
WHAT IS HE TALKING ABOUT?
THE OFFICE IS NOW CLOSED.
TICK
PHEW.
I'M BEAT.
KAIN-SAMA, I CAN'T BELIEVE THE NERVE OF THOSE POOR PEOPLE.

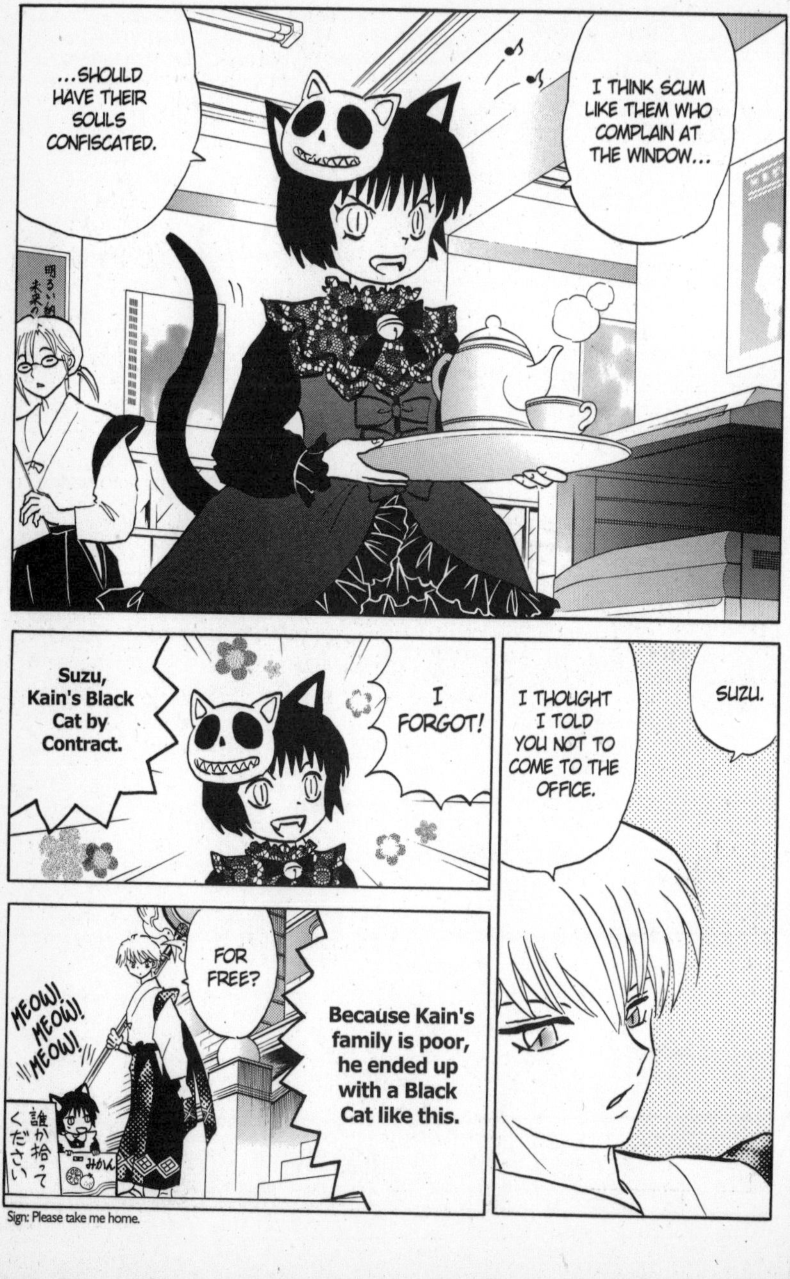
I THINK SCUM LIKE THEM WHO COMPLAIN AT THE WINDOW...
...SHOULD HAVE THEIR SOULS CONFISCATED.
SUZU.
I THOUGHT I TOLD YOU NOT TO COME TO THE OFFICE.
I FORGOT!
Suzu, Kain's Black Cat by Contract.
FOR FREE?
Because Kain's family is poor, he ended up with a Black Cat like this.
MEOW! MEOW! MEOW!
誰か拾ってください
みかん

Sign: Please take me home.

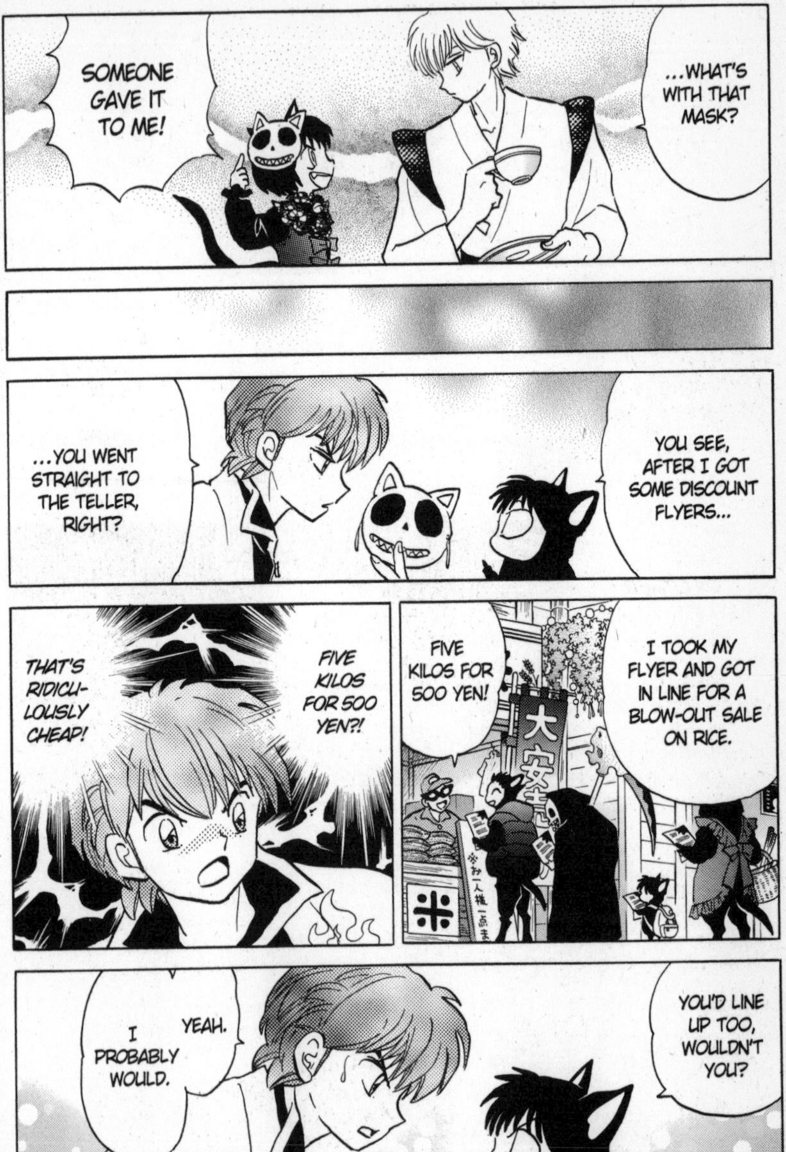
...WHAT'S WITH THAT MASK?
SOMEONE GAVE IT TO ME!
YOU SEE, AFTER I GOT SOME DISCOUNT FLYERS...
...YOU WENT STRAIGHT TO THE TELLER, RIGHT?
I TOOK MY FLYER AND GOT IN LINE FOR A BLOW-OUT SALE ON RICE.
FIVE KILOS FOR 500 YEN!
FIVE KILOS FOR 500 YEN?!
THAT'S RIDICU-LOUSLY CHEAP!
YOU'D LINE UP TOO, WOULDN'T YOU?
YEAH.
I PROBABLY WOULD.

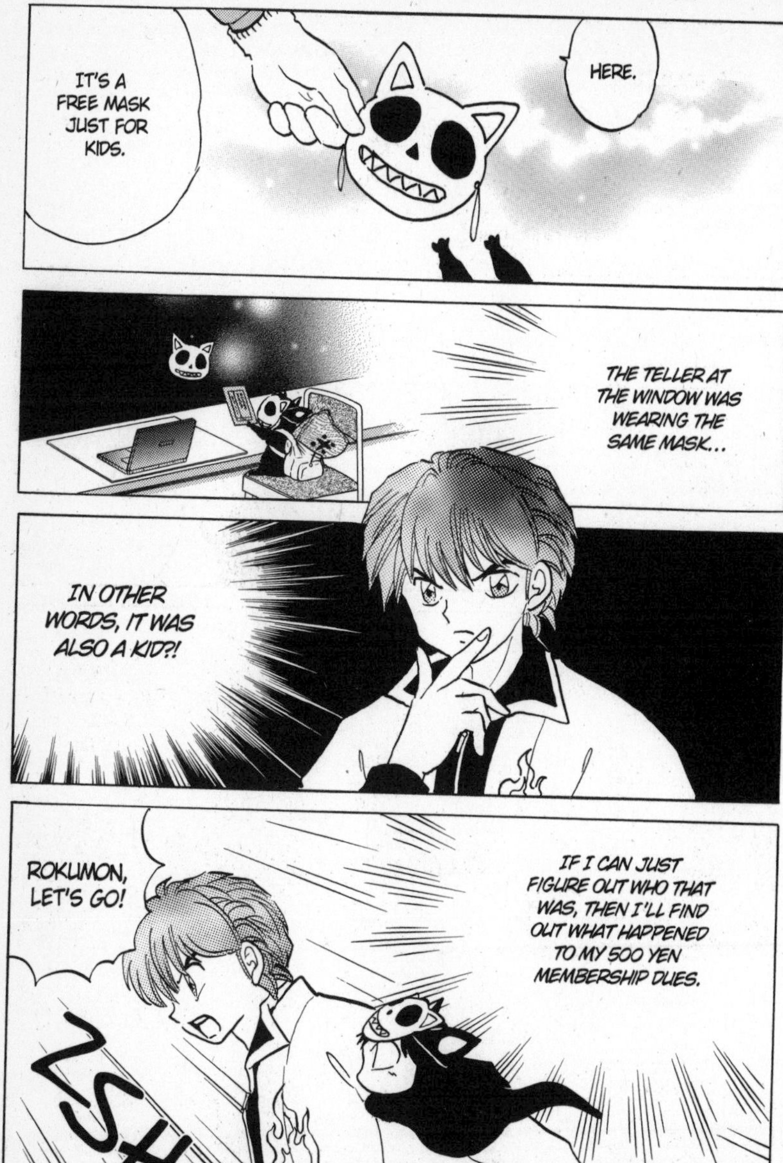
HERE.
IT'S A FREE MASK JUST FOR KIDS.
THE TELLER AT THE WINDOW WAS WEARING THE SAME MASK...
IN OTHER WORDS, IT WAS ALSO A KID?!
IF I CAN JUST FIGURE OUT WHO THAT WAS, THEN I'LL FIND OUT WHAT HAPPENED TO MY 500 YEN MEMBERSHIP DUES.
ROKUMON, LET'S GO!
ZSH

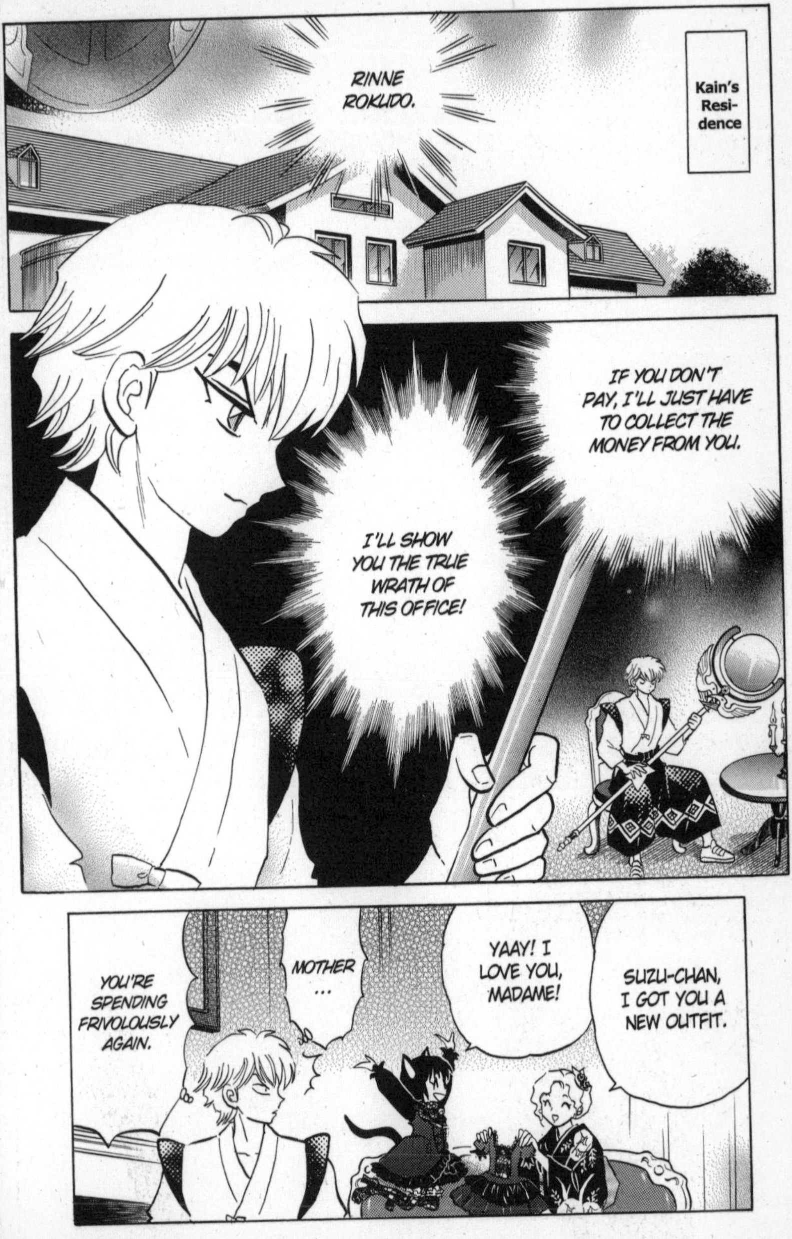
Kain's Residence
RINNE ROKUDO.
IF YOU DON'T PAY, I'LL JUST HAVE TO COLLECT THE MONEY FROM YOU.
I'LL SHOW YOU THE TRUE WRATH OF THIS OFFICE!
SUZU-CHAN, I GOT YOU A NEW OUTFIT.
YAAY! I LOVE YOU, MADAME!
MOTHER...
YOU'RE SPENDING FRIVOLOUSLY AGAIN.

CHAPTER 95: THE PRICE OF PRIDE

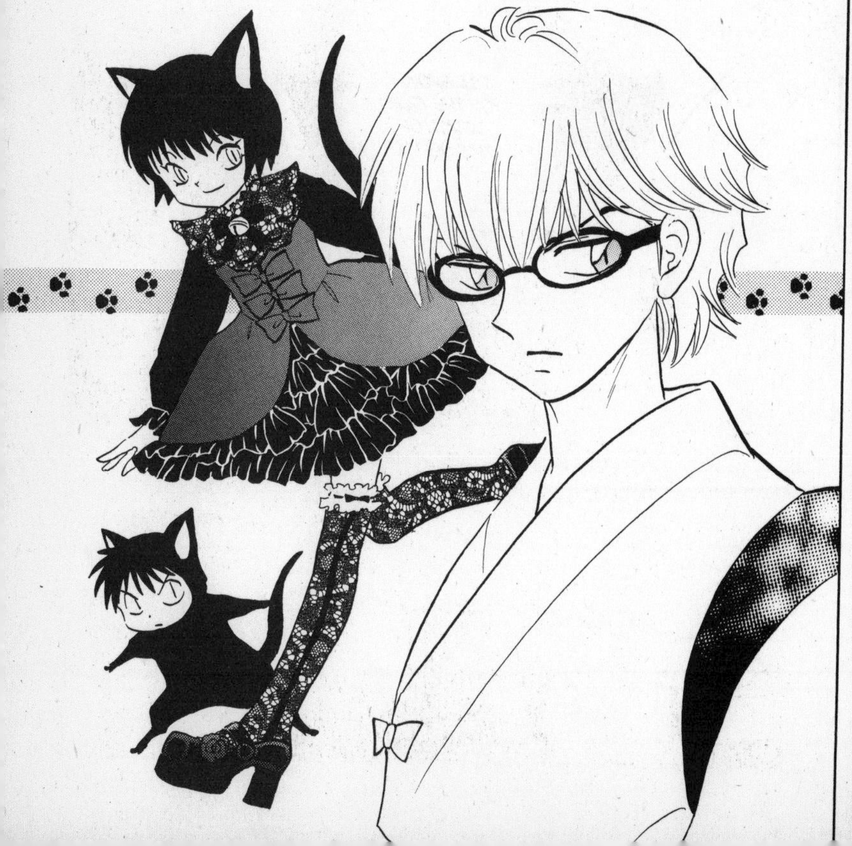

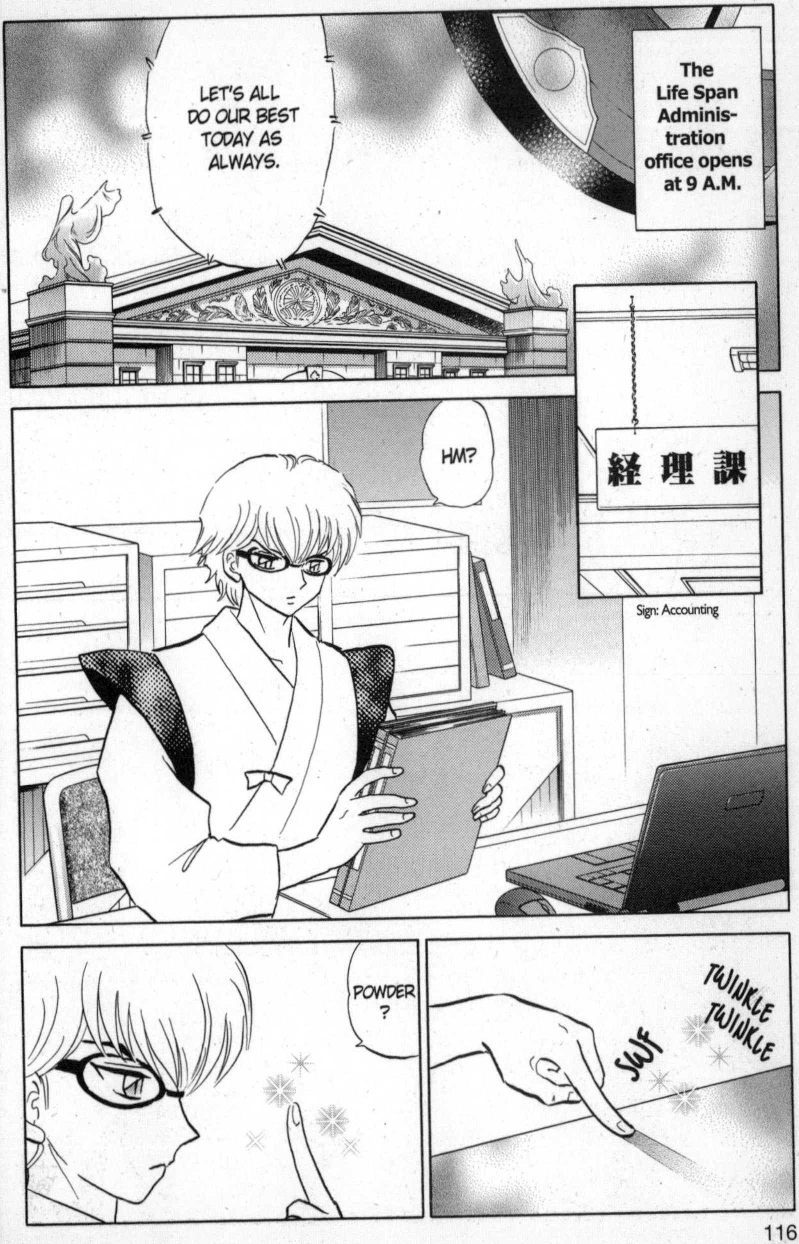
The Life Span Administration office opens at 9 A.M.
LET'S ALL DO OUR BEST TODAY AS ALWAYS.
経理課
HM?
TWINKLE TWINKLE
SWF
POWDER?
Sign: Accounting

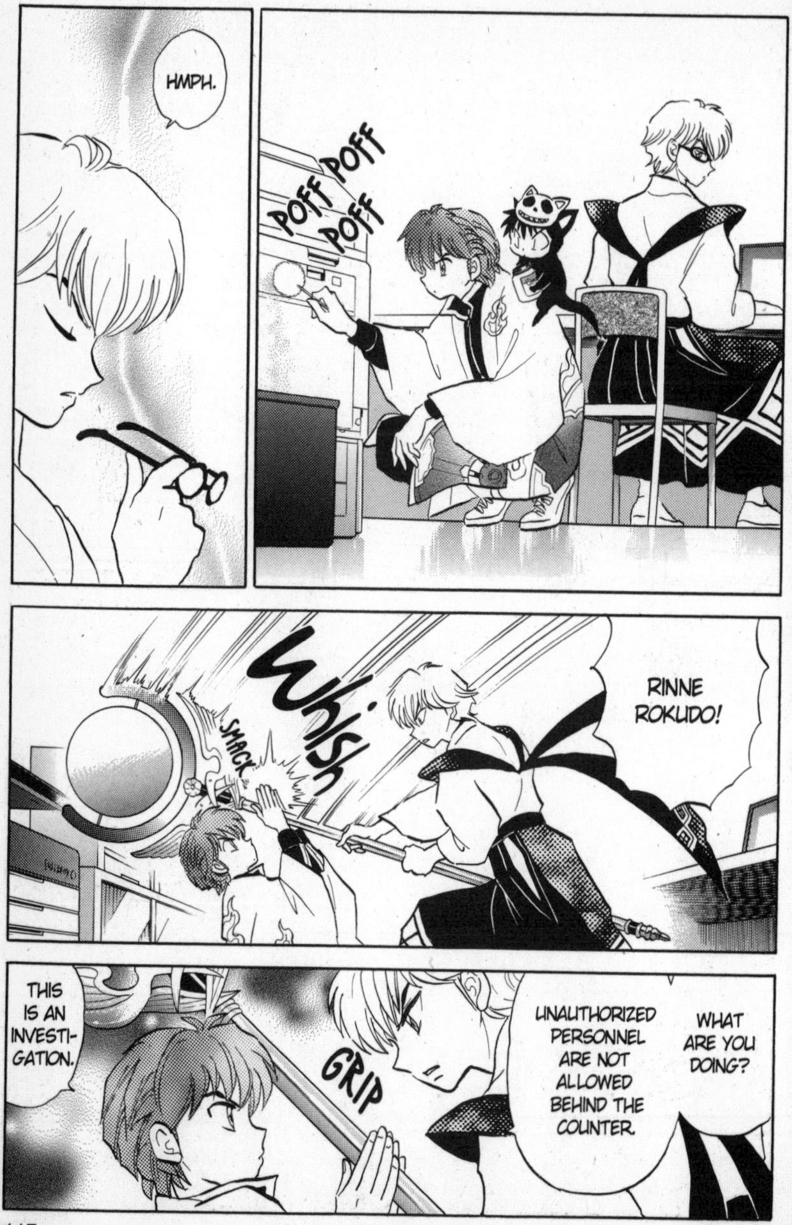
POFF POFF
POFF POFF
HMPH.
RINNE ROKUDO!
Whish
SMACK
WHAT ARE YOU DOING?
UNAUTHORIZED PERSONNEL ARE NOT ALLOWED BEHIND THE COUNTER.
GRIP
THIS IS AN INVESTI-GATION.

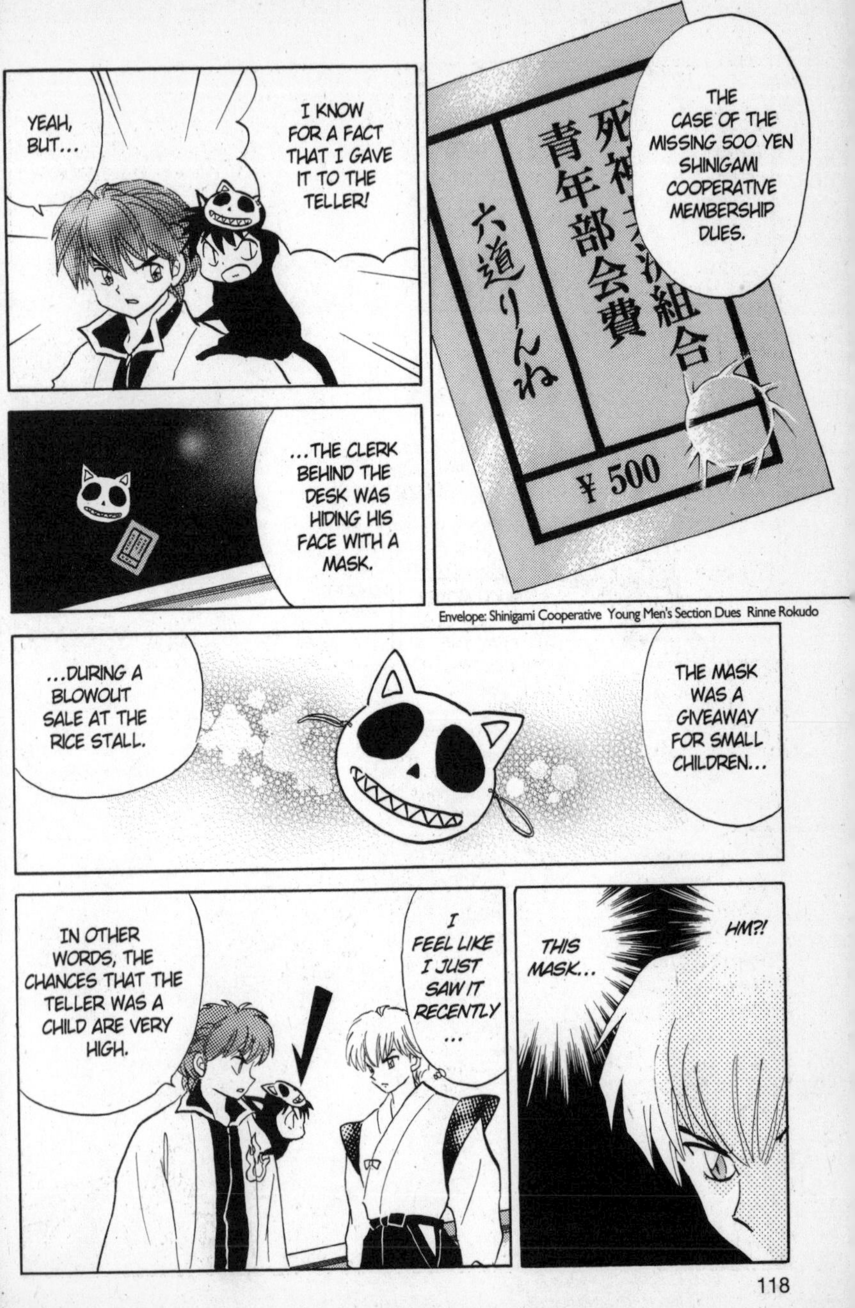
THE CASE OF THE MISSING 500 YEN SHINIGAMI COOPERATIVE MEMBERSHIP DUES.
青年部会費
六道りんね
¥ 500
I KNOW FOR A FACT THAT I GAVE IT TO THE TELLER!
YEAH, BUT...
...THE CLERK BEHIND THE DESK WAS HIDING HIS FACE WITH A MASK.
Envelope: Shinigami Cooperative Young Men's Section Dues Rinne Rokudo
THE MASK WAS A GIVEAWAY FOR SMALL CHILDREN...
...DURING A BLOWOUT SALE AT THE RICE STALL.
HM?!
THIS MASK...
I FEEL LIKE I JUST SAW IT RECENTLY...
IN OTHER WORDS, THE CHANCES THAT THE TELLER WAS A CHILD ARE VERY HIGH.

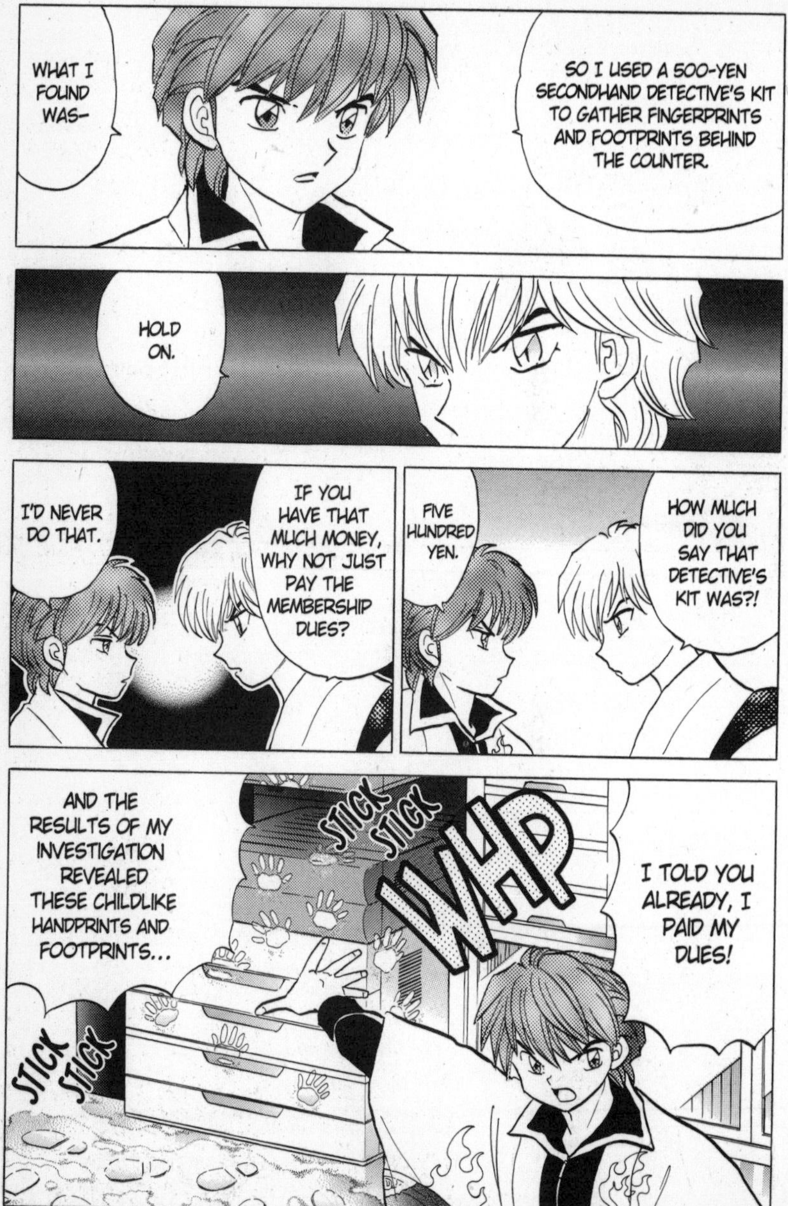
SO I USED A 500-YEN SECONDHAND DETECTIVE'S KIT TO GATHER FINGERPRINTS AND FOOTPRINTS BEHIND THE COUNTER.
WHAT I FOUND WAS-
HOLD ON.
HOW MUCH DID YOU SAY THAT DETECTIVE'S KIT WAS?!
FIVE HUNDRED YEN.
IF YOU HAVE THAT MUCH MONEY, WHY NOT JUST PAY THE MEMBERSHIP DUES?
I'D NEVER DO THAT.
I TOLD YOU ALREADY, I PAID MY DUES!
WHP
STICK STICK
AND THE RESULTS OF MY INVESTIGATION REVEALED THESE CHILDLIKE HANDPRINTS AND FOOTPRINTS...
STICK STICK

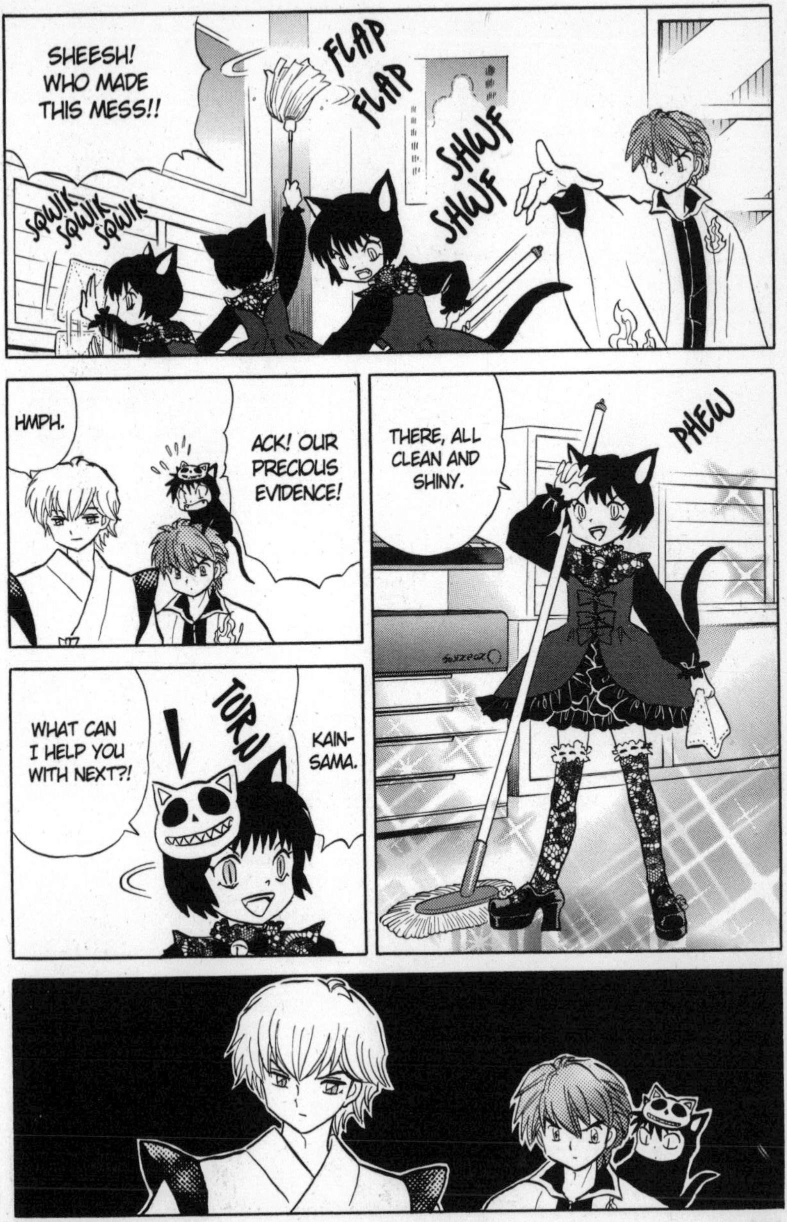
FLAP FLAP
SHWF SHWF
SHEESH! WHO MADE THIS MESS!!
SQWIK SQWIK SQWIK
PHEW
THERE, ALL CLEAN AND SHINY.
ACK! OUR PRECIOUS EVIDENCE!
HMPH.
KAIN-SAMA.
TURN
WHAT CAN I HELP YOU WITH NEXT?!

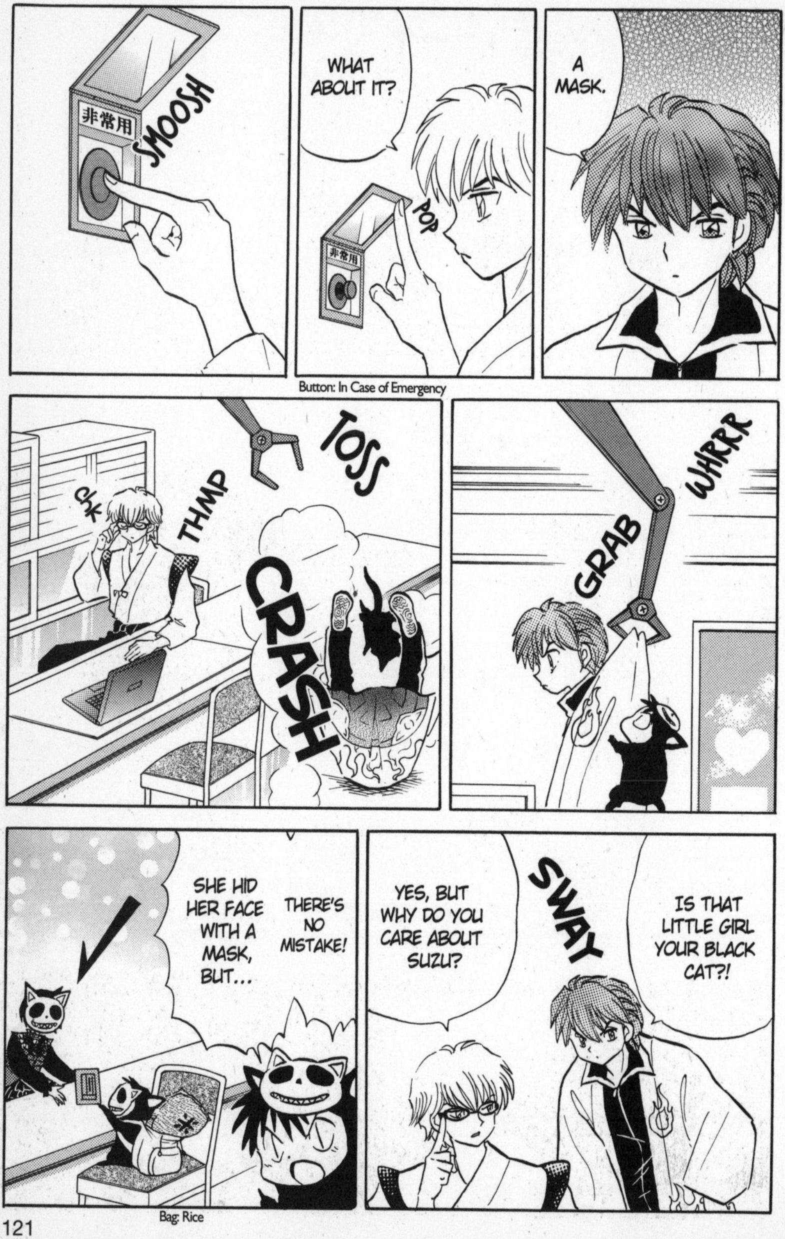
A MASK.
WHAT ABOUT IT?
POP
非常用
SMOOSH
非常用
WHRRR
GRAB
TOSS
THMP
CHK
CRASH
IS THAT LITTLE GIRL YOUR BLACK CAT?!
SWAY
YES, BUT WHY DO YOU CARE ABOUT SUZU?
THERE'S NO MISTAKE!
SHE HID HER FACE WITH A MASK, BUT…

Button: In Case of Emergency

Bag: Rice

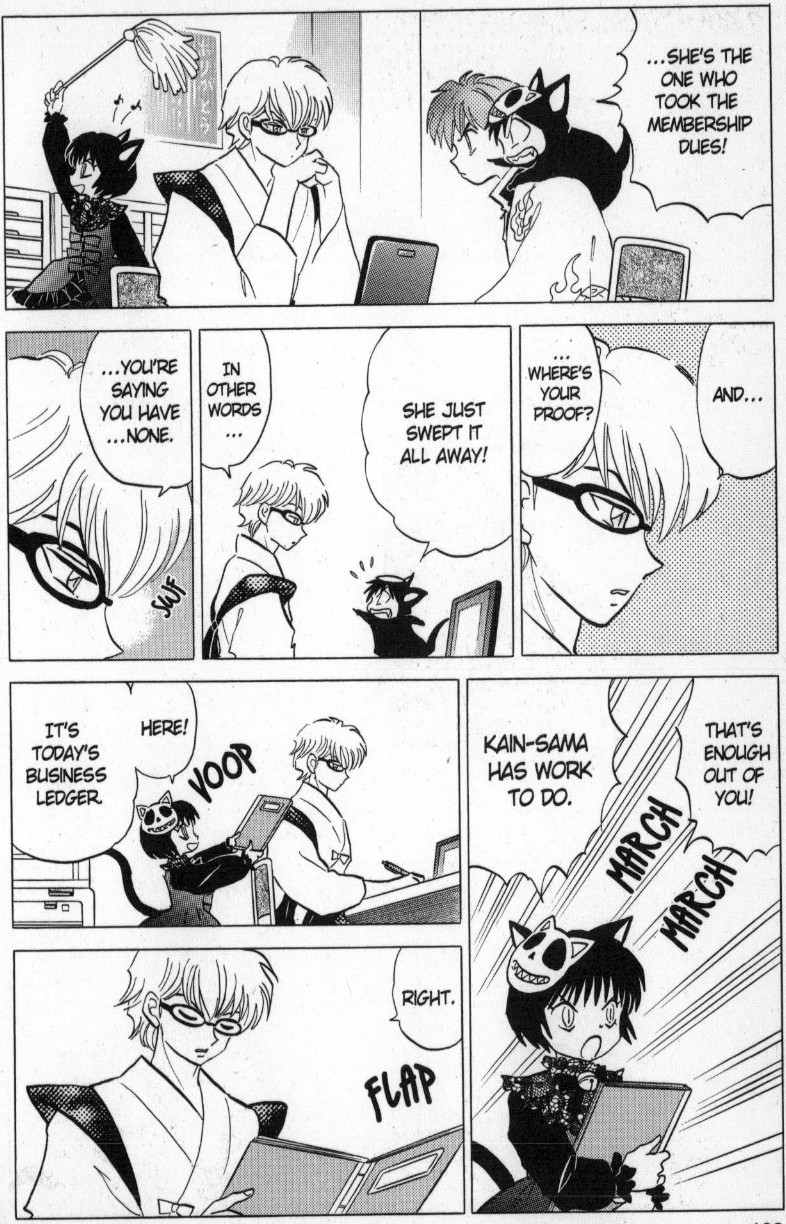
...SHE'S THE ONE WHO TOOK THE MEMBERSHIP DUES!
AND...
...WHERE'S YOUR PROOF?
SHE JUST SWEPT IT ALL AWAY!
IN OTHER WORDS ...
...YOU'RE SAYING YOU HAVE ...NONE.
SWF
THAT'S ENOUGH OUT OF YOU!
KAIN-SAMA HAS WORK TO DO.
MARCH
MARCH
HERE!
IT'S TODAY'S BUSINESS LEDGER.
VOOP
RIGHT.
FLAP

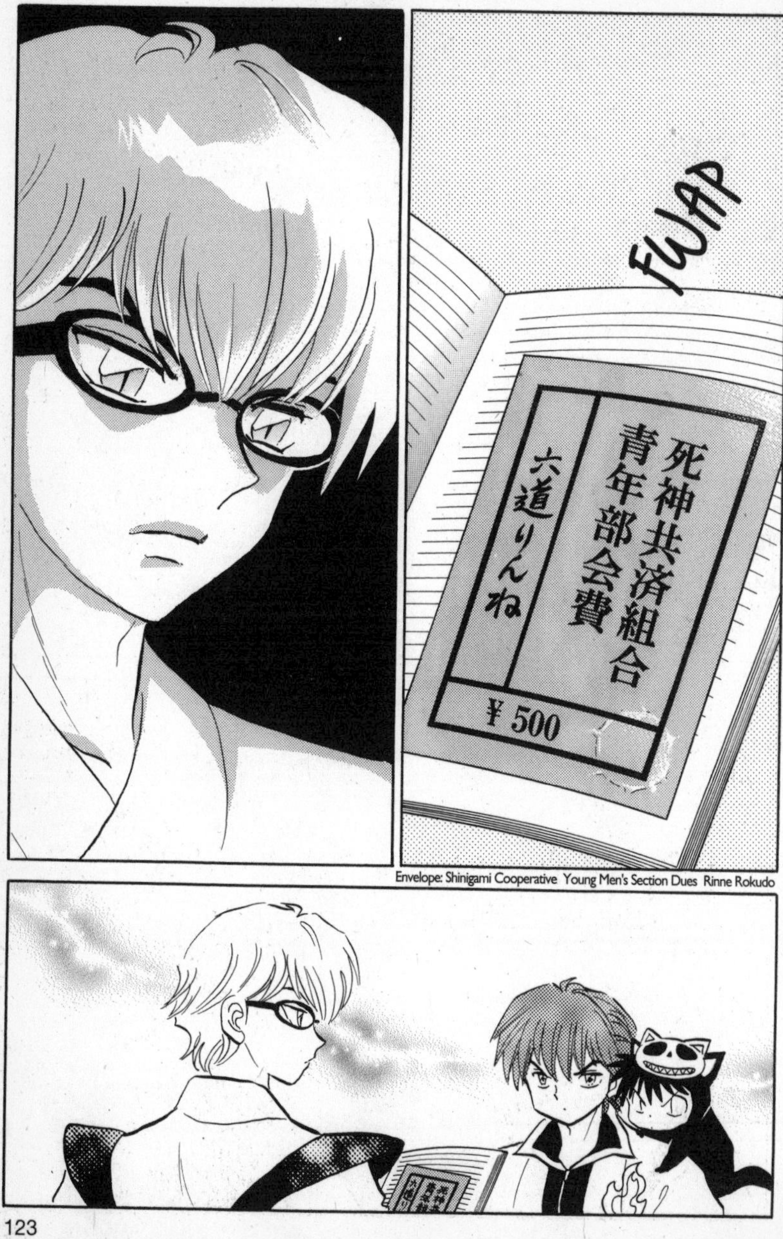
FWAP
死神共済組合青年部会費
六道りんね
¥ 500
Envelope: Shinigami Cooperative Young Men's Section Dues Rinne Rokudo

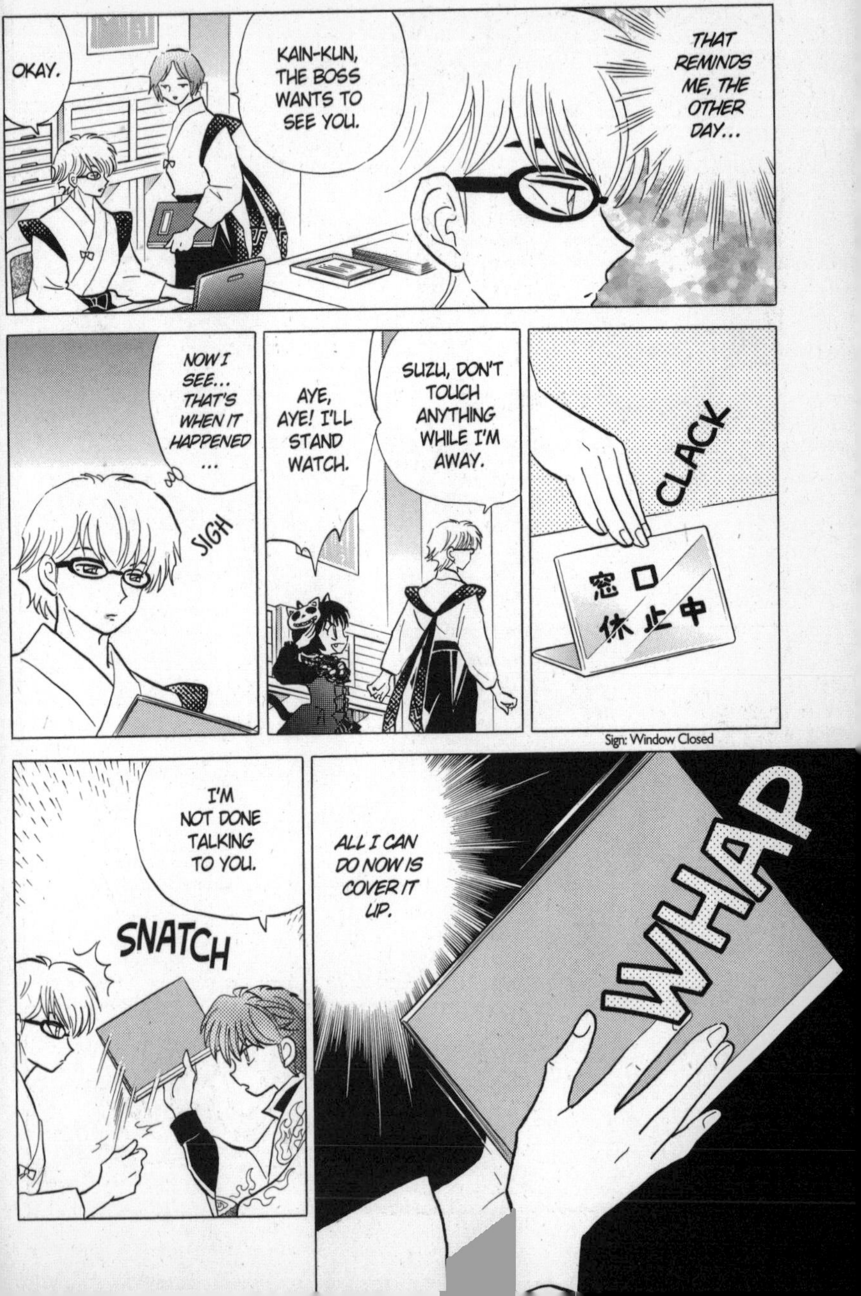
THAT REMINDS ME, THE OTHER DAY...
KAIN-KUN, THE BOSS WANTS TO SEE YOU.
OKAY.
CLACK
窓口
休止中
SUZU, DON'T TOUCH ANYTHING WHILE I'M AWAY.
AYE, AYE! I'LL STAND WATCH.
NOW I SEE... THAT'S WHEN IT HAPPENED...
SIGH
ALL I CAN DO NOW IS COVER IT UP.
WHAP
I'M NOT DONE TALKING TO YOU.
SNATCH

Sign: Window Closed

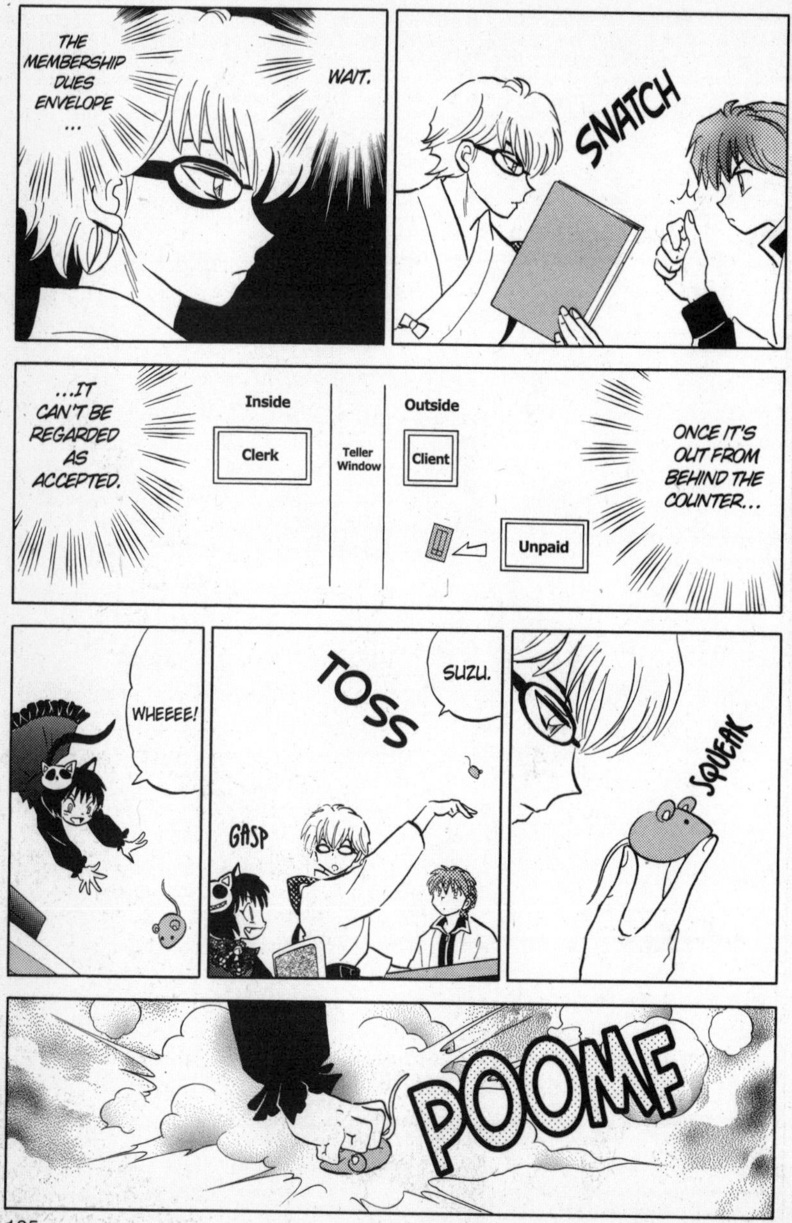
SNATCH
WAIT.
THE MEMBERSHIP DUES ENVELOPE ...
ONCE IT'S OUT FROM BEHIND THE COUNTER...
Outside
Client
Unpaid
Teller Window
Inside
Clerk
...IT CAN'T BE REGARDED AS ACCEPTED.
SQUEAK
SUZU.
TOSS
GASP
WHEEEE!
POOMF

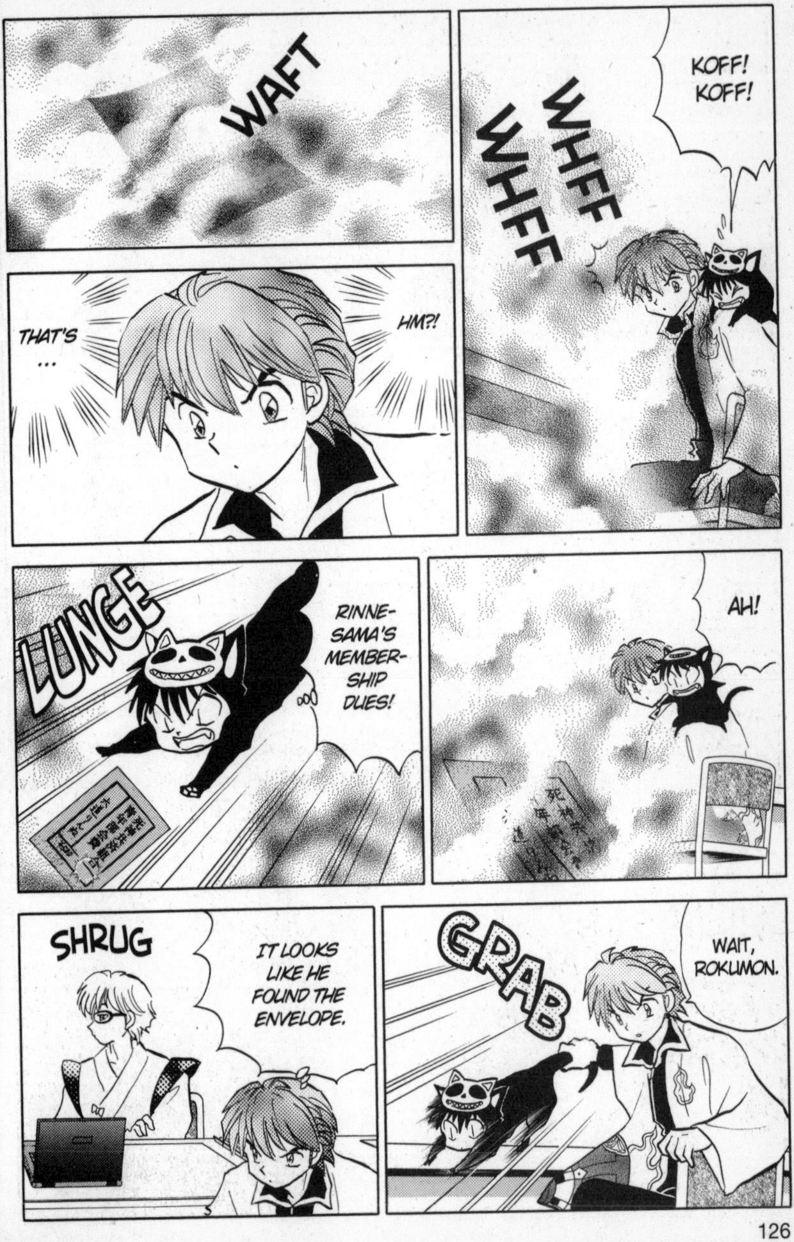
KOFF! KOFF!
WHFF WHFF
WAFT
HM?!
THAT'S ...
AH!
RINNE-SAMA'S MEMBERSHIP DUES!
LUNGE
WAIT, ROKUMON.
GRAB
IT LOOKS LIKE HE FOUND THE ENVELOPE.
SHRUG

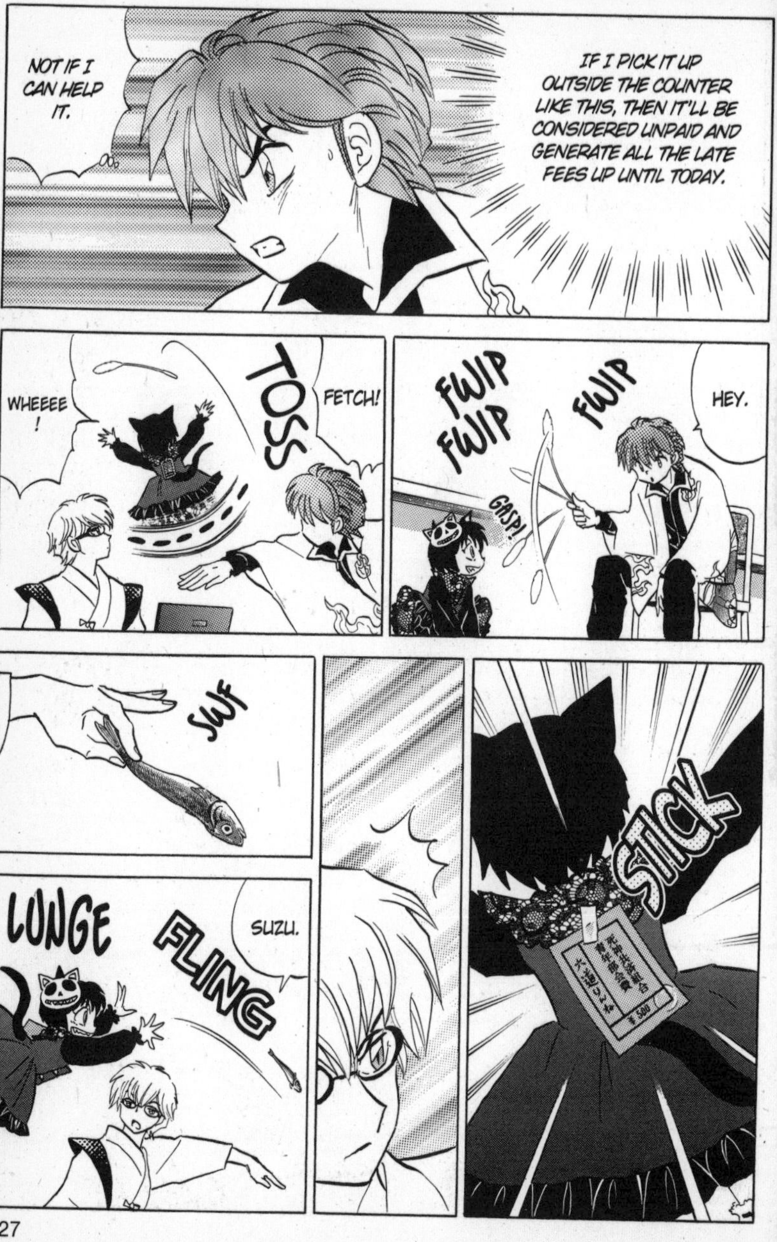
IF I PICK IT UP OUTSIDE THE COUNTER LIKE THIS, THEN IT'LL BE CONSIDERED UNPAID AND GENERATE ALL THE LATE FEES UP UNTIL TODAY.
NOT IF I CAN HELP IT.
HEY.
FWIP
FWIP FWIP
GASP!
FETCH!
TOSS
WHEEEE !
STICK
SWF
SUZU.
FLING
LUNGE

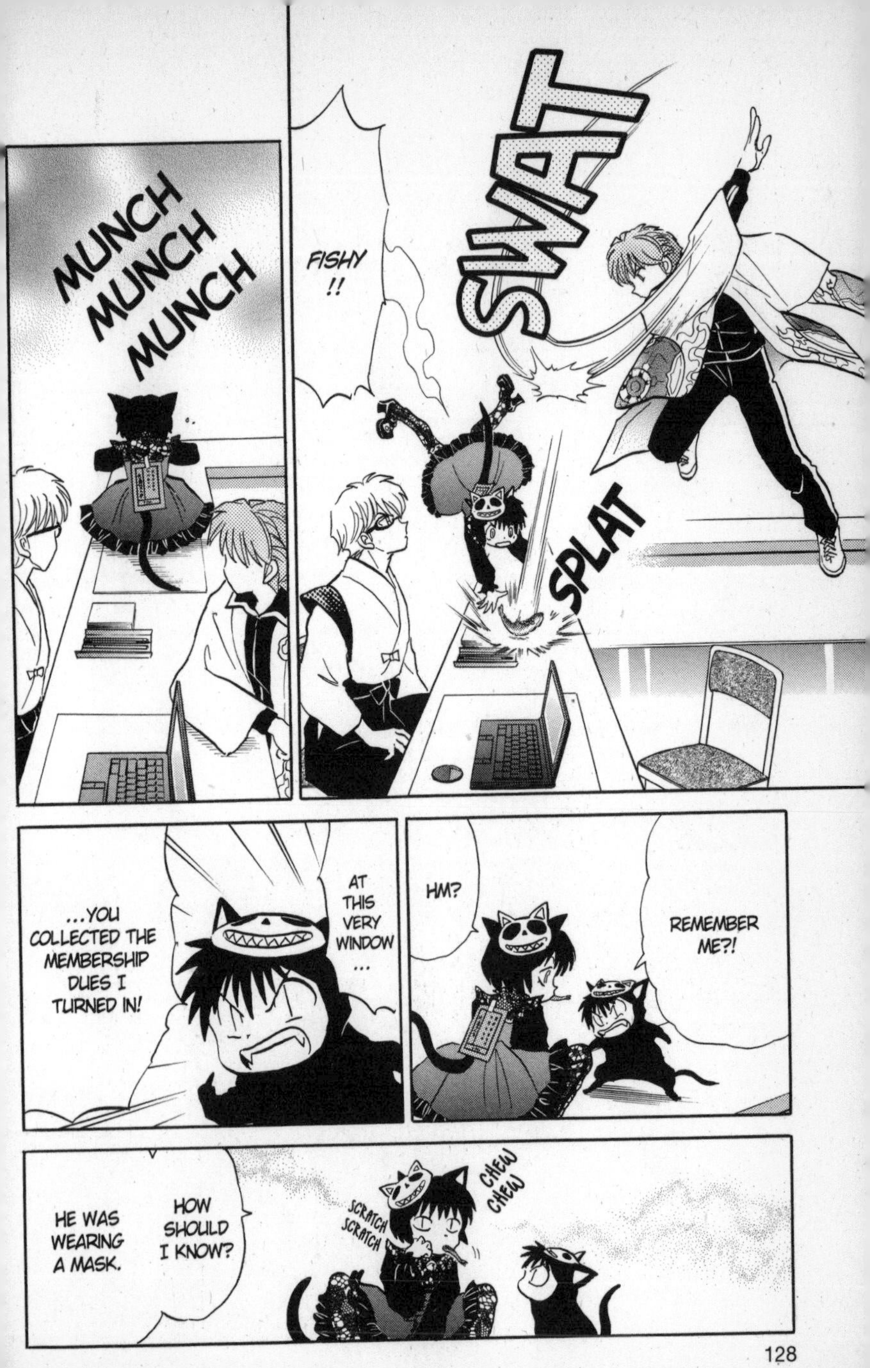
SWAT
FISHY !!
SPLAT
MUNCH MUNCH MUNCH
REMEMBER ME?!
HM?
AT THIS VERY WINDOW ...
...YOU COLLECTED THE MEMBERSHIP DUES I TURNED IN!
CHEW CHEW
SCRATCH SCRATCH
HOW SHOULD I KNOW?
HE WAS WEARING A MASK.

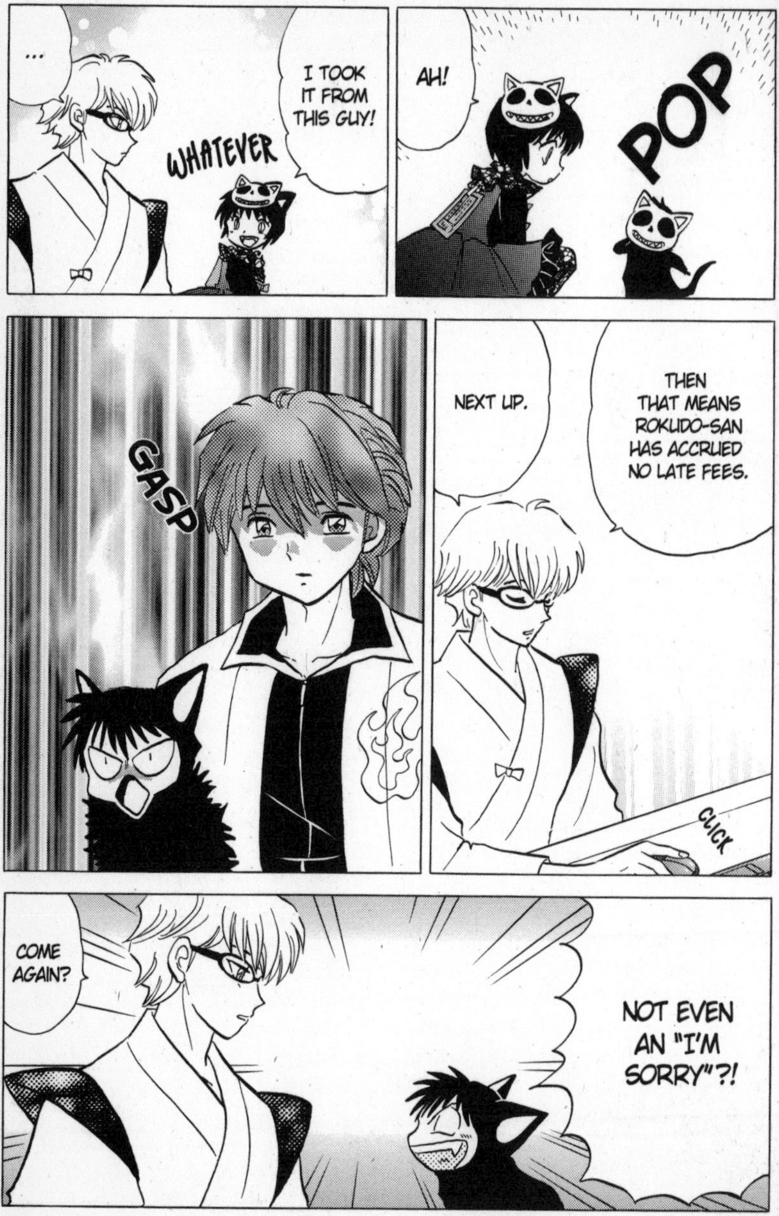
POP
AH!
I TOOK IT FROM THIS GUY!
...
WHATEVER
THEN THAT MEANS ROKUDO-SAN HAS ACCRUED NO LATE FEES.
NEXT UP.
CLICK
GASP
NOT EVEN AN "I'M SORRY"?!
COME AGAIN?

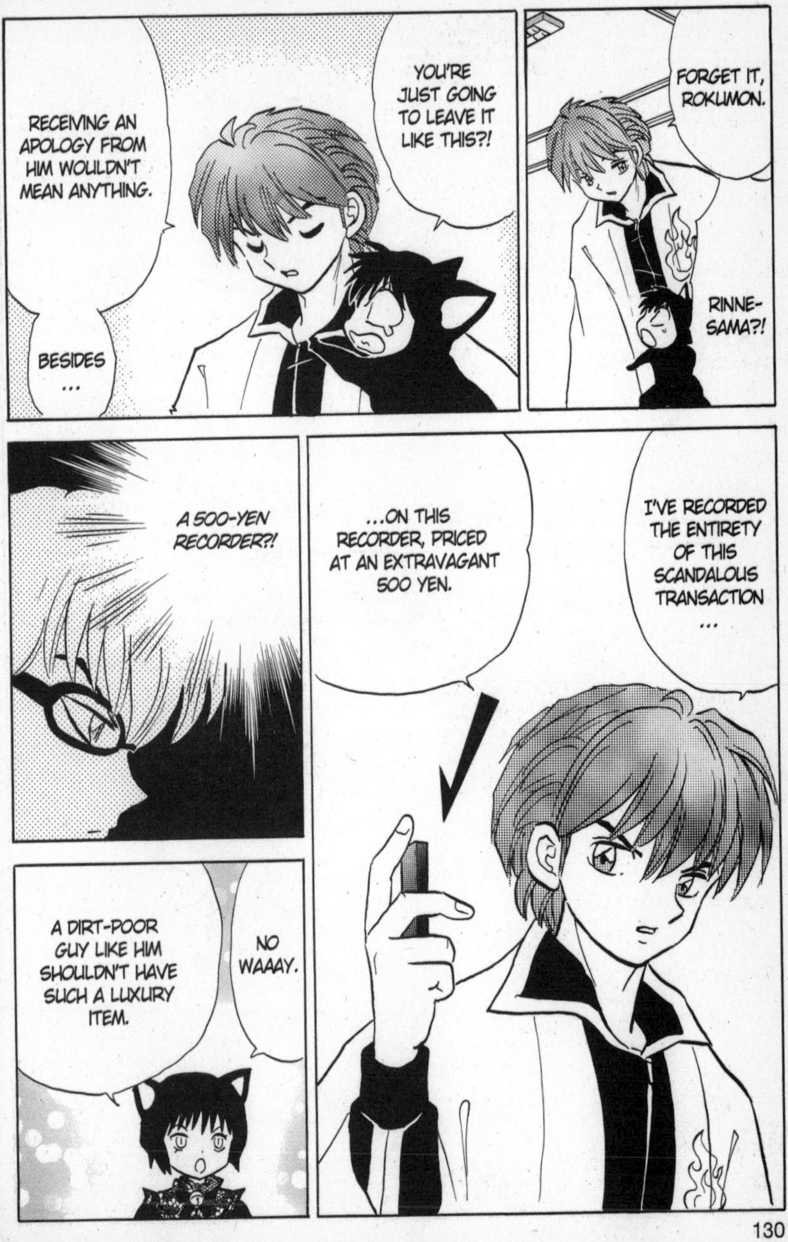
FORGET IT, ROKUMON.
RINNE-SAMA?!
YOU'RE JUST GOING TO LEAVE IT LIKE THIS?!
RECEIVING AN APOLOGY FROM HIM WOULDN'T MEAN ANYTHING.
BESIDES ...
I'VE RECORDED THE ENTIRETY OF THIS SCANDALOUS TRANSACTION ...
...ON THIS RECORDER, PRICED AT AN EXTRAVAGANT 500 YEN.
A 500-YEN RECORDER?!
NO WAAAY.
A DIRT-POOR GUY LIKE HIM SHOULDN'T HAVE SUCH A LUXURY ITEM.

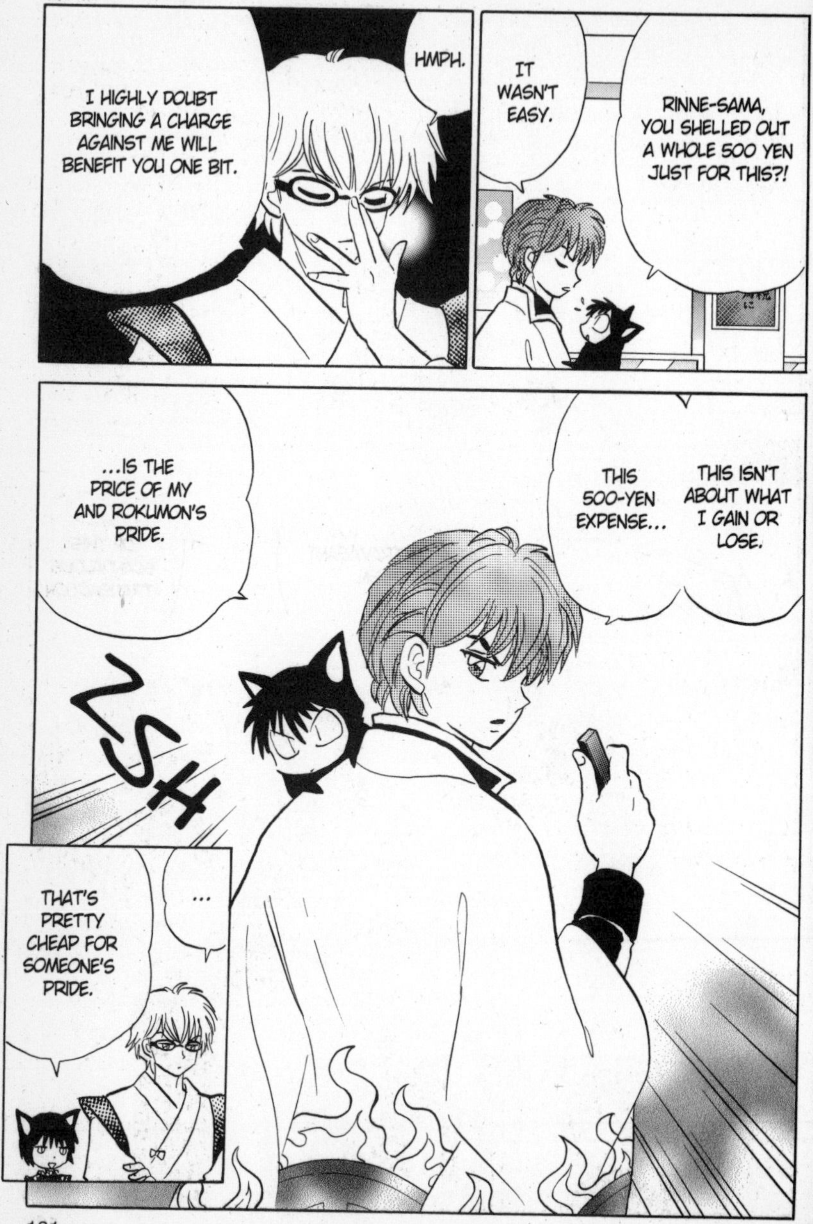
RINNE-SAMA, YOU SHELLED OUT A WHOLE 500 YEN JUST FOR THIS?!
IT WASN'T EASY.
HMPH.
I HIGHLY DOUBT BRINGING A CHARGE AGAINST ME WILL BENEFIT YOU ONE BIT.
THIS ISN'T ABOUT WHAT I GAIN OR LOSE.
THIS 500-YEN EXPENSE...
...IS THE PRICE OF MY AND ROKUMON'S PRIDE.
ZSH
...
THAT'S PRETTY CHEAP FOR SOMEONE'S PRIDE.

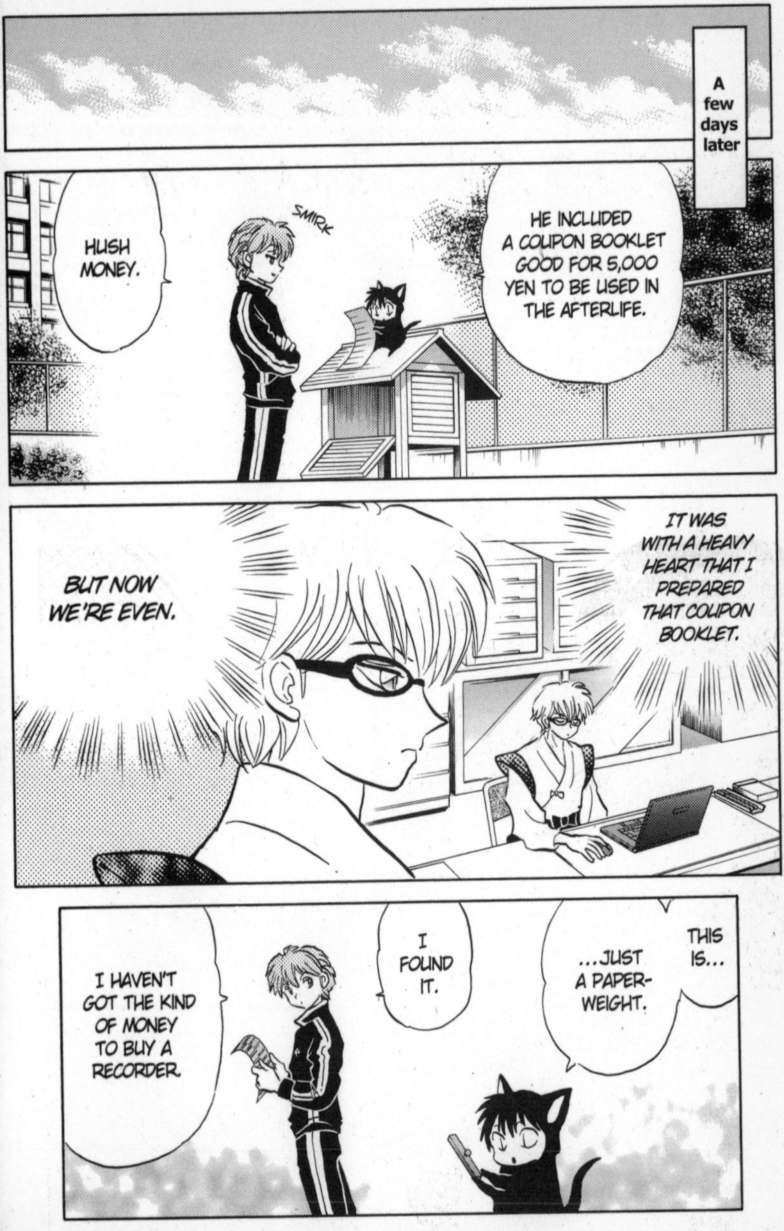
A few days later
HE INCLUDED A COUPON BOOKLET GOOD FOR 5,000 YEN TO BE USED IN THE AFTERLIFE.
SMIRK
HUSH MONEY.
IT WAS WITH A HEAVY HEART THAT I PREPARED THAT COUPON BOOKLET.
BUT NOW WE'RE EVEN.
THIS IS...
...JUST A PAPER-WEIGHT.
I FOUND IT.
I HAVEN'T GOT THE KIND OF MONEY TO BUY A RECORDER.

CHAPTER 96: THE DREAM COURT

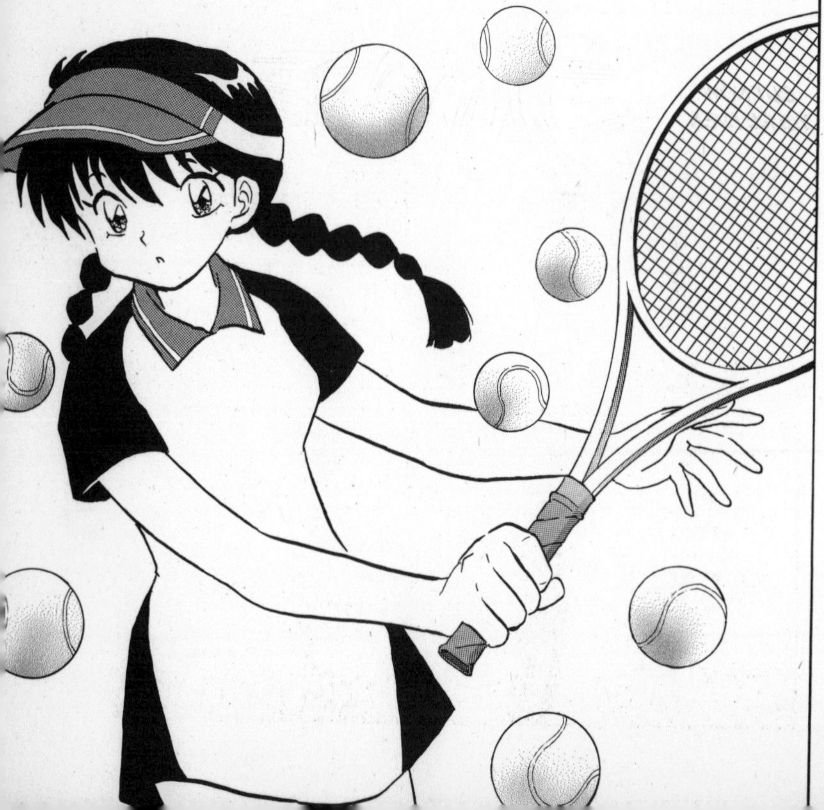

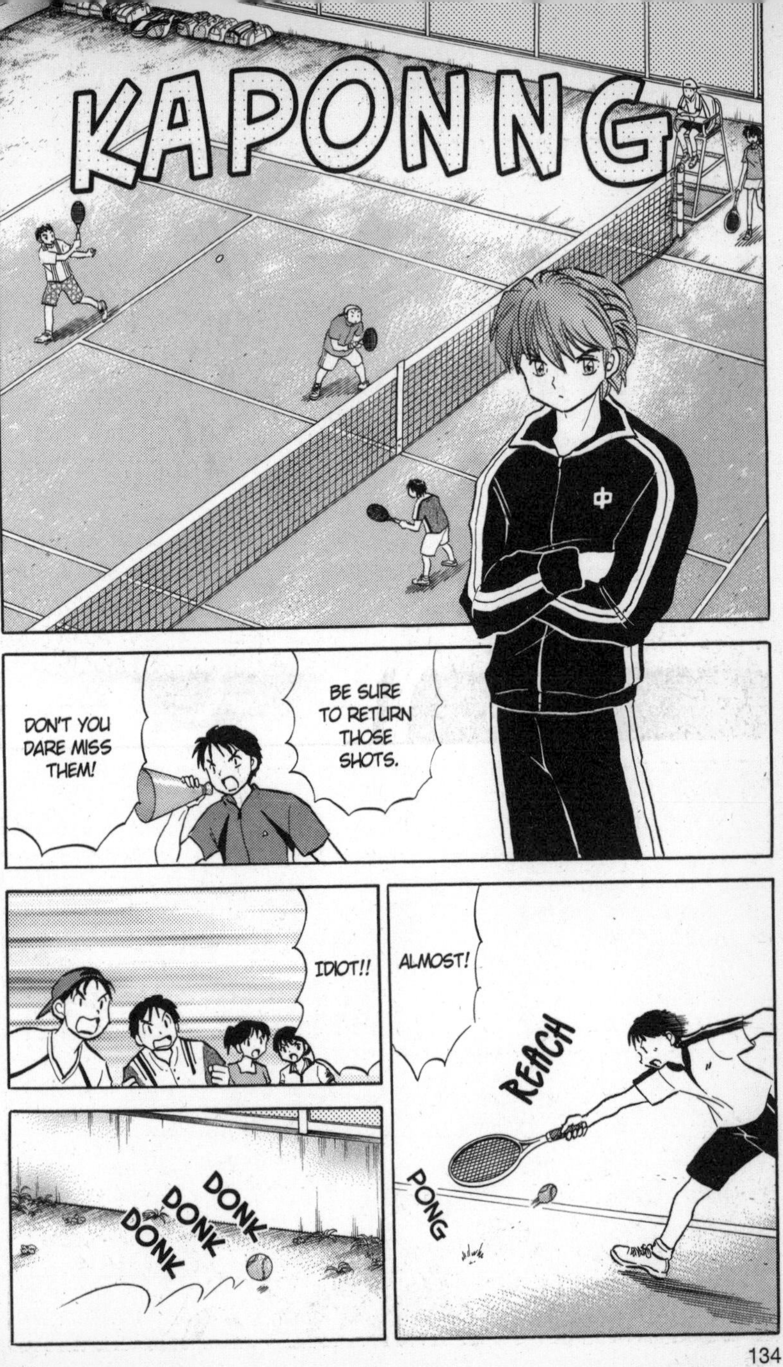
KAPONNG
BE SURE TO RETURN THOSE SHOTS.
DON'T YOU DARE MISS THEM!
ALMOST!
REACH
PONG
IDIOT!!
DONK
DONK
DONK

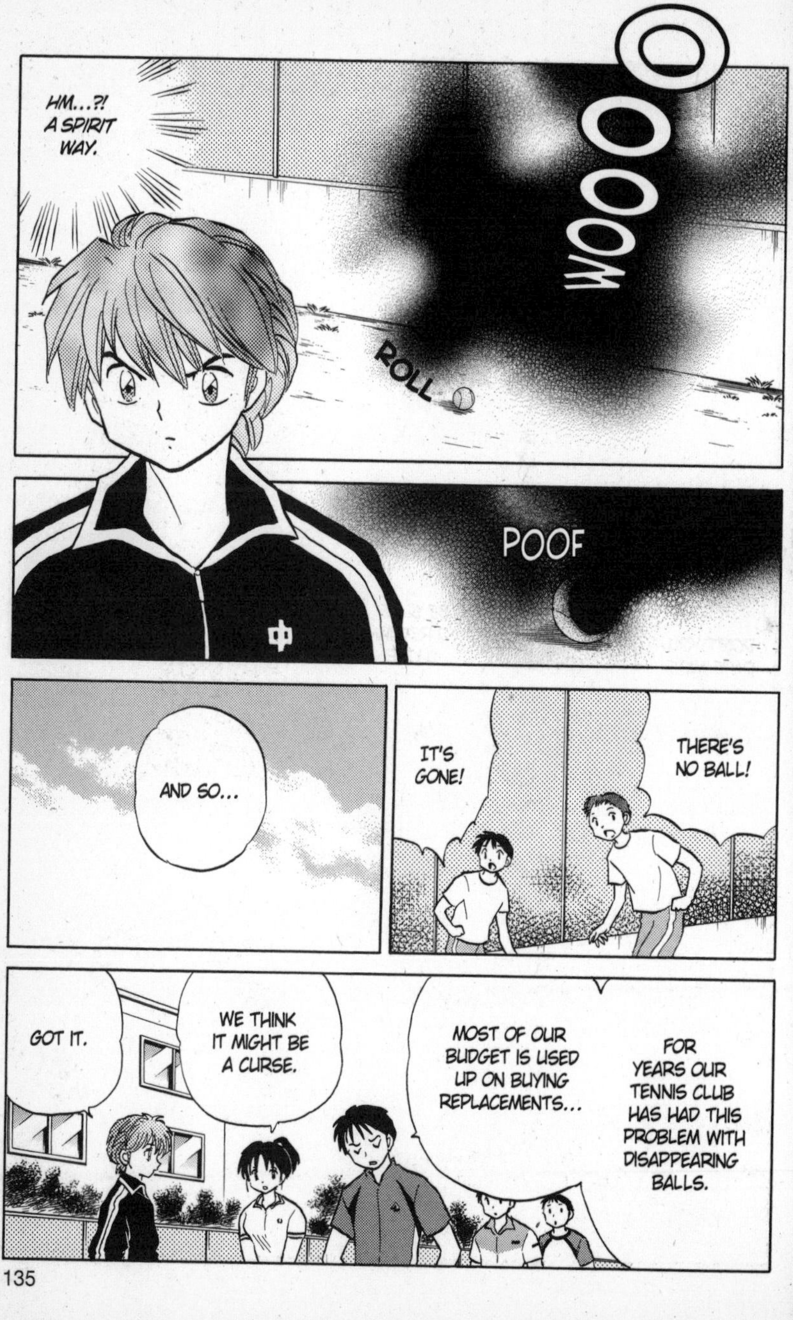
OOOOM
ROLL
HM...?! A SPIRIT WAY.
POOF
THERE'S NO BALL!
IT'S GONE!
AND SO...
FOR YEARS OUR TENNIS CLUB HAS HAD THIS PROBLEM WITH DISAPPEARING BALLS.
MOST OF OUR BUDGET IS USED UP ON BUYING REPLACEMENTS...
WE THINK IT MIGHT BE A CURSE.
GOT IT.

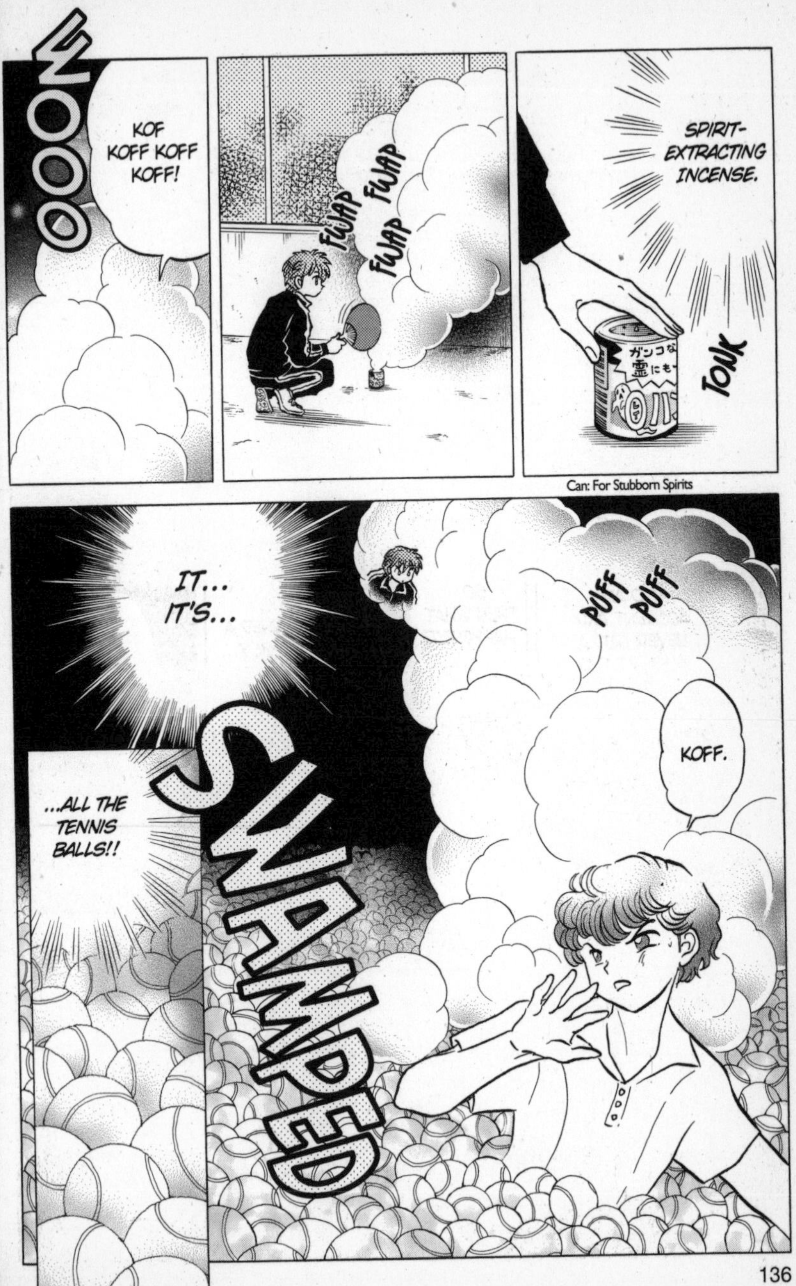
SPIRIT-EXTRACTING INCENSE.
ガンコな霊にも
TOUK
Can: For Stubborn Spirits
FWAP FWAP FWAP
KOF KOFF KOFF KOFF!
WOOOO
PUFF PUFF
IT... IT'S...
KOFF.
SWAMPED
...ALL THE TENNIS BALLS!!

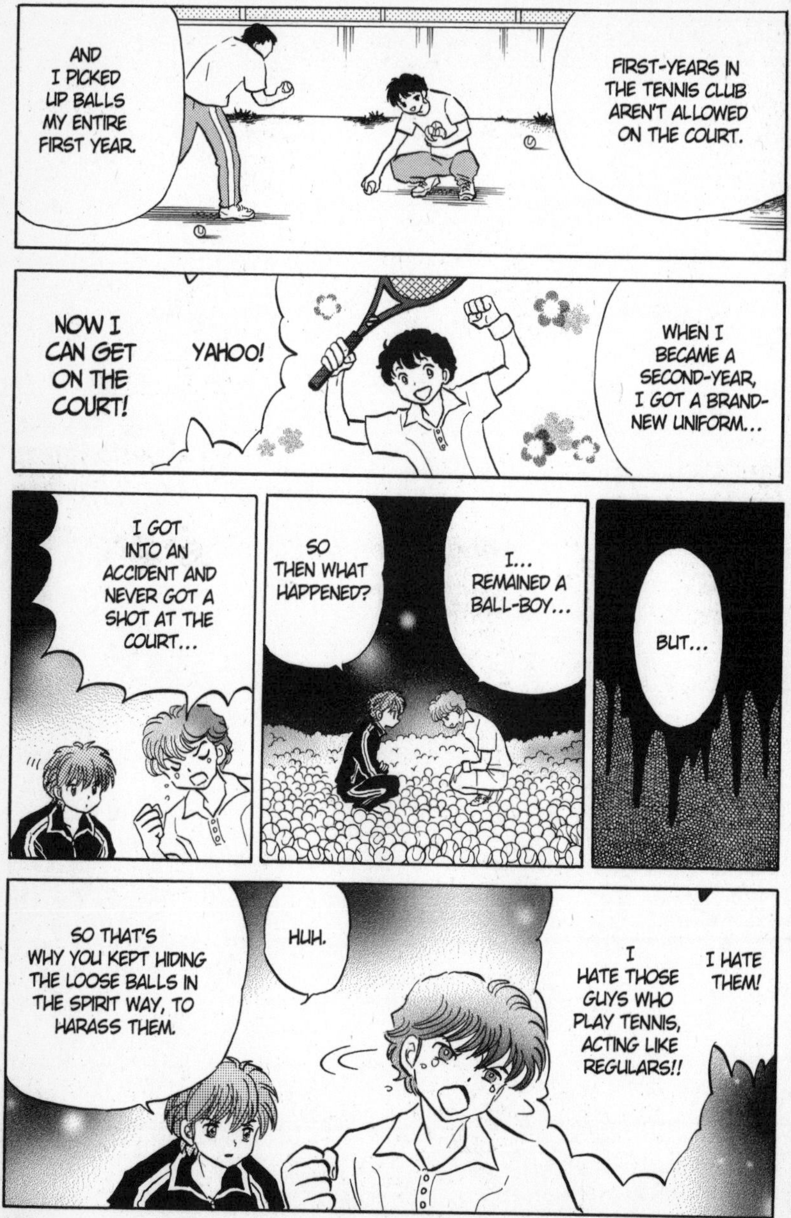
FIRST-YEARS IN THE TENNIS CLUB AREN'T ALLOWED ON THE COURT.
AND I PICKED UP BALLS MY ENTIRE FIRST YEAR.
WHEN I BECAME A SECOND-YEAR, I GOT A BRAND-NEW UNIFORM...
YAHOO!
NOW I CAN GET ON THE COURT!
BUT...
I... REMAINED A BALL-BOY...
SO THEN WHAT HAPPENED?
I GOT INTO AN ACCIDENT AND NEVER GOT A SHOT AT THE COURT...
I HATE THEM!
I HATE THOSE GUYS WHO PLAY TENNIS, ACTING LIKE REGULARS!!
HUH.
SO THAT'S WHY YOU KEPT HIDING THE LOOSE BALLS IN THE SPIRIT WAY, TO HARASS THEM.

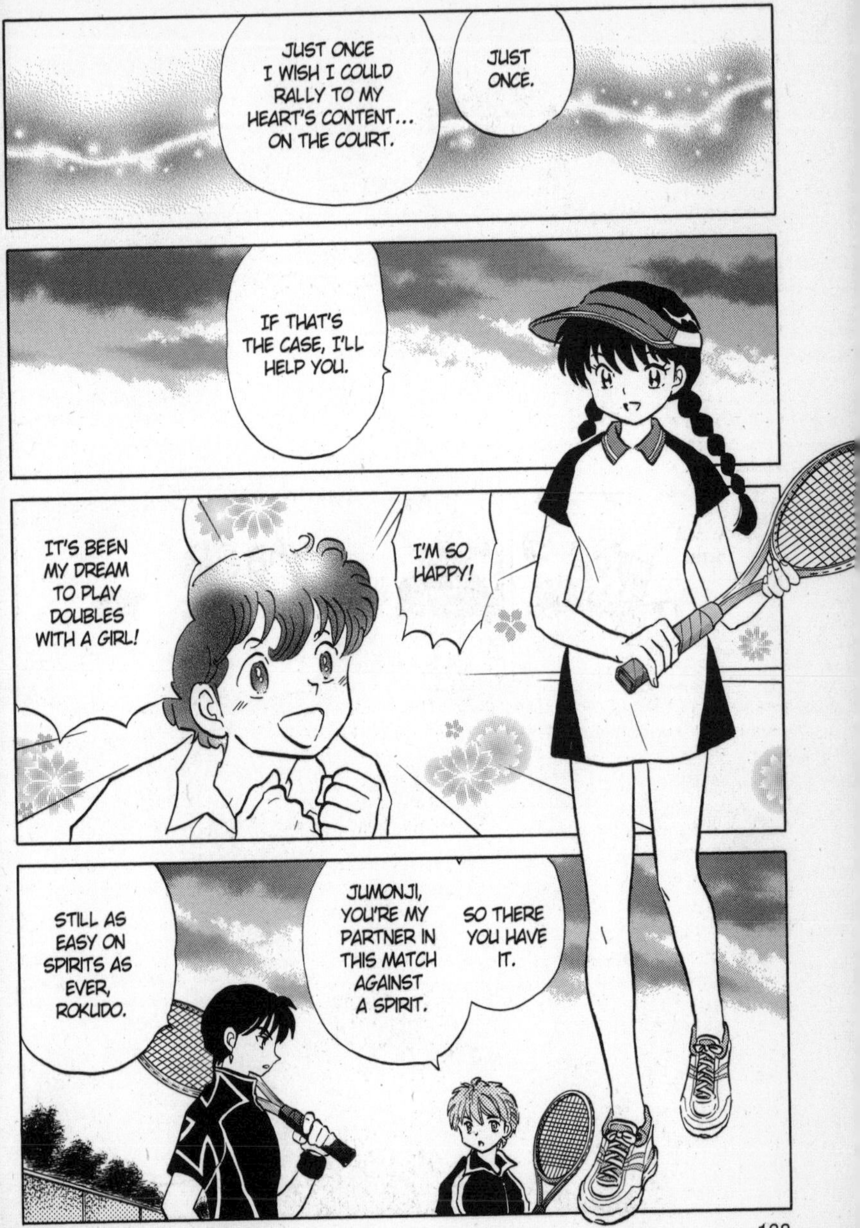
JUST ONCE.
JUST ONCE I WISH I COULD RALLY TO MY HEART'S CONTENT... ON THE COURT.
IF THAT'S THE CASE, I'LL HELP YOU.
I'M SO HAPPY!
IT'S BEEN MY DREAM TO PLAY DOUBLES WITH A GIRL!
SO THERE YOU HAVE IT.
JUMONJI, YOU'RE MY PARTNER IN THIS MATCH AGAINST A SPIRIT.
STILL AS EASY ON SPIRITS AS EVER, ROKUDO.

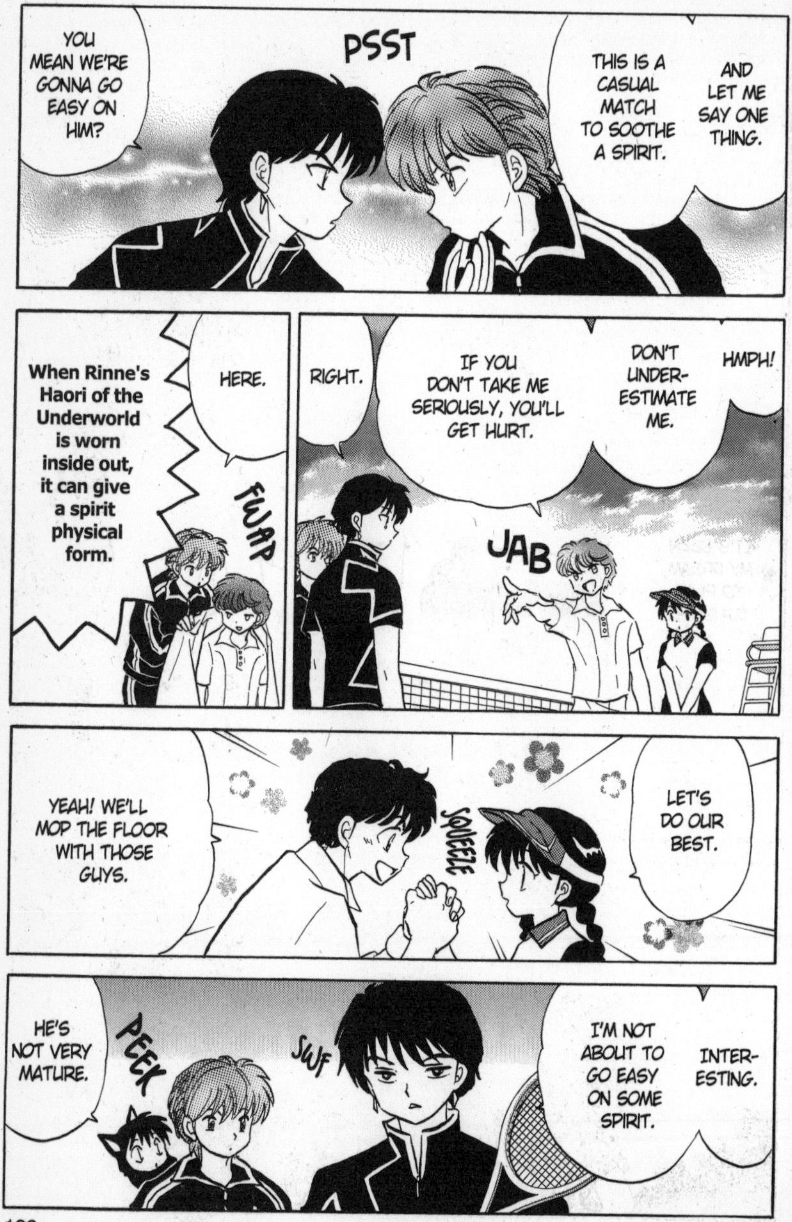
AND LET ME SAY ONE THING.
THIS IS A CASUAL MATCH TO SOOTHE A SPIRIT.
PSST
YOU MEAN WE'RE GONNA GO EASY ON HIM?
HMPH!
DON'T UNDER-ESTIMATE ME.
IF YOU DON'T TAKE ME SERIOUSLY, YOU'LL GET HURT.
JAB
RIGHT.
HERE.
FWAP
When Rinne's Haori of the Underworld is worn inside out, it can give a spirit physical form.
LET'S DO OUR BEST.
SQUEEZE
YEAH! WE'LL MOP THE FLOOR WITH THOSE GUYS.
INTER-ESTING.
I'M NOT ABOUT TO GO EASY ON SOME SPIRIT.
SWF
PEEK
HE'S NOT VERY MATURE.

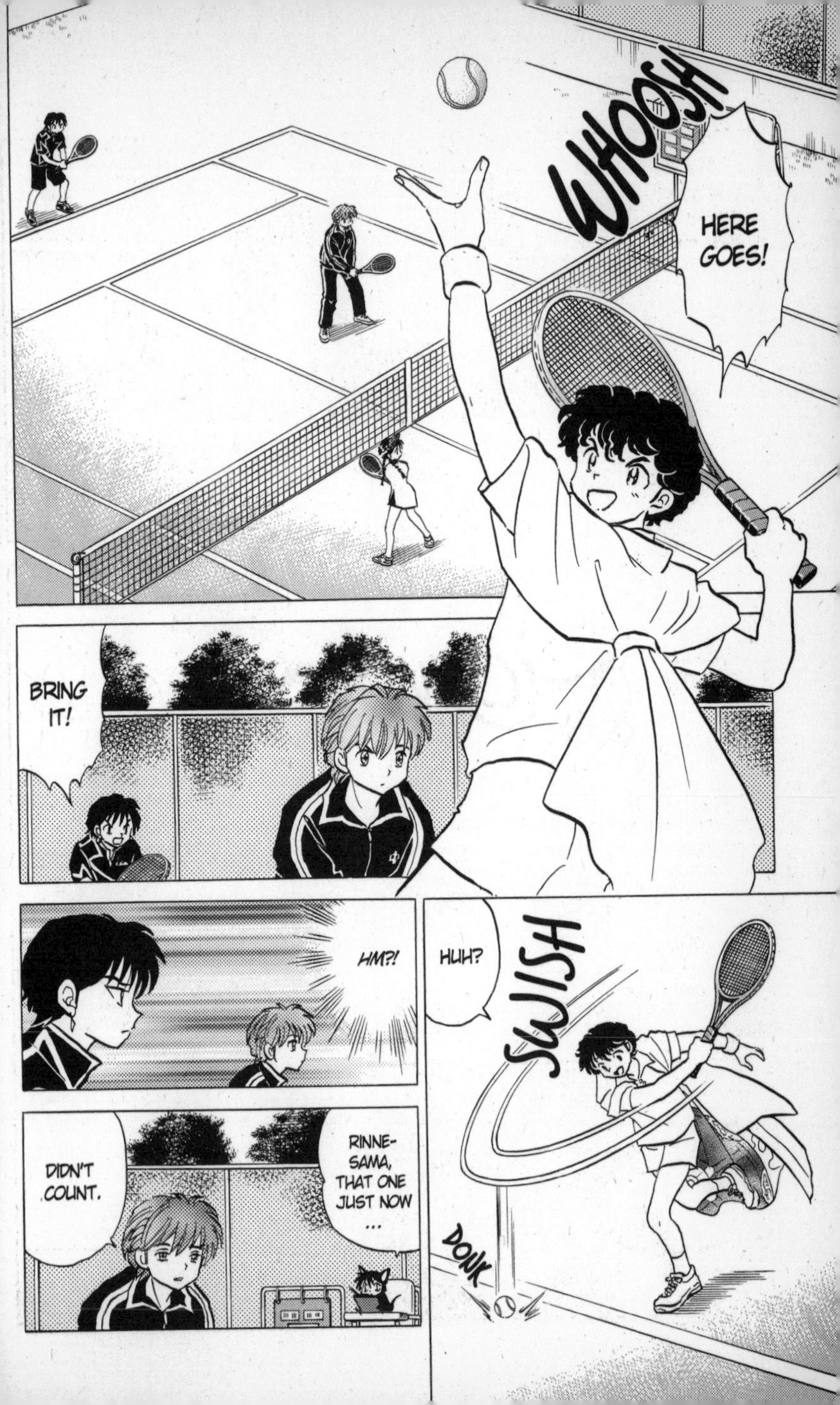
WHOOSH
HERE GOES!
BRING IT!
HUH?
SWISH
DONK
HM?!
RINNE-SAMA, THAT ONE JUST NOW ...
DIDN'T COUNT.

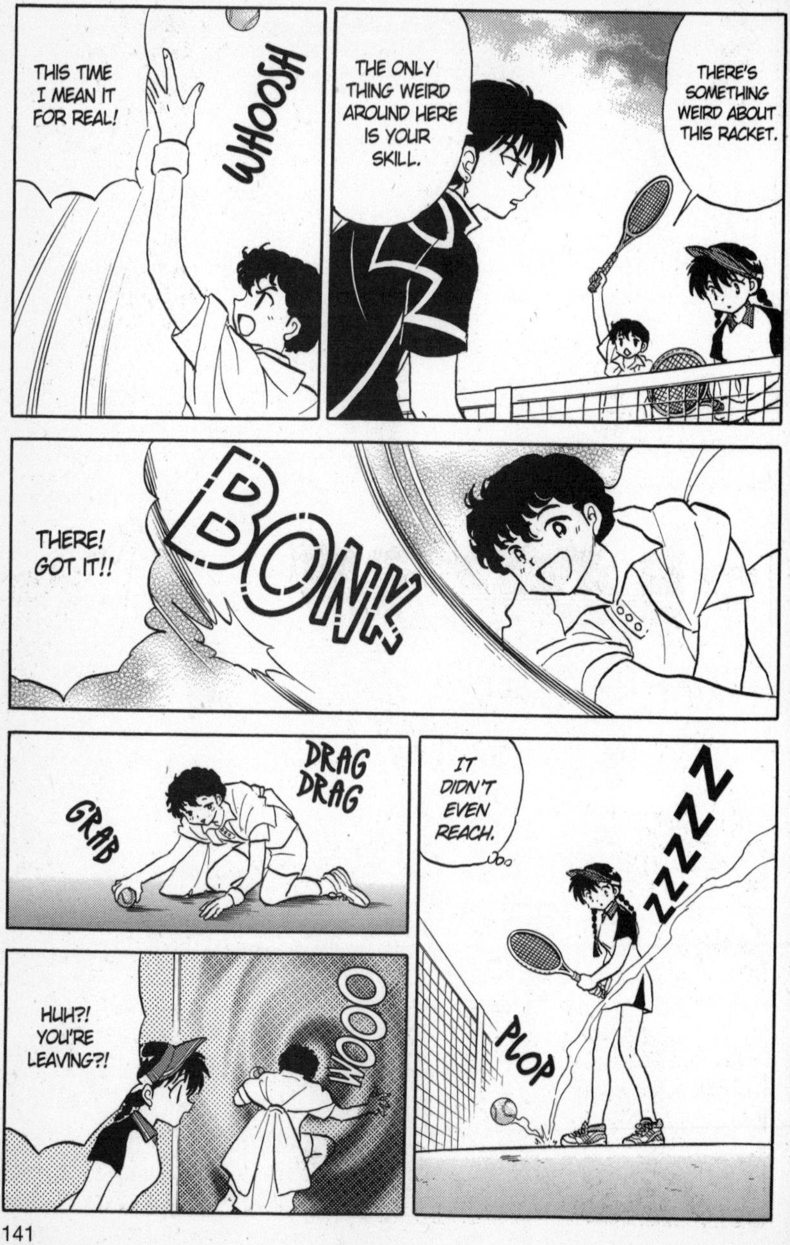
THERE'S SOMETHING WEIRD ABOUT THIS RACKET.
THE ONLY THING WEIRD AROUND HERE IS YOUR SKILL.
WHOOSH
THIS TIME I MEAN IT FOR REAL!
BONK
THERE! GOT IT!!
ZZZZZ
IT DIDN'T EVEN REACH.
PLOP
DRAG DRAG
GRAB
WOOOO
HUH?! YOU'RE LEAVING?!

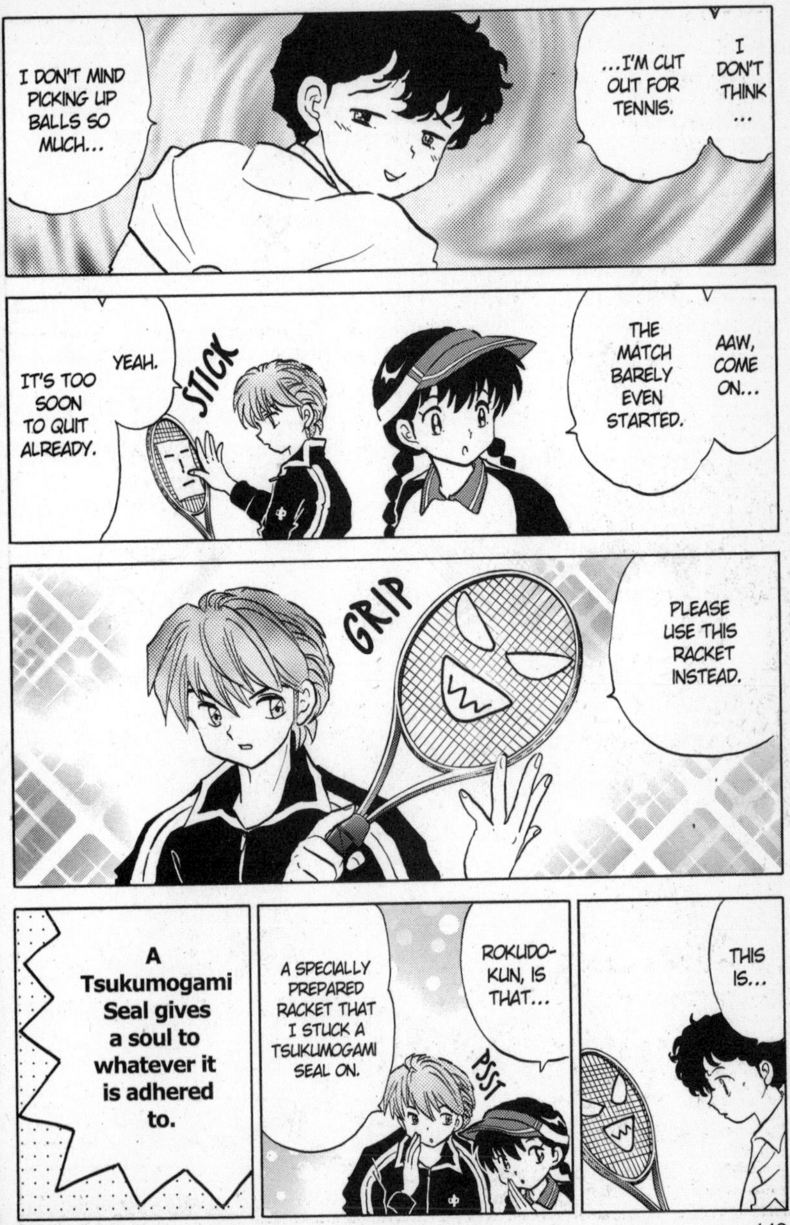
I DON'T THINK ... ...I'M CUT OUT FOR TENNIS.
I DON'T MIND PICKING UP BALLS SO MUCH...
AAW, COME ON... THE MATCH BARELY EVEN STARTED.
STICK
YEAH. IT'S TOO SOON TO QUIT ALREADY.
PLEASE USE THIS RACKET INSTEAD.
GRIP
THIS IS...
ROKUDO-KUN, IS THAT...
PSST
A SPECIALLY PREPARED RACKET THAT I STUCK A TSUKUMOGAMI SEAL ON.
A Tsukumogami Seal gives a soul to whatever it is adhered to.

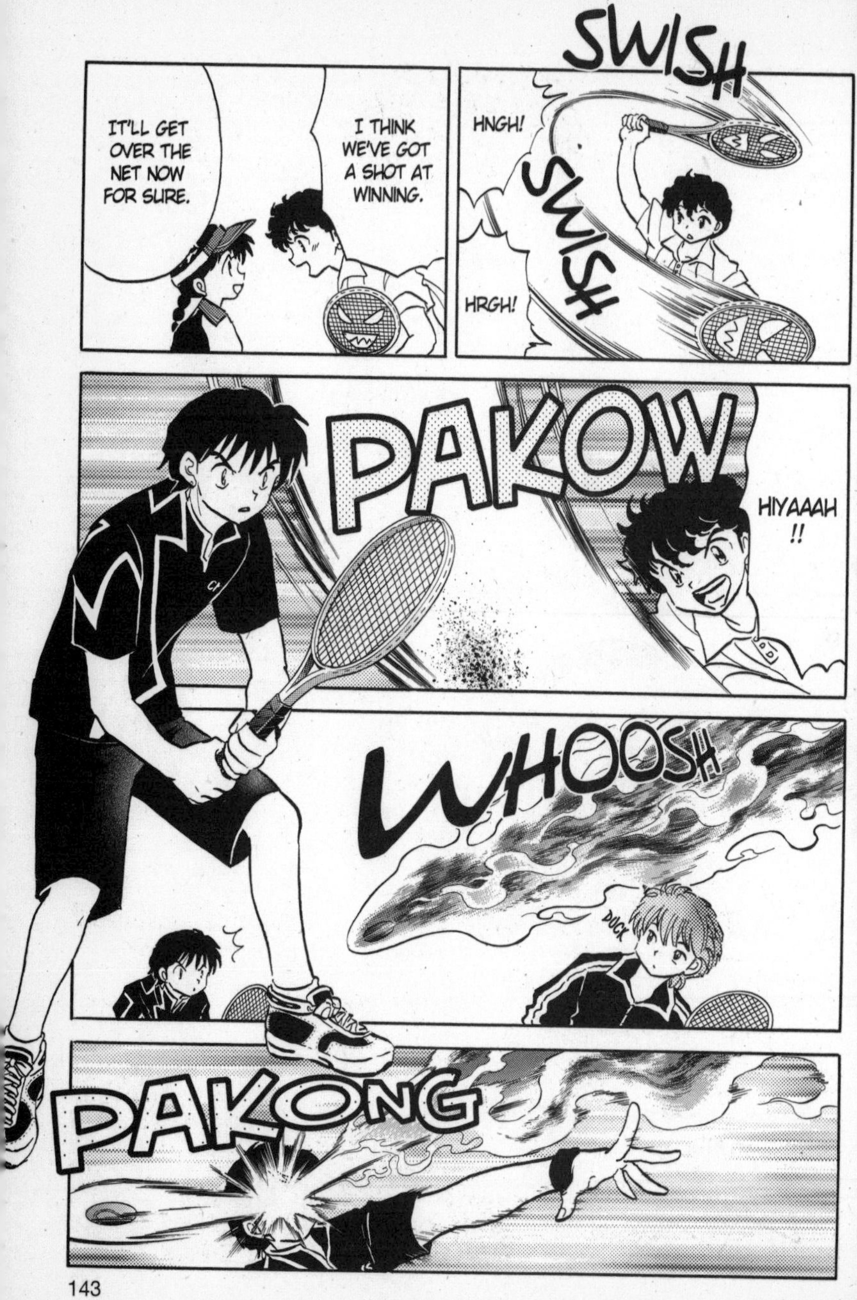
SWISH
HNGH!
SWISH
HRGH!
I THINK WE'VE GOT A SHOT AT WINNING.
IT'LL GET OVER THE NET NOW FOR SURE.
PAKOW
HIYAAAH !!
WHOOSH
DUCK
PAKONG

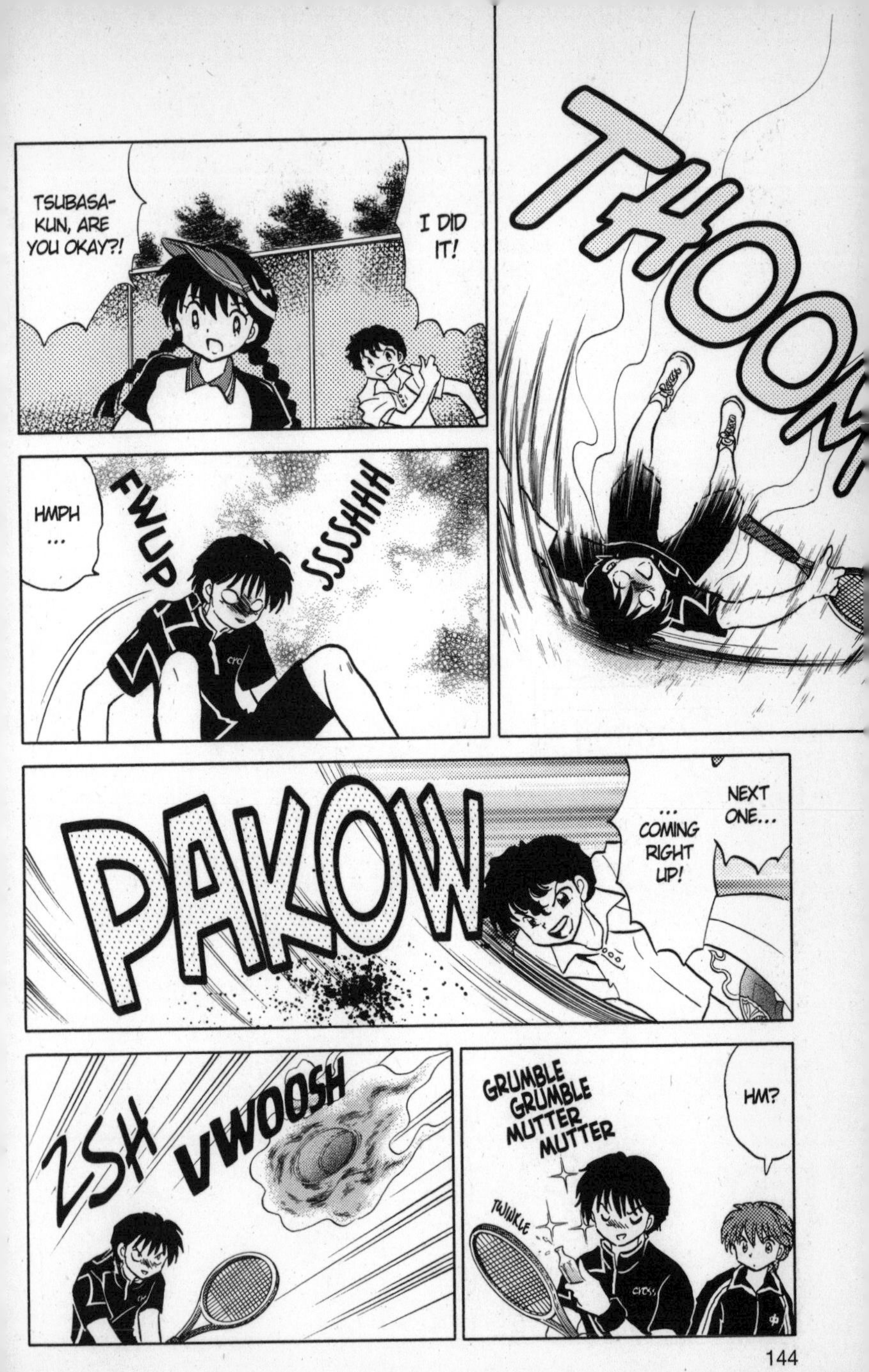
THOOM
I DID IT!
TSUBASA-KUN, ARE YOU OKAY?!
HMPH ...
FWUP
JSSSHHH
NEXT ONE...
... COMING RIGHT UP!
PAKOW
HM?
GRUMBLE GRUMBLE MUTTER MUTTER
TWINKLE
VWOOSH
ZSH

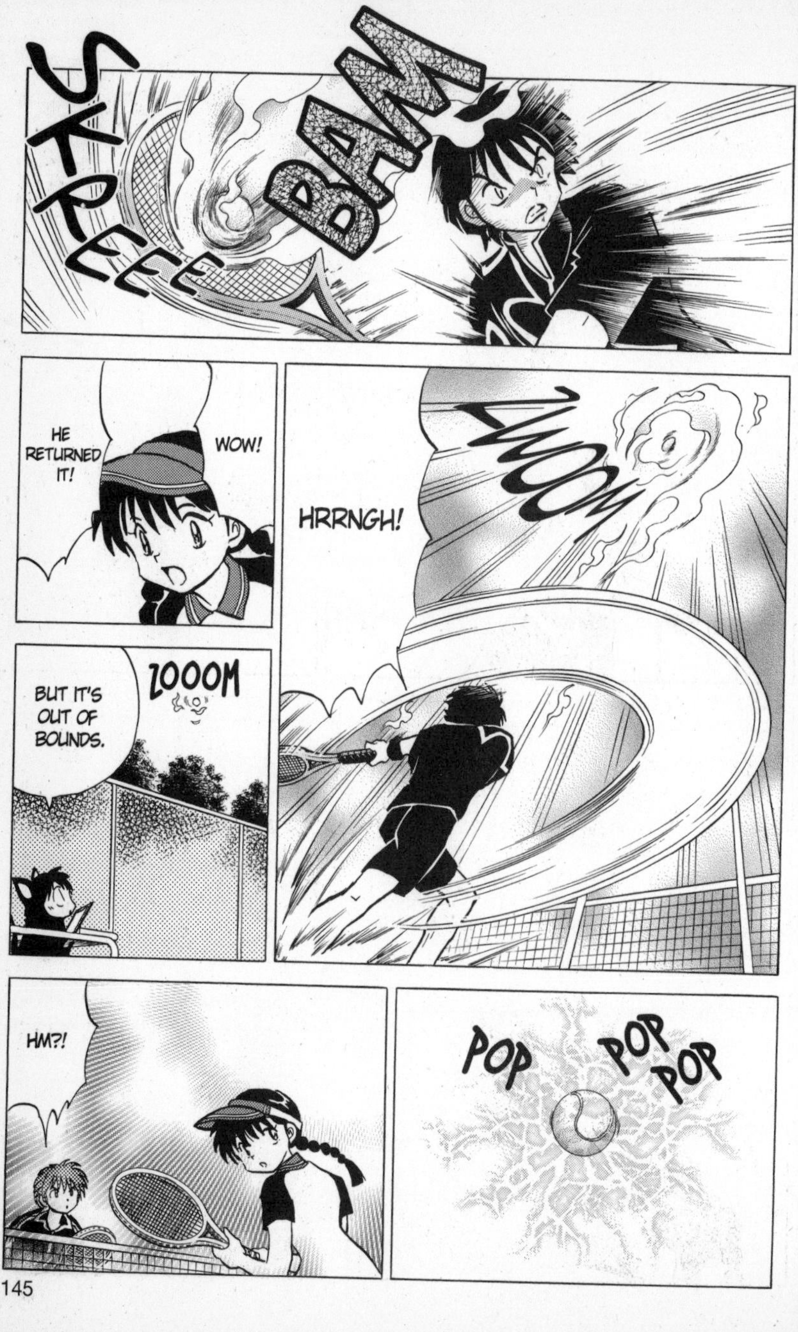
SKREEE
BAM
HRRNGH!
ZWOOM
WOW!
HE RETURNED IT!
BUT IT'S OUT OF BOUNDS.
ZOOOM
POP
POP
POP
HM?!

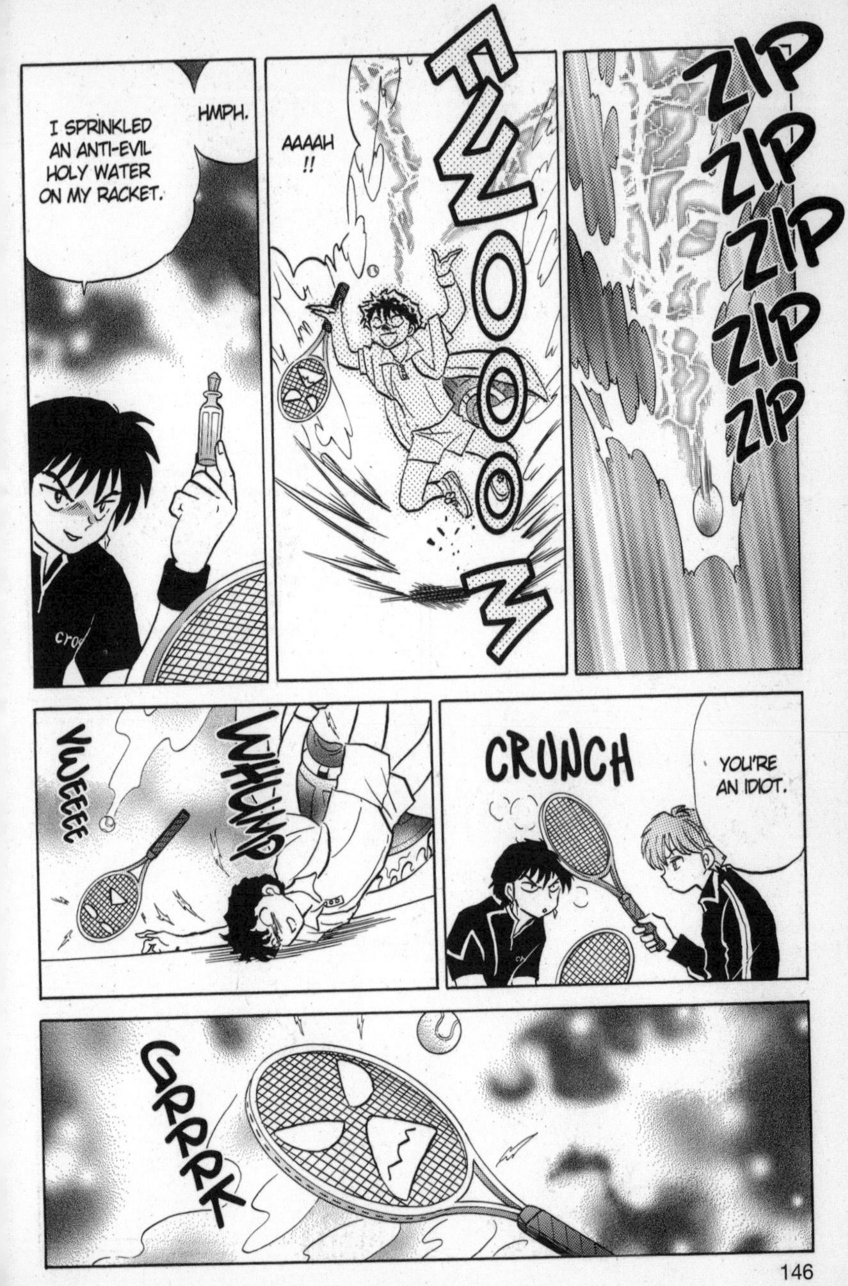
ZIP
ZIP
ZIP
ZIP
ZIP
FWOOOM
AAAAH !!
HMPH.
I SPRINKLED AN ANTI-EVIL HOLY WATER ON MY RACKET.
YOU'RE AN IDIOT.
CRUNCH
WHUMP
VWEEEEE
GRRRK

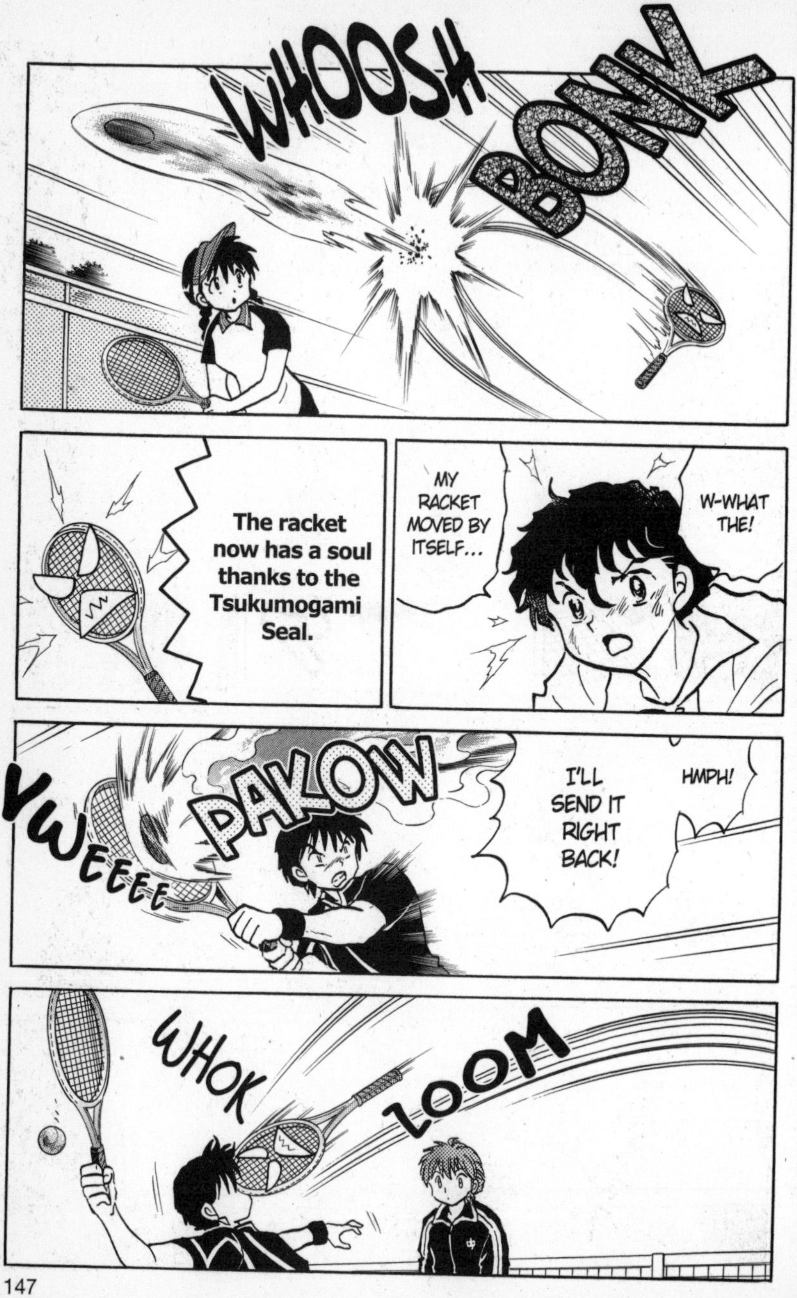
BONK
WHOOSH
W-WHAT THE!
MY RACKET MOVED BY ITSELF...
The racket now has a soul thanks to the Tsukumogami Seal.
HMPH!
I'LL SEND IT RIGHT BACK!
PAKOW
YWEEEEE
ZOOM
WHOK

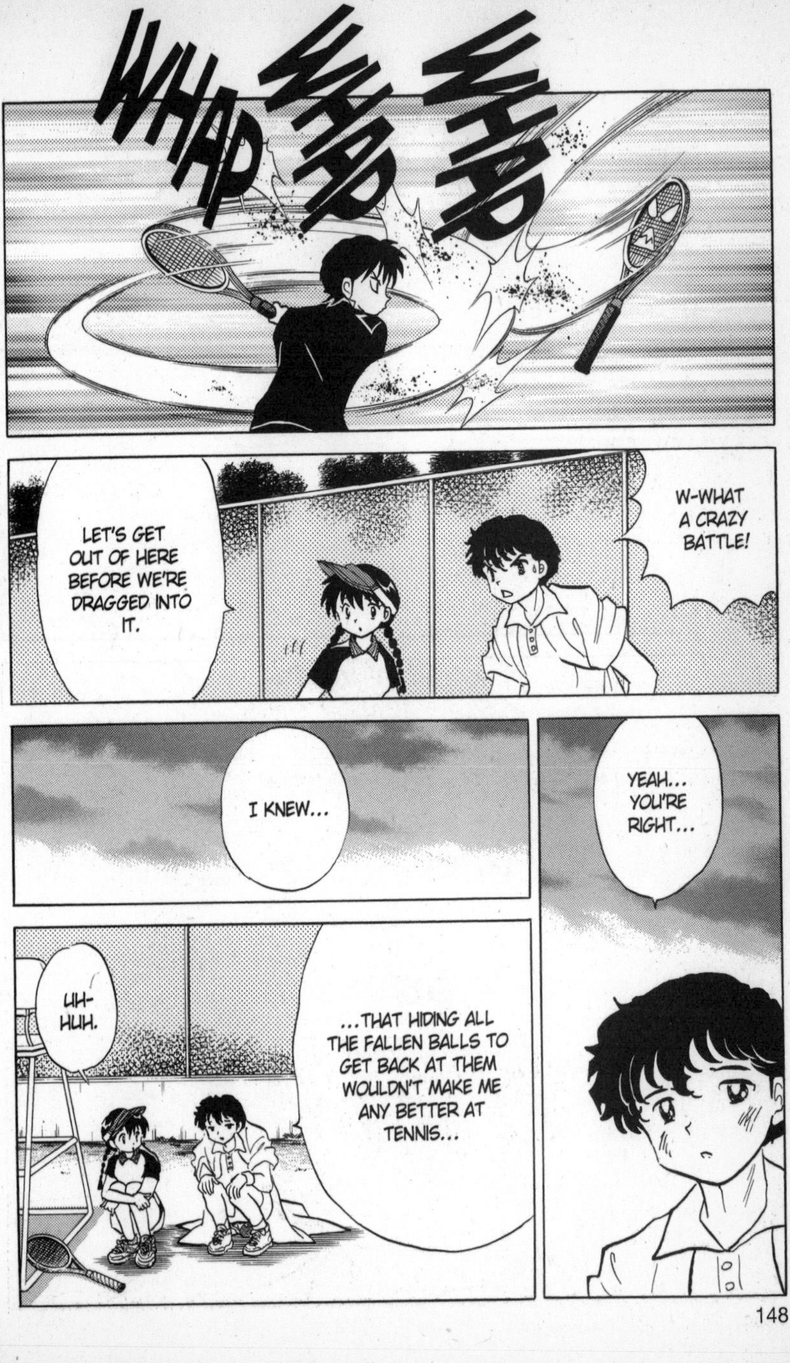
WHAP WHAP WHAP
W-WHAT A CRAZY BATTLE!
LET'S GET OUT OF HERE BEFORE WE'RE DRAGGED INTO IT.
YEAH... YOU'RE RIGHT...
I KNEW...
...THAT HIDING ALL THE FALLEN BALLS TO GET BACK AT THEM WOULDN'T MAKE ME ANY BETTER AT TENNIS...
UH-HUH.

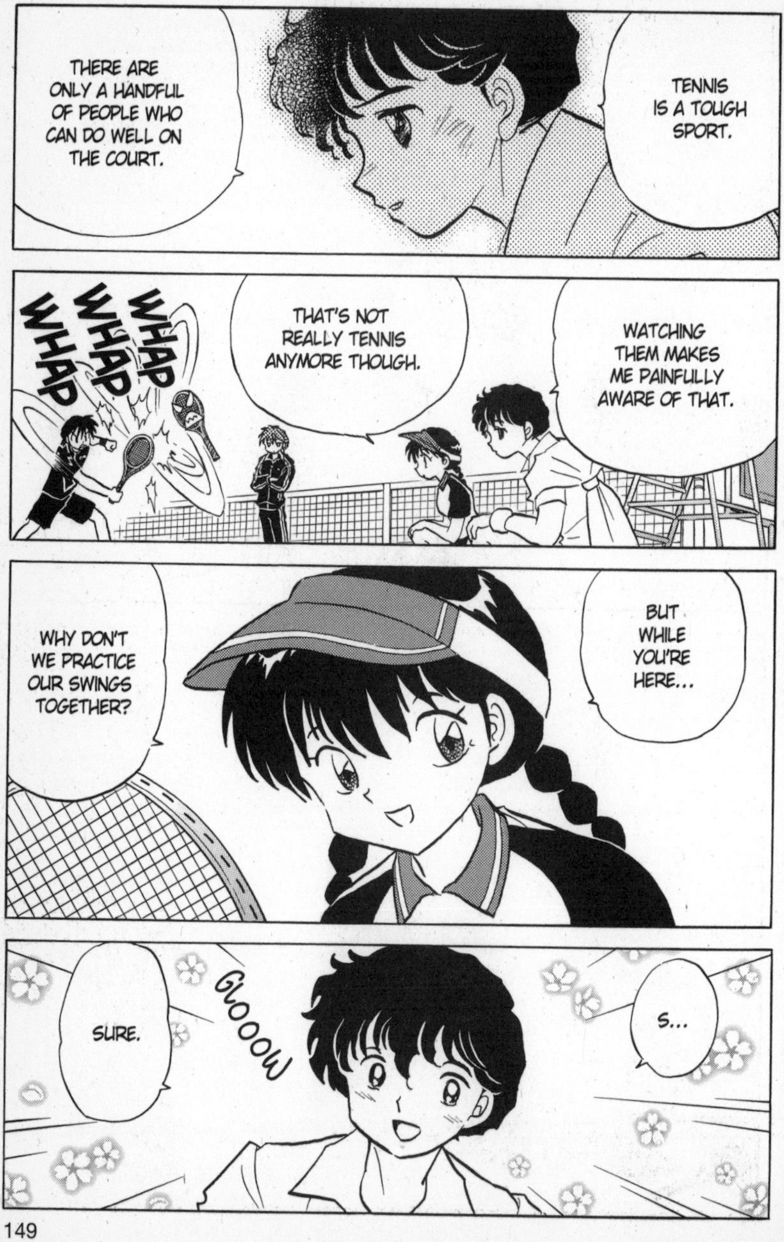
TENNIS IS A TOUGH SPORT.
THERE ARE ONLY A HANDFUL OF PEOPLE WHO CAN DO WELL ON THE COURT.
WATCHING THEM MAKES ME PAINFULLY AWARE OF THAT.
THAT'S NOT REALLY TENNIS ANYMORE THOUGH.
WHAP WHAP WHAP
BUT WHILE YOU'RE HERE...
WHY DON'T WE PRACTICE OUR SWINGS TOGETHER?
S...
GLOOOW
SURE.

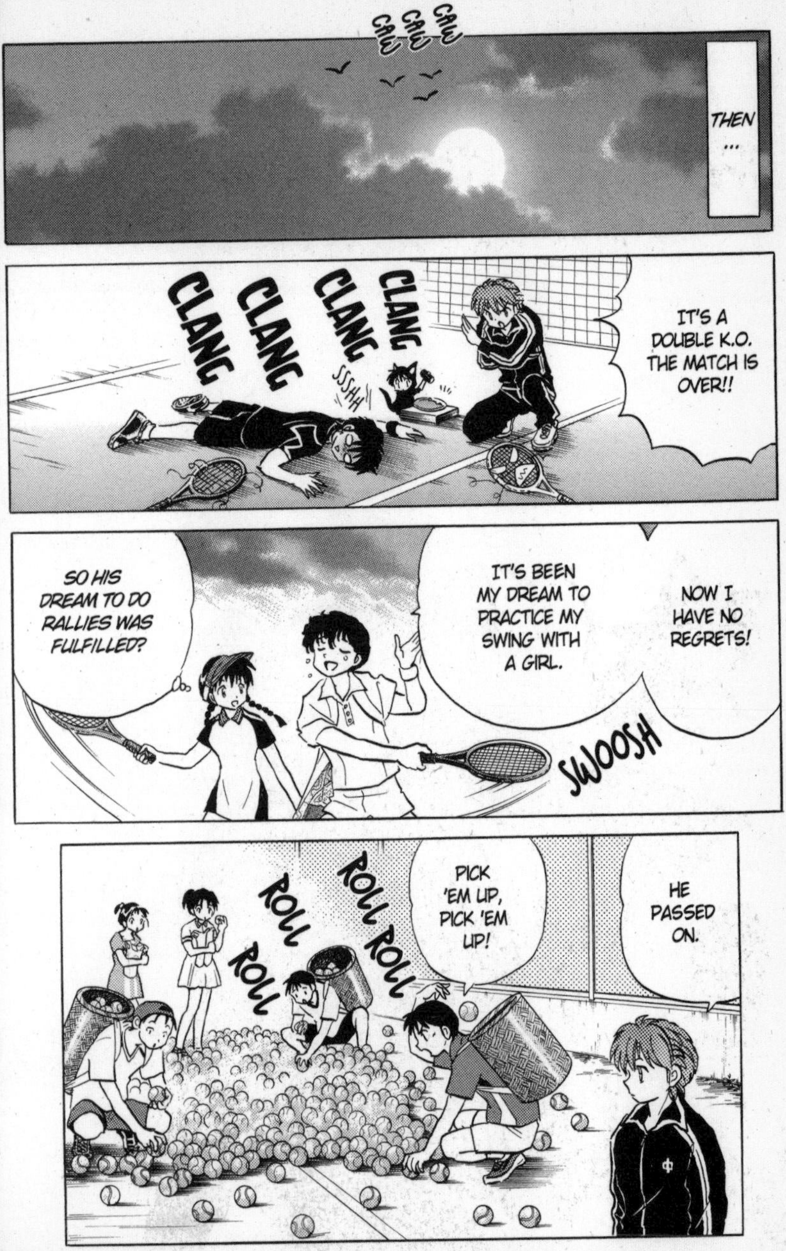
CAW CAW CAW
THEN...
IT'S A DOUBLE K.O. THE MATCH IS OVER!!
CLANG CLANG CLANG CLANG
SSSHH
IT'S BEEN MY DREAM TO PRACTICE MY SWING WITH A GIRL.
NOW I HAVE NO REGRETS!
SWOOSH
SO HIS DREAM TO DO RALLIES WAS FULFILLED?
HE PASSED ON.
PICK 'EM UP, PICK 'EM UP!
ROLL ROLL ROLL ROLL

CHAPTER 97: THE TABOOS OF THE SHINIGAMI WORLD

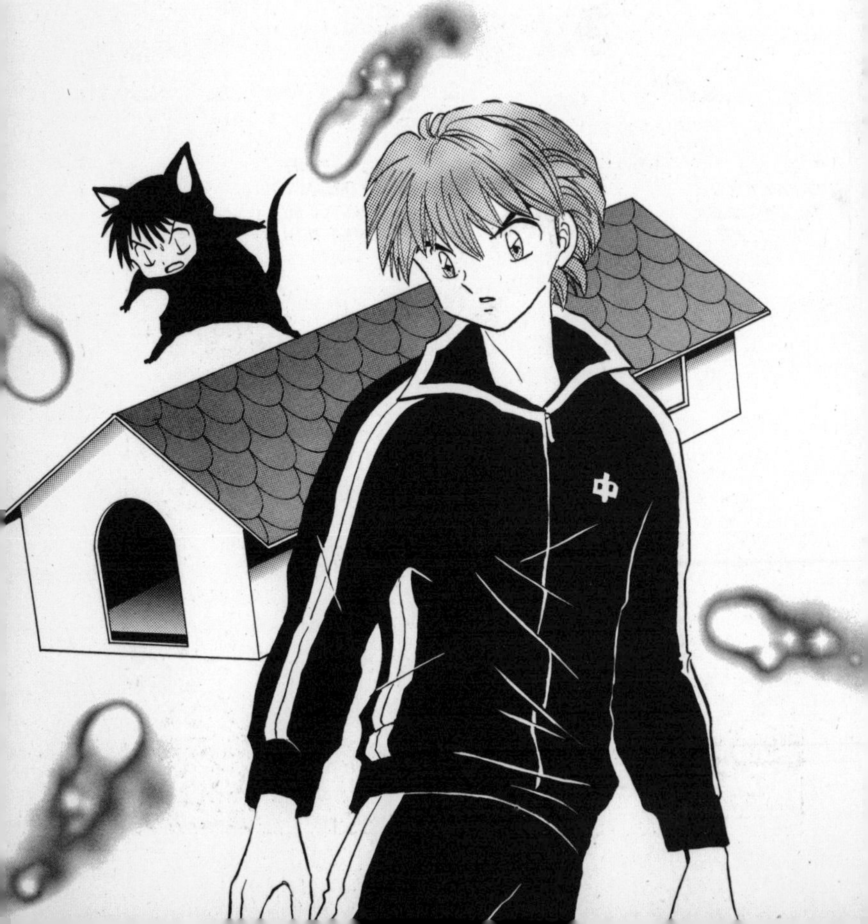

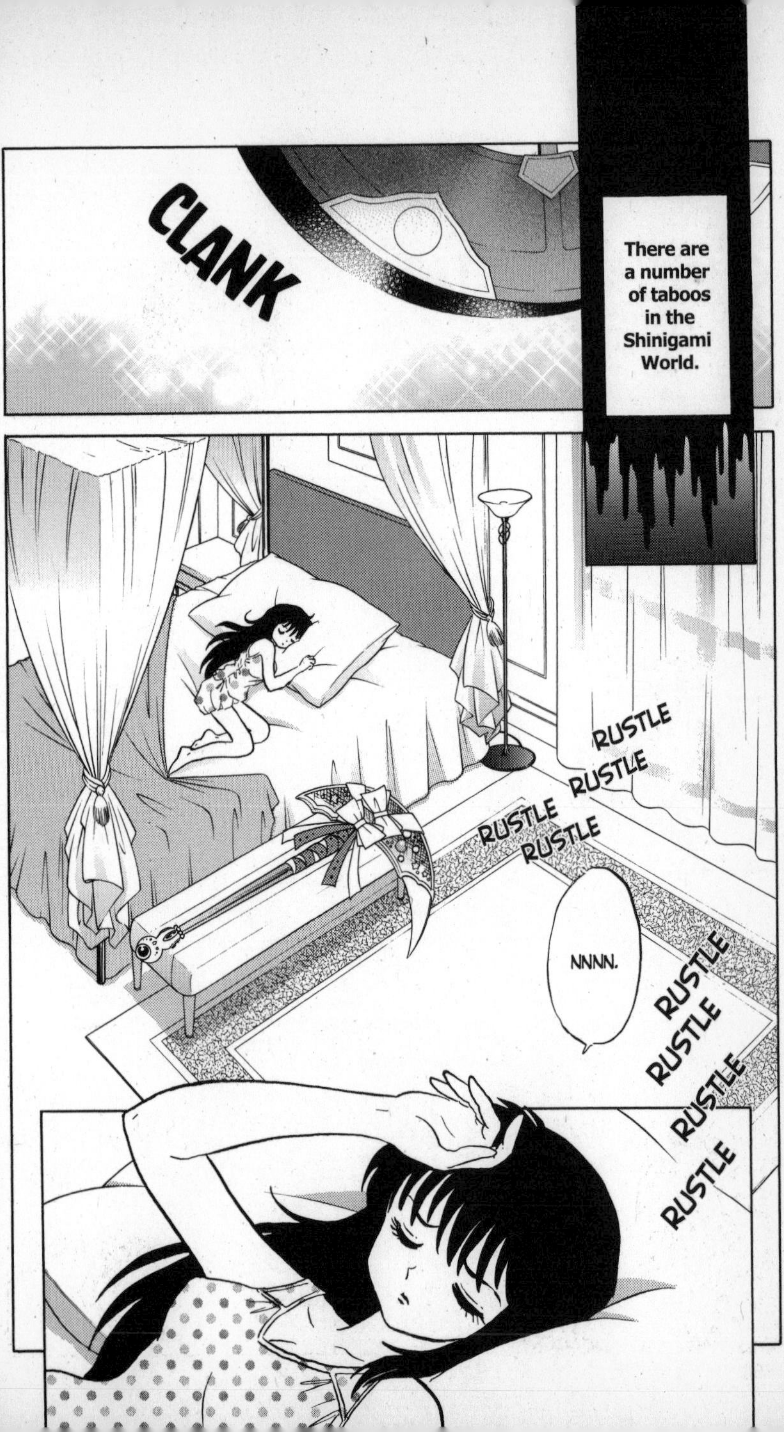
There are a number of taboos in the Shinigami World.
CLANK
RUSTLE RUSTLE
RUSTLE RUSTLE
NNNN.
RUSTLE RUSTLE RUSTLE RUSTLE

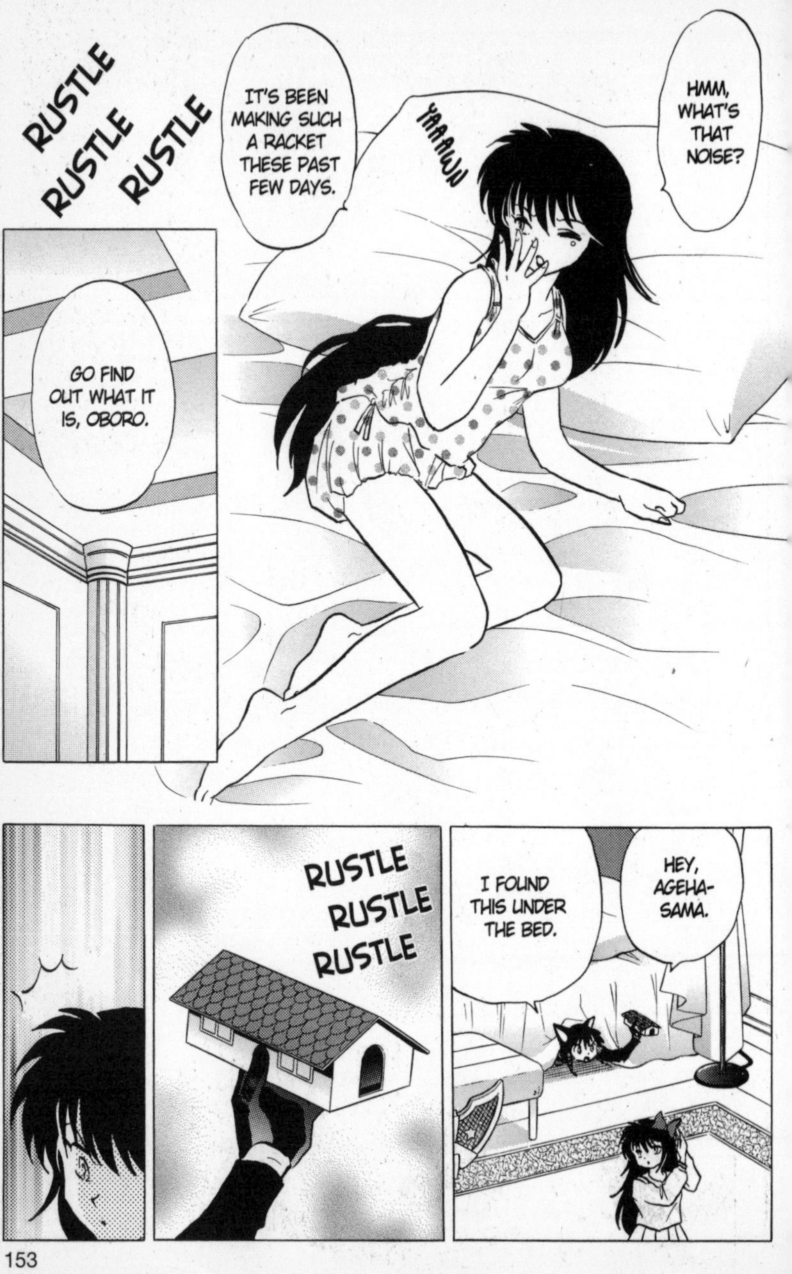
HMM, WHAT'S THAT NOISE?
YAAAWN
IT'S BEEN MAKING SUCH A RACKET THESE PAST FEW DAYS.
RUSTLE RUSTLE RUSTLE
GO FIND OUT WHAT IT IS, OBORO.
HEY, AGEHA-SAMA.
I FOUND THIS UNDER THE BED.
RUSTLE RUSTLE RUSTLE

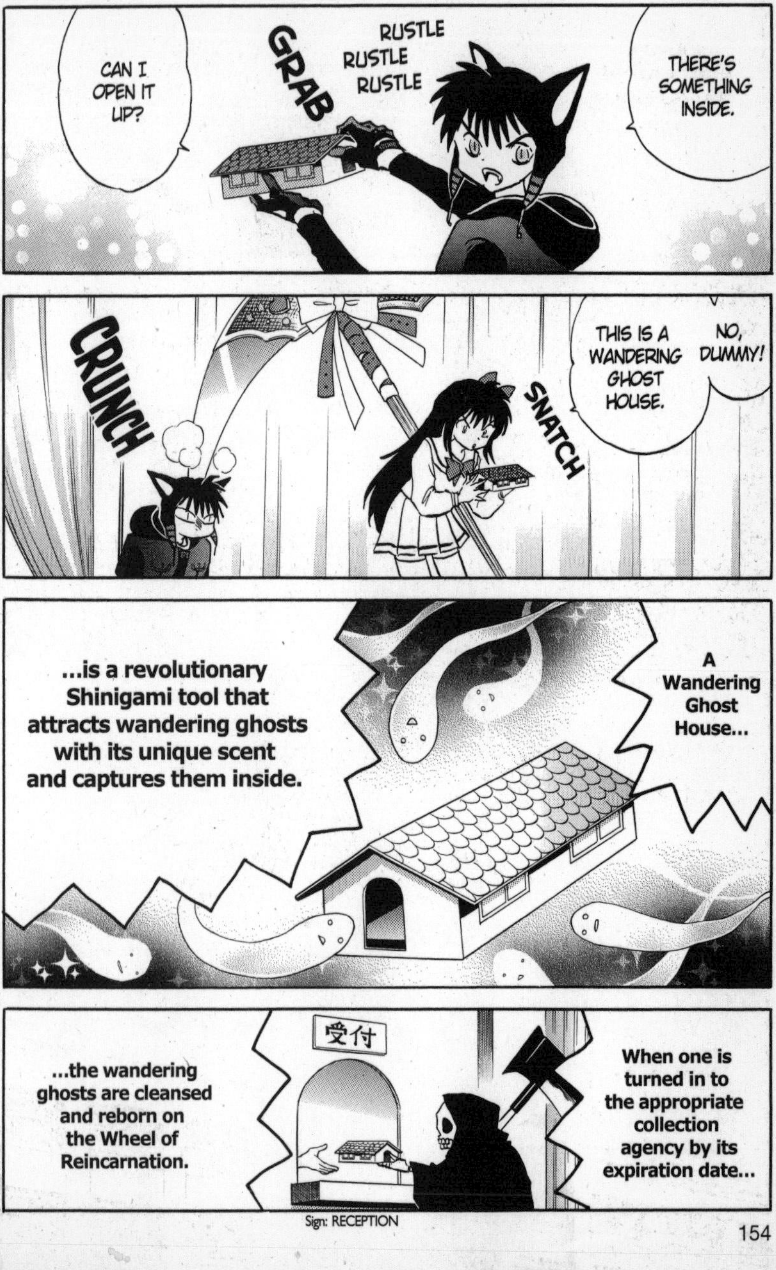
THERE'S SOMETHING INSIDE.
RUSTLE
RUSTLE
RUSTLE
GRAB
CAN I OPEN IT UP?
NO, DUMMY!
THIS IS A WANDERING GHOST HOUSE.
SNATCH
CRUNCH
A Wandering Ghost House...
...is a revolutionary Shinigami tool that attracts wandering ghosts with its unique scent and captures them inside.
When one is turned in to the appropriate collection agency by its expiration date...
受付
...the wandering ghosts are cleansed and reborn on the Wheel of Reincarnation.
Sign: RECEPTION

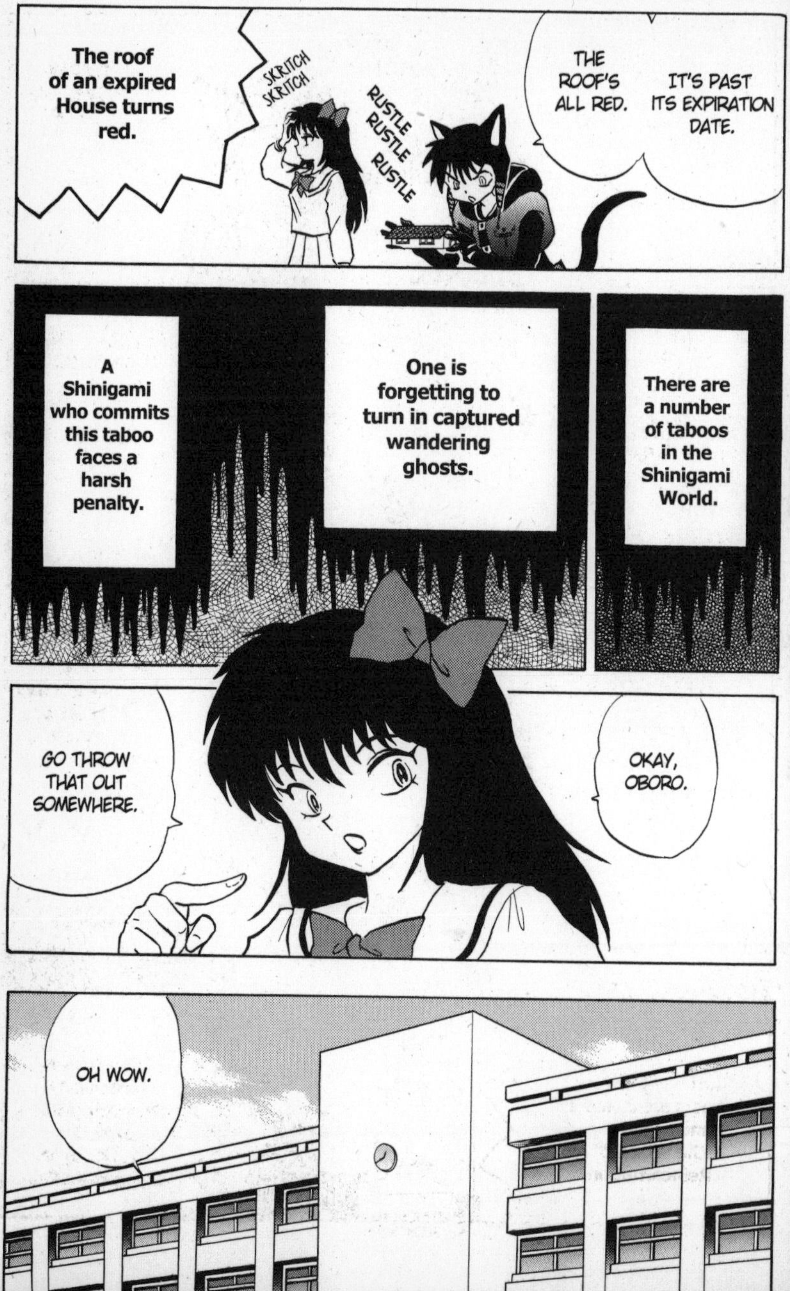
IT'S PAST ITS EXPIRATION DATE.
THE ROOF'S ALL RED.
RUSTLE RUSTLE RUSTLE
SKRITCH SKRITCH
The roof of an expired House turns red.
There are a number of taboos in the Shinigami World.
One is forgetting to turn in captured wandering ghosts.
A Shinigami who commits this taboo faces a harsh penalty.
OKAY, OBORO.
GO THROW THAT OUT SOMEWHERE.
OH WOW.

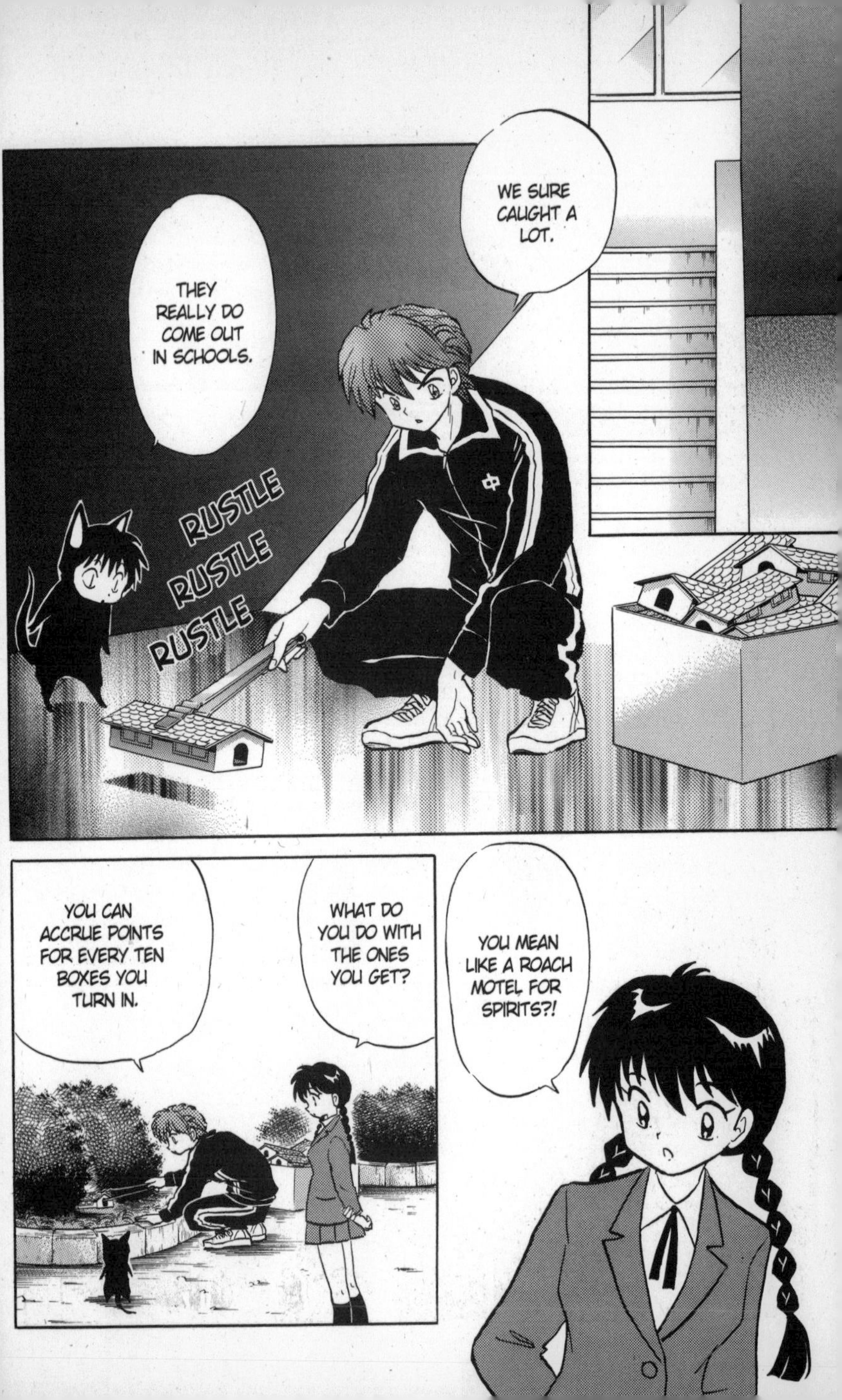
WE SURE CAUGHT A LOT.
THEY REALLY DO COME OUT IN SCHOOLS.
RUSTLE RUSTLE RUSTLE
YOU MEAN LIKE A ROACH MOTEL FOR SPIRITS?!
WHAT DO YOU DO WITH THE ONES YOU GET?
YOU CAN ACCRUE POINTS FOR EVERY TEN BOXES YOU TURN IN.

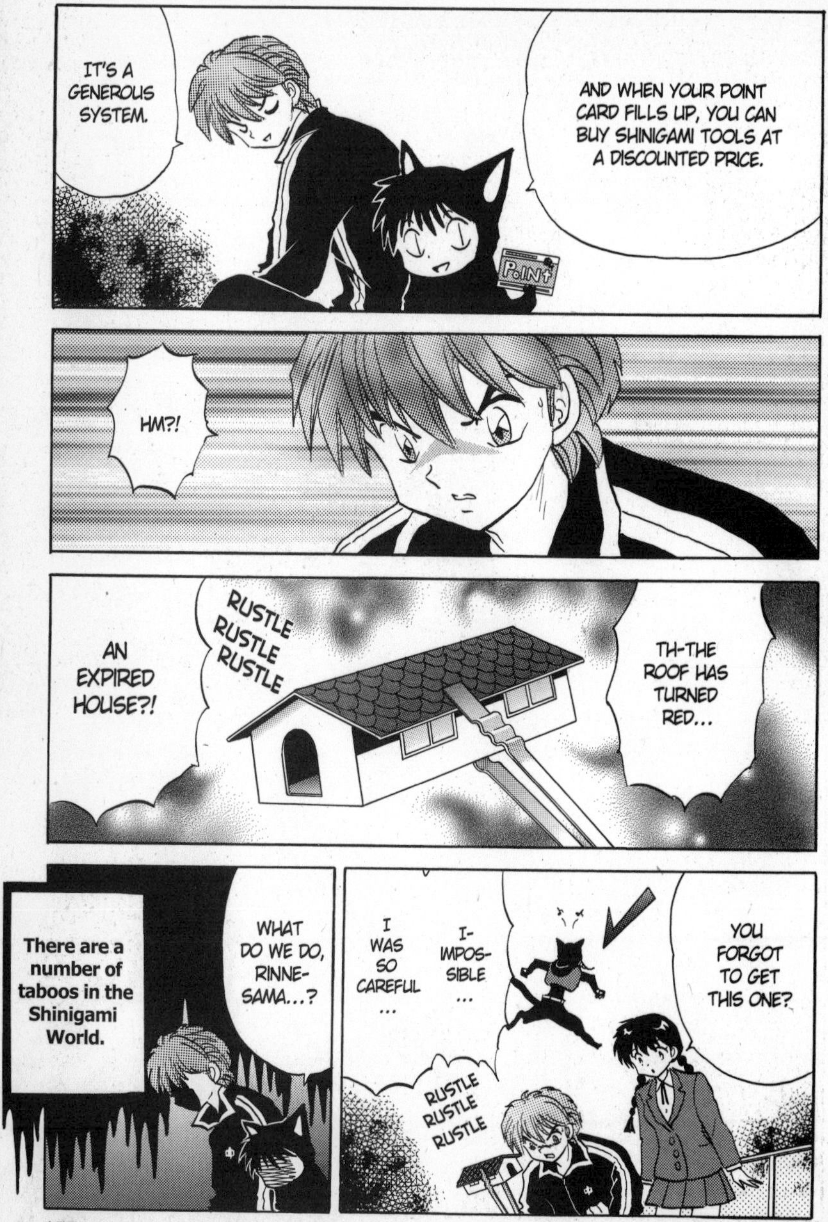
AND WHEN YOUR POINT CARD FILLS UP, YOU CAN BUY SHINIGAMI TOOLS AT A DISCOUNTED PRICE.
POINT
IT'S A GENEROUS SYSTEM.
HM?!
TH-THE ROOF HAS TURNED RED...
RUSTLE RUSTLE RUSTLE
AN EXPIRED HOUSE?!
YOU FORGOT TO GET THIS ONE?
I- IMPOSSIBLE...
I WAS SO CAREFUL...
RUSTLE RUSTLE RUSTLE
WHAT DO WE DO, RINNE-SAMA...?
There are a number of taboos in the Shinigami World.

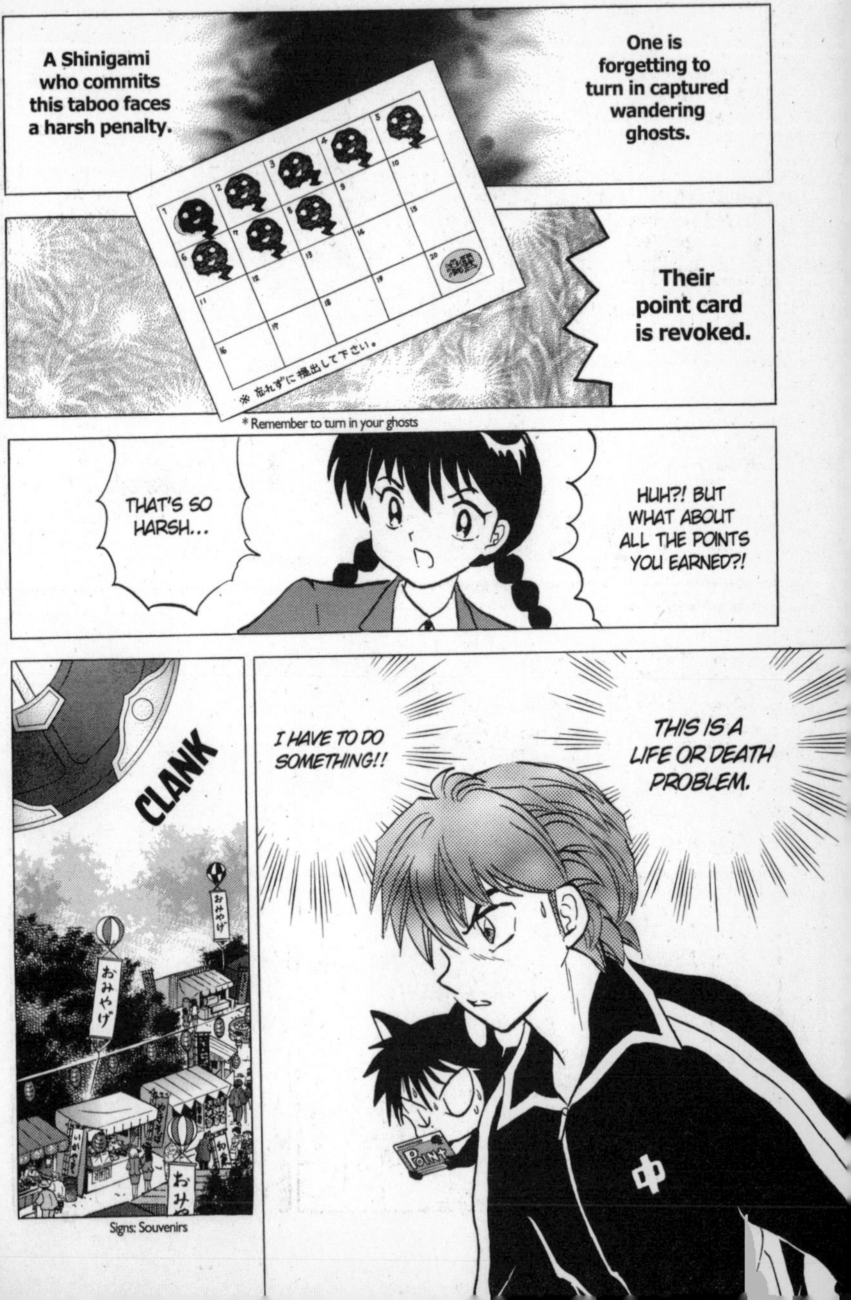
One is forgetting to turn in captured wandering ghosts.
A Shinigami who commits this taboo faces a harsh penalty.
Their point card is revoked.
※ 忘れずに提出して下さい。
HUH?! BUT WHAT ABOUT ALL THE POINTS YOU EARNED?!
THAT'S SO HARSH...
THIS IS A LIFE OR DEATH PROBLEM.
I HAVE TO DO SOMETHING!!
POINT
CLANK
おみやげ
おみやげ
* Remember to turn in your ghosts

Signs: Souvenirs

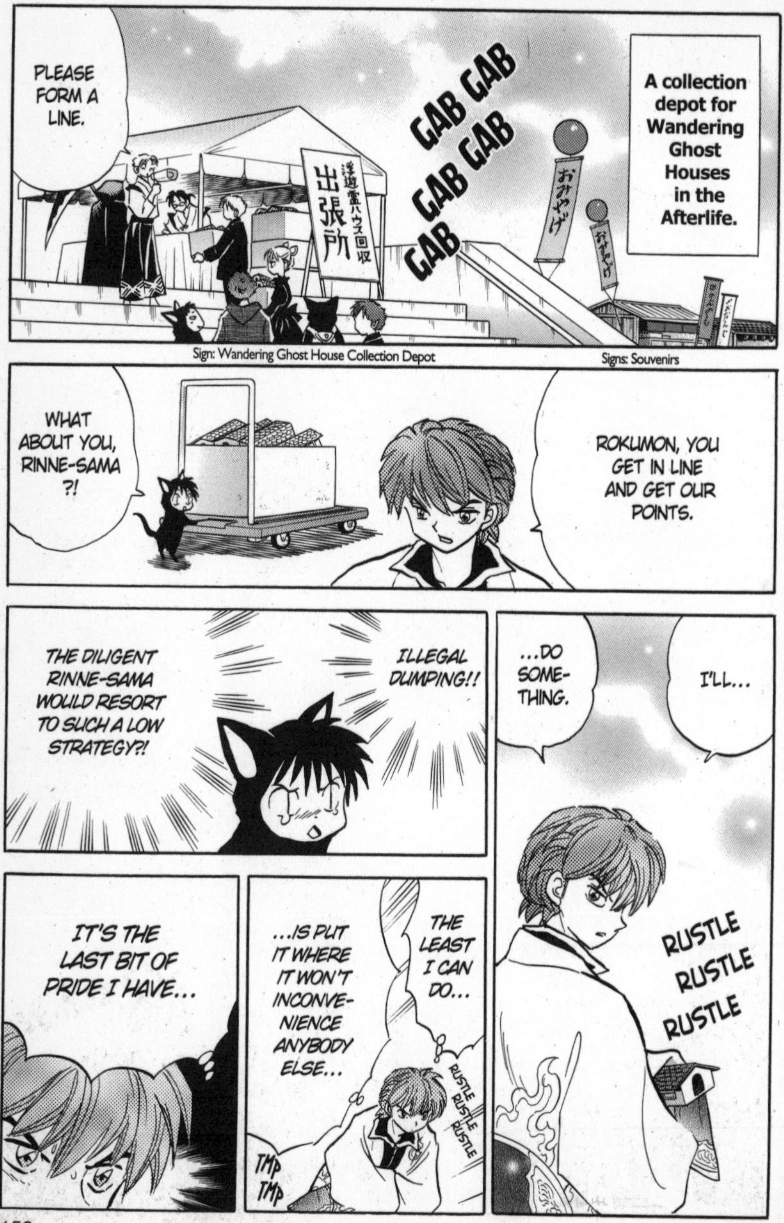
A collection depot for Wandering Ghost Houses in the Afterlife.
GAB GAB GAB GAB GAB
PLEASE FORM A LINE.
Sign: Wandering Ghost House Collection Depot
Signs: Souvenirs
ROKUMON, YOU GET IN LINE AND GET OUR POINTS.
WHAT ABOUT YOU, RINNE-SAMA?!
I'LL...
...DO SOME-THING.
RUSTLE RUSTLE RUSTLE
ILLEGAL DUMPING!!
THE DILIGENT RINNE-SAMA WOULD RESORT TO SUCH A LOW STRATEGY?!
THE LEAST I CAN DO...
...IS PUT IT WHERE IT WON'T INCONVE-NIENCE ANYBODY ELSE...
RUSTLE RUSTLE RUSTLE
TMP TMP
IT'S THE LAST BIT OF PRIDE I HAVE...

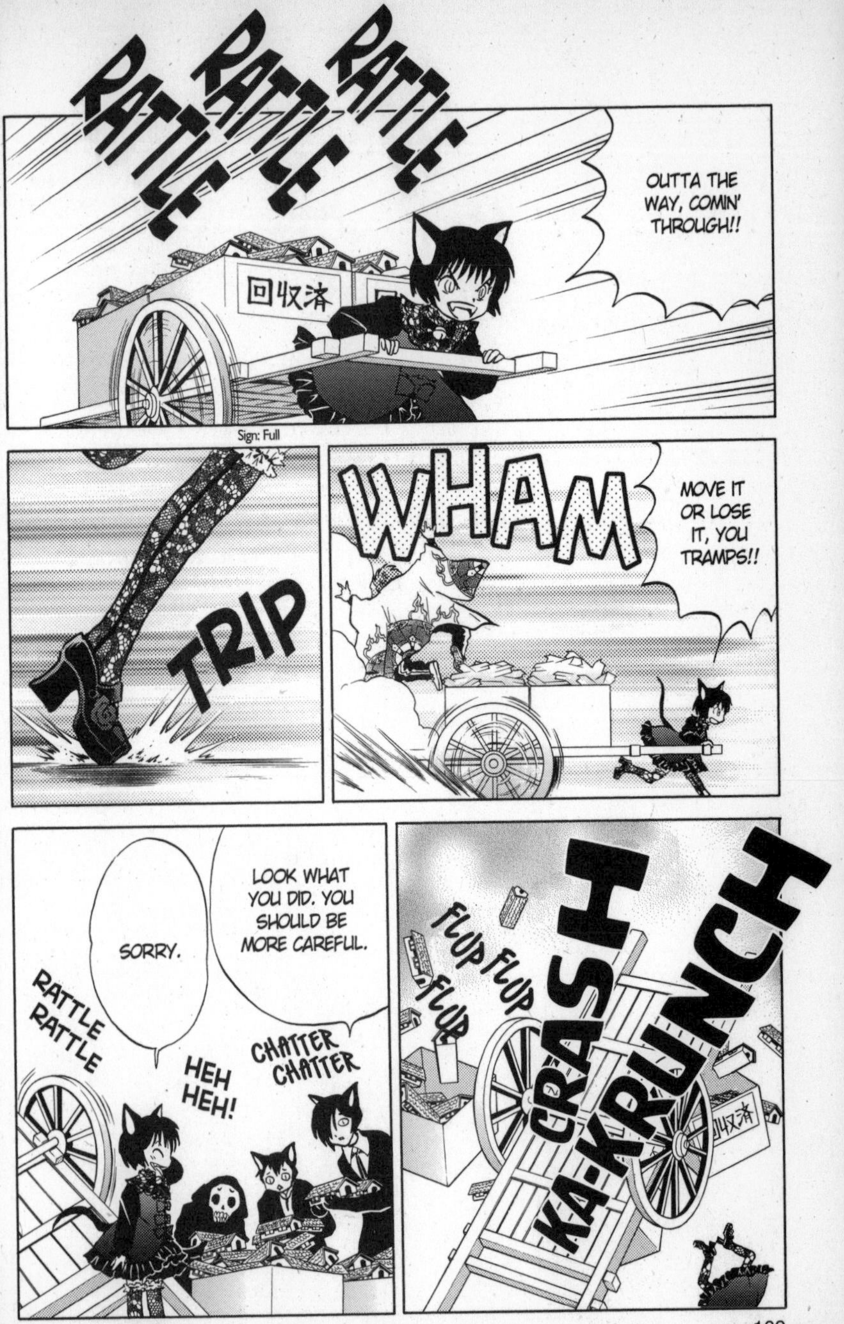
RATTLE RATTLE RATTLE
OUTTA THE WAY, COMIN' THROUGH!!
回収済
Sign: Full
WHAM
MOVE IT OR LOSE IT, YOU TRAMPS!!
TRIP
FLUP FLUP FLUP
CRASH
KA-KRUNCH
LOOK WHAT YOU DID. YOU SHOULD BE MORE CAREFUL.
SORRY.
RATTLE RATTLE
HEH HEH!
CHATTER CHATTER

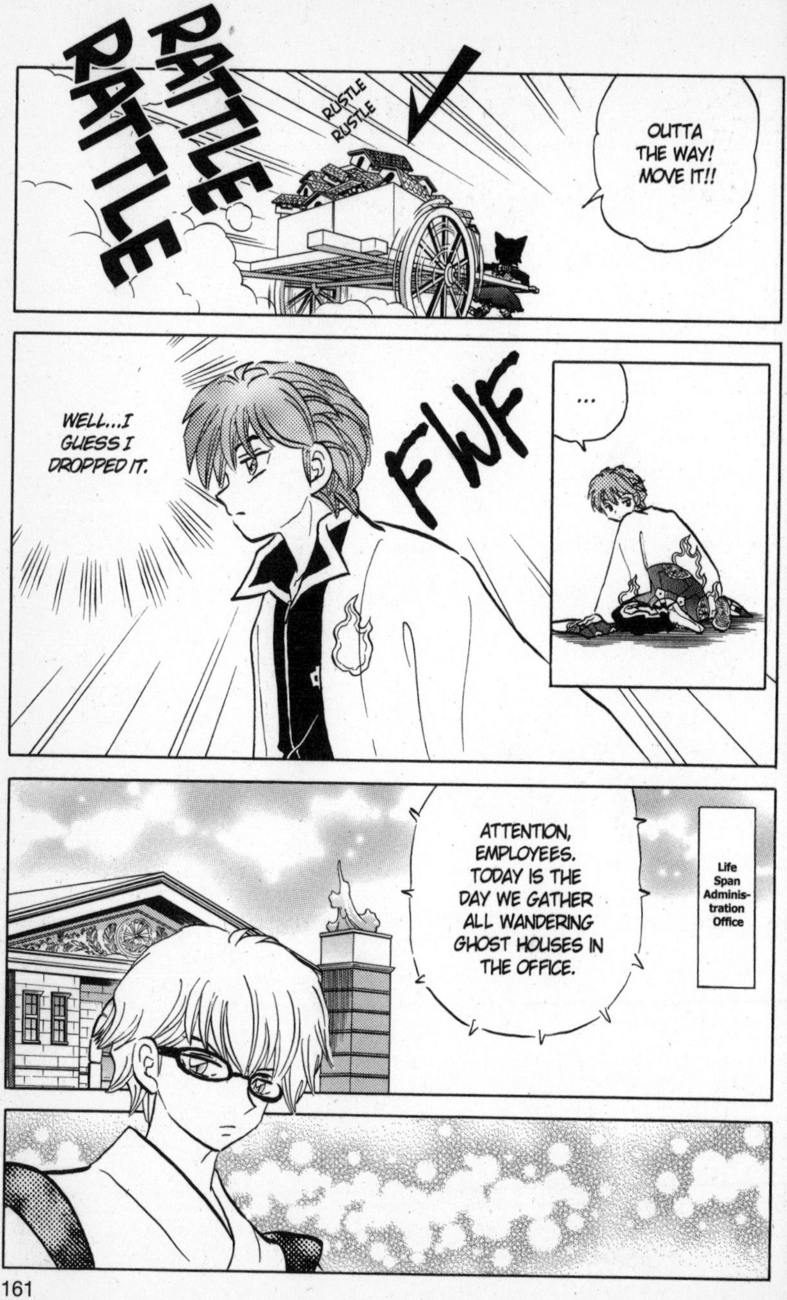
OUTTA THE WAY! MOVE IT!!
RUSTLE RUSTLE
RATTLE RATTLE
...
FWF
WELL...I GUESS I DROPPED IT.
Life Span Adminis-tration Office
ATTENTION, EMPLOYEES. TODAY IS THE DAY WE GATHER ALL WANDERING GHOST HOUSES IN THE OFFICE.

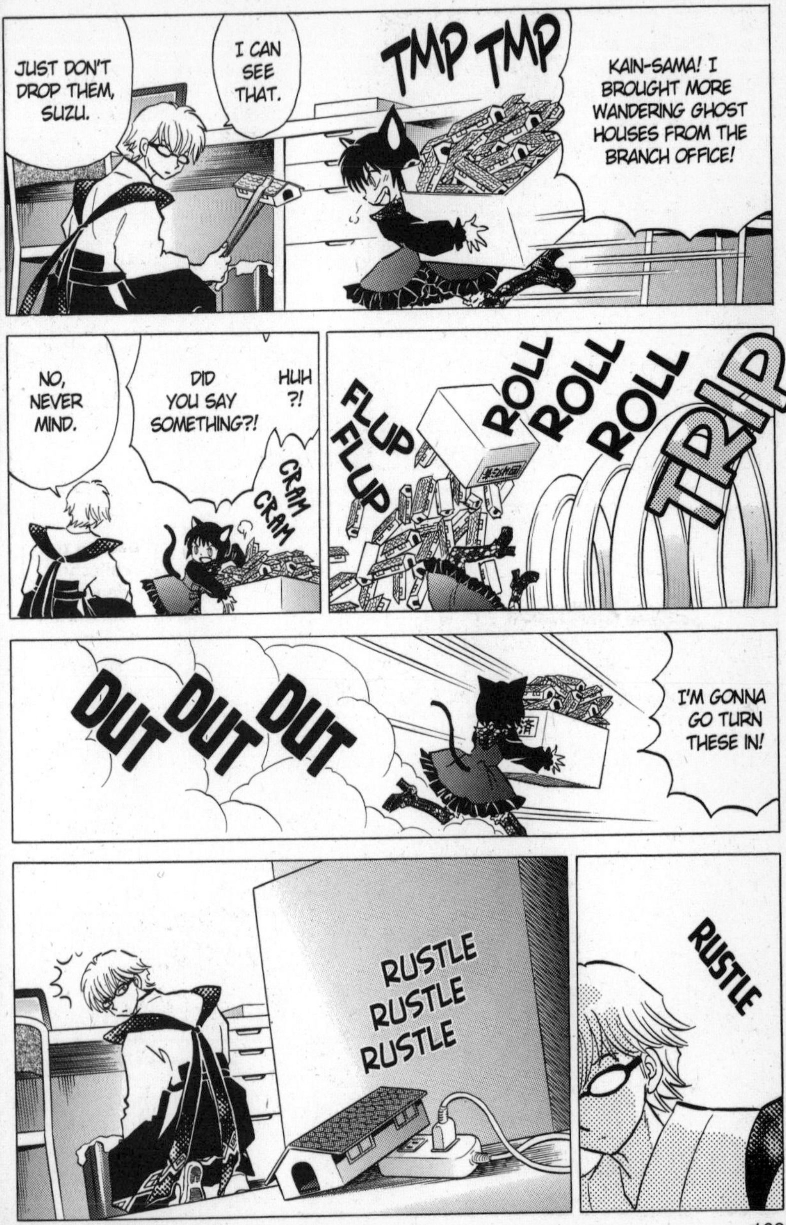
KAIN-SAMA! I BROUGHT MORE WANDERING GHOST HOUSES FROM THE BRANCH OFFICE!
TMP TMP
I CAN SEE THAT.
JUST DON'T DROP THEM, SUZU.
TRIP
ROLL ROLL ROLL
FLUP FLUP
HUH ?!
DID YOU SAY SOMETHING?!
CRAM CRAM
NO, NEVER MIND.
I'M GONNA GO TURN THESE IN!
OUT OUT OUT
RUSTLE
RUSTLE RUSTLE RUSTLE

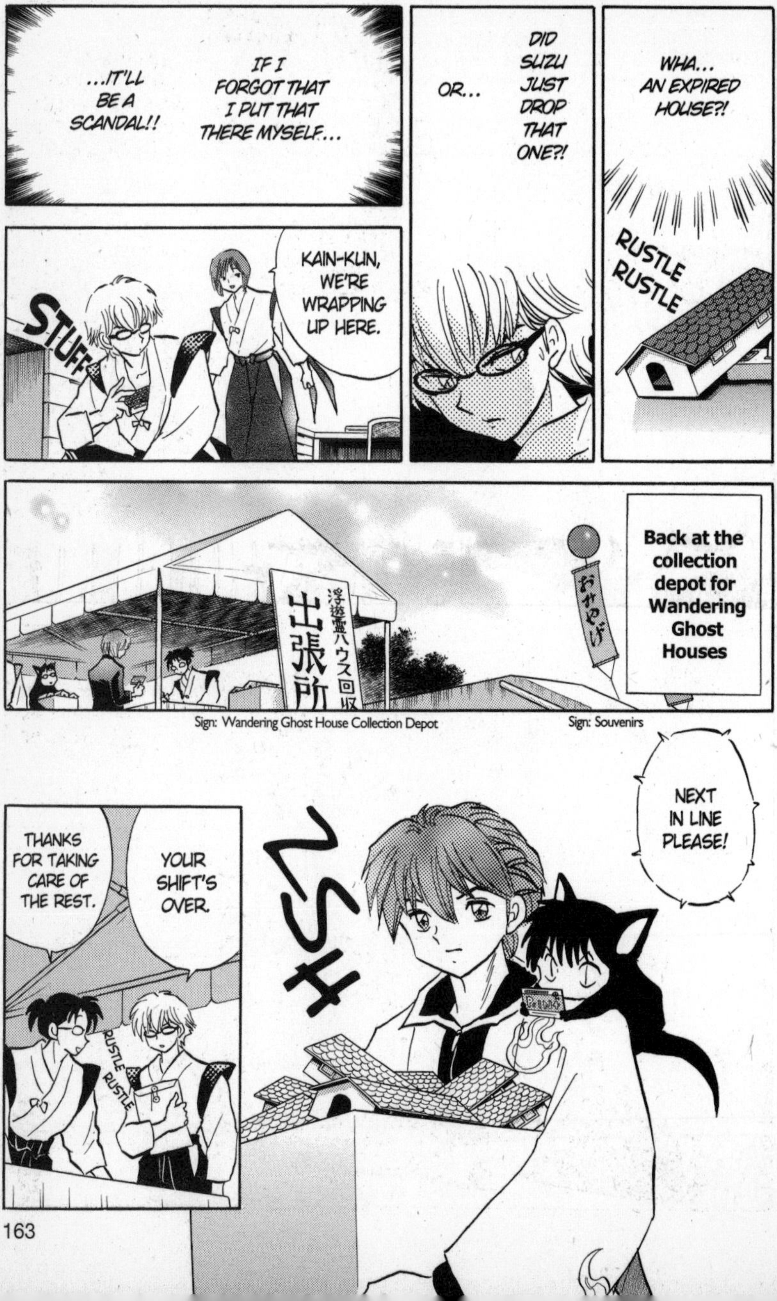
WHA... AN EXPIRED HOUSE?!
RUSTLE RUSTLE
DID SUZU JUST DROP THAT ONE?!
OR...
IF I FORGOT THAT I PUT THAT THERE MYSELF...
...IT'LL BE A SCANDAL!!
KAIN-KUN, WE'RE WRAPPING UP HERE.
STUFF
Back at the collection depot for Wandering Ghost Houses
おみやげ
浮遊霊ハウス回収出張所
Sign: Wandering Ghost House Collection Depot
Sign: Souvenirs
NEXT IN LINE PLEASE!
ZSH
YOUR SHIFT'S OVER.
THANKS FOR TAKING CARE OF THE REST.
RUSTLE RUSTLE

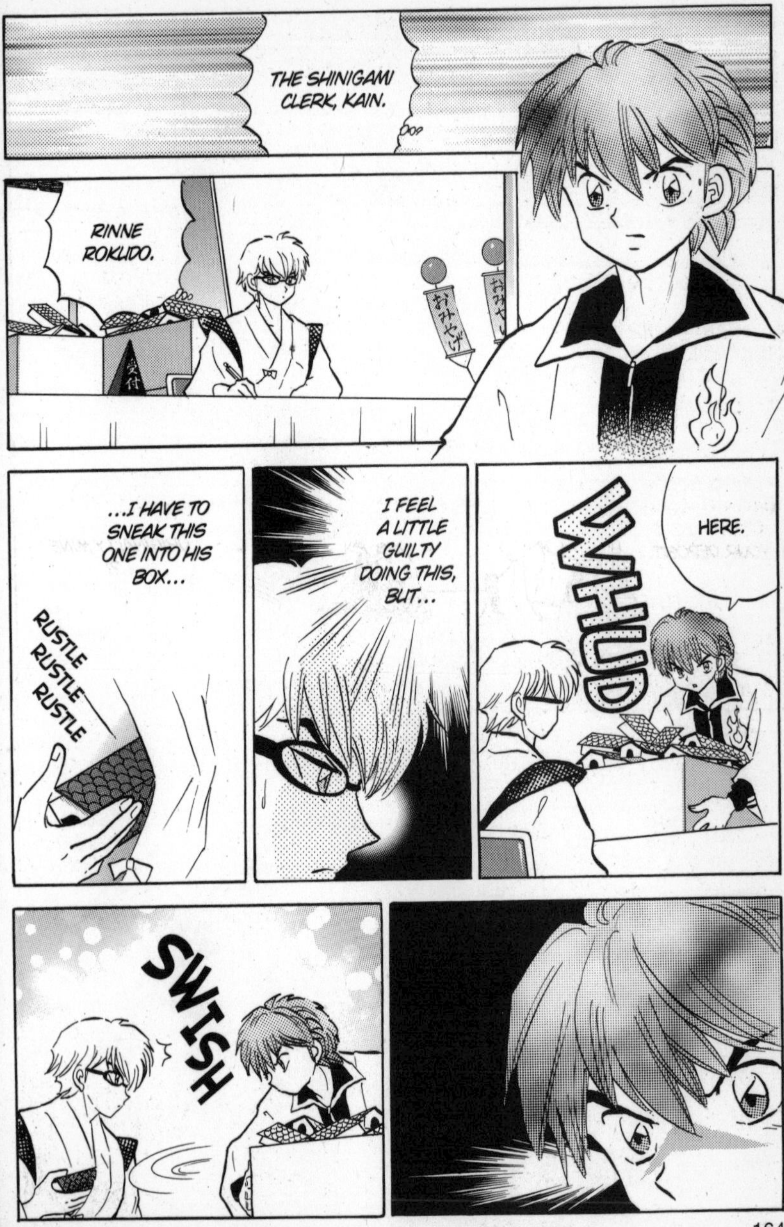
THE SHINIGAMI CLERK, KAIN.
RINNE ROKUDO.
HERE.
WHUD
I FEEL A LITTLE GUILTY DOING THIS, BUT...
...I HAVE TO SNEAK THIS ONE INTO HIS BOX...
RUSTLE RUSTLE RUSTLE
SWISH

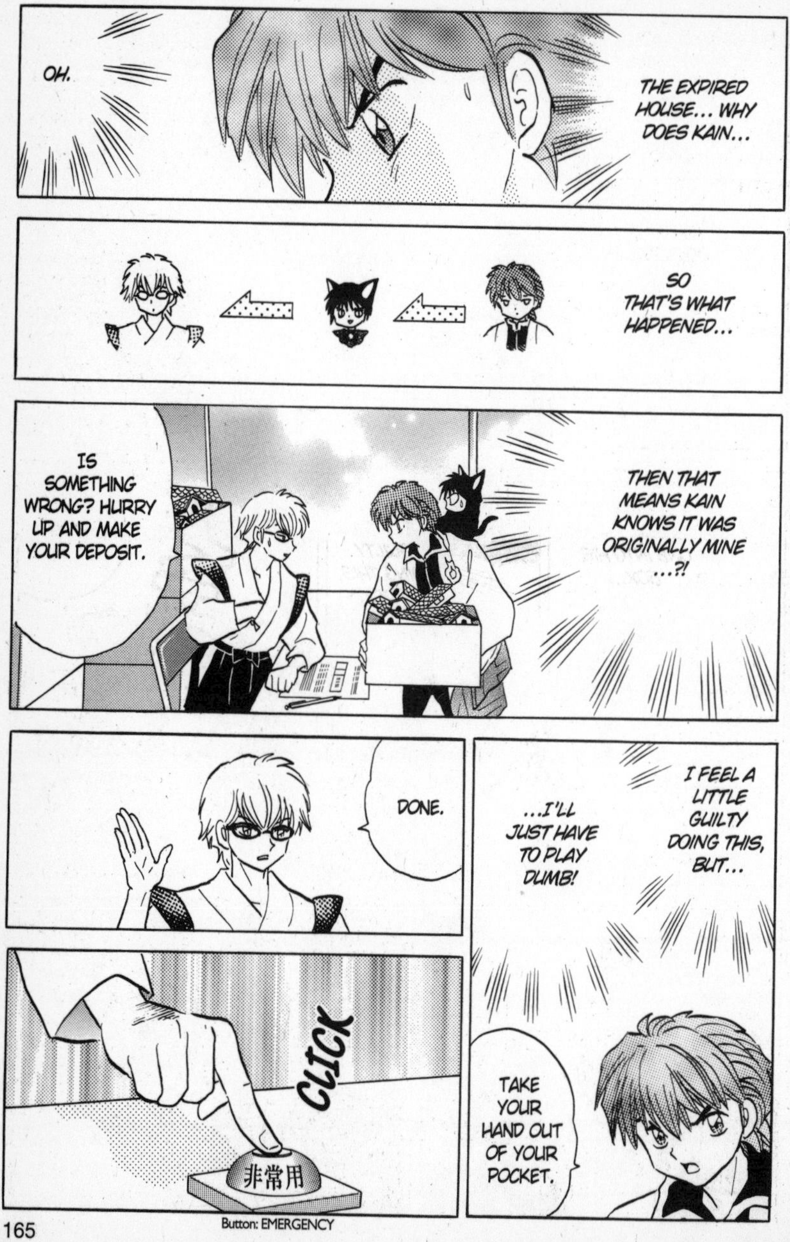
THE EXPIRED HOUSE... WHY DOES KAIN...
OH.
SO THAT'S WHAT HAPPENED...
THEN THAT MEANS KAIN KNOWS IT WAS ORIGINALLY MINE...?!
IS SOMETHING WRONG? HURRY UP AND MAKE YOUR DEPOSIT.
I FEEL A LITTLE GUILTY DOING THIS, BUT...
...I'LL JUST HAVE TO PLAY DUMB!
TAKE YOUR HAND OUT OF YOUR POCKET.
DONE.
CLICK
非常用
Button: EMERGENCY

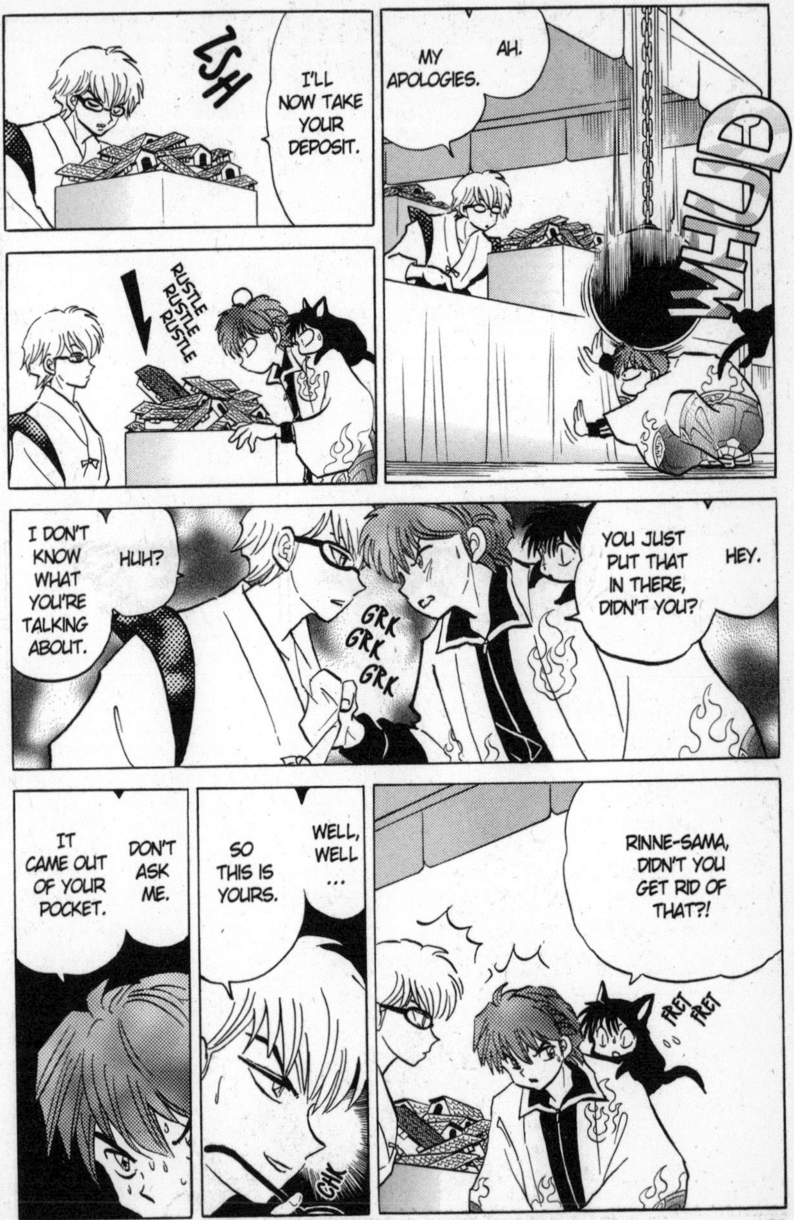
AH.
MY APOLOGIES.
WHUD
I'LL NOW TAKE YOUR DEPOSIT.
LSH
RUSTLE RUSTLE
HEY.
YOU JUST PUT THAT IN THERE, DIDN'T YOU?
GRK GRK GRK
HUH?
I DON'T KNOW WHAT YOU'RE TALKING ABOUT.
RINNE-SAMA, DIDN'T YOU GET RID OF THAT?!
FRET FRET
WELL, WELL...
SO THIS IS YOURS.
CHK
DON'T ASK ME.
IT CAME OUT OF YOUR POCKET.

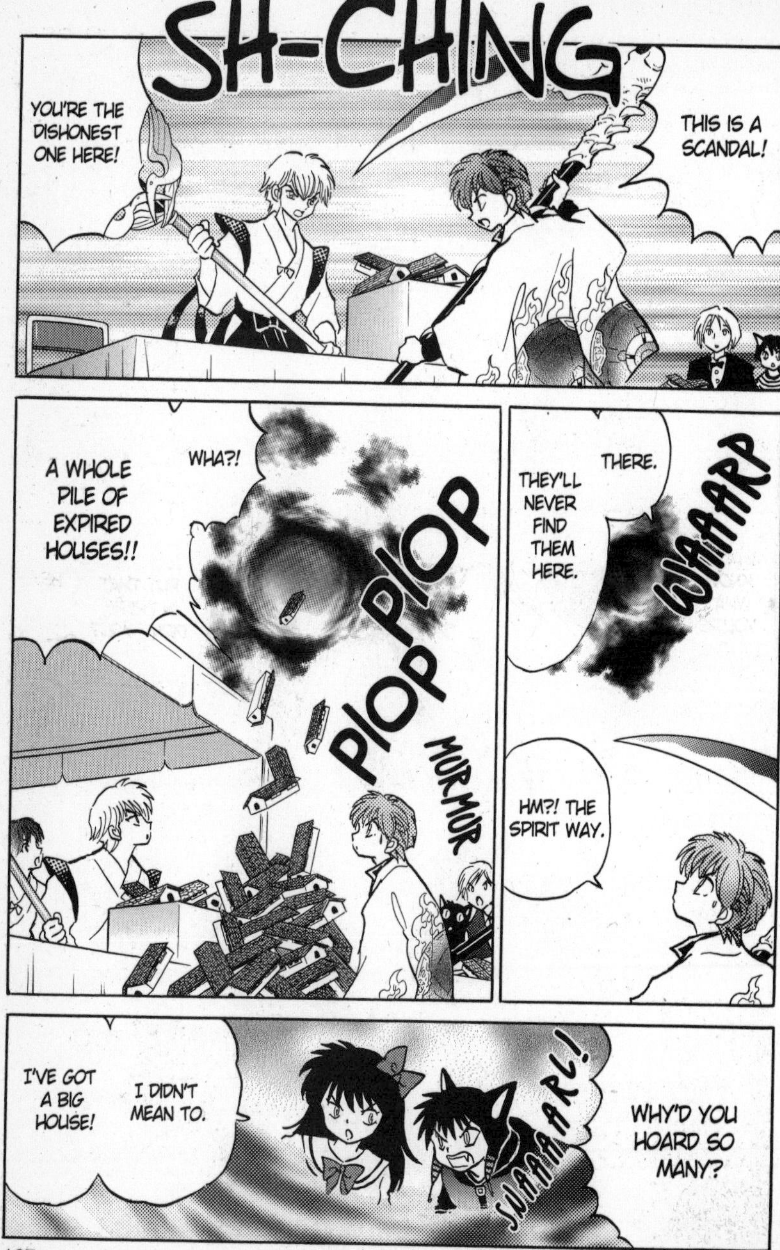
THIS IS A SCANDAL!
SH-CHING
YOU'RE THE DISHONEST ONE HERE!
WAAARP
THERE.
THEY'LL NEVER FIND THEM HERE.
HM?! THE SPIRIT WAY.
WHA?!
PLOP PLOP
A WHOLE PILE OF EXPIRED HOUSES!!
MUR MUR
WHY'D YOU HOARD SO MANY?
SNAAARL!
I DIDN'T MEAN TO.
I'VE GOT A BIG HOUSE!

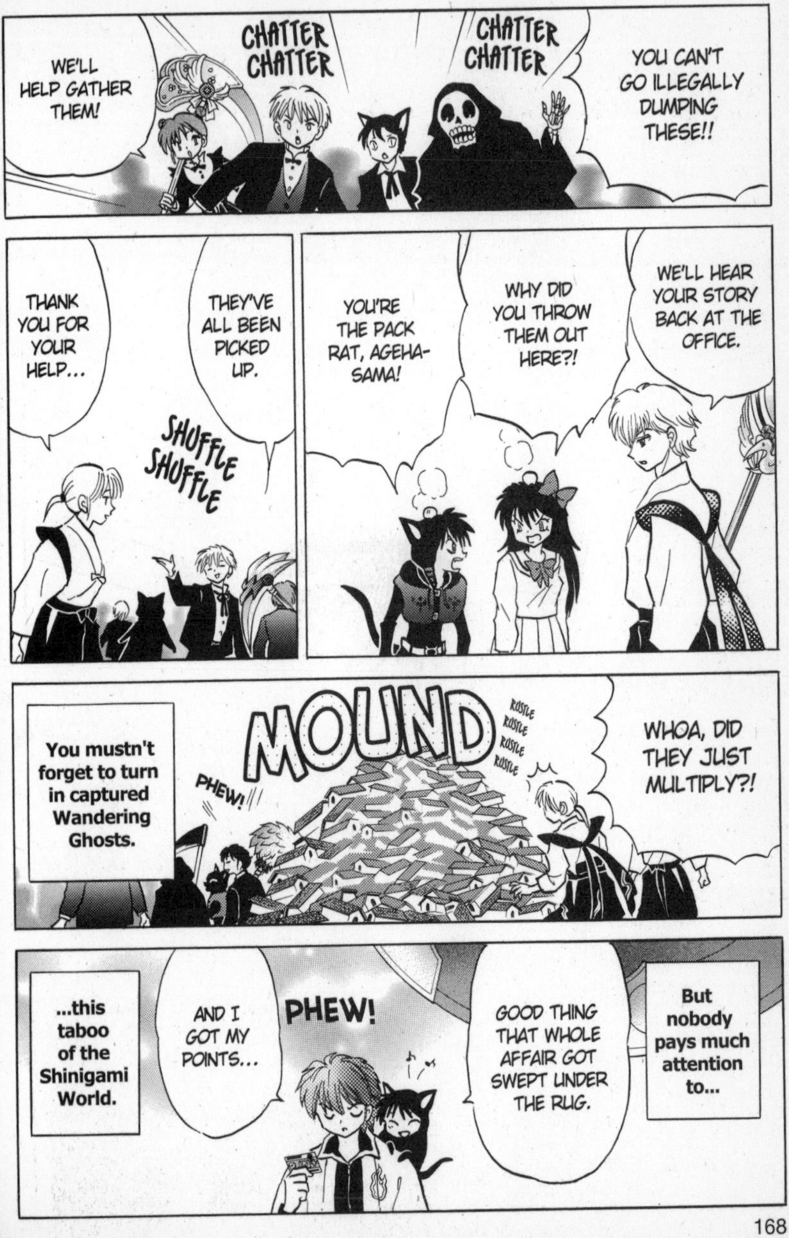
YOU CAN'T GO ILLEGALLY DUMPING THESE!!
CHATTER CHATTER
CHATTER CHATTER
WE'LL HELP GATHER THEM!
WE'LL HEAR YOUR STORY BACK AT THE OFFICE.
WHY DID YOU THROW THEM OUT HERE?!
YOU'RE THE PACK RAT, AGEHA-SAMA!
THEY'VE ALL BEEN PICKED UP.
THANK YOU FOR YOUR HELP...
SHUFFLE SHUFFLE
WHOA, DID THEY JUST MULTIPLY?!
RUSTLE RUSTLE RUSTLE RUSTLE
MOUND
PHEW!
You mustn't forget to turn in captured Wandering Ghosts.
But nobody pays much attention to...
GOOD THING THAT WHOLE AFFAIR GOT SWEPT UNDER THE RUG.
PHEW!
AND I GOT MY POINTS...
...this taboo of the Shinigami World.

CHAPTER 98: POLTERGEIST

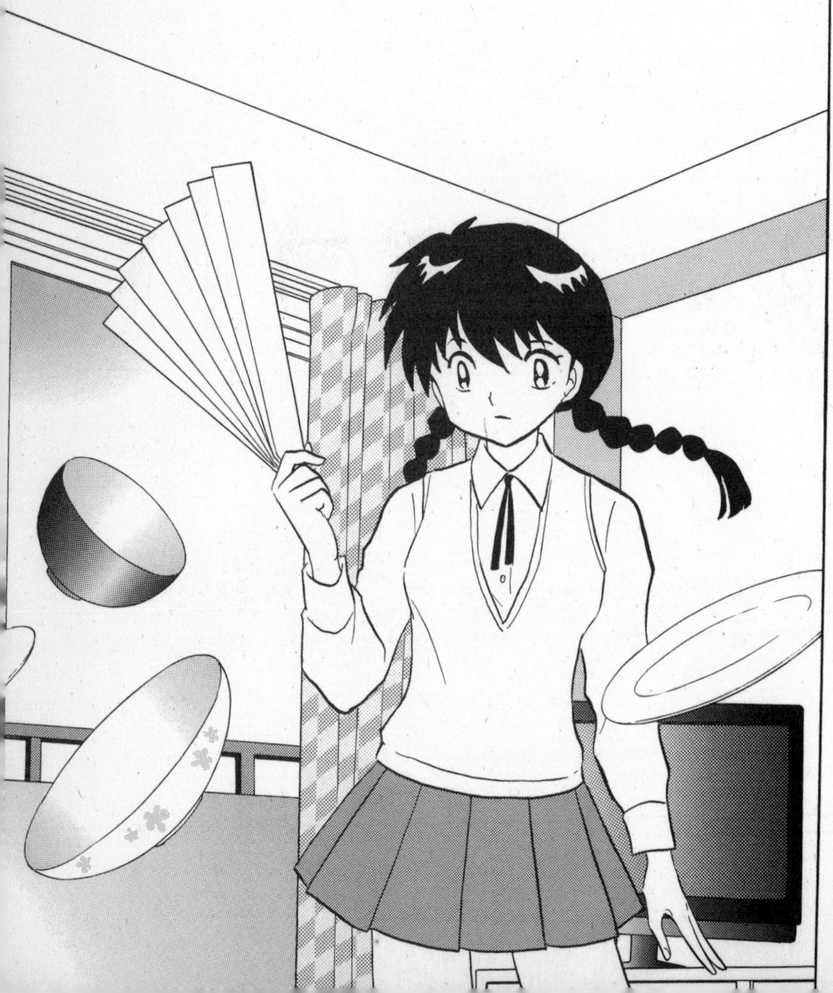

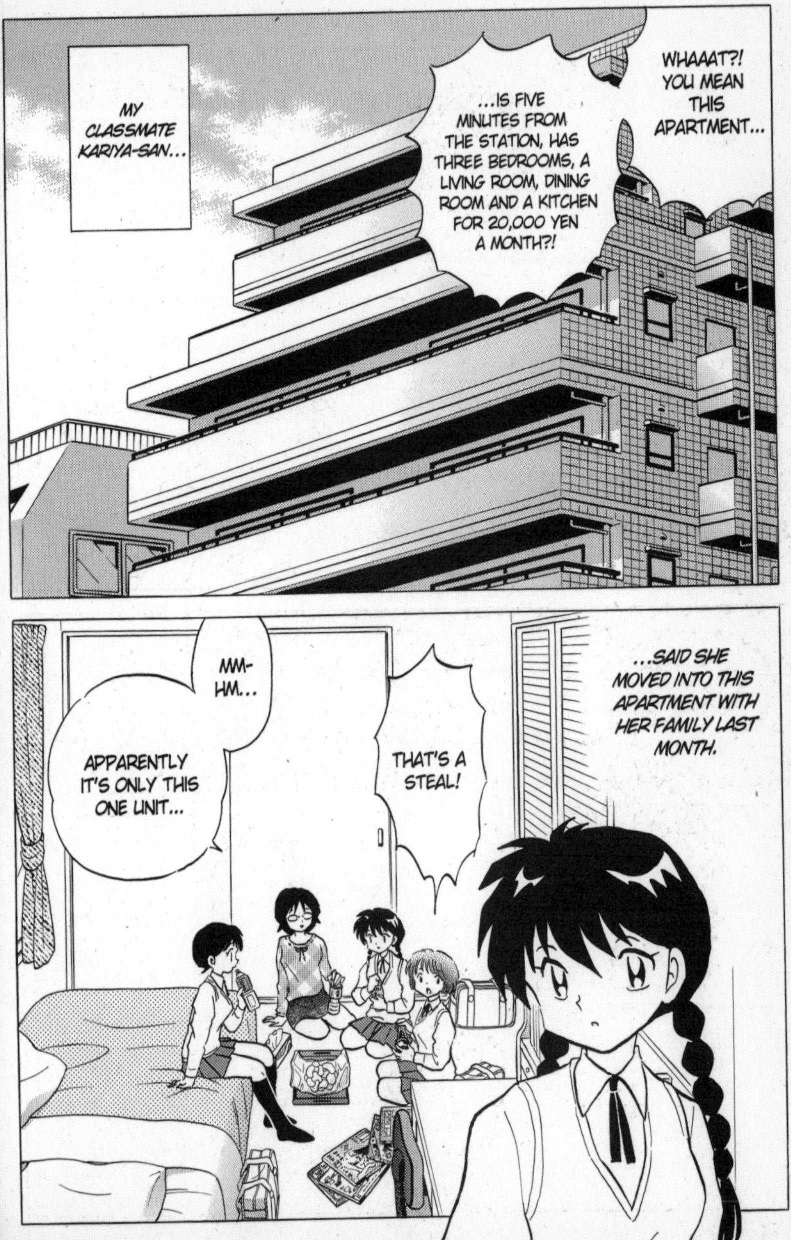
WHAAAT?! YOU MEAN THIS APARTMENT...
...IS FIVE MINUTES FROM THE STATION, HAS THREE BEDROOMS, A LIVING ROOM, DINING ROOM AND A KITCHEN FOR 20,000 YEN A MONTH?!
MY CLASSMATE KARIYA-SAN...
...SAID SHE MOVED INTO THIS APARTMENT WITH HER FAMILY LAST MONTH.
THAT'S A STEAL!
MM-HM...
APPARENTLY IT'S ONLY THIS ONE UNIT...

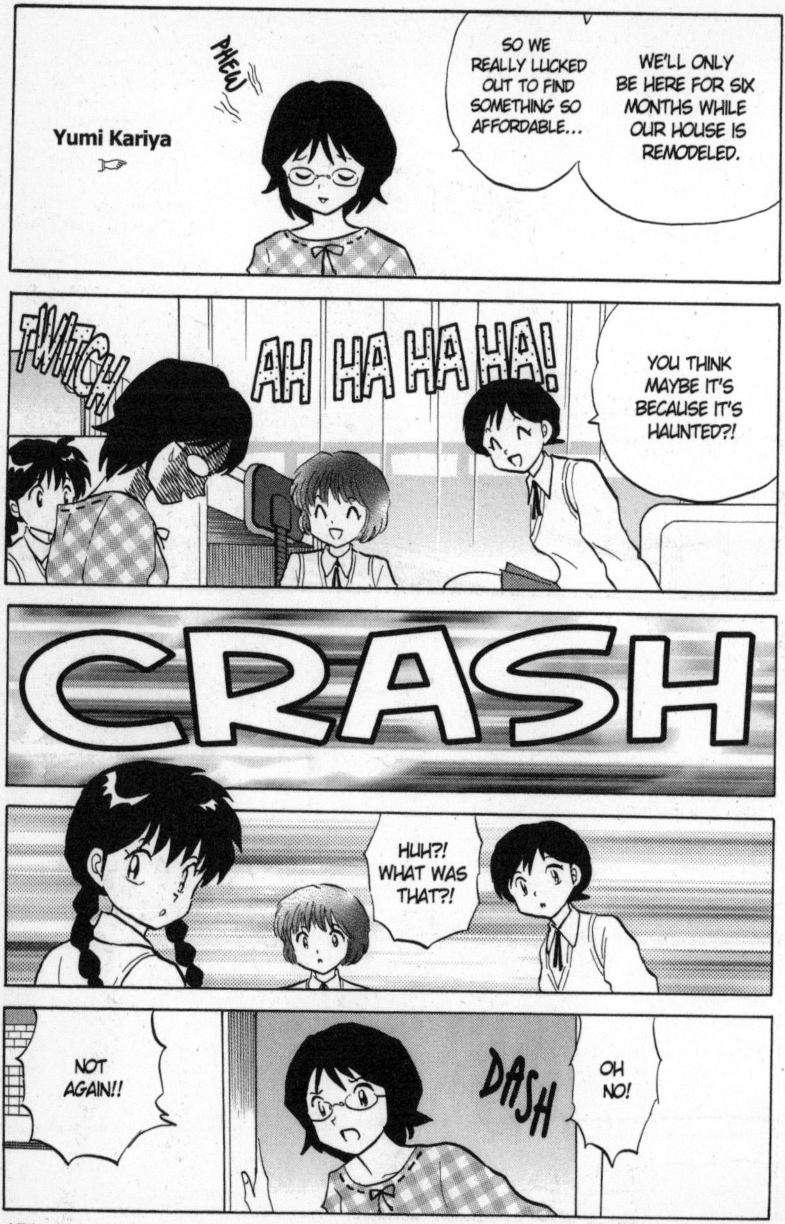
WE'LL ONLY BE HERE FOR SIX MONTHS WHILE OUR HOUSE IS REMODELED.
SO WE REALLY LUCKED OUT TO FIND SOMETHING SO AFFORDABLE...
PHEW
Yumi Kariya
YOU THINK MAYBE IT'S BECAUSE IT'S HAUNTED?!
AH HA HA HA!
TWITCH
CRASH
HUH?! WHAT WAS THAT?!
OH NO!
DASH
NOT AGAIN!!

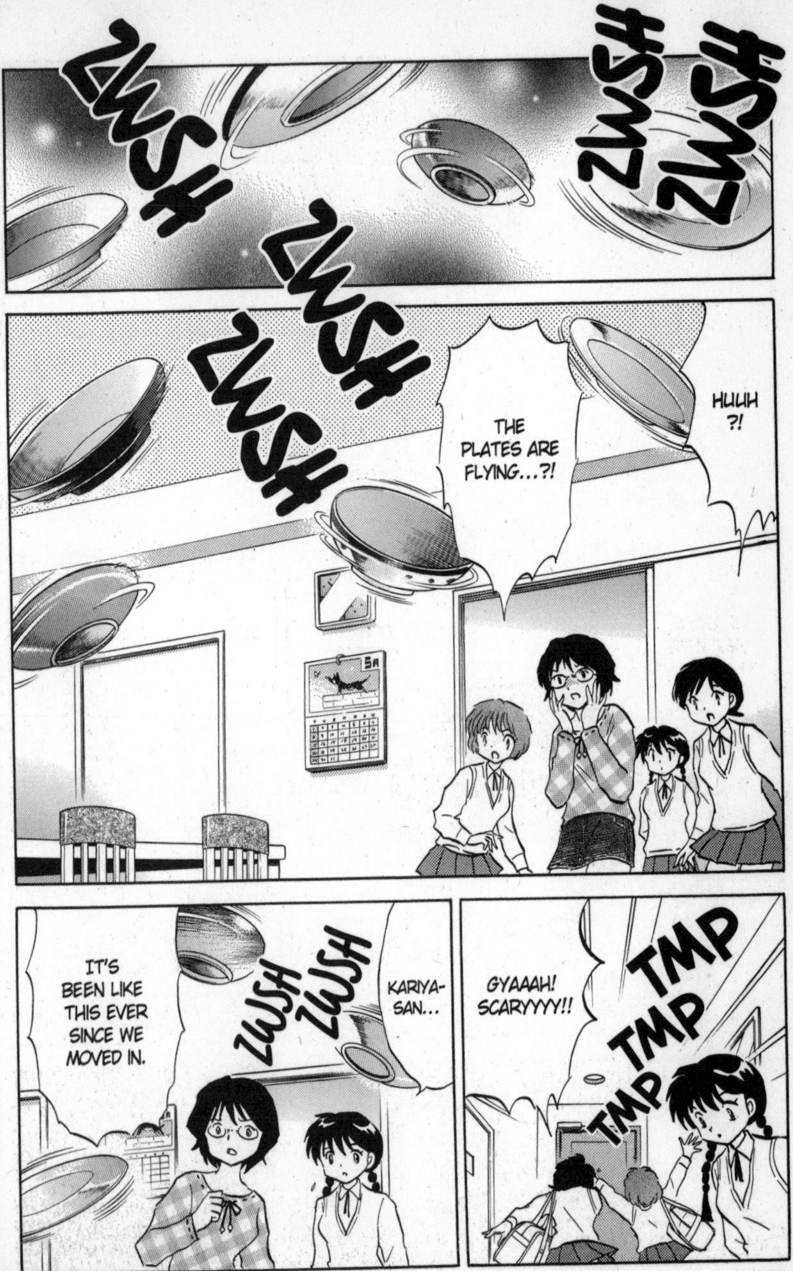
ZWSH ZWSH
ZWSH
ZWSH
HUUH ?!
THE PLATES ARE FLYING...?!
ZWSH ZWSH
TMP TMP TMP
GYAAAH! SCARYYYY!!
KARIYA-SAN...
ZWSH ZWSH
IT'S BEEN LIKE THIS EVER SINCE WE MOVED IN.

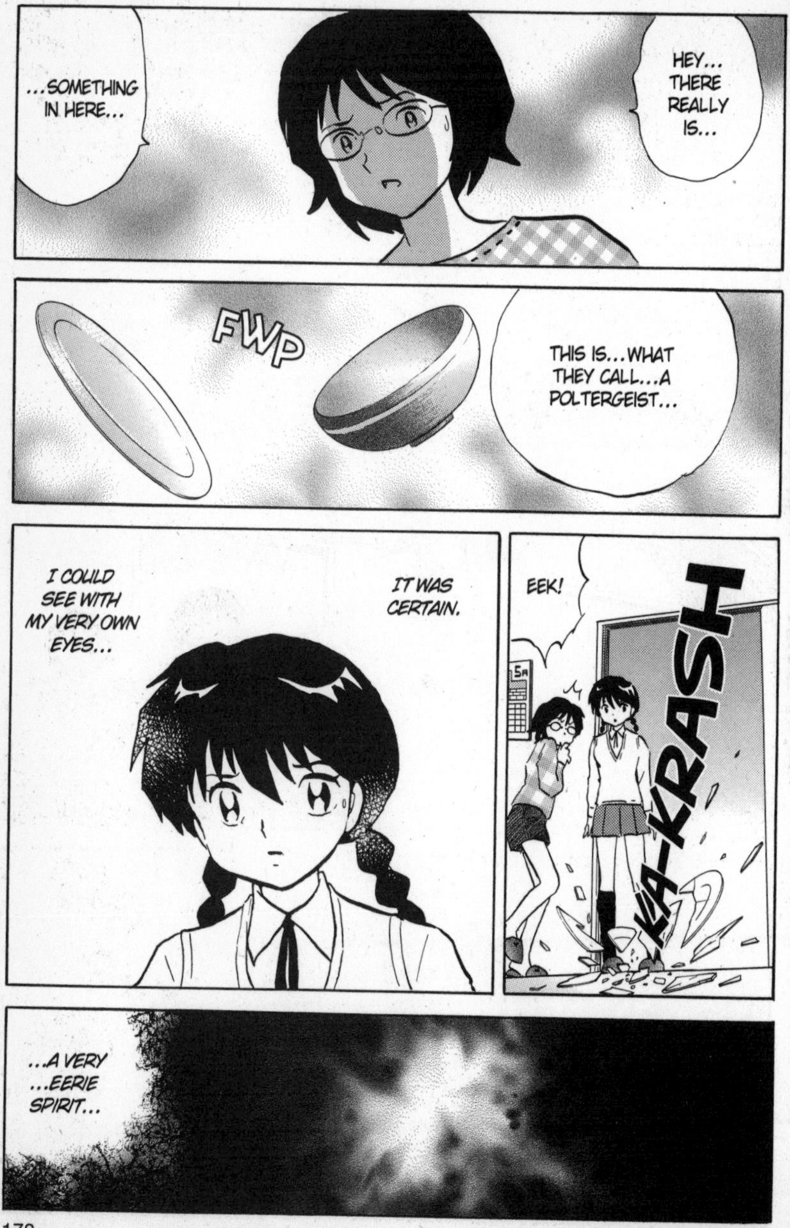
HEY... THERE REALLY IS...
...SOMETHING IN HERE...
THIS IS...WHAT THEY CALL...A POLTERGEIST...
FWP
EEK!
KA-KRASH
IT WAS CERTAIN.
I COULD SEE WITH MY VERY OWN EYES...
...A VERY ...EERIE SPIRIT...

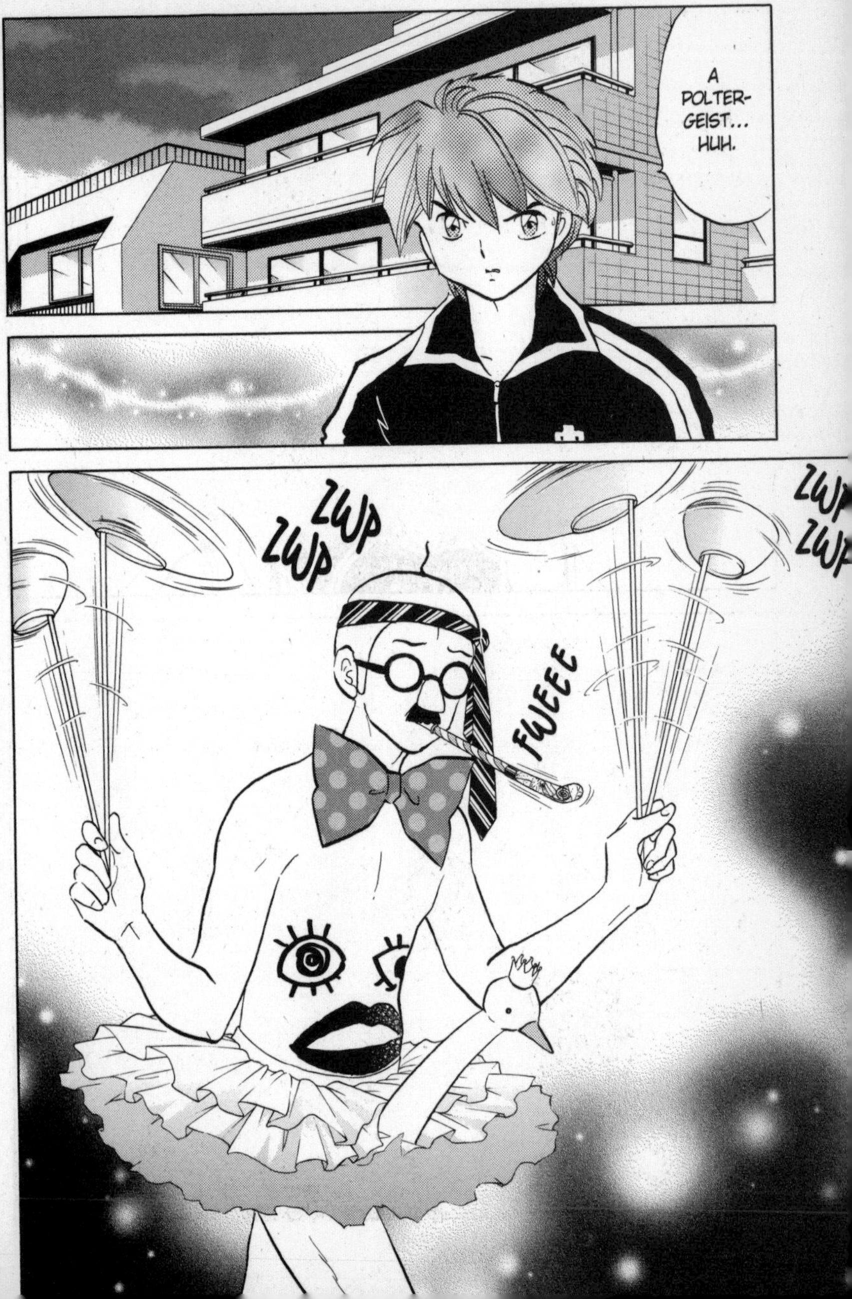
A POLTER-GEIST… HUH.
ZWP ZWP
ZWP ZWP
FWEEE

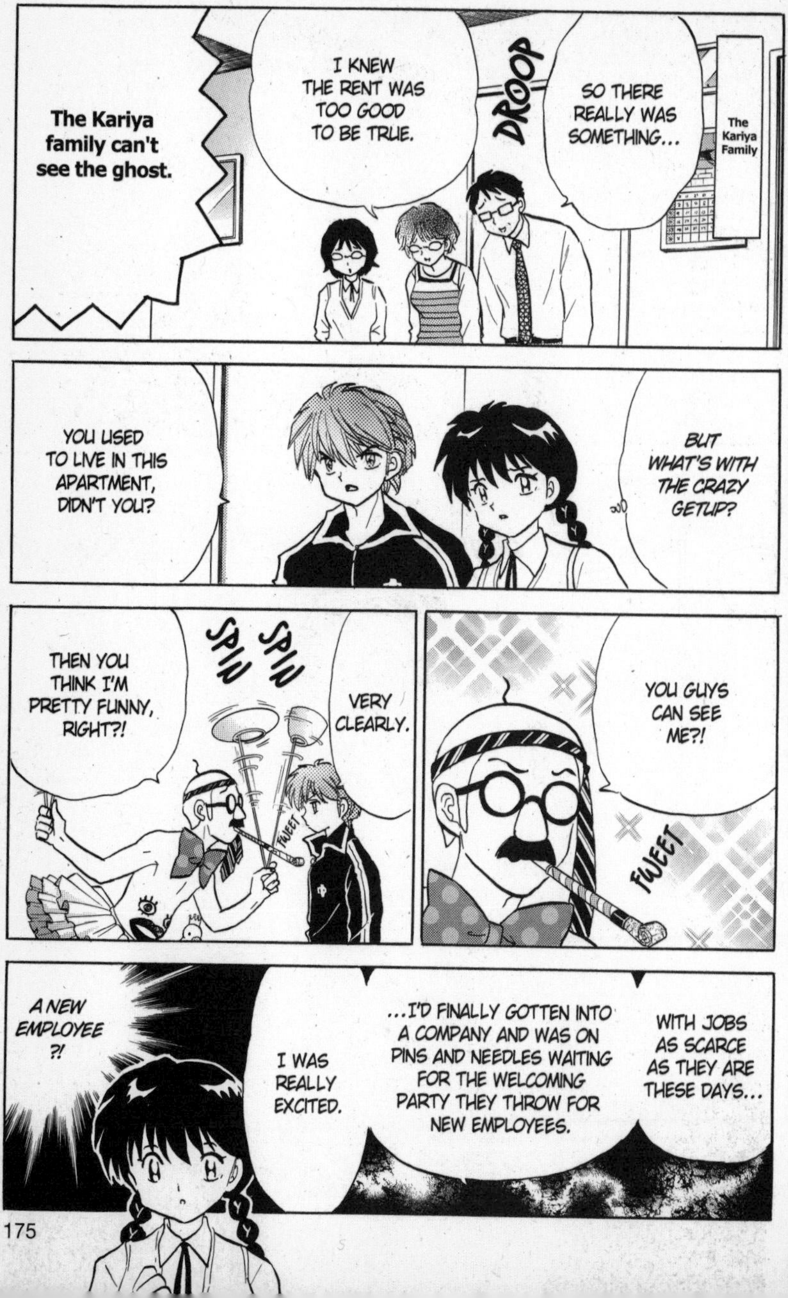
The Kariya Family
SO THERE REALLY WAS SOMETHING...
DROOP
I KNEW THE RENT WAS TOO GOOD TO BE TRUE.
The Kariya family can't see the ghost.
BUT WHAT'S WITH THE CRAZY GETUP?
YOU USED TO LIVE IN THIS APARTMENT, DIDN'T YOU?
YOU GUYS CAN SEE ME?!
FWEET
VERY CLEARLY.
SPIN SPIN
THEN YOU THINK I'M PRETTY FUNNY, RIGHT?!
FWEET
WITH JOBS AS SCARCE AS THEY ARE THESE DAYS...
...I'D FINALLY GOTTEN INTO A COMPANY AND WAS ON PINS AND NEEDLES WAITING FOR THE WELCOMING PARTY THEY THROW FOR NEW EMPLOYEES.
I WAS REALLY EXCITED.
A NEW EMPLOYEE ?!

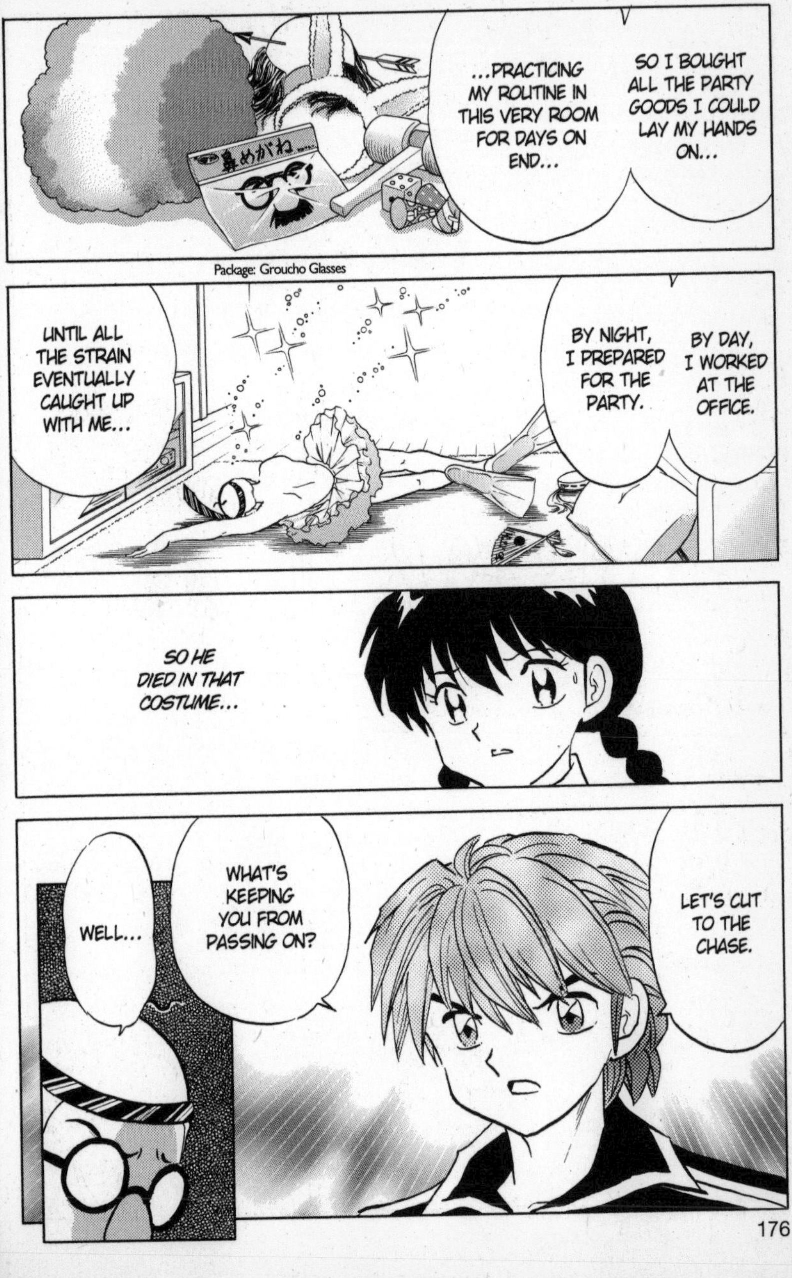
SO I BOUGHT ALL THE PARTY GOODS I COULD LAY MY HANDS ON...
...PRACTICING MY ROUTINE IN THIS VERY ROOM FOR DAYS ON END...
鼻めがね
Package: Groucho Glasses
BY DAY, I WORKED AT THE OFFICE.
BY NIGHT, I PREPARED FOR THE PARTY.
UNTIL ALL THE STRAIN EVENTUALLY CAUGHT UP WITH ME...
SO HE DIED IN THAT COSTUME...
LET'S CUT TO THE CHASE.
WHAT'S KEEPING YOU FROM PASSING ON?
WELL...

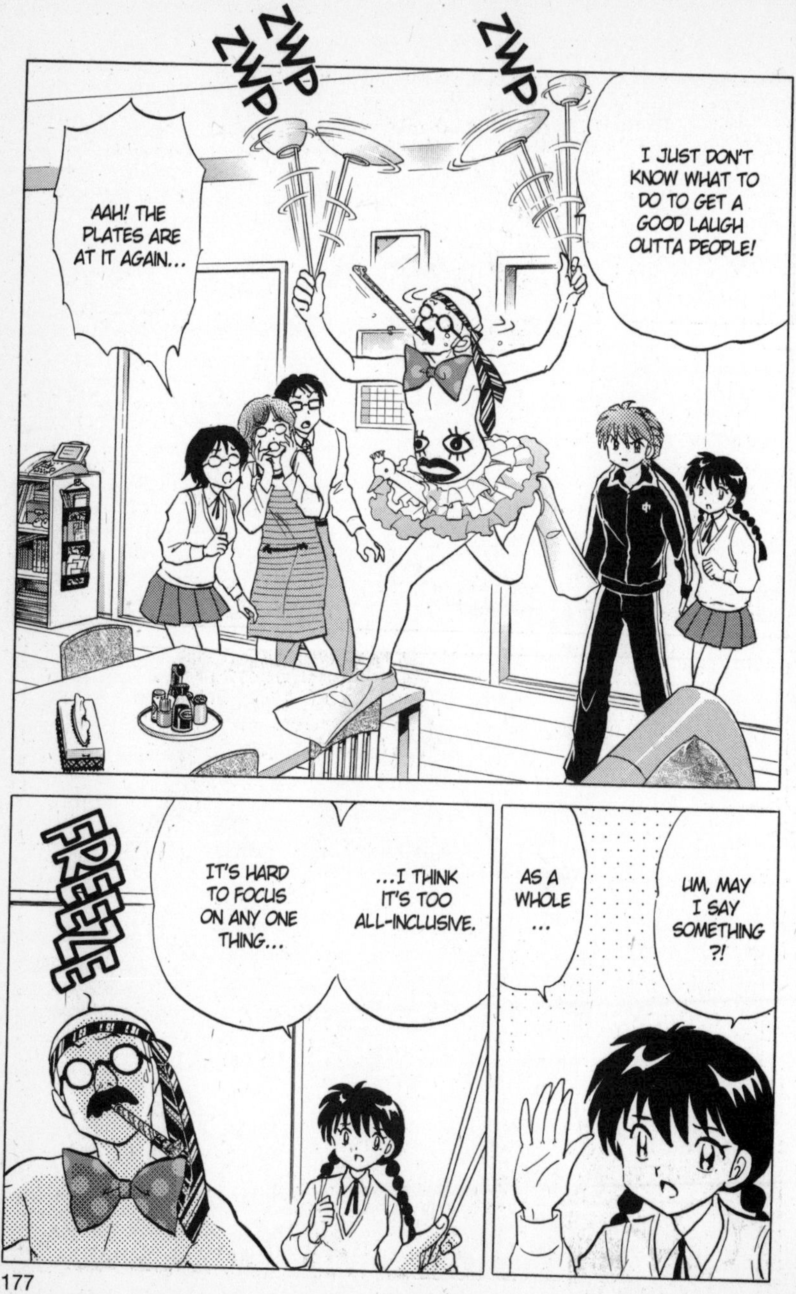
ZWP
ZWP ZWP
I JUST DON'T KNOW WHAT TO DO TO GET A GOOD LAUGH OUTTA PEOPLE!
AAH! THE PLATES ARE AT IT AGAIN...
UM, MAY I SAY SOMETHING?!
AS A WHOLE...
...I THINK IT'S TOO ALL-INCLUSIVE.
IT'S HARD TO FOCUS ON ANY ONE THING...
FREEZE

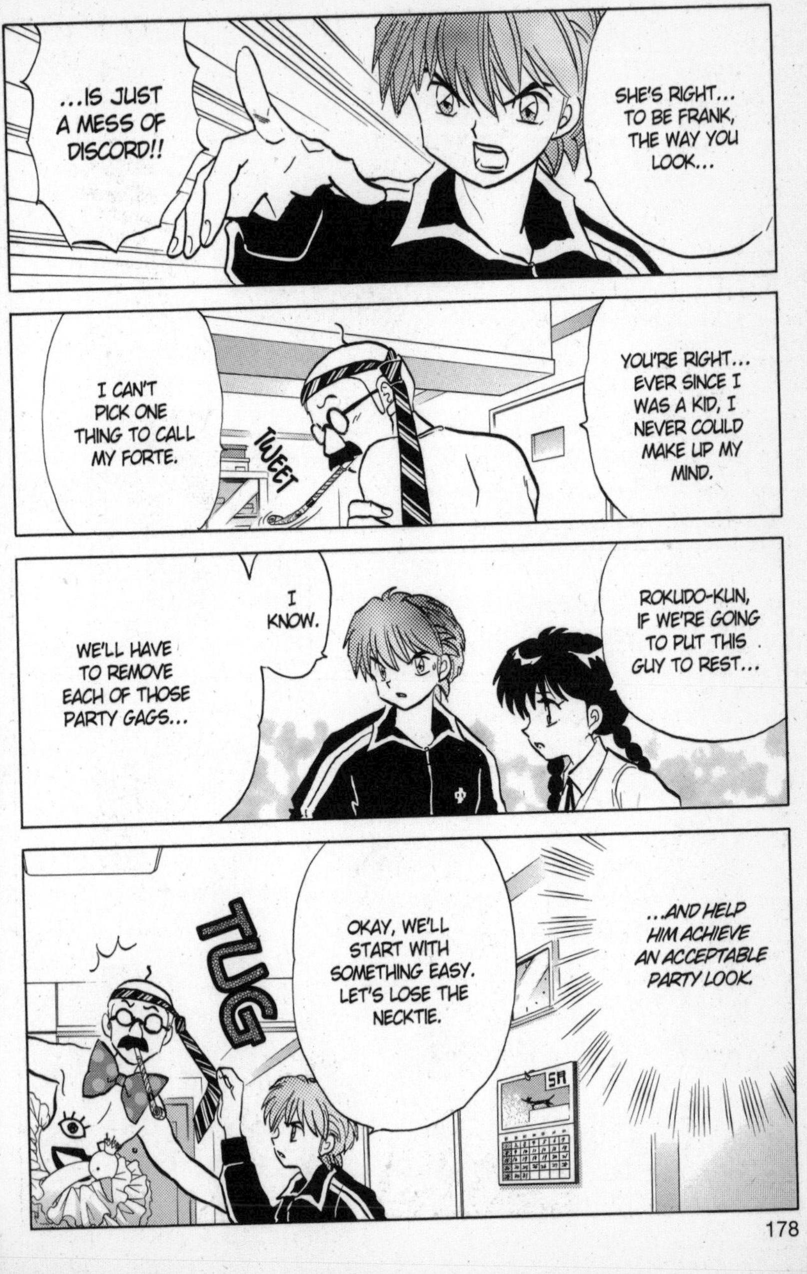
SHE'S RIGHT... TO BE FRANK, THE WAY YOU LOOK...
...IS JUST A MESS OF DISCORD!!
YOU'RE RIGHT... EVER SINCE I WAS A KID, I NEVER COULD MAKE UP MY MIND.
TWEET
I CAN'T PICK ONE THING TO CALL MY FORTE.
ROKUDO-KUN, IF WE'RE GOING TO PUT THIS GUY TO REST...
I KNOW.
WE'LL HAVE TO REMOVE EACH OF THOSE PARTY GAGS...
...AND HELP HIM ACHIEVE AN ACCEPTABLE PARTY LOOK.
OKAY, WE'LL START WITH SOMETHING EASY. LET'S LOSE THE NECKTIE.
TUG

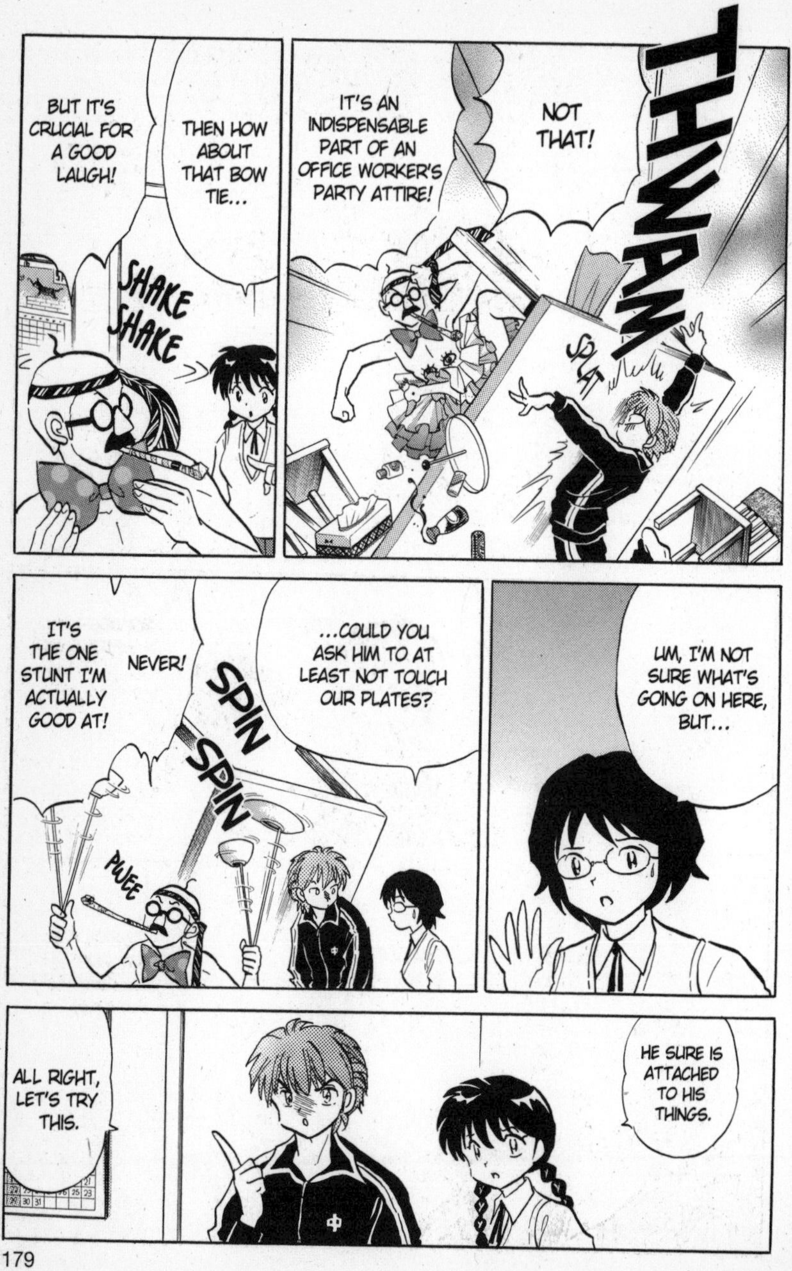
NOT THAT!
IT'S AN INDISPENSABLE PART OF AN OFFICE WORKER'S PARTY ATTIRE!
THWAM
SPLAT
THEN HOW ABOUT THAT BOW TIE...
BUT IT'S CRUCIAL FOR A GOOD LAUGH!
SHAKE SHAKE
UM, I'M NOT SURE WHAT'S GOING ON HERE, BUT...
...COULD YOU ASK HIM TO AT LEAST NOT TOUCH OUR PLATES?
SPIN SPIN
NEVER!
IT'S THE ONE STUNT I'M ACTUALLY GOOD AT!
PWEE
HE SURE IS ATTACHED TO HIS THINGS.
ALL RIGHT, LET'S TRY THIS.

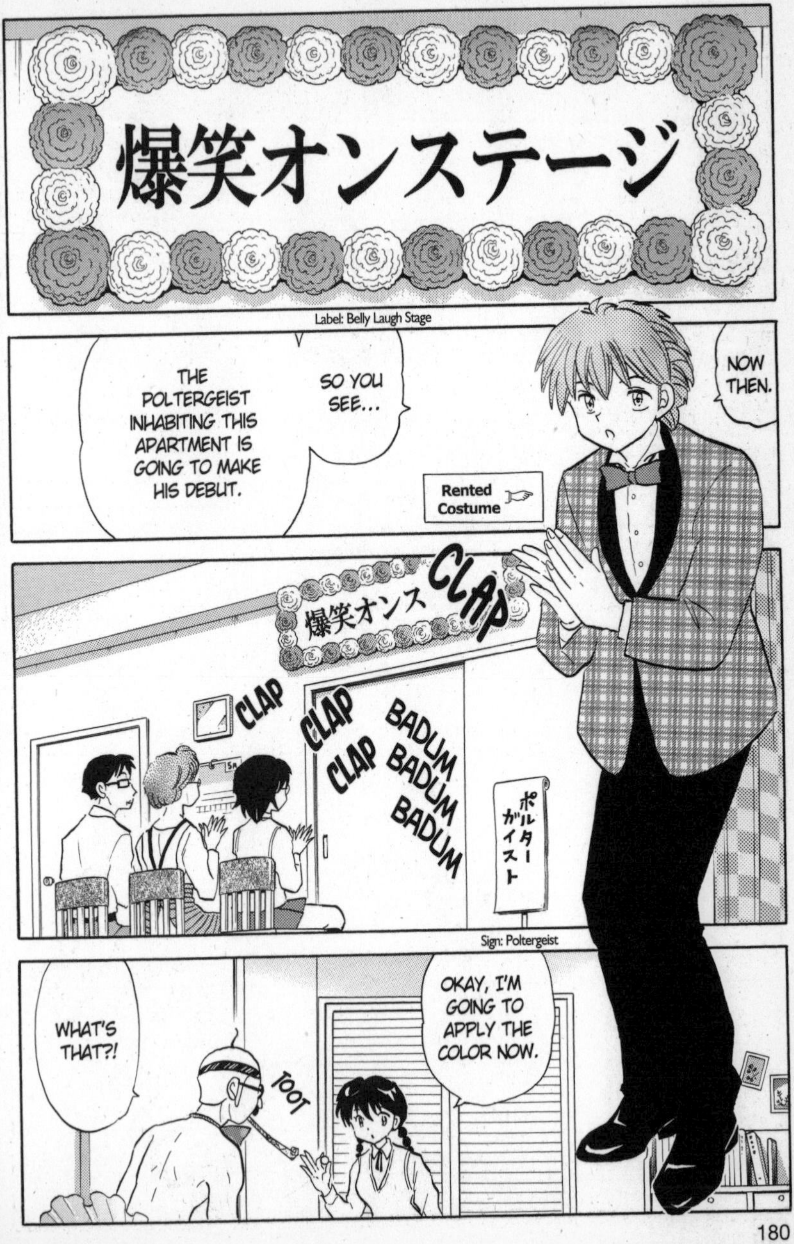
爆笑オンステージ
Label: Belly Laugh Stage
NOW THEN.
SO YOU SEE...
THE POLTERGEIST INHABITING THIS APARTMENT IS GOING TO MAKE HIS DEBUT.
Rented Costume
CLAP
爆笑オンス
CLAP
CLAP
CLAP
BADUM BADUM BADUM BADUM
ポルターガイスト
Sign: Poltergeist
OKAY, I'M GOING TO APPLY THE COLOR NOW.
TOOT
WHAT'S THAT?!

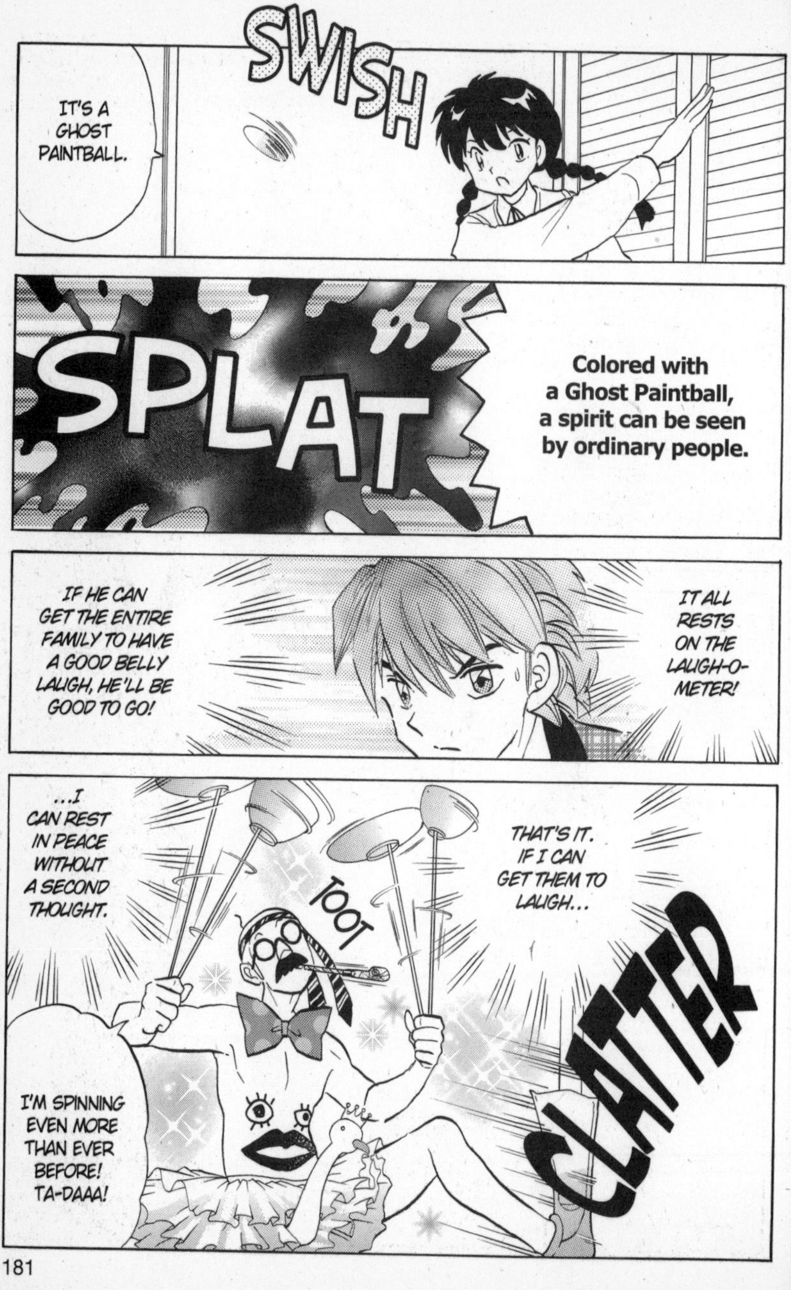
SWISH
IT'S A GHOST PAINTBALL.
Colored with a Ghost Paintball, a spirit can be seen by ordinary people.
SPLAT
IT ALL RESTS ON THE LAUGH-O-METER!
IF HE CAN GET THE ENTIRE FAMILY TO HAVE A GOOD BELLY LAUGH, HE'LL BE GOOD TO GO!
THAT'S IT. IF I CAN GET THEM TO LAUGH...
...I CAN REST IN PEACE WITHOUT A SECOND THOUGHT.
TOOT
CLATTER
I'M SPINNING EVEN MORE THAN EVER BEFORE! TA-DAAA!

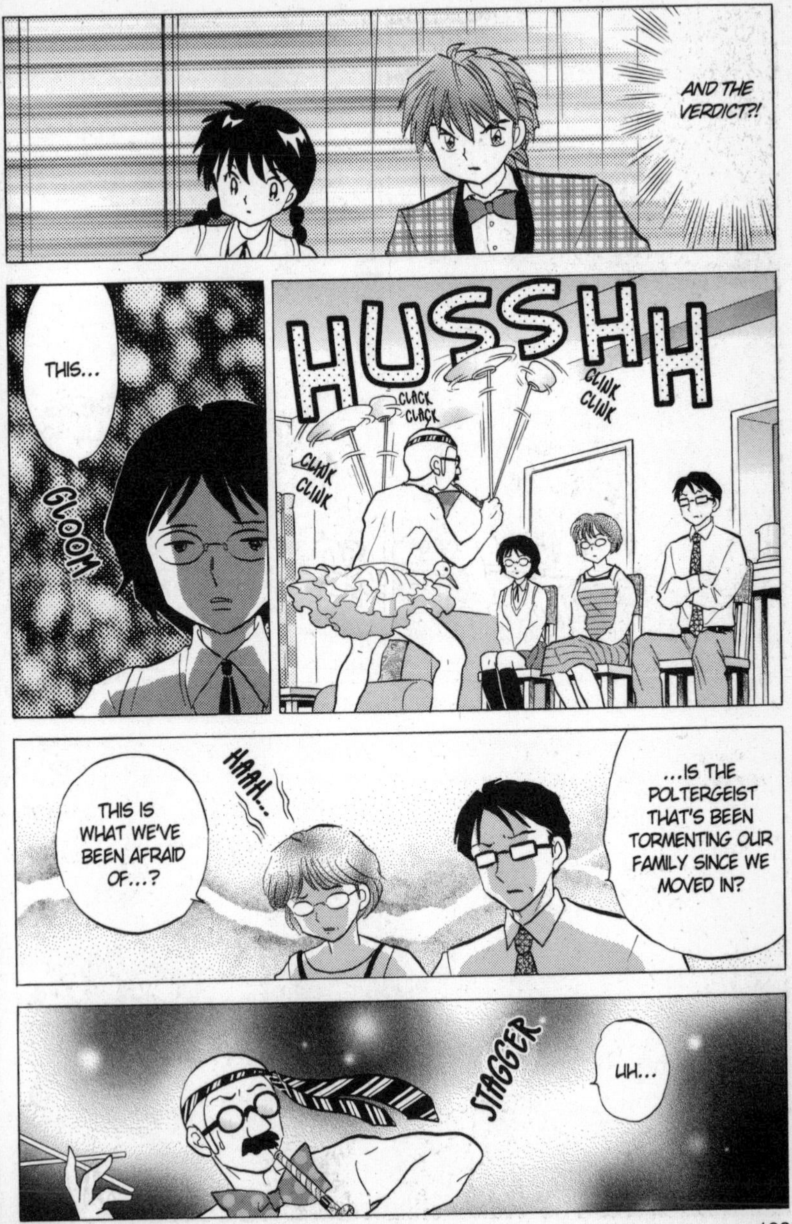
AND THE VERDICT?!
HUSSHH
CLINK CLINK
CLACK CLACK
CLINK CLINK
THIS...
GLOOM
...IS THE POLTERGEIST THAT'S BEEN TORMENTING OUR FAMILY SINCE WE MOVED IN?
HAAAH...
THIS IS WHAT WE'VE BEEN AFRAID OF...?
UH...
STAGGER

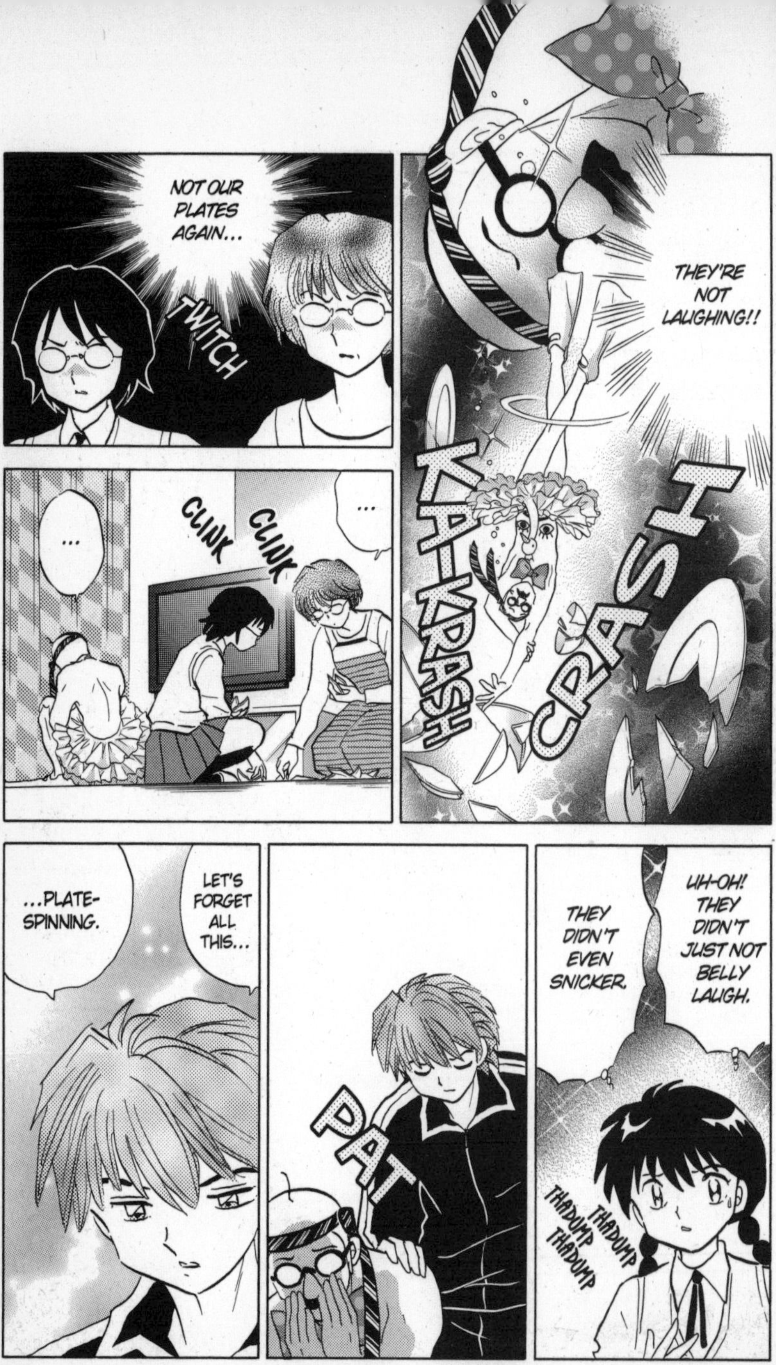
THEY'RE NOT LAUGHING!!
CRASH
KA-KRASH
NOT OUR PLATES AGAIN...
TWITCH
...
CLINK
CLINK
...
UH-OH! THEY DIDN'T JUST NOT BELLY LAUGH.
THEY DIDN'T EVEN SNICKER.
THADUMP THADUMP THADUMP
PAT
LET'S FORGET ALL THIS...
...PLATE-SPINNING.

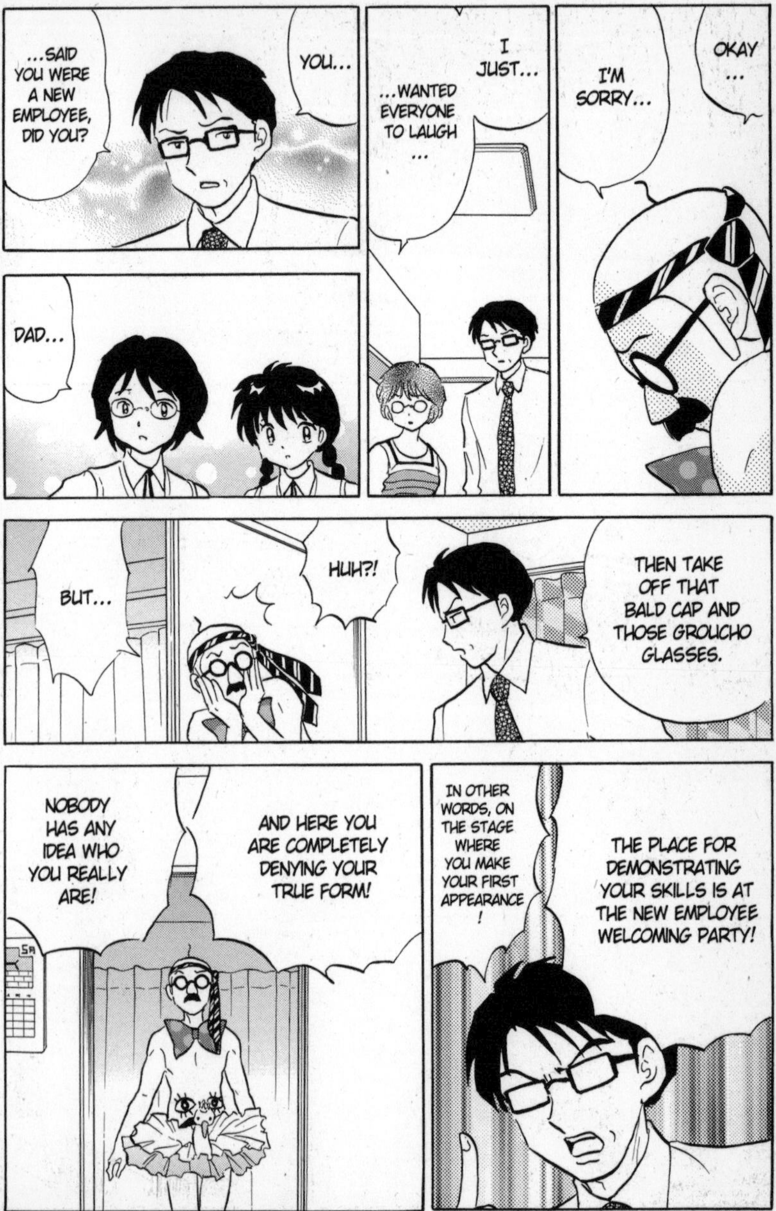
OKAY ...
I'M SORRY...
I JUST...
...WANTED EVERYONE TO LAUGH ...
YOU...
...SAID YOU WERE A NEW EMPLOYEE, DID YOU?
DAD...
THEN TAKE OFF THAT BALD CAP AND THOSE GROUCHO GLASSES.
HUH?!
BUT...
THE PLACE FOR DEMONSTRATING YOUR SKILLS IS AT THE NEW EMPLOYEE WELCOMING PARTY!
IN OTHER WORDS, ON THE STAGE WHERE YOU MAKE YOUR FIRST APPEARANCE !
AND HERE YOU ARE COMPLETELY DENYING YOUR TRUE FORM!
NOBODY HAS ANY IDEA WHO YOU REALLY ARE!

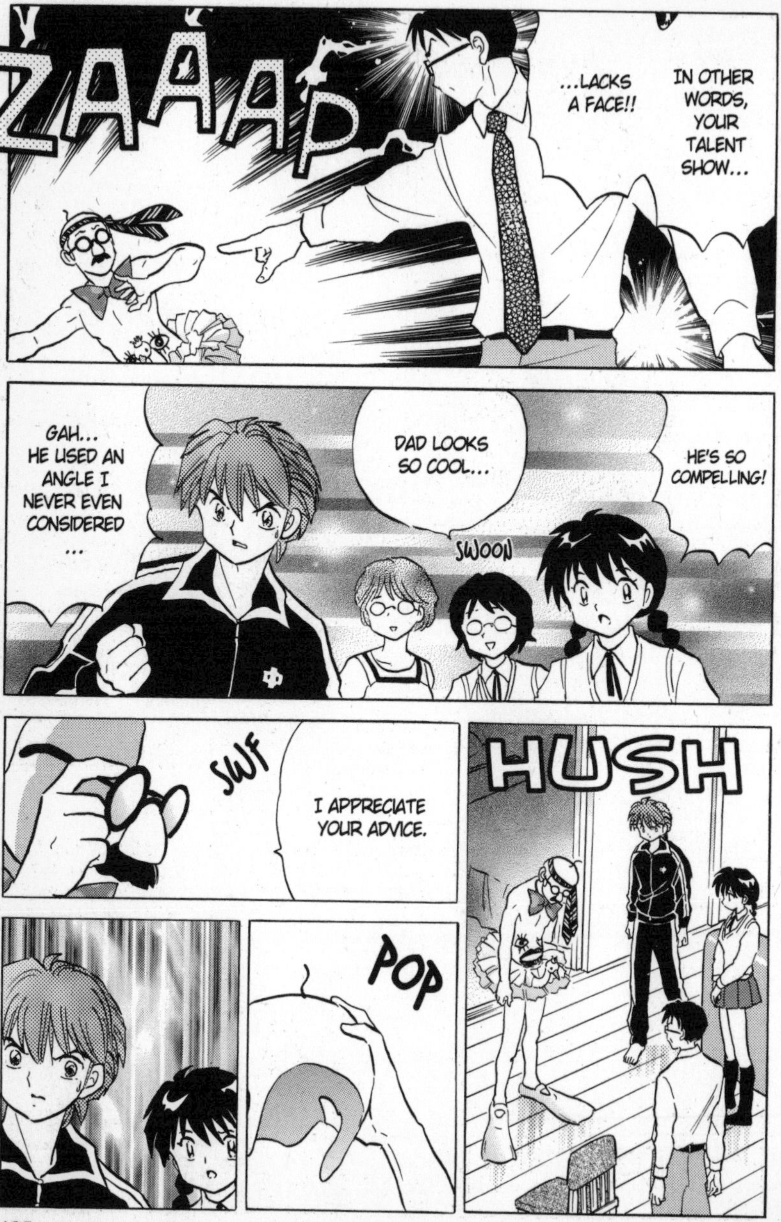
IN OTHER WORDS, YOUR TALENT SHOW...
...LACKS A FACE!!
ZAAAAP
HE'S SO COMPELLING!
DAD LOOKS SO COOL...
SWOON
GAH... HE USED AN ANGLE I NEVER EVEN CONSIDERED ...
HUSH
I APPRECIATE YOUR ADVICE.
SWF
POP

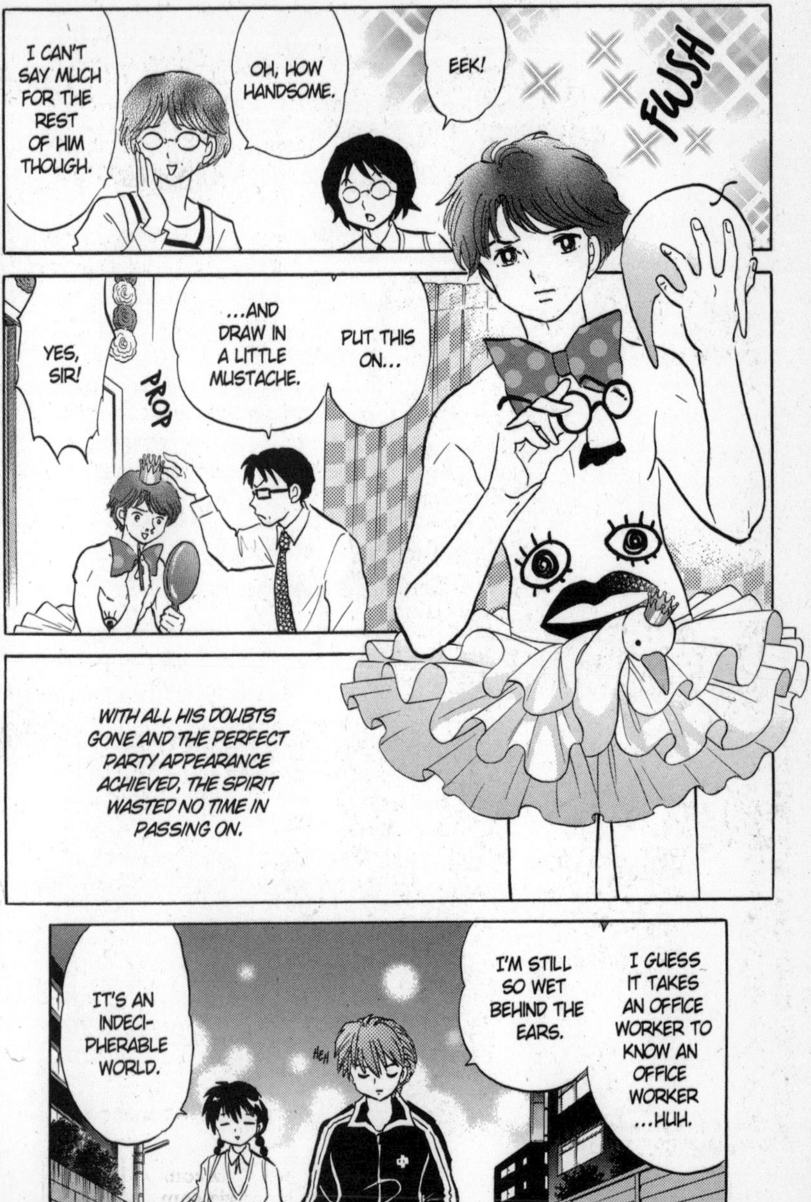
FUSH
EEK!
OH, HOW HANDSOME.
I CAN'T SAY MUCH FOR THE REST OF HIM THOUGH.
PUT THIS ON...
...AND DRAW IN A LITTLE MUSTACHE.
PROP
YES, SIR!
WITH ALL HIS DOUBTS GONE AND THE PERFECT PARTY APPEARANCE ACHIEVED, THE SPIRIT WASTED NO TIME IN PASSING ON.
I GUESS IT TAKES AN OFFICE WORKER TO KNOW AN OFFICE WORKER ...HUH.
I'M STILL SO WET BEHIND THE EARS.
HEH
IT'S AN INDECI-PHERABLE WORLD.

RIN-NE VOLUME 10 -END-

Half Human, Half Demon— ALL ACTION!

Relive the feudal fairy tale with the new VIZBIG Editions featuring:

· Three volumes in one
  for $17.99 US / $24.00 CAN
· Larger trim size with premium paper
· Now unflipped! Pages read
  Right-to-Left as the creator intended

Change Your Perspective—Get BIG

大VIZBIG EDITION

INUYASHA

ISBN-13: 978-1-4215-3280-6

INUYASHA

Story and Art by Rumiko Takahashi

On sale at
store.viz.com
Also available at your local
bookstore and comic store

MANGA STARTS ON SUNDAY
SHONENSUNDAY.COM

Freshly Baked from Japan!

It's 16-year-old Kazuma Azuma's dream to use his otherworldly baking powers to create Ja-pan, the national bread of the land of the rising sun. But in a nation known for rice and seafood delicacies, the stakes are high. Can Kazuma rise to the occasion before his dreams fall flat?

Find out in Yakitate!! Japan—buy the manga today!

Yakitate!! Japan™

$9.99

www.viz.com

Hey! You're Reading in the Wrong Direction!

This is the end of this graphic novel!

To properly enjoy this VIZ graphic novel, please turn it around and begin reading from right to left. Unlike English, Japanese is read right to left, so Japanese comics are read in reverse order from the way English comics are typically read.

This book has been printed in the original Japanese format in order to preserve the orientation of the original artwork. Have fun with it!

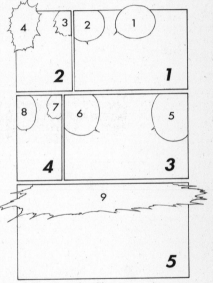

Follow the action this way